Senza Parole

Lubok
Galerie Kleindienst
Leipzig 2015

Tilo Baumgärtel

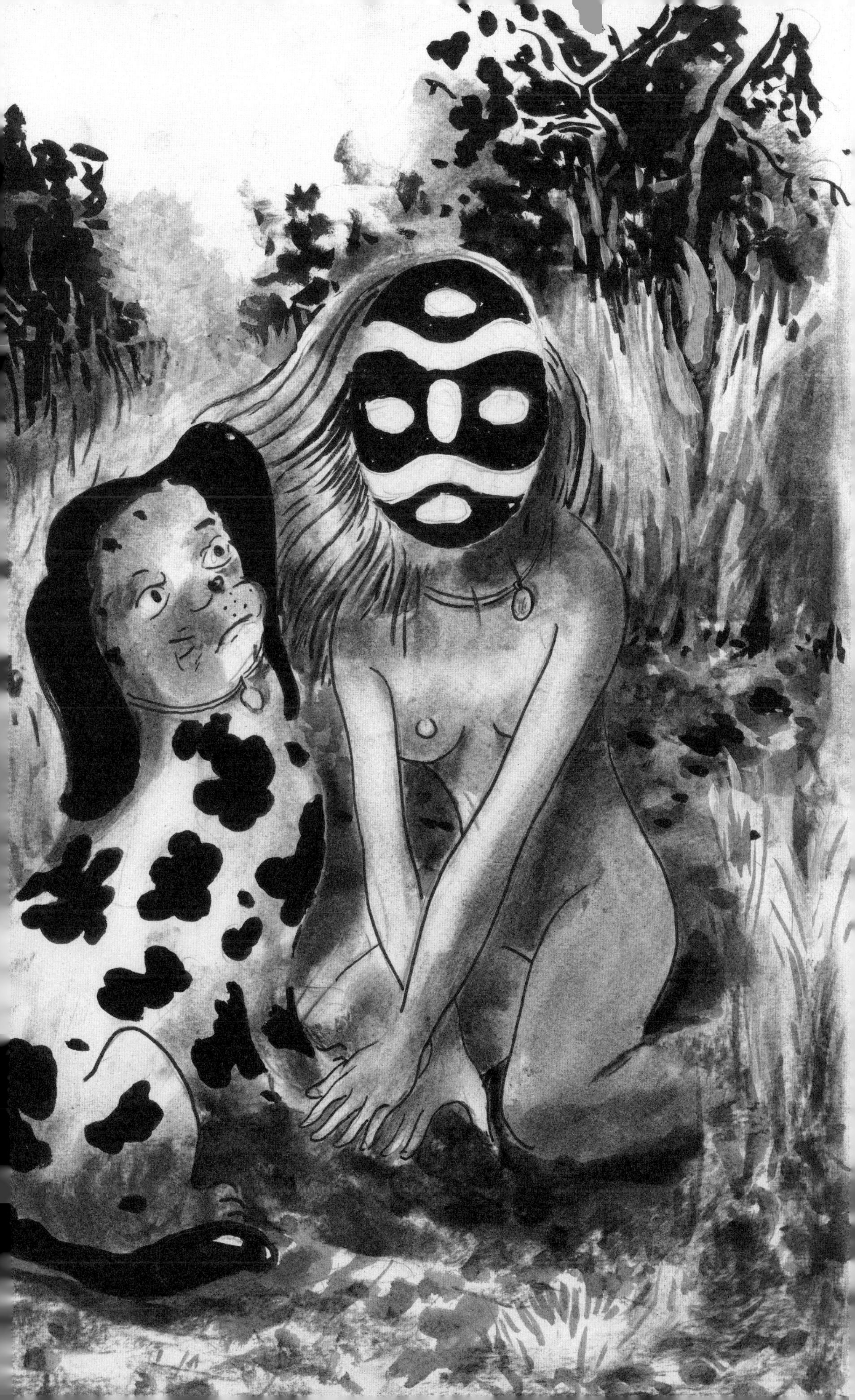

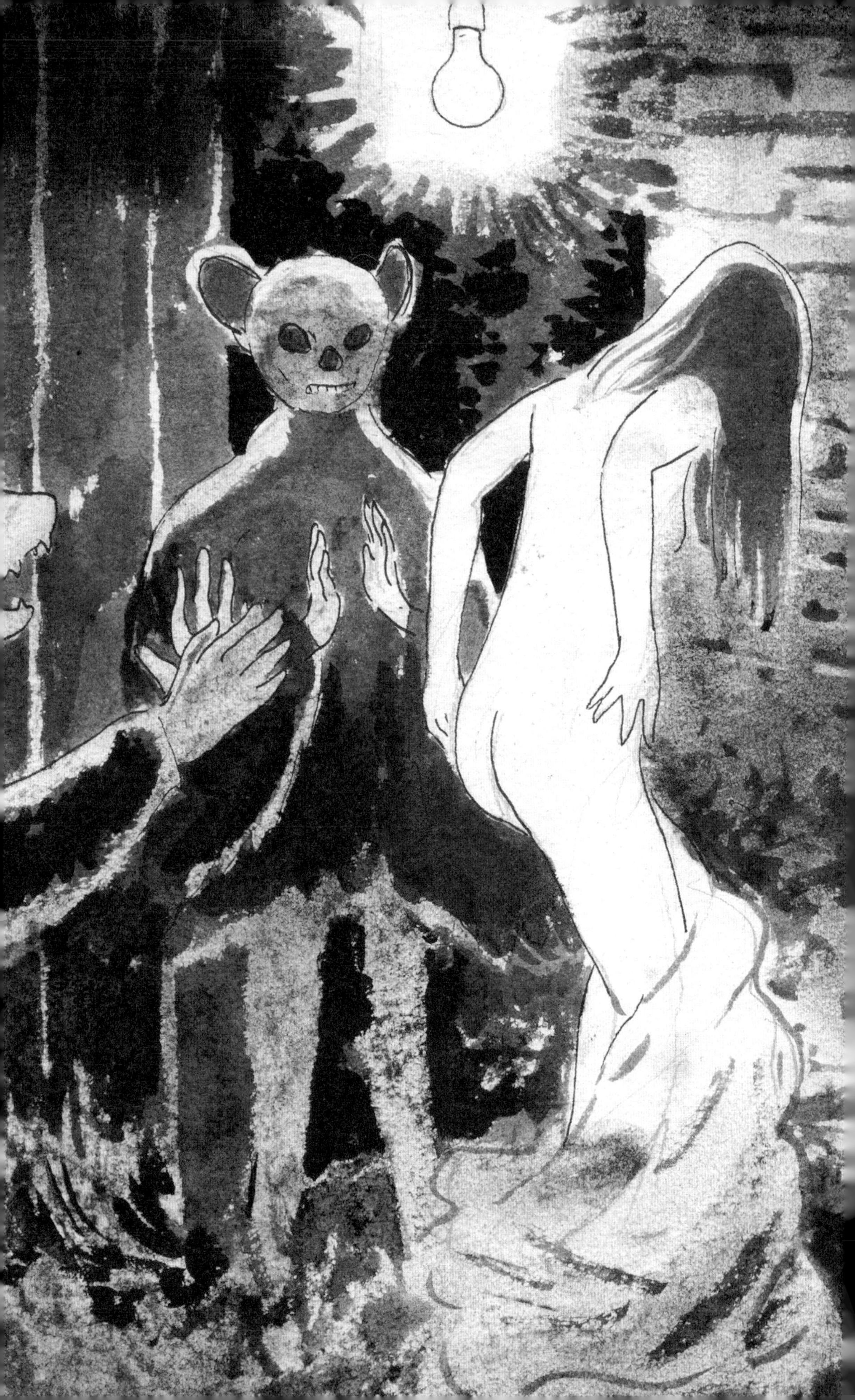

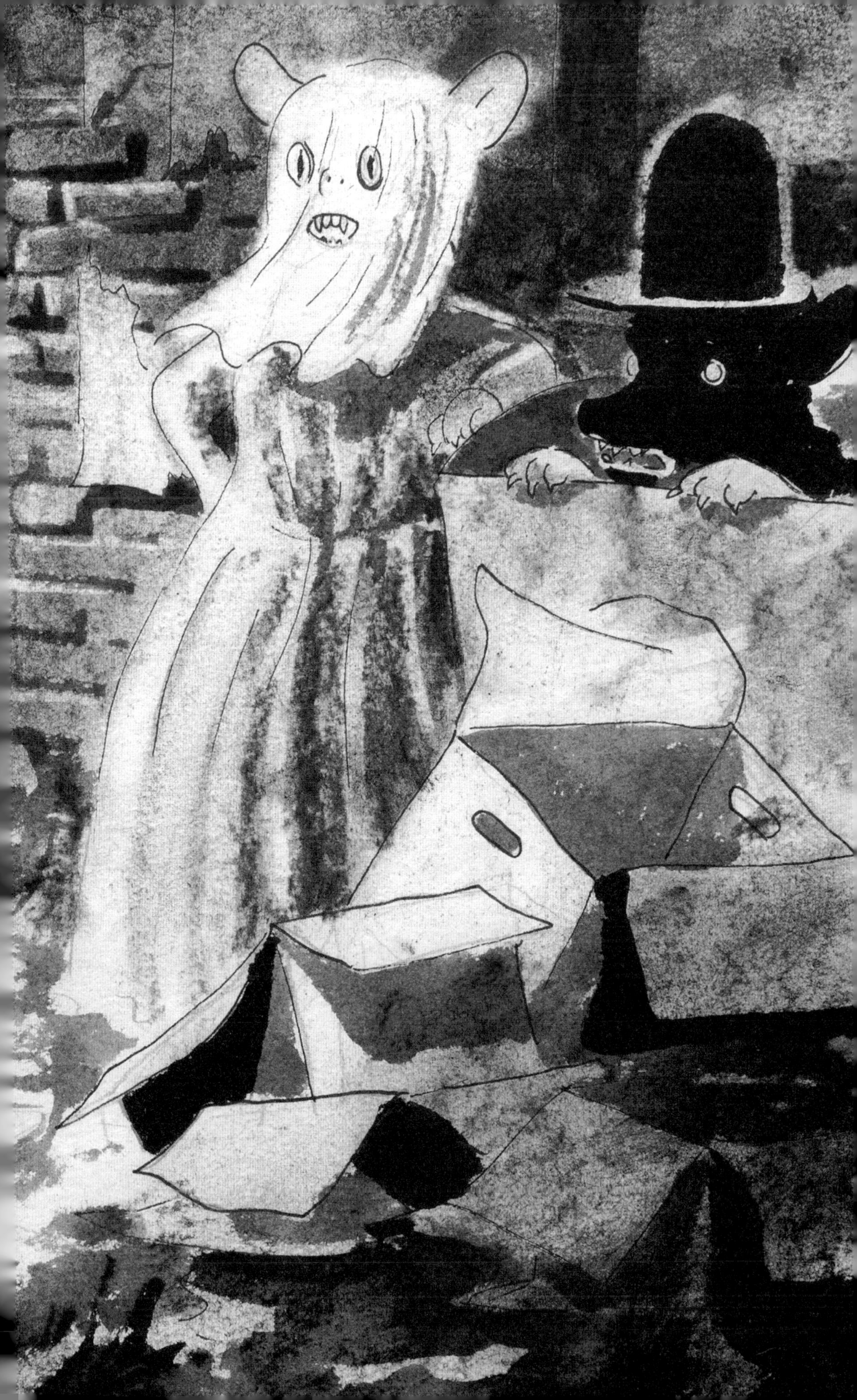

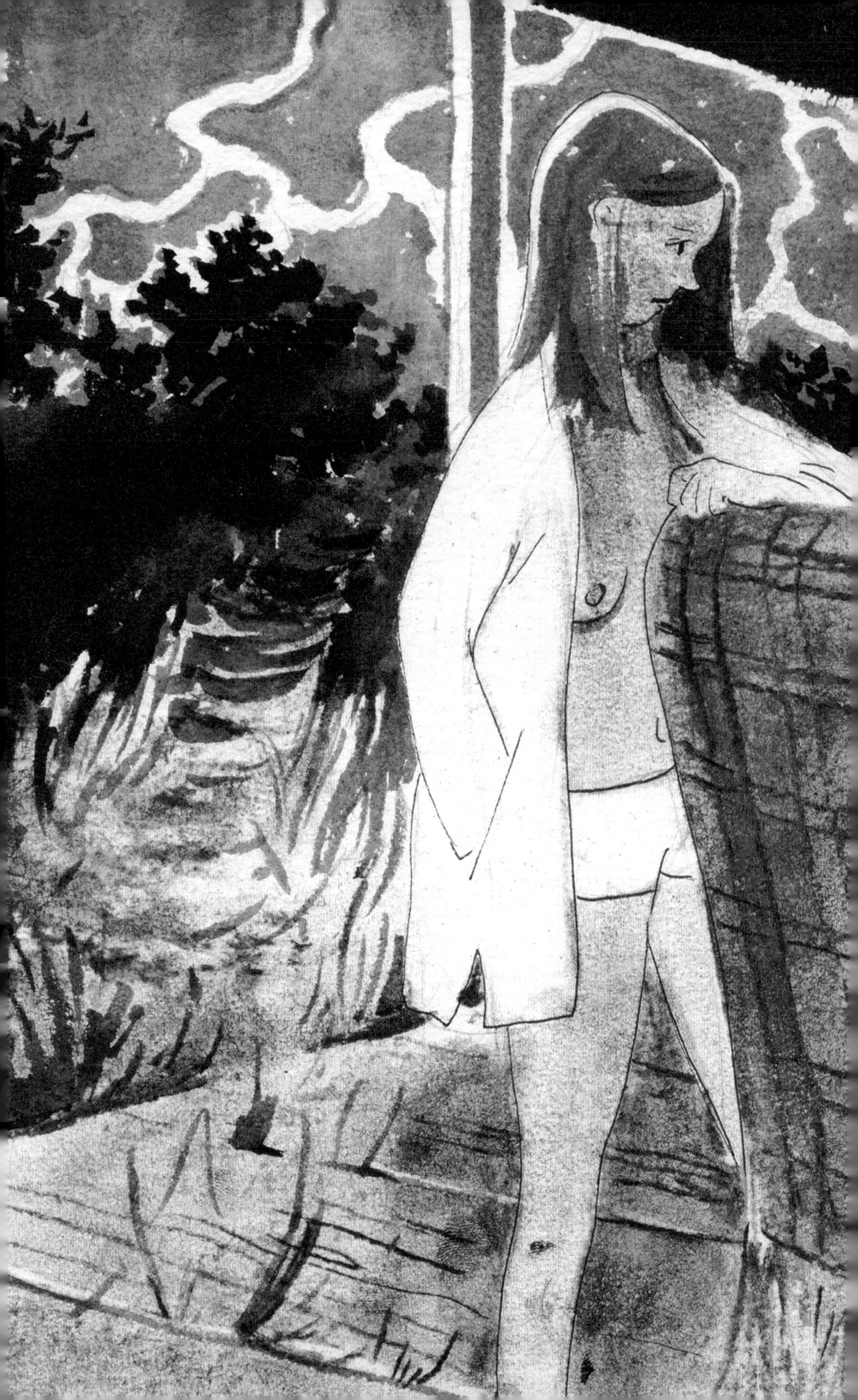

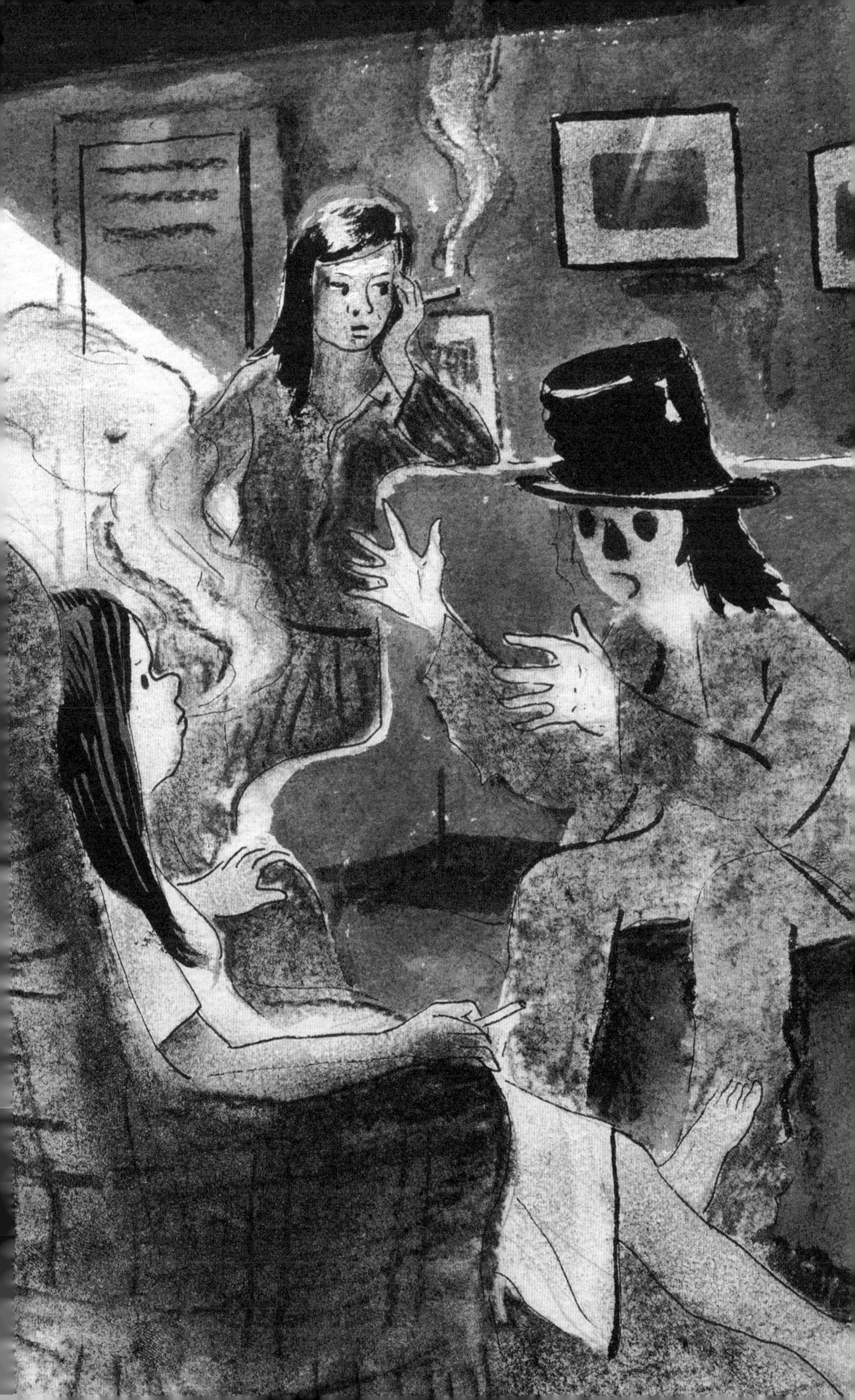

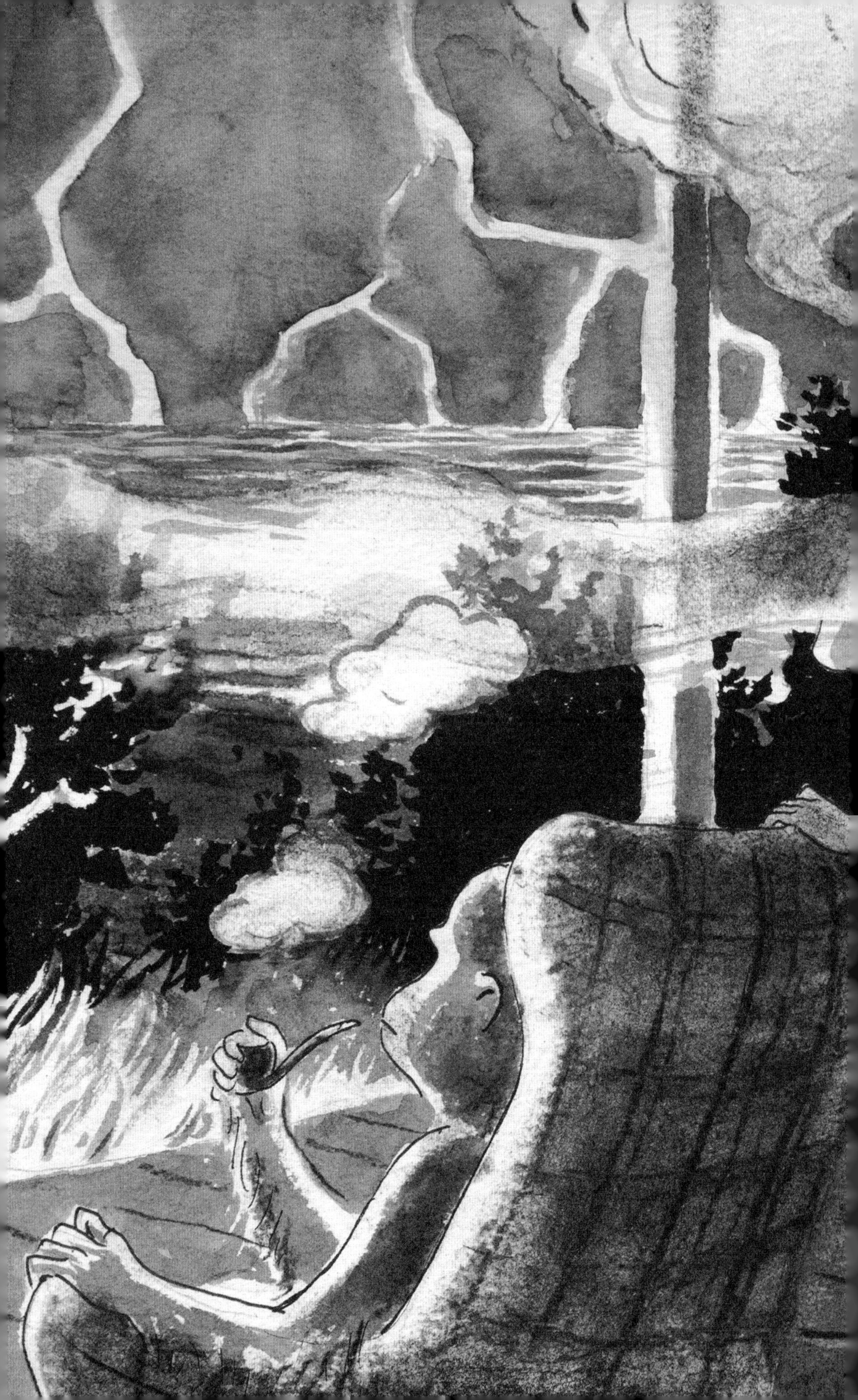

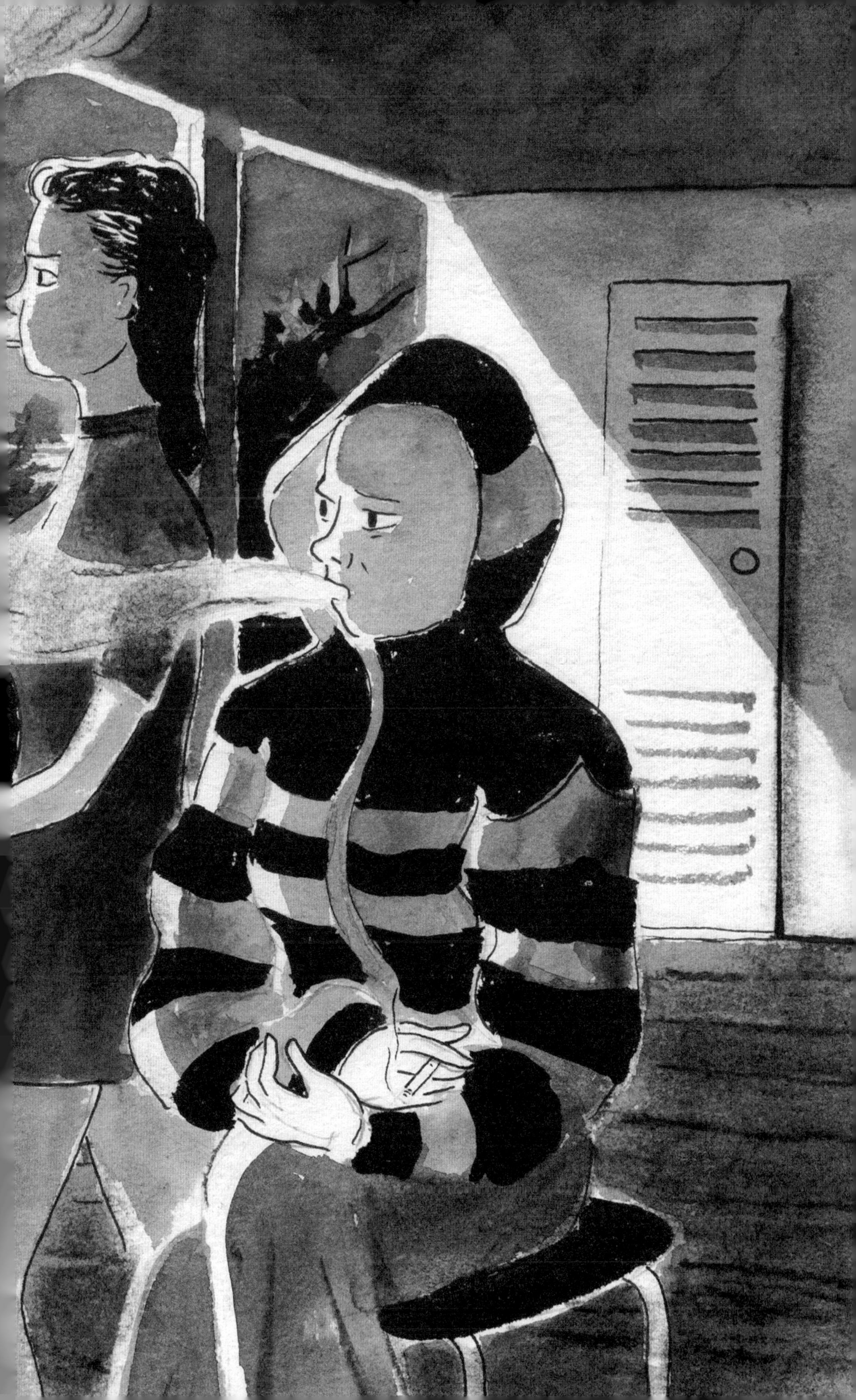

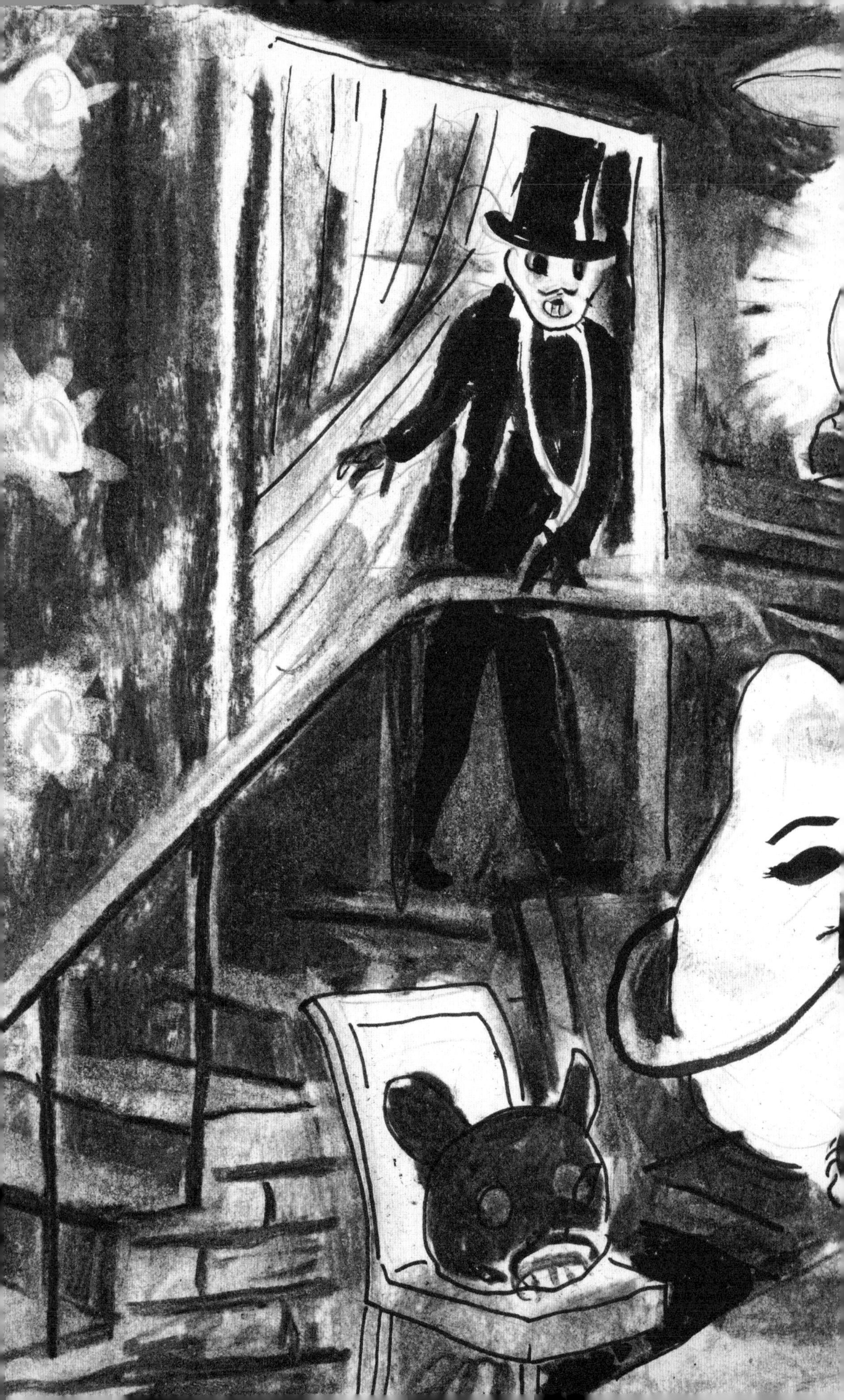

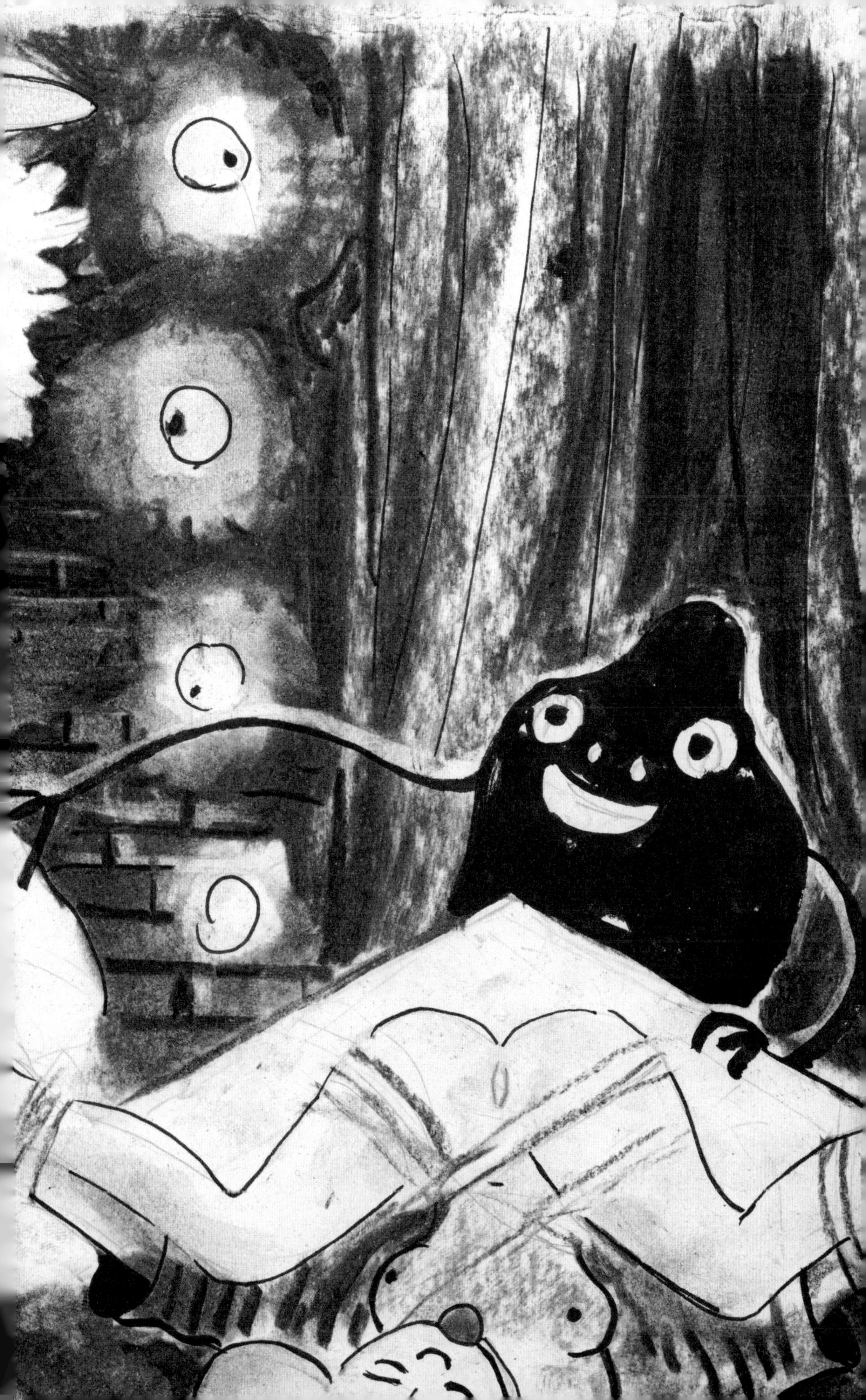

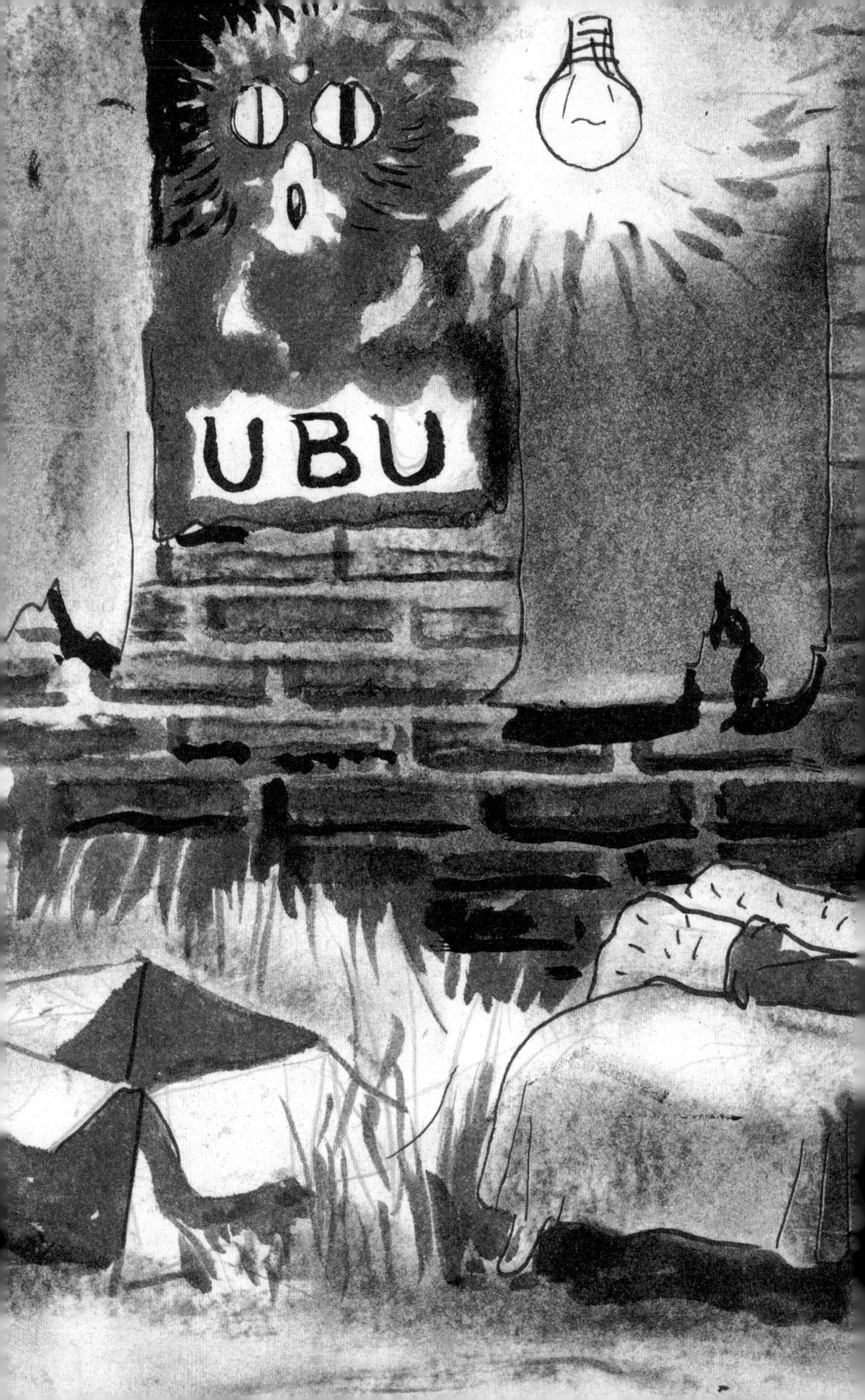
UBU

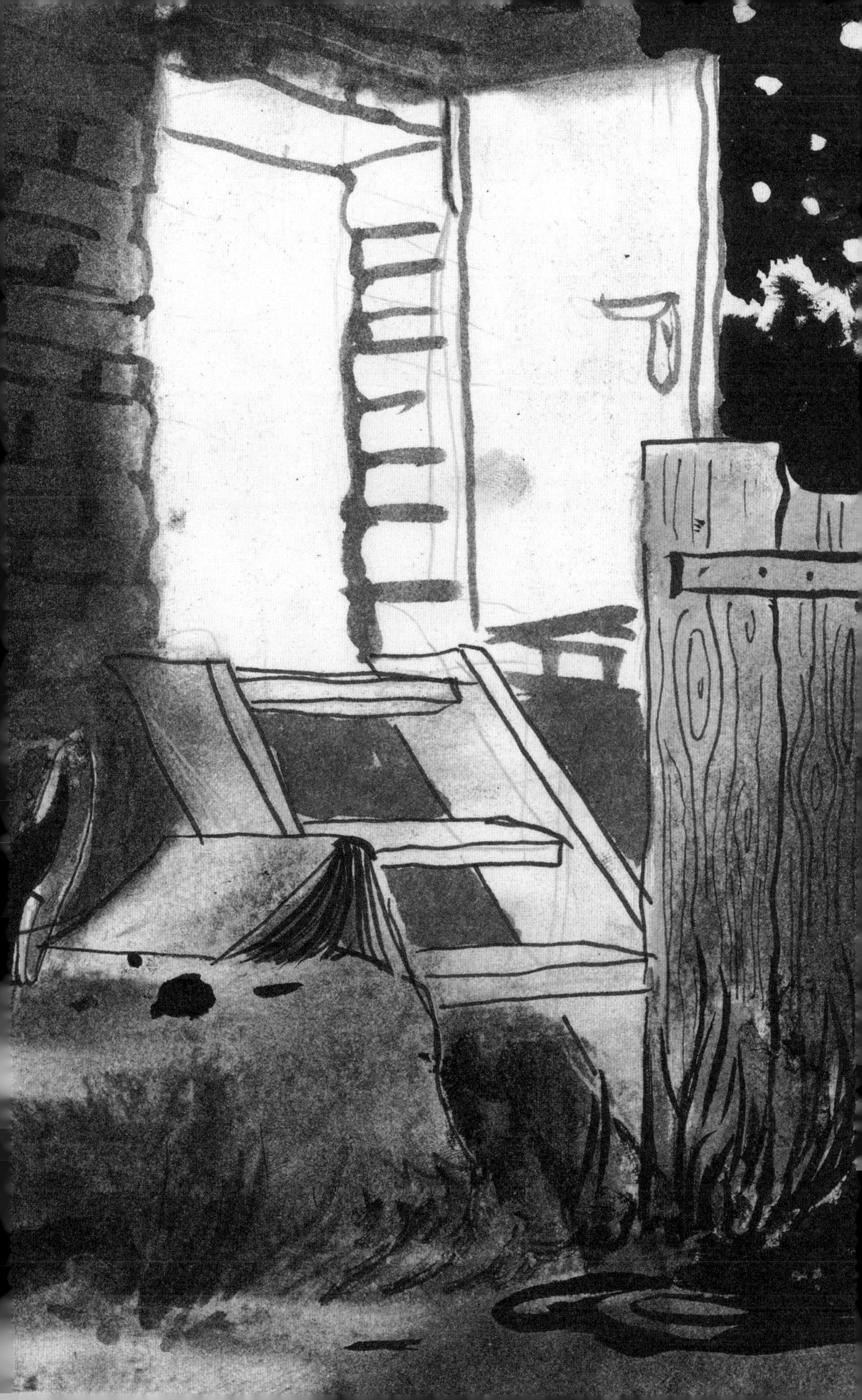

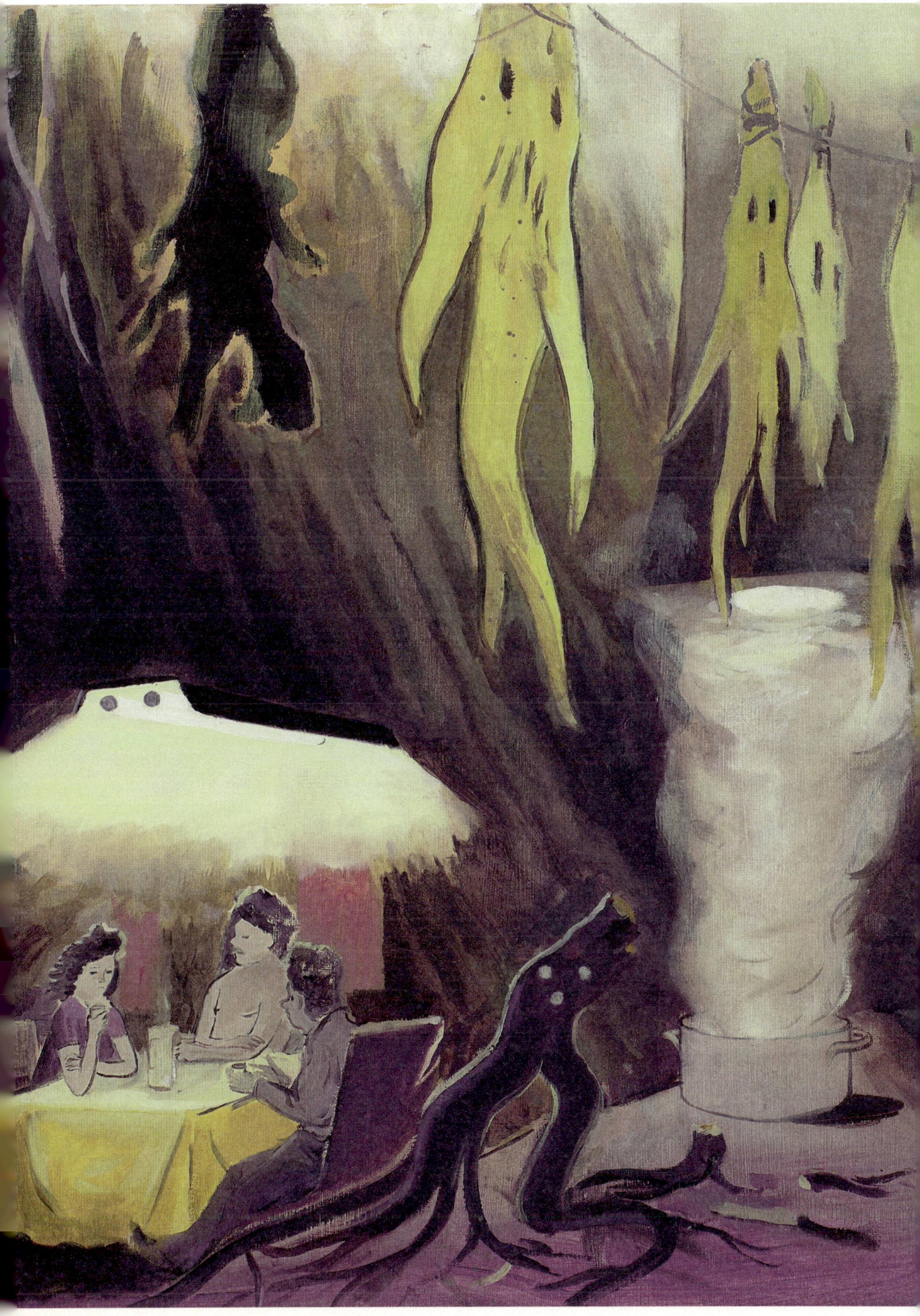

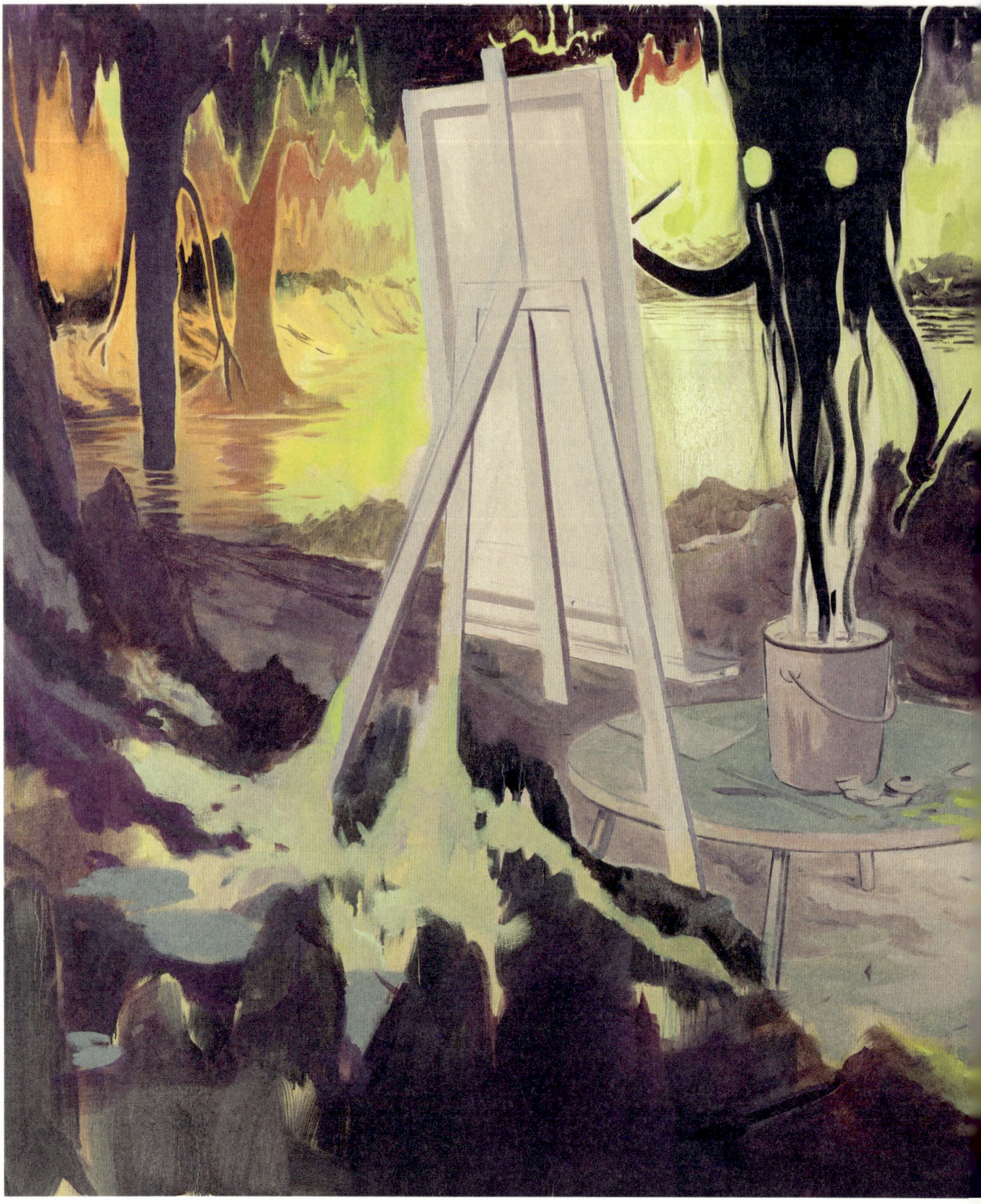

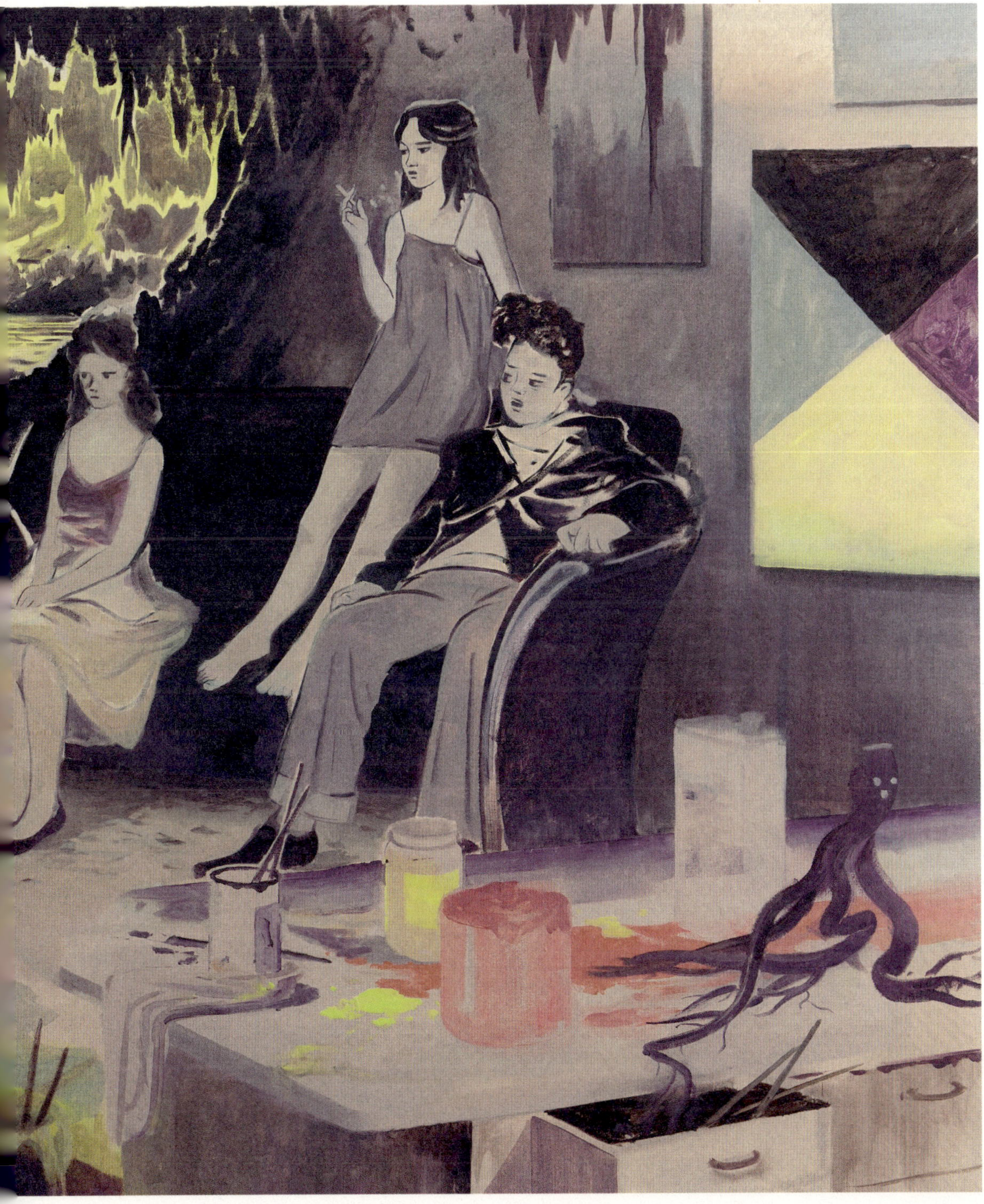

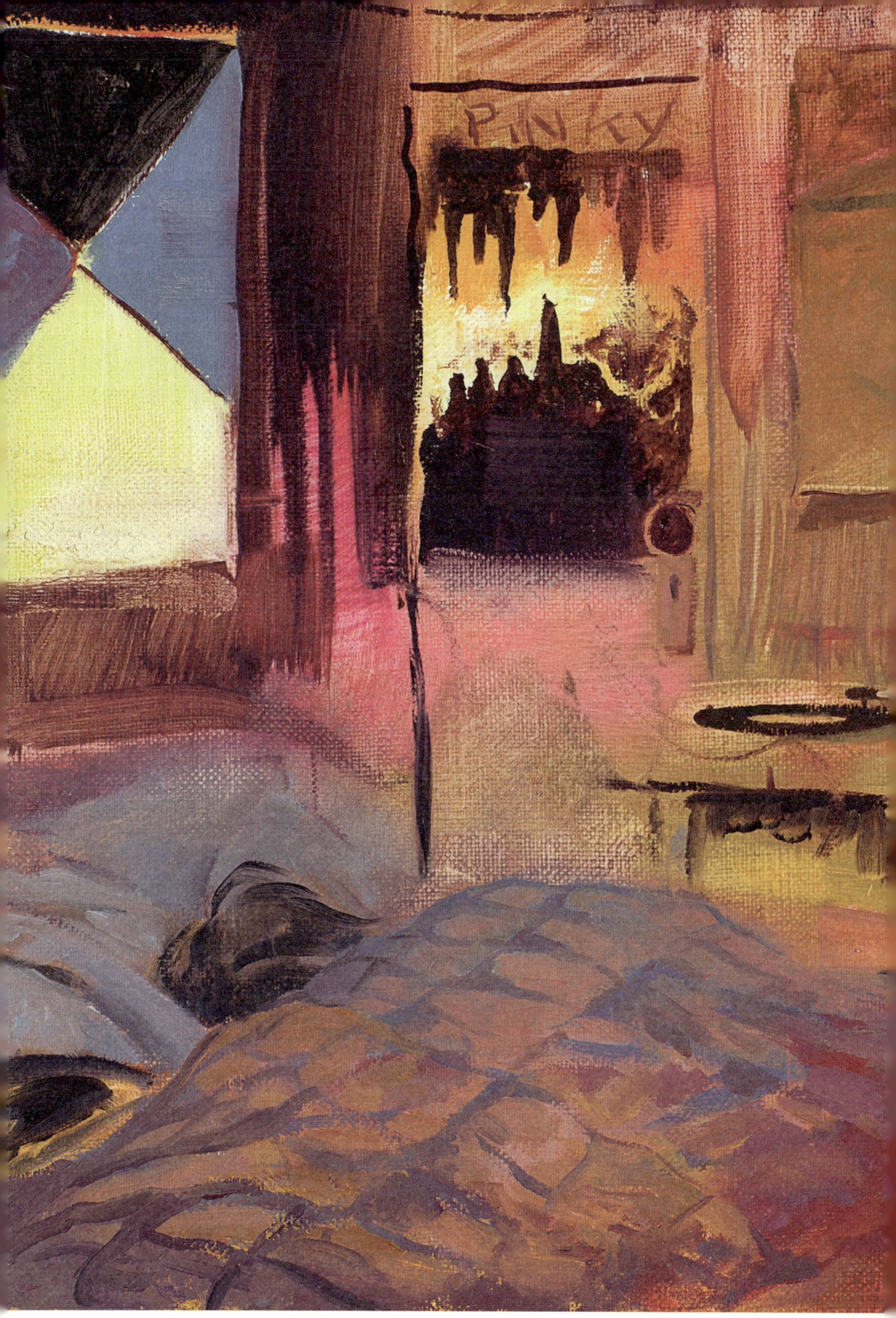
PINKY

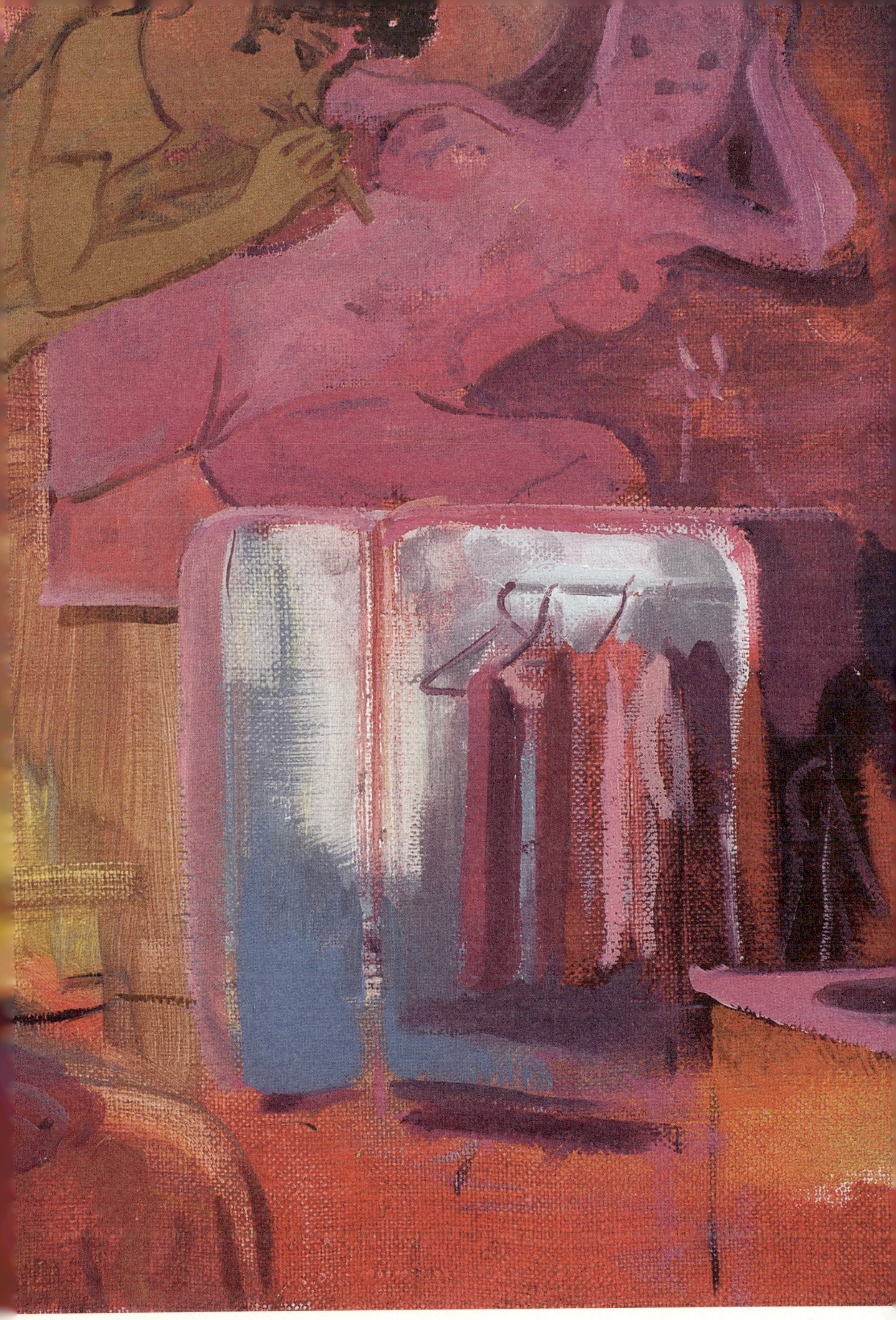

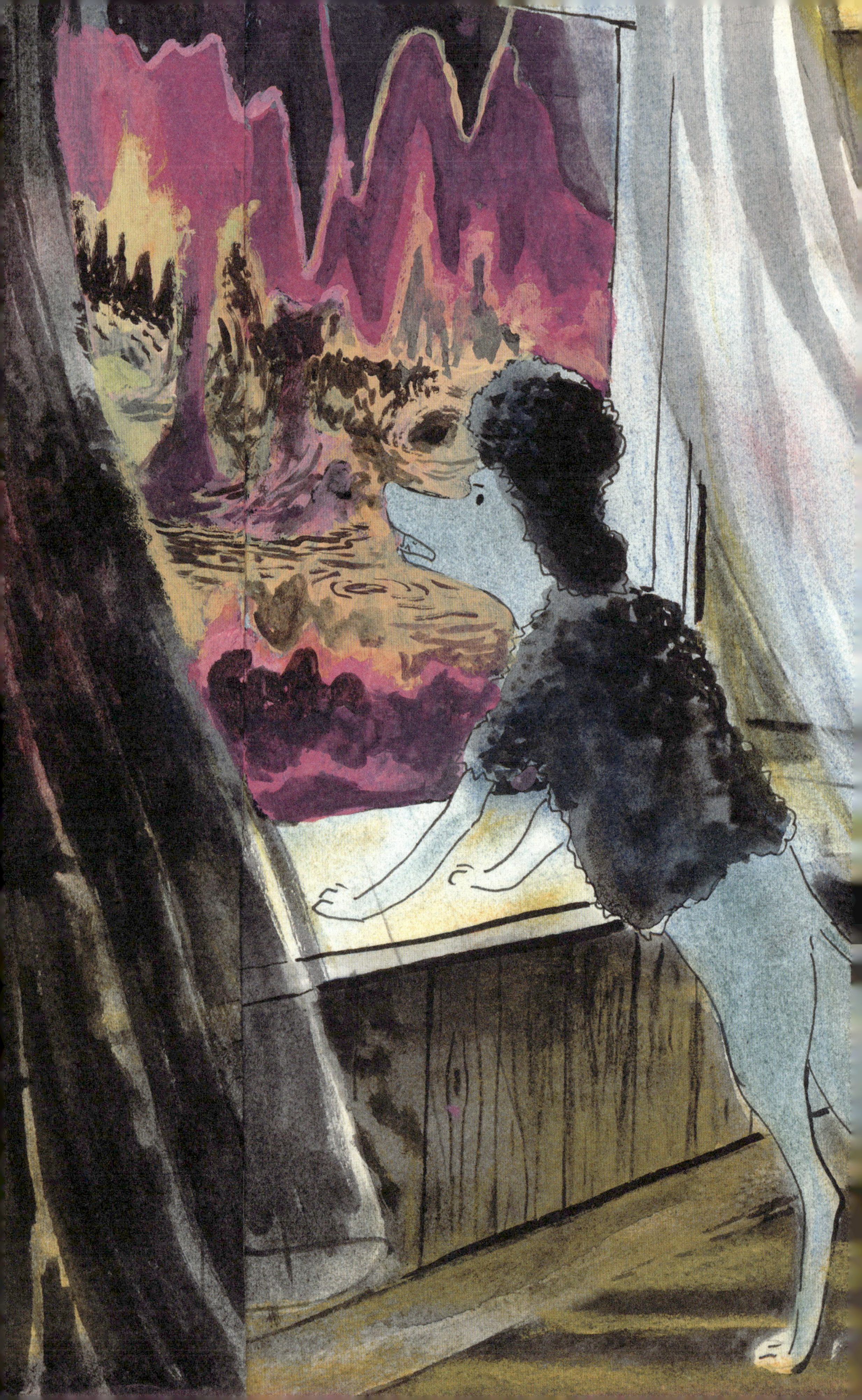

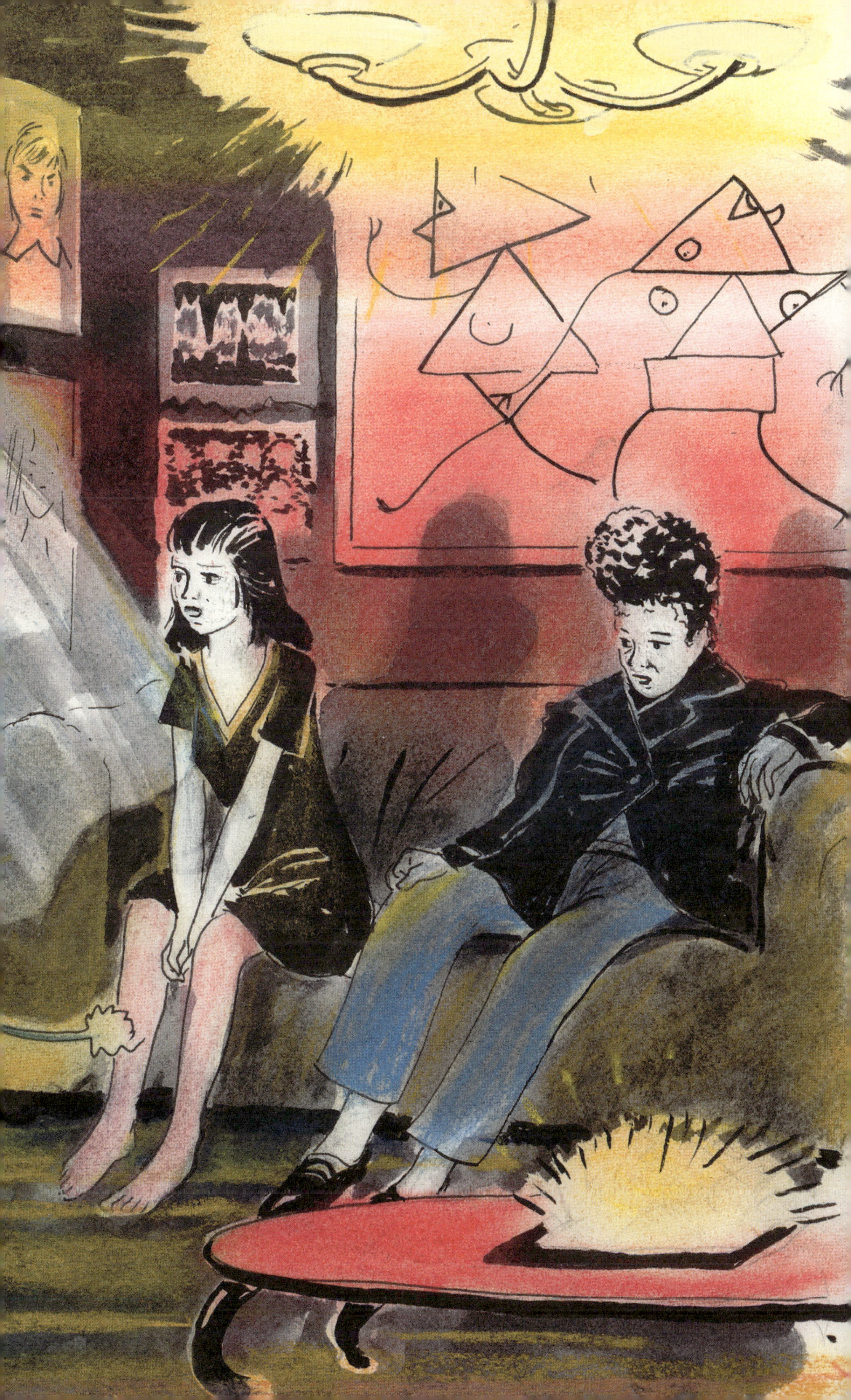

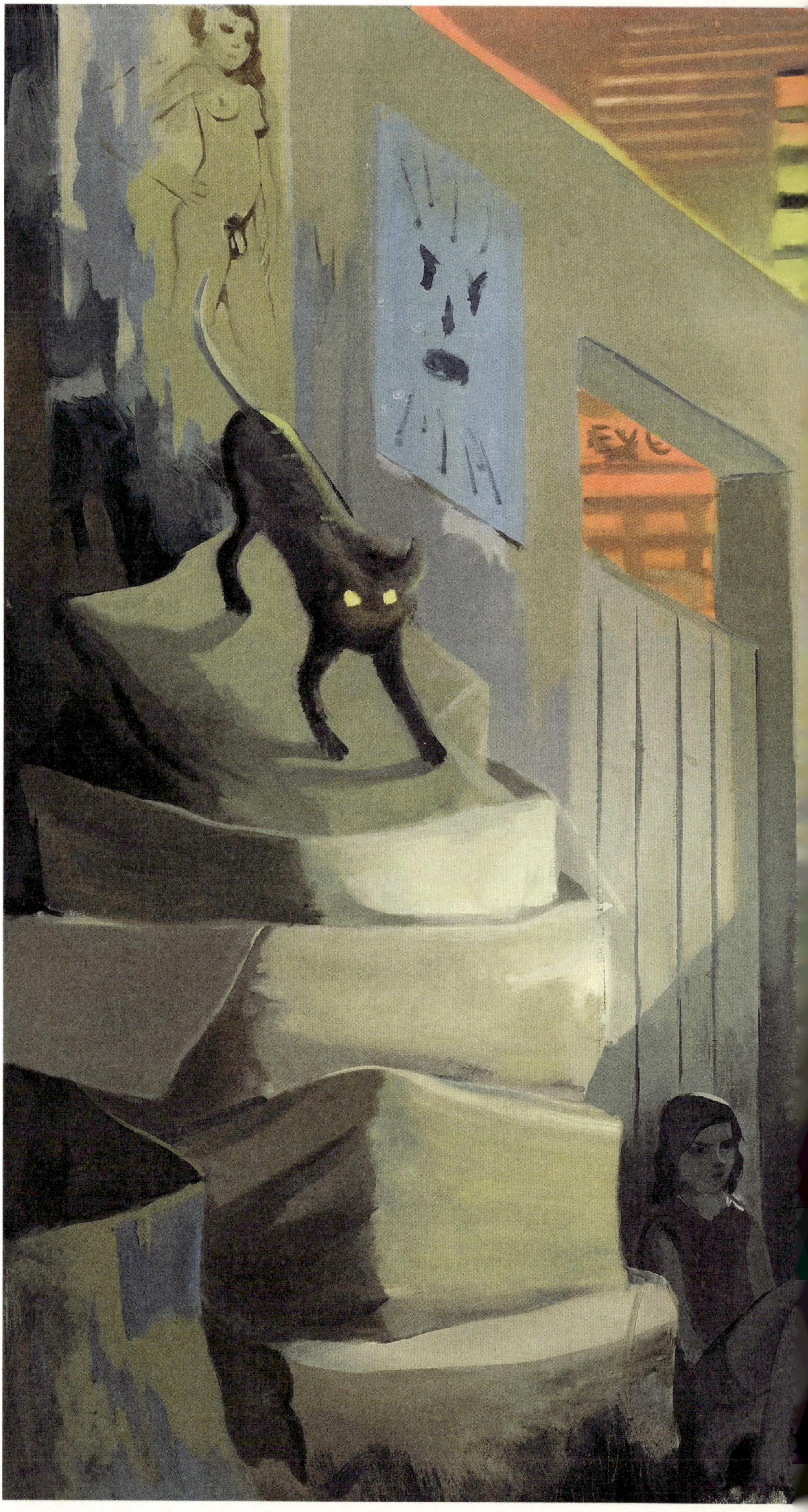

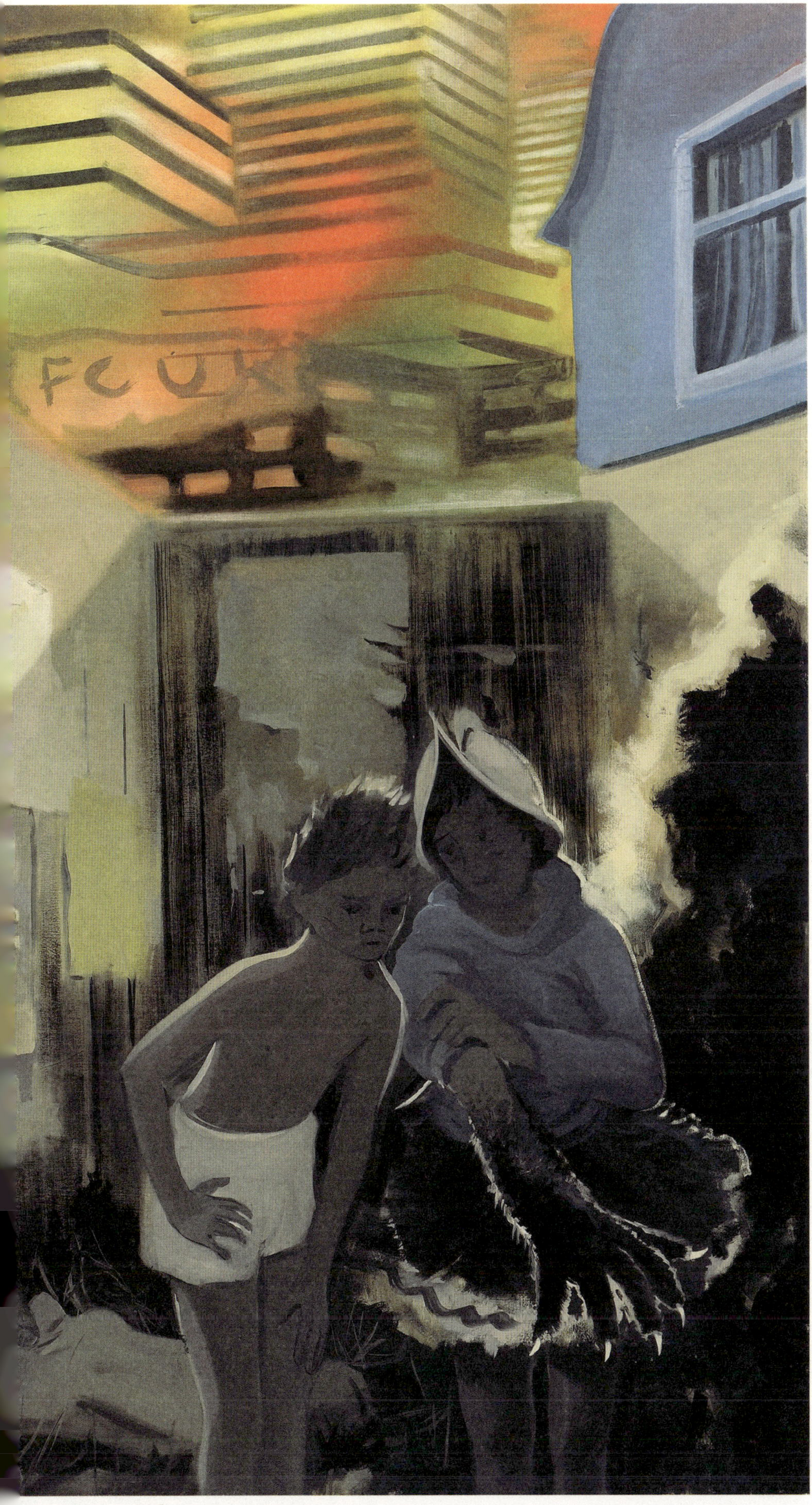
FCU

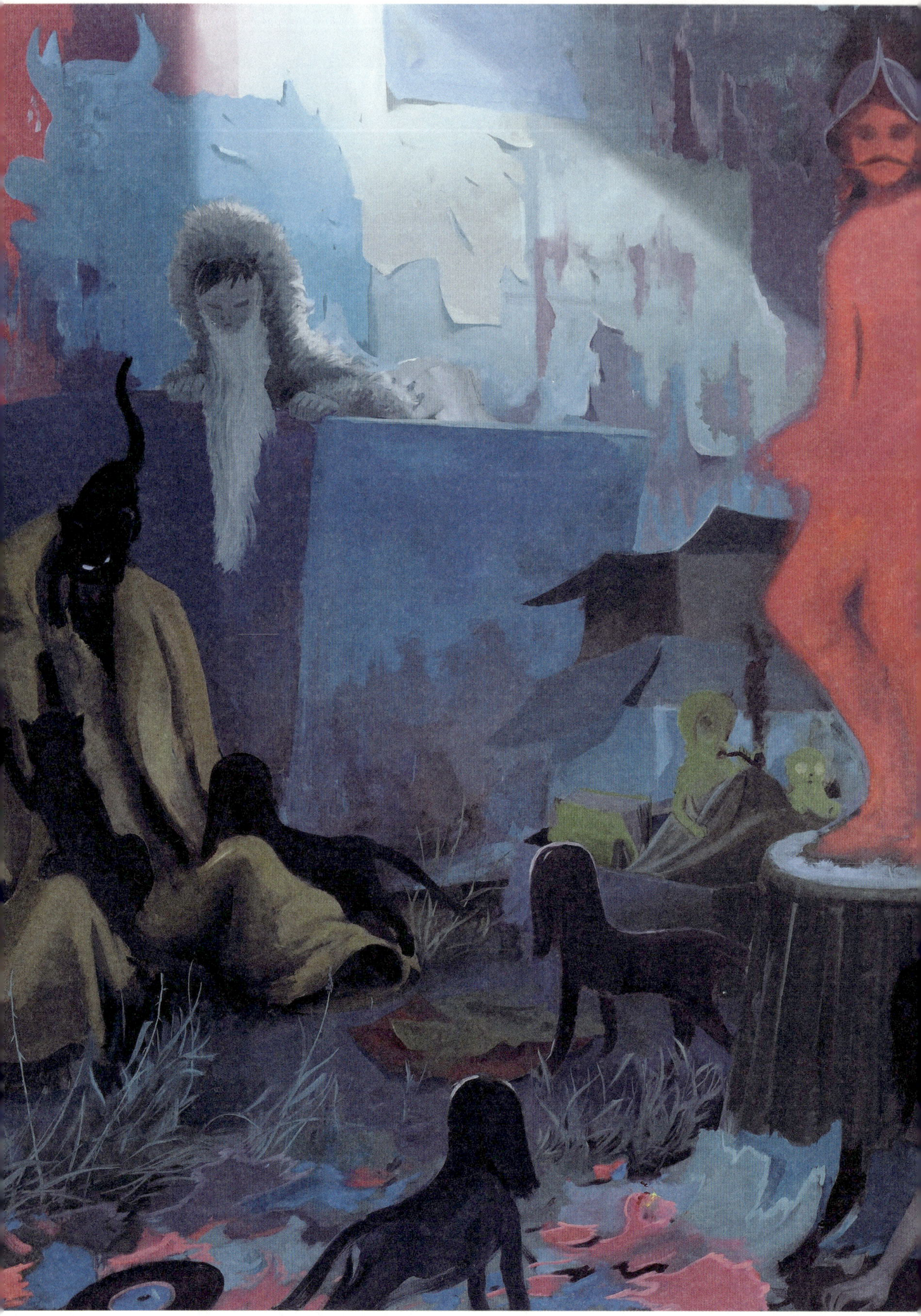

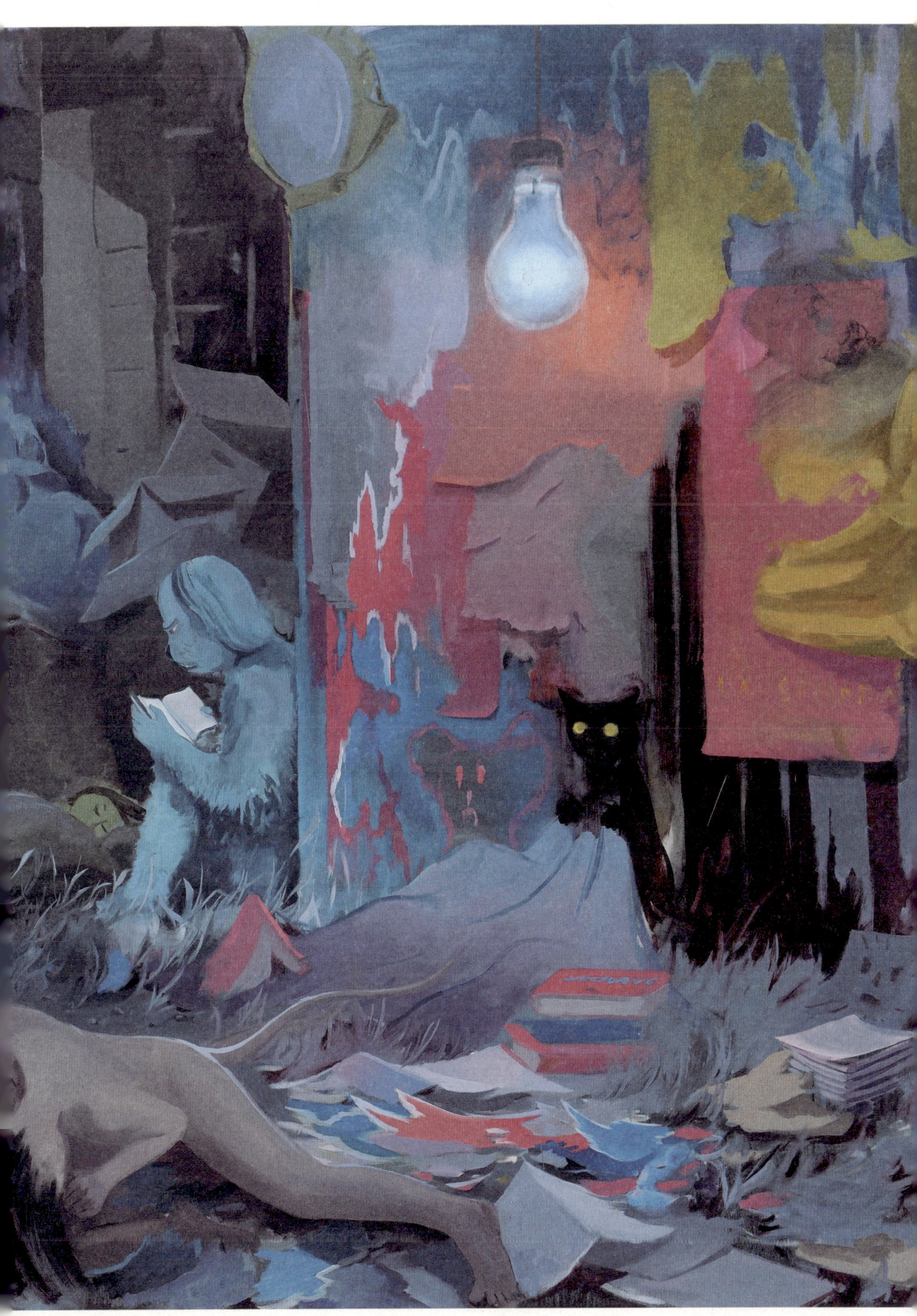

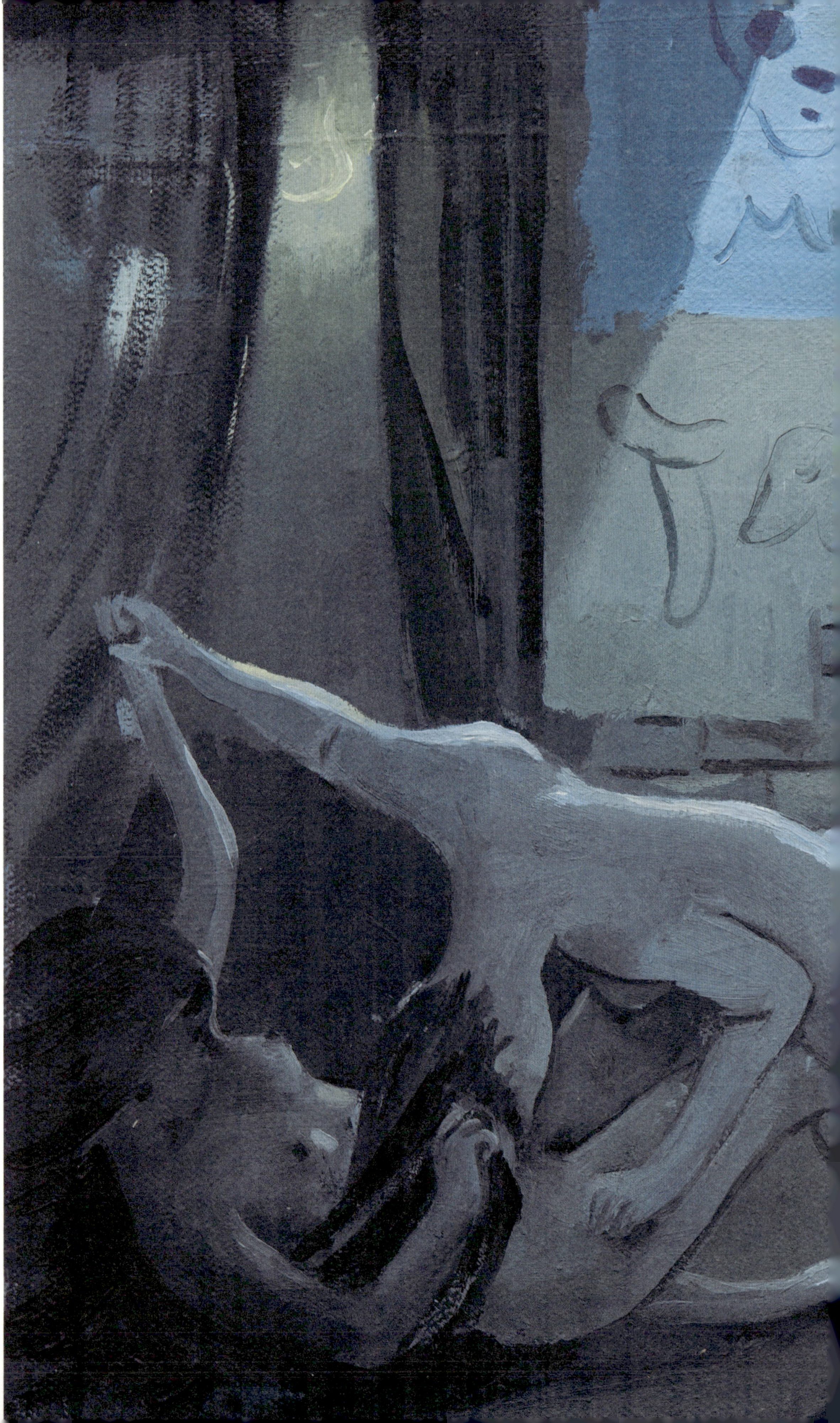

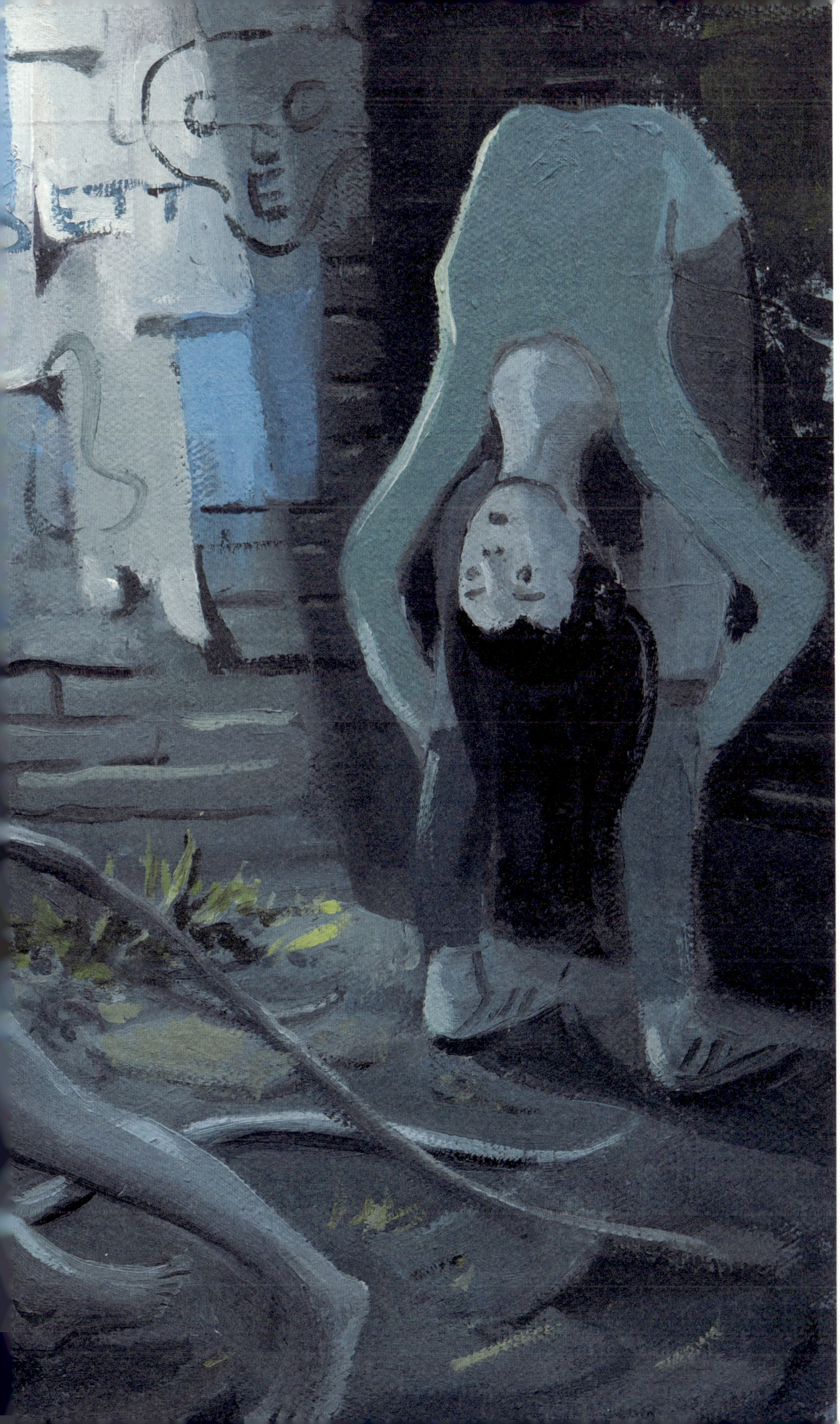

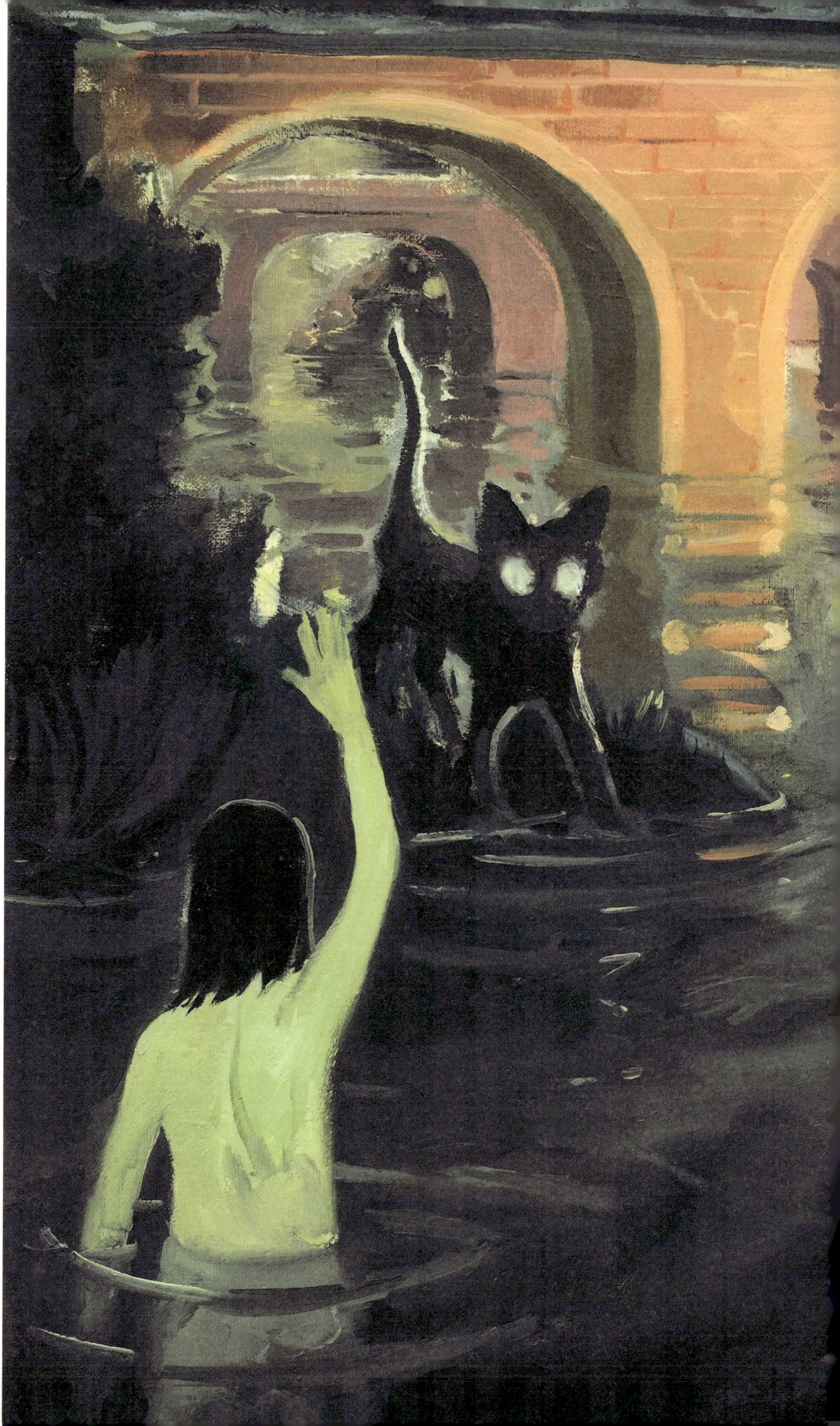

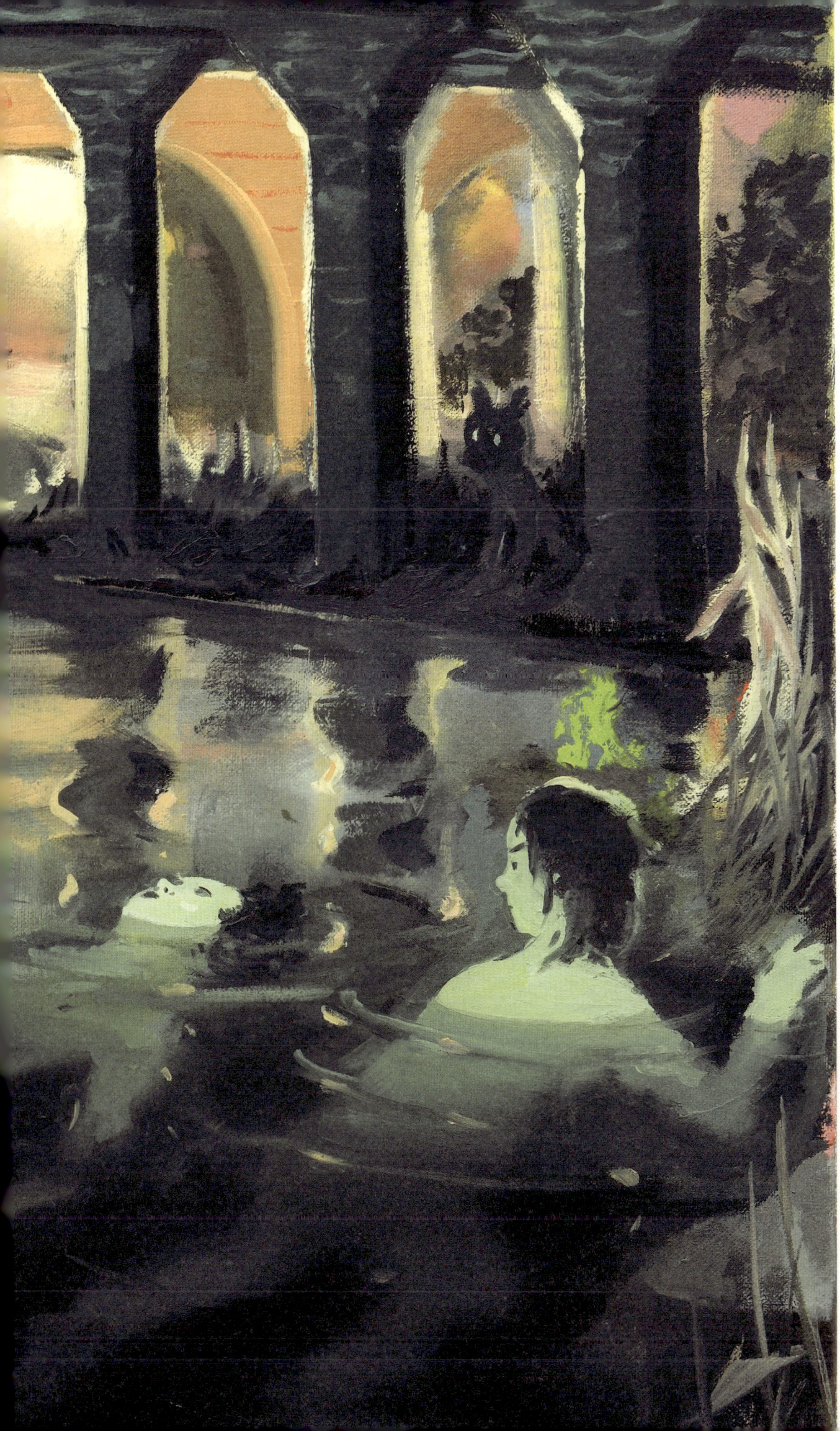

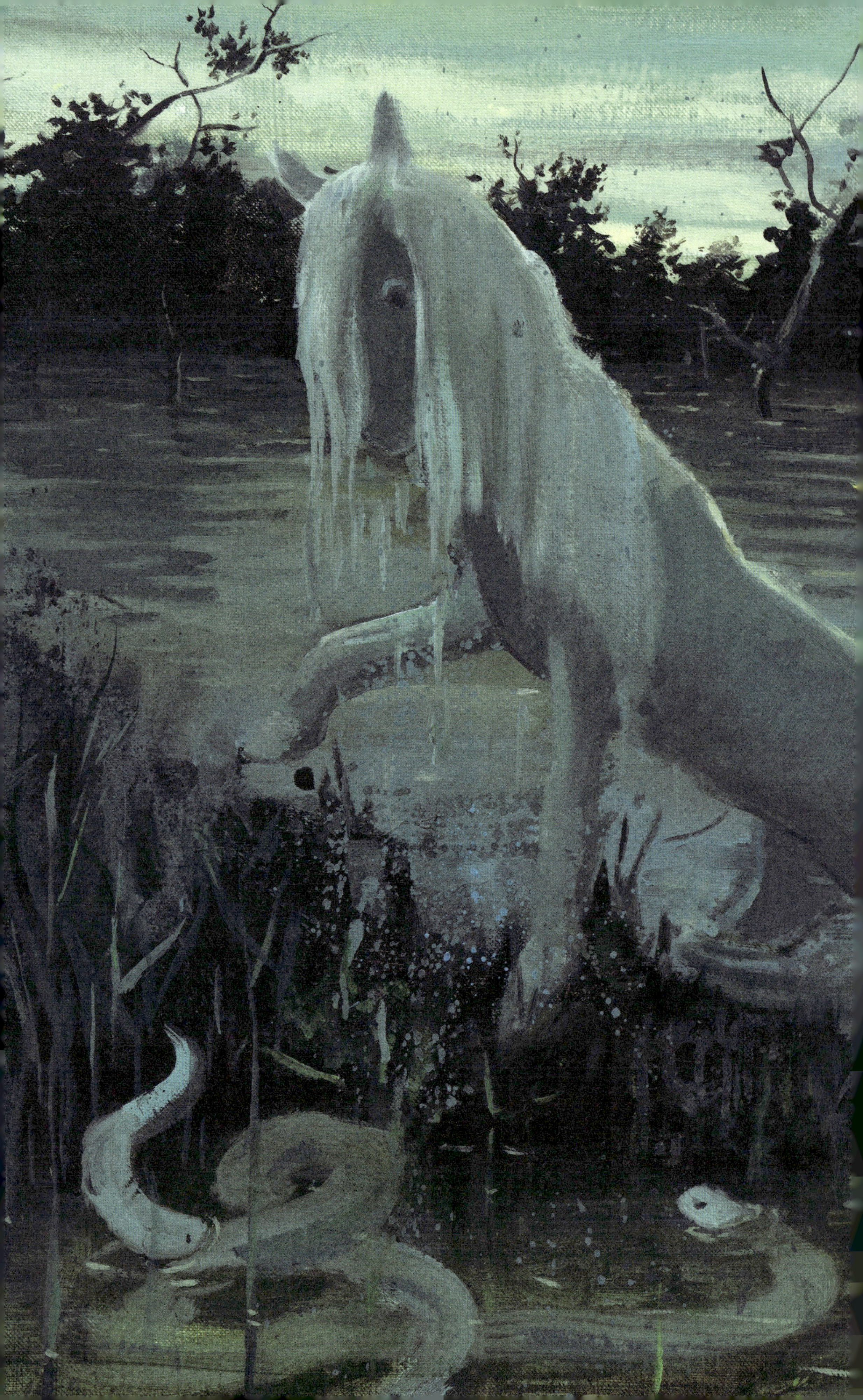

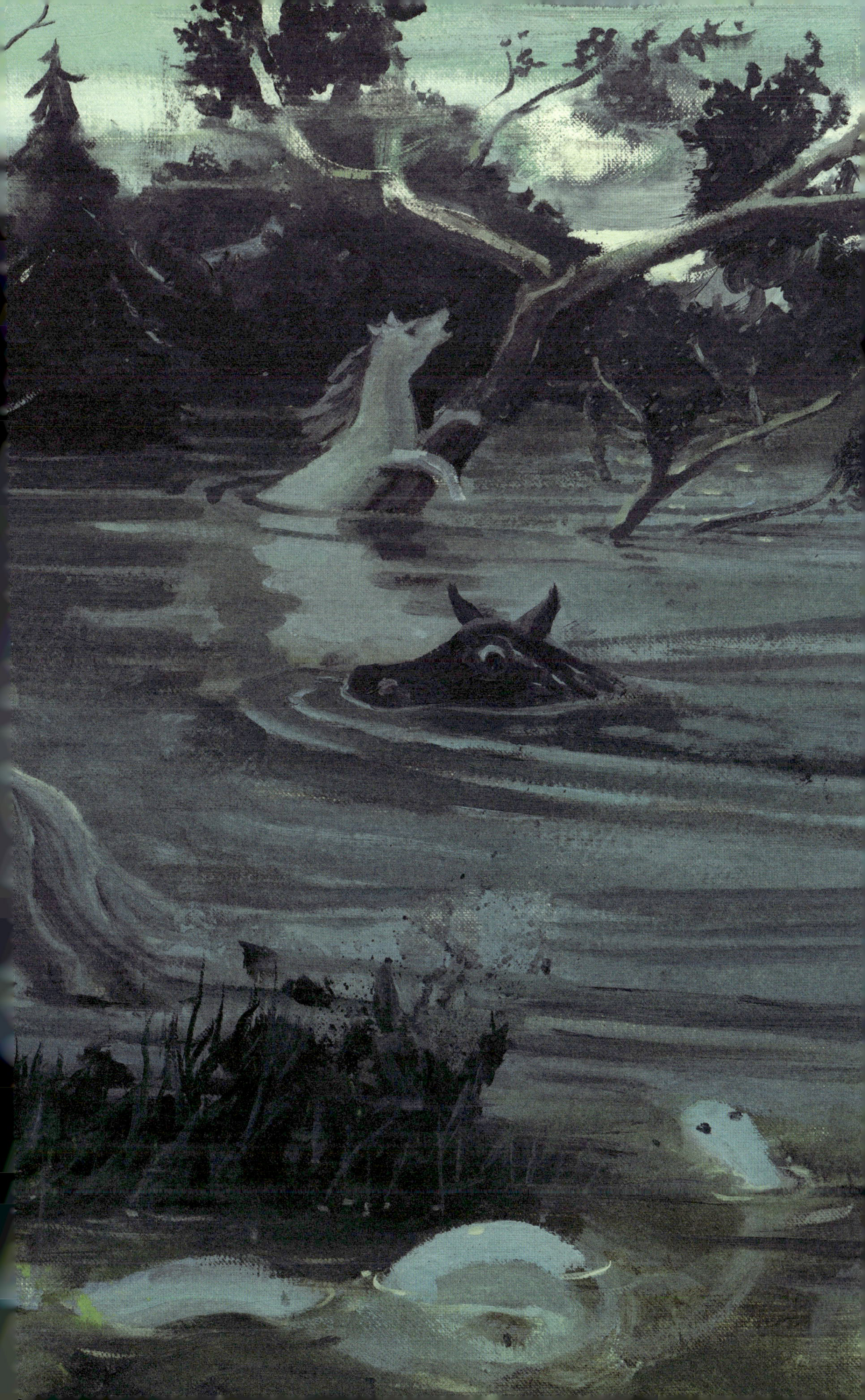

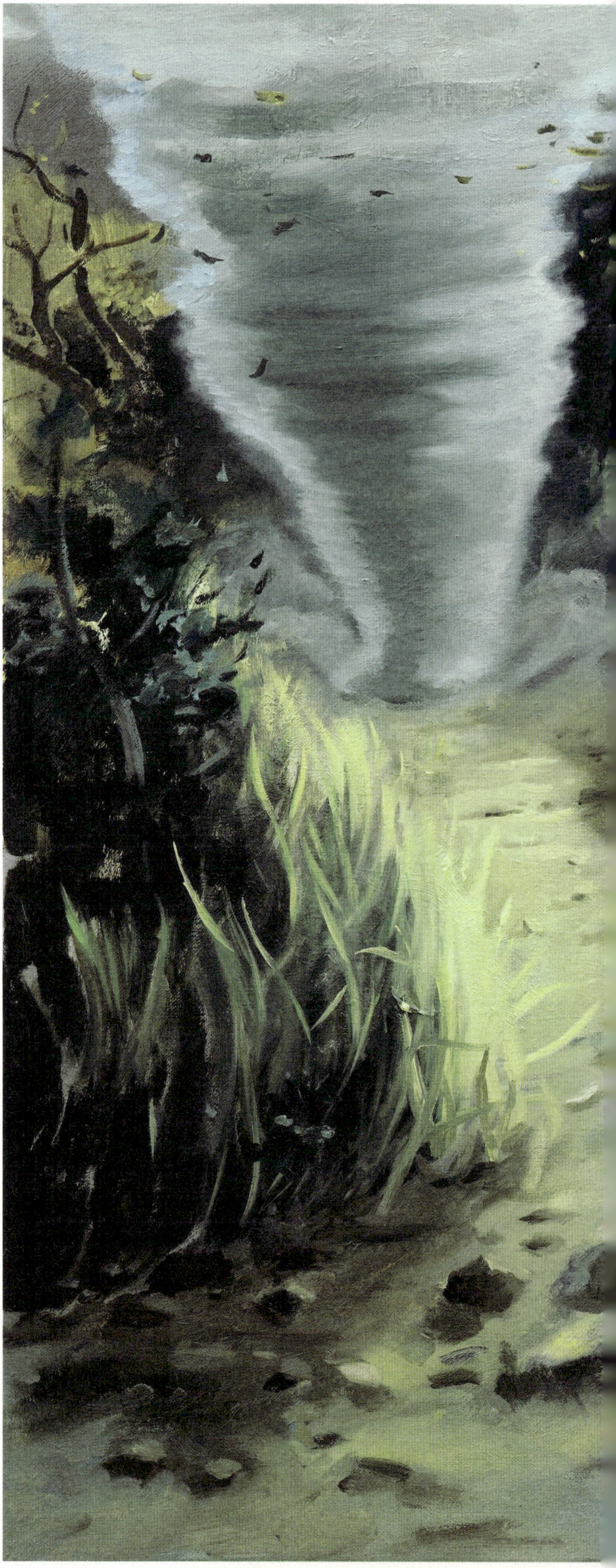

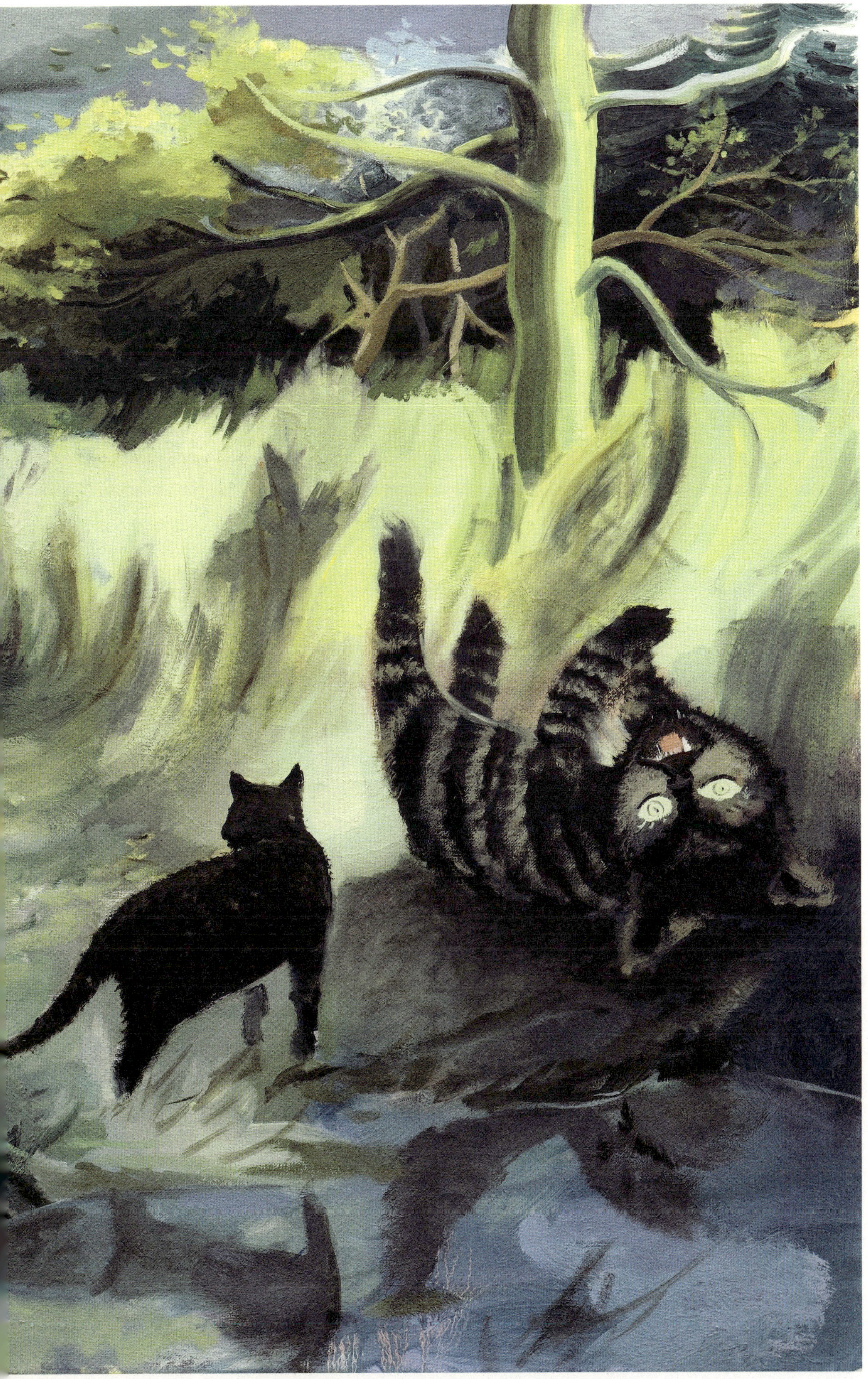

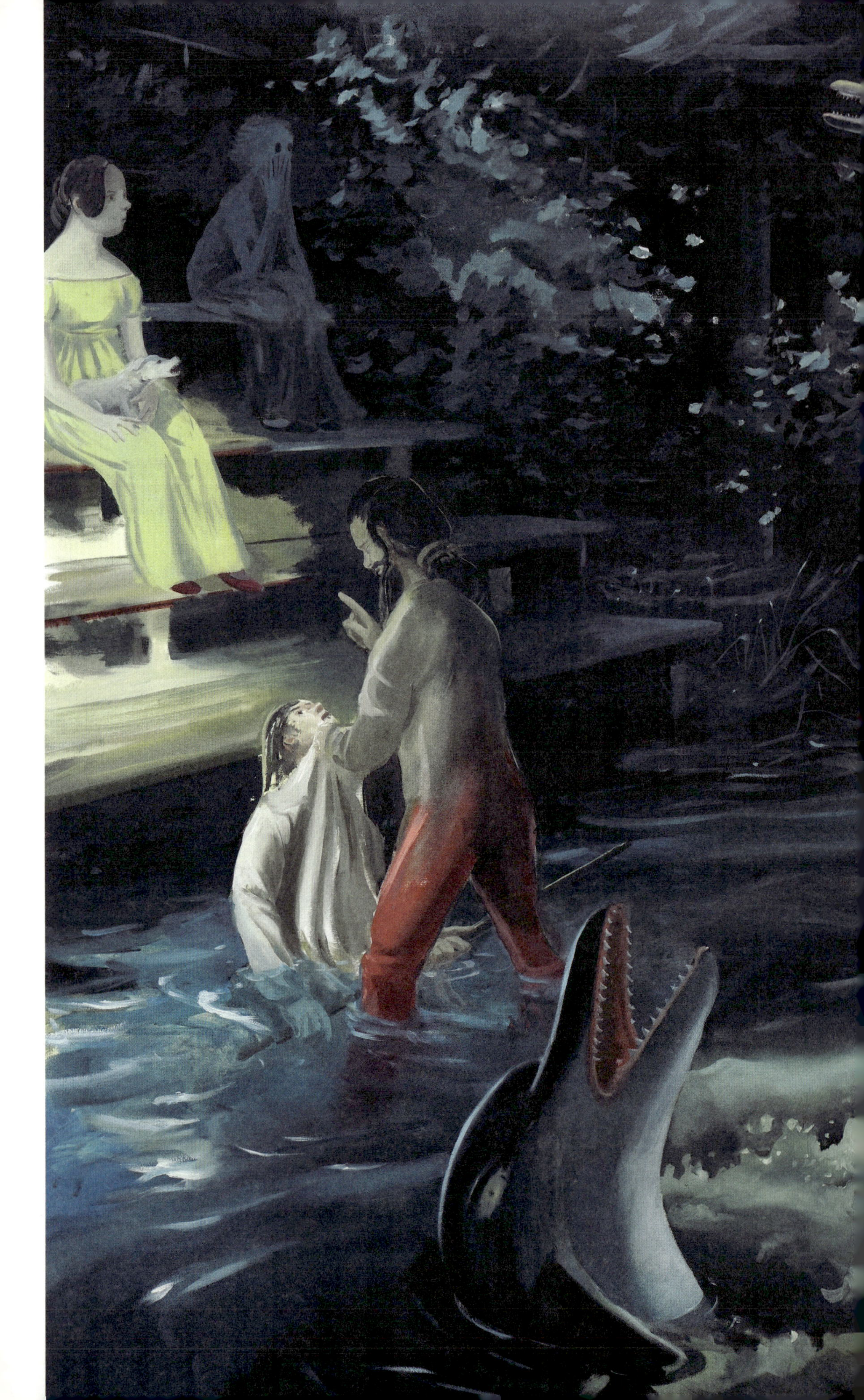

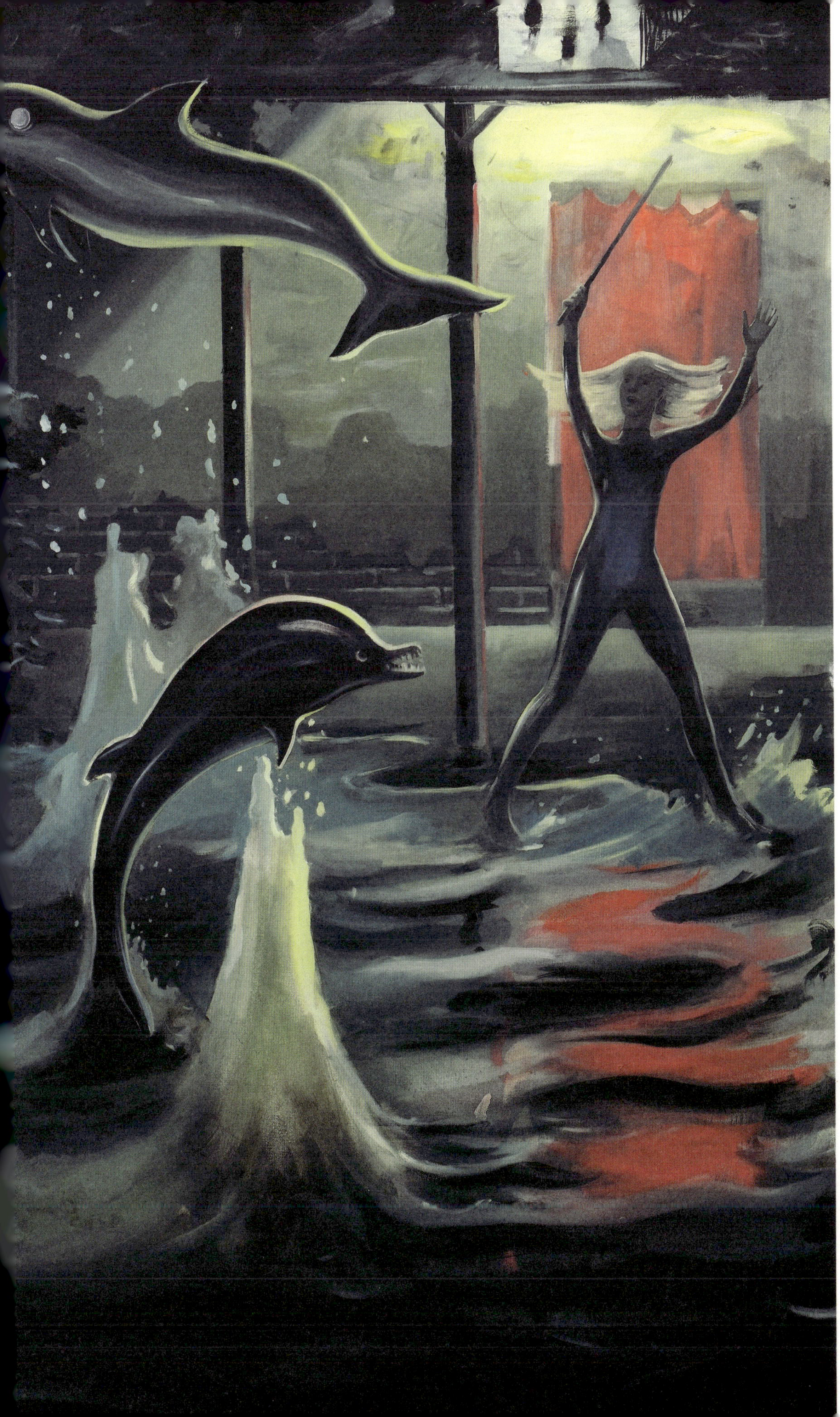

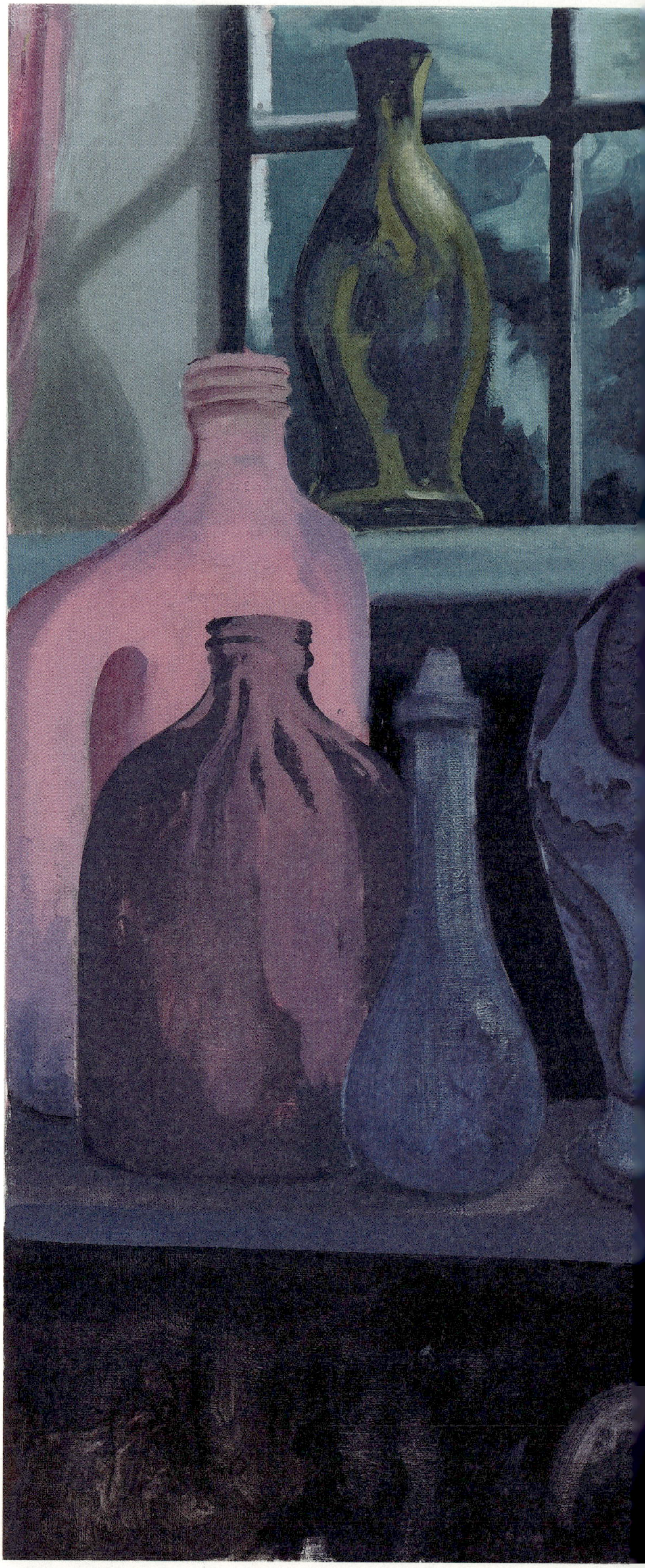

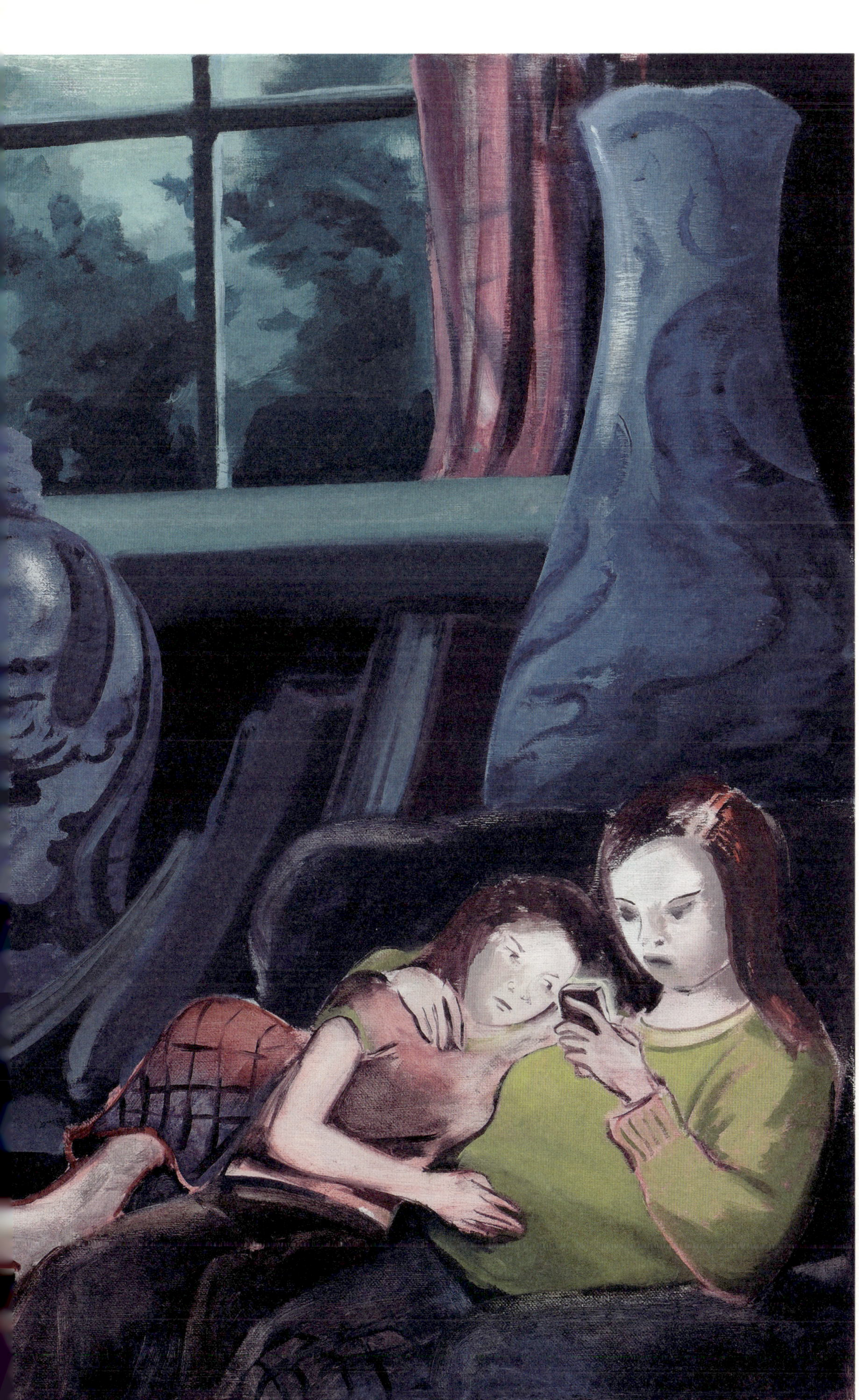

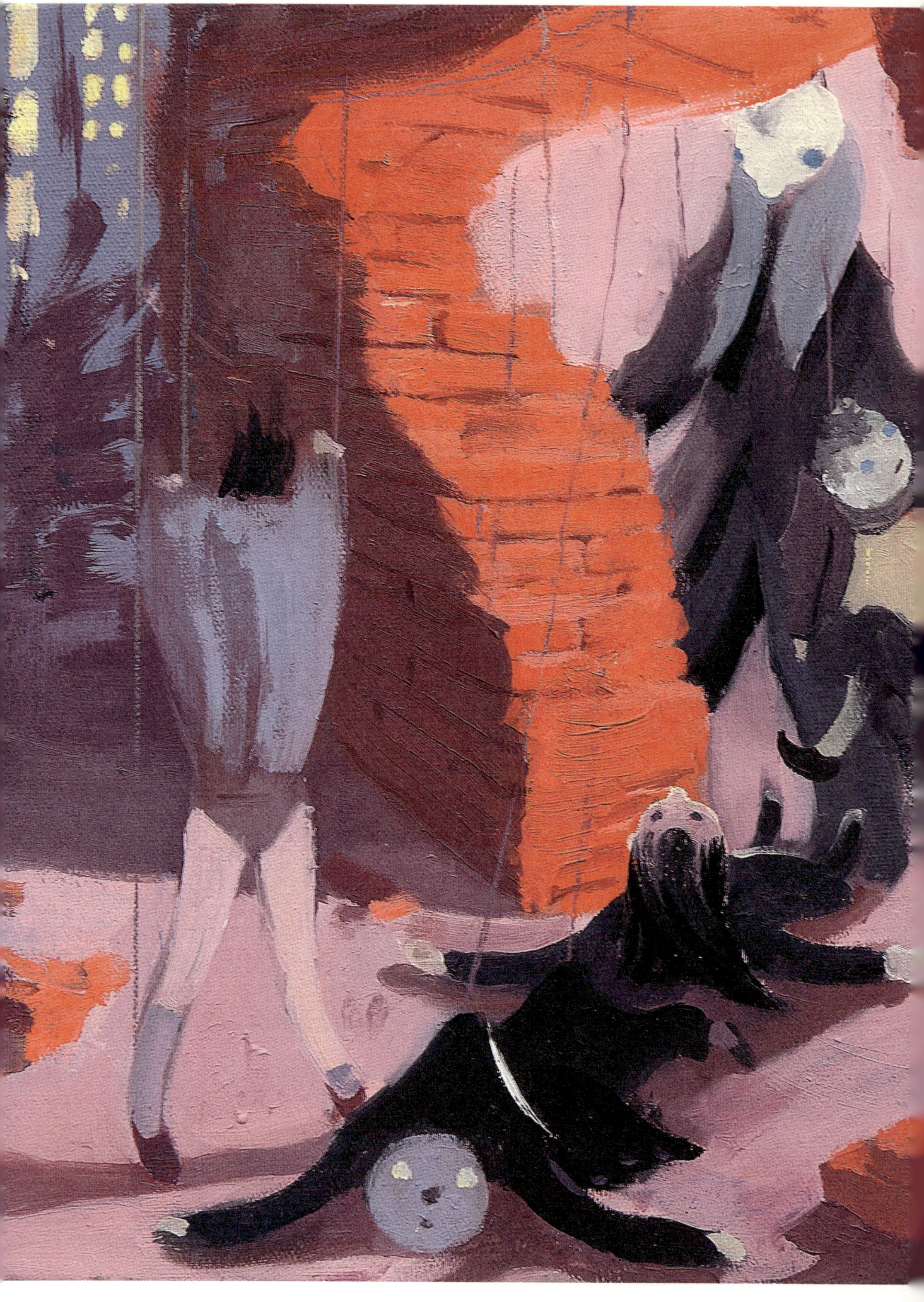

SCHEINTORE

Ich zünde die vier mal fünf Tageslichtstreifen, der Glasglockenchor spielt sein Fünfsekundenstück und schafft ein kühles Morgenstreulicht unter dem Betonhimmel. Salpetrige Steine schlagen unzählige Landschaften vor. Ein Andrew Bird singt „Give it away" dazu. Neben dem Projektfriedhof an der großen Wand hängen die Leinwandgevierte – Scheintore, die es zu öffnen gilt. Geduldig versuche ich zu verstehen, wann sie die Wand durchdringen können. Ein Optimist steht vor der Mauer, denn der Tag ist noch voller Stunden. Potentiale wirken groß, bevor man sie auszuschöpfen versucht, und ein genialer Verdacht hält, solange noch nichts getan ist. Das Kaninchen mit den rotierenden Gänseblümchenaugen muss zuerst aus dem Kopf. Das Getümmel der Gedanken, die wie abgeklärte, aufgeklärte kleine Äffchen Kopfstände und Salti schlagen und plappern, was ich schon weiß. Ein Gedanke reicht völlig. Die anderen mit Nachdruck aus dem Oberstübchen zu bitten ist der erste Schritt. Es braucht Atem, Abstände und Vitaminquellen. Verkleidet und durchsichtig sollen sie mein Gefühl in die Welt flüstern. Ich warte auf die kleine Wolke mit der Matrix. Auf den Gedanken, der sich unterscheidet, den man heraushören will aus den Spatzengesängen auf den Dächern. Ein kleines Intromotiv, das sich wiederholt und Bestand hat. Doch Geduld sei die Uniform des Tages. Die Gedankenblase ist auf 20 Grad abgekühlt. Zwei Kammern ist sie entschlüpft. Die eine lodert und die andere friert. Das ovale Gebilde über meinem Kopf hat hohes Gras und Gebüsche. Ein pferdeartiger Kopf starrt heraus. Sein Blick ist hypnotisch, unverbindlich und schwer deutbar. Seine Fragen und Antworten verschmelzen zu einem Summton, unterlegt mit einer Bassline. Ich versuche die Gedankenblase zu greifen und wie ein Schild vor meine Leinwand zu schieben. Dabei entstehen Risse und Verrutschungen. Schnell erstmal was aufs Papier, bevor es weghuscht wie die Eidechse, wenn man den Stein hebt. Das Papier ist hellhörig, die Leinwand stolz. Nähert man sich tanzend oder schlafend? Die Kühlkammer leitet zum Nachdenksessel und die Brennkammer dreht die Regler auf. Ein Metronom kreist um meinen Kopf und taktet ruhig in die zweite Tageshälfte. Die wird es bringen und zur Not borge ich mir was von morgen. Alles, nur nicht mit hängendem Kopf das Bergwerk aus Backstein verlassen. Sei es nur ein Stäubchen, nur ein paar Sekunden aus dem gewissen Fenster blicken, so ist der Tag gerettet. Liegt dann ein Bauplan vor, reimen sich nur zwei Worte, kommen die nächsten Verse wie von selbst. Das kann ich beim Auftritt verkünden. Zwei Helfer sollen es sein. Rechtecke, die noch wirken, wenn der Strom abgestellt ist. Screenshots aus dem Kopfkino, Gebrauchsgegenstände, Geheimnisse. Ich male, das Bild bleibt und ich gehe weiter. So läuft das.

IMAGINARY PORTALS

I let in the four times five beams of daylight, the glass bell choir performs its 5 second piece and creates a cool diffused morning light below the concrete sky. Nitrous rocks suggest innumerable landscapes. One Andrew Bird chants -give it away- on top of it all. Next to the graveyard of projects on the large wall there are the canvas frames, imaginary portals that demand to be opened. Patiently I try to fathom when they are ready to pierce through the wall. An optimist before the wall, since the day is still full of hours. Potentials seem huge before you try to tap them, and a brilliant doubt persists as long as nothing has been done. First, you need to get the rabbit with the rotating daisy eyes out of your head. The bustle of thoughts, which, like tiny jaded, sophisticated monkeys engage in somersaults and headstands, blabber about things I already know. A single thought is enough. The first step is to persistently ask the others to leave your mind. You require breath, distance and vitamin sources. Disguised and transparent they should whisper my feeling to the world. I am waiting for the tiny cloud that holds the matrix. For the thought that is different, the one you want to make out among the sparrow songs from the roofs. A minuscule introductory motif that repeats itself and has an enduring quality. But patience be the uniform of the day. The bubble of thought has cooled down to 20 degrees. It has slipped from two chambers. One of them blazing, the other freezing. The oval shape above my head has high grass and shrubs. A horse-like head stares down from it. His gaze is hypnotic, noncommittal and well tough to interpret. His questions and answers merge into a humming sound accompanied by a bass line. I try to get a hold of the thought bubble and to push it before my canvas like a shield. This causes tears and slips. Let's put something down on paper real quick, before it rushes away like a lizard when you lift the rock. The paper is only paper-thin, the canvas proud. To approach it dancing or sleeping? The cooling chamber directs you to the contemplation chair and the furnace chamber turns the controls to maximum. A metronome circles around my head and tick tick ticks me softly into the second half of the day. This will certainly spawn something and in case I'll borrow something off tomorrow. Everything, but don't leave this mine of bricks with your head bent down. If it's just a brief dream, just a view from that particular window for a few seconds the day is saved. Then if there's a blueprint. If only two words rhyme, the next verses will come by themselves. This I can announce at my next appearance. Two assistants is all it takes. Rectangles that continue to resonate when the power is cut. Screenshots of the films in your mind, basic commodities. Secrets. I paint, the picture remains and I go on. That's how it's done.

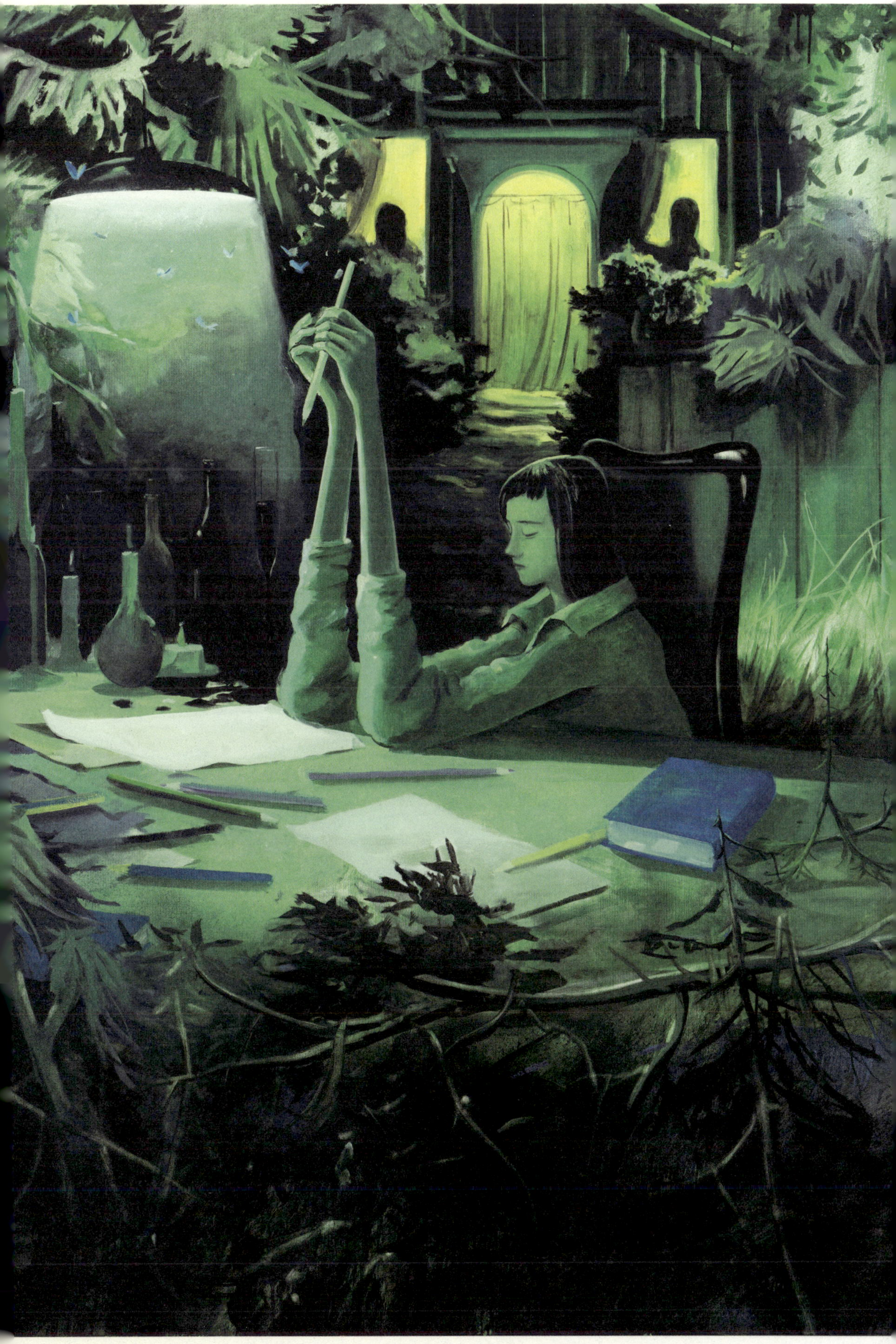

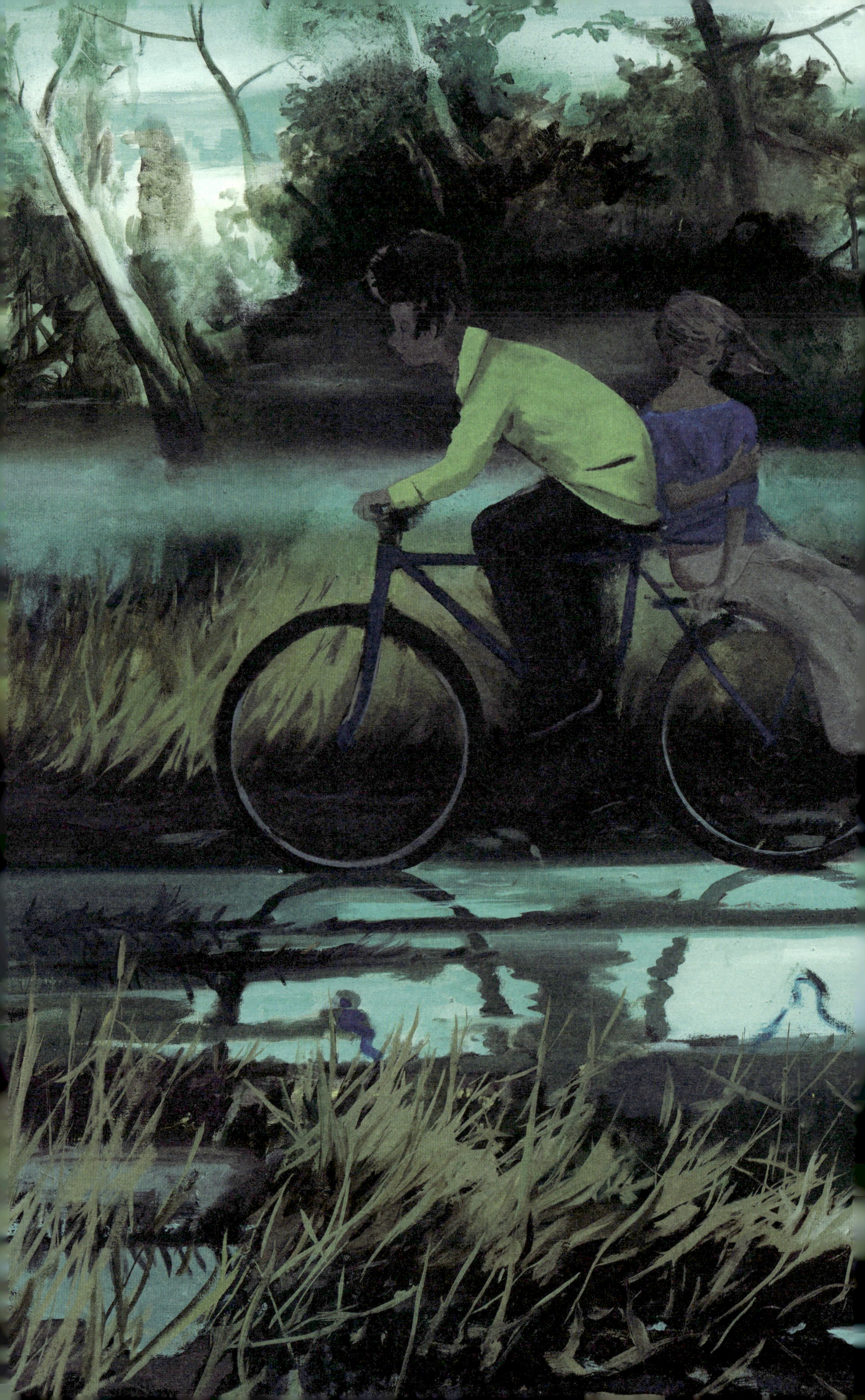

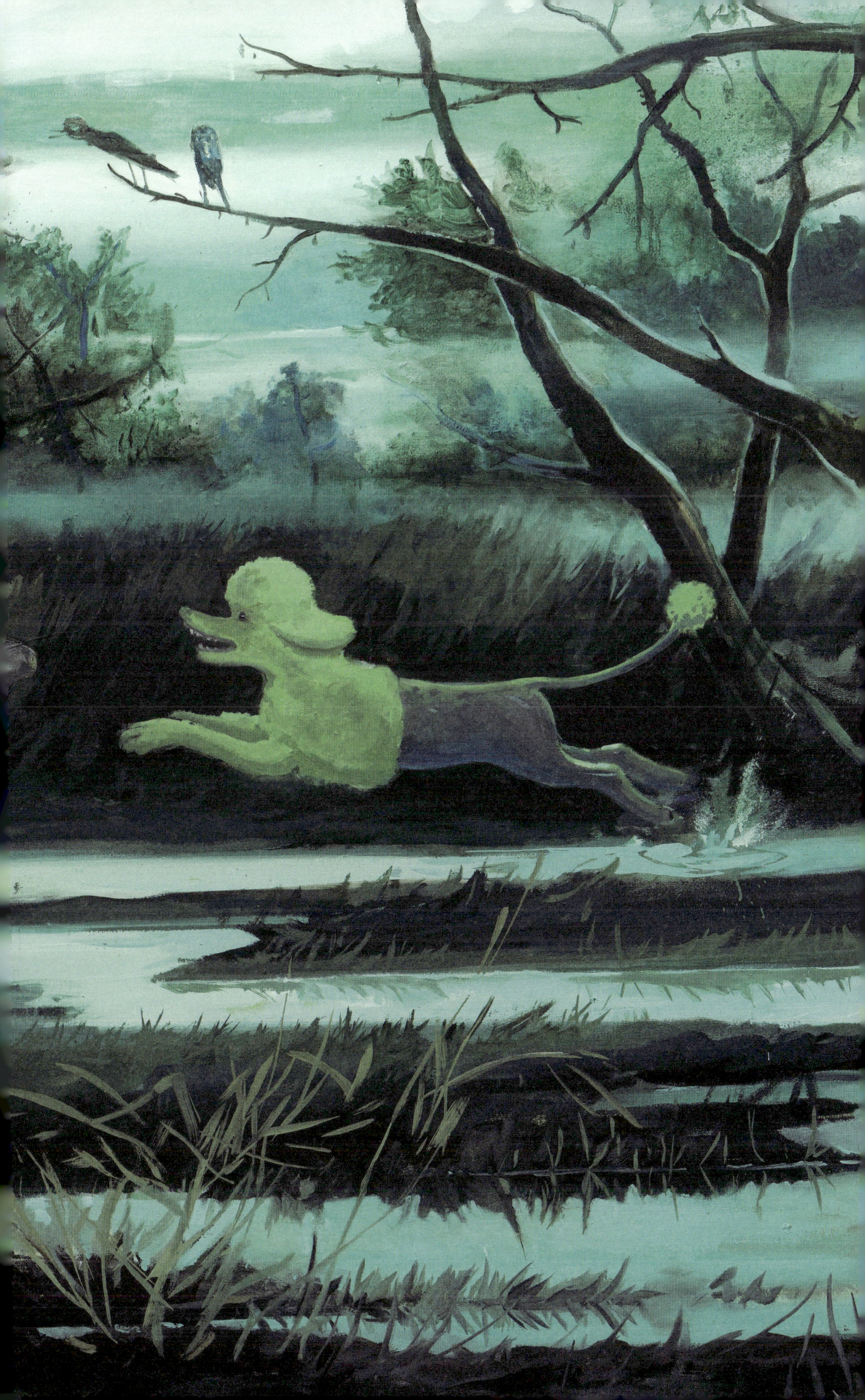

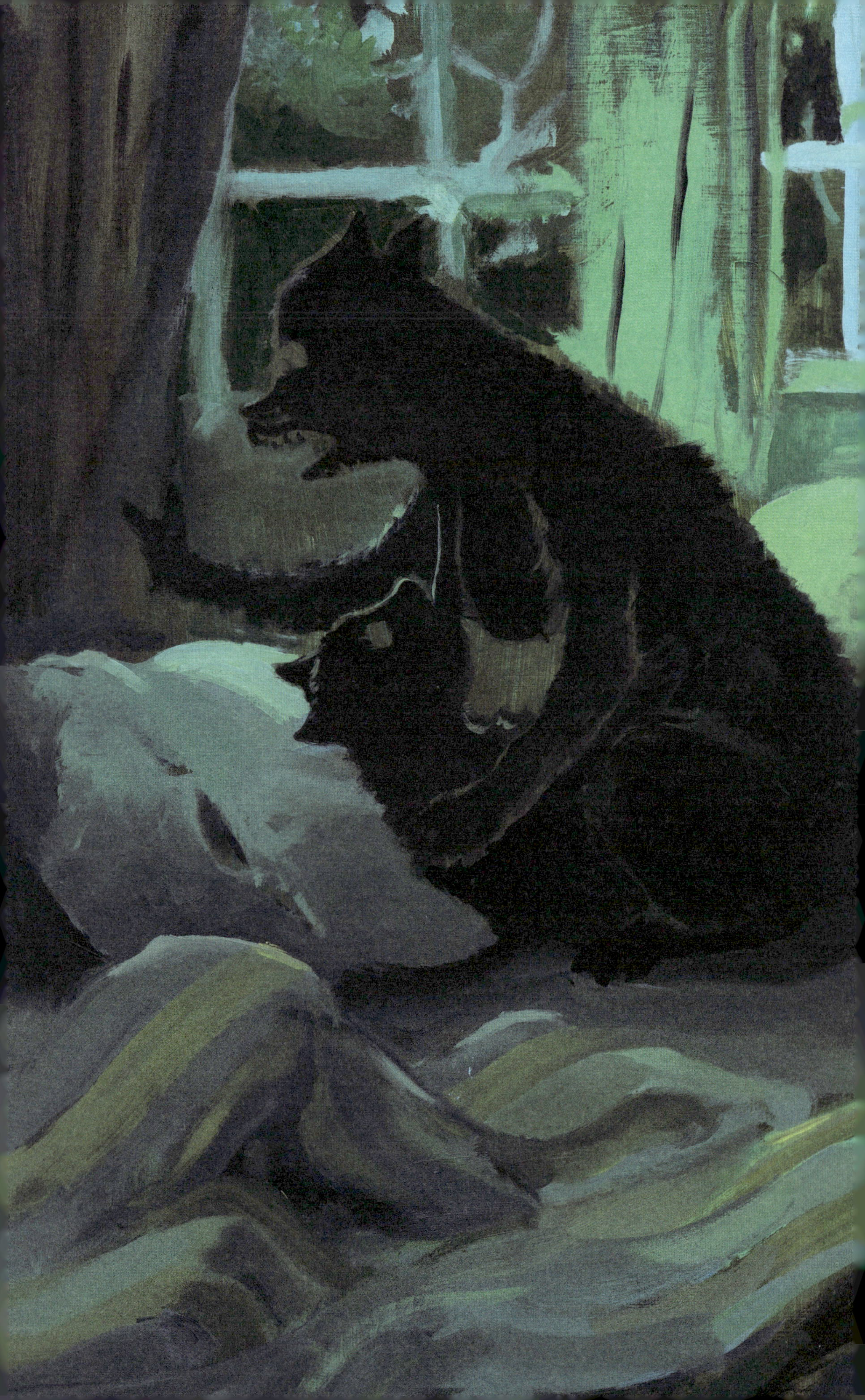

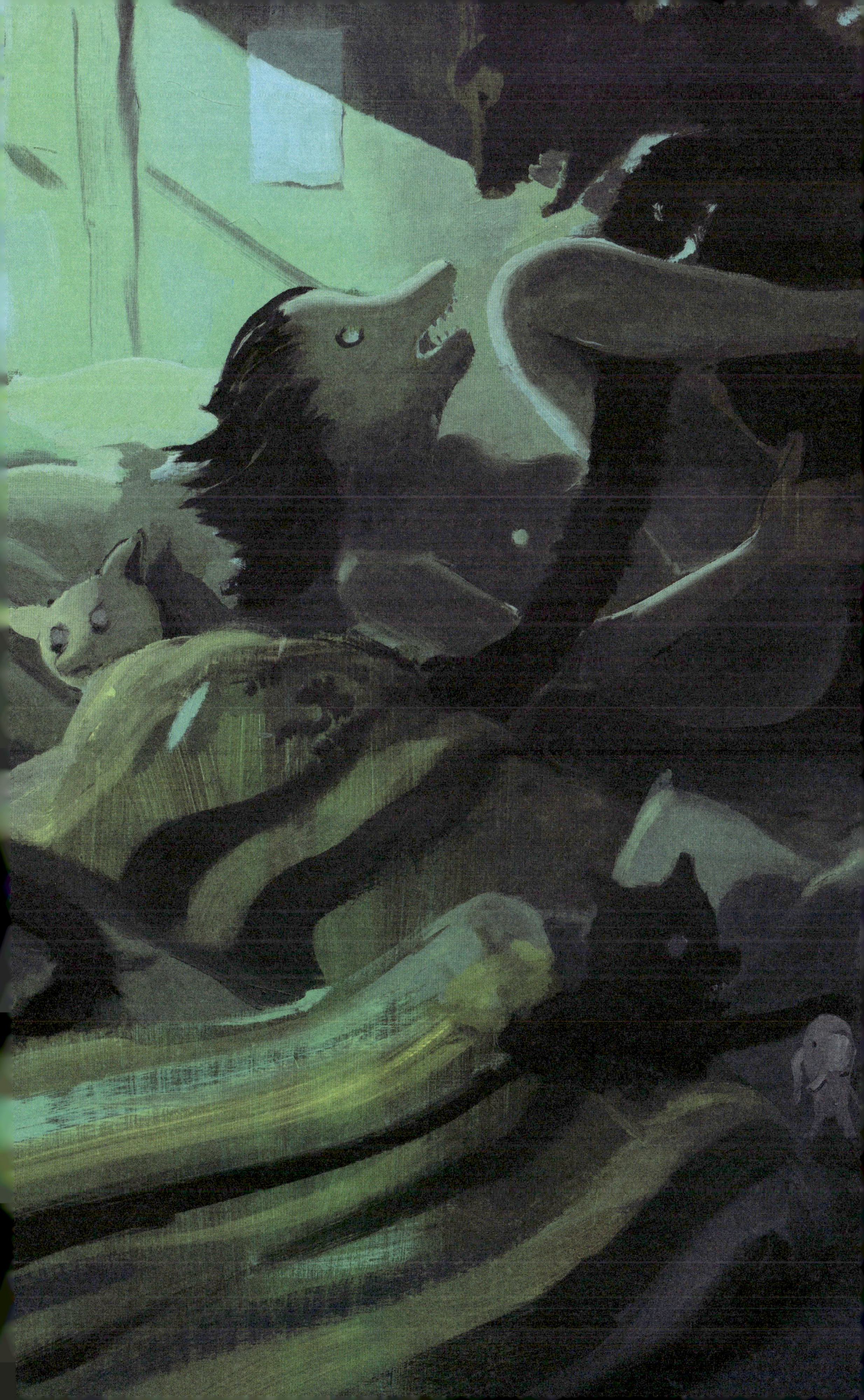

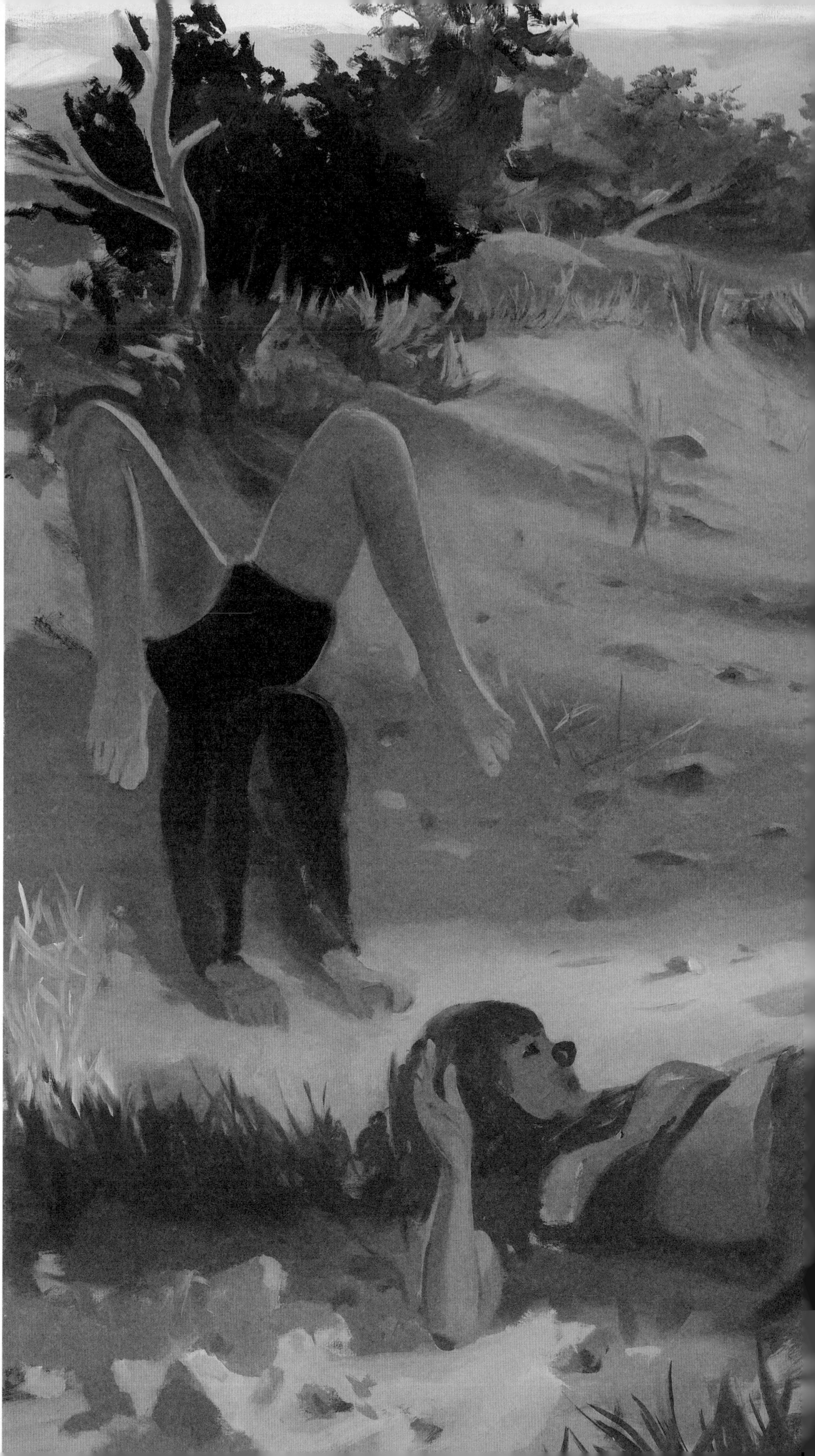

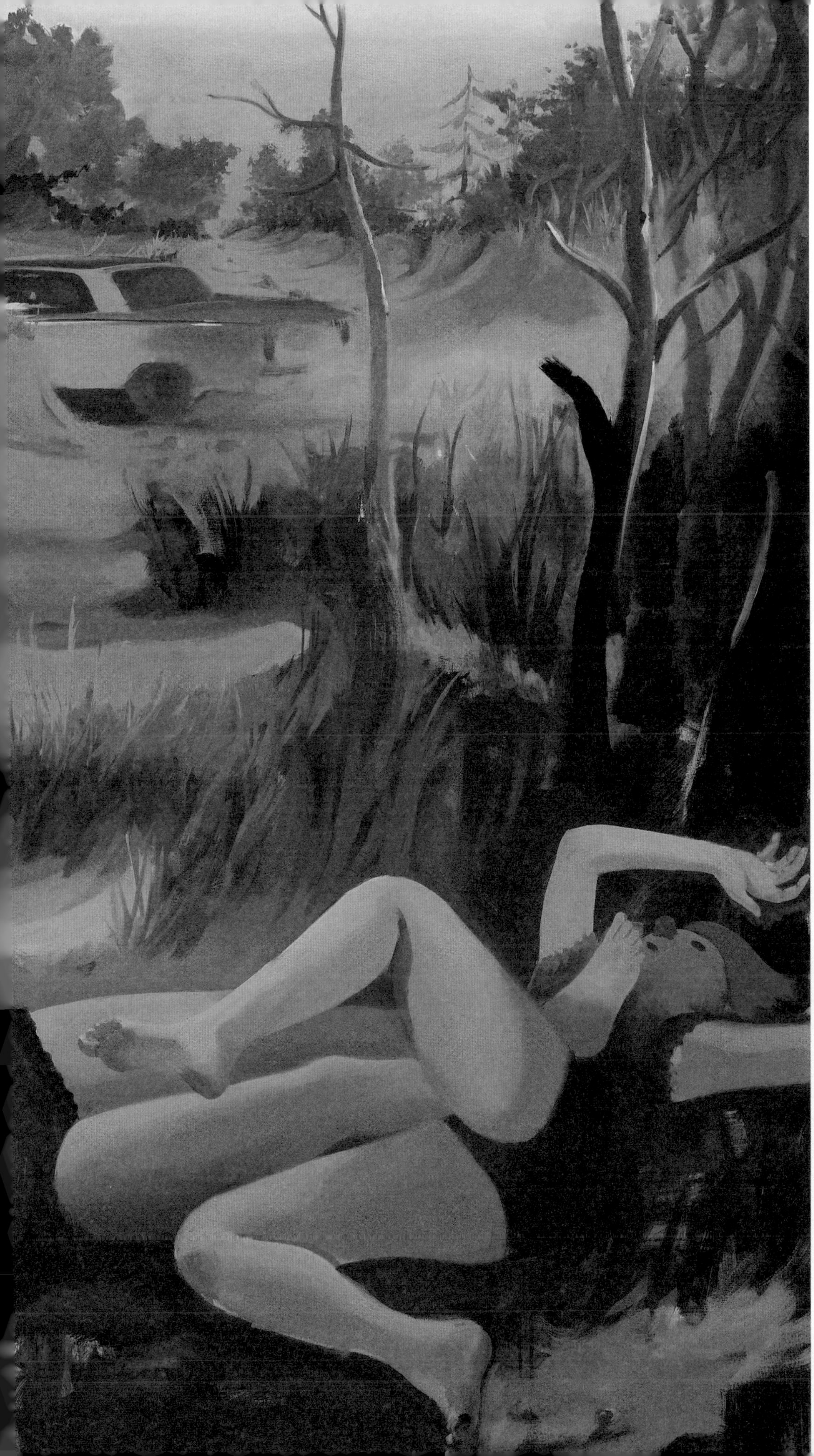

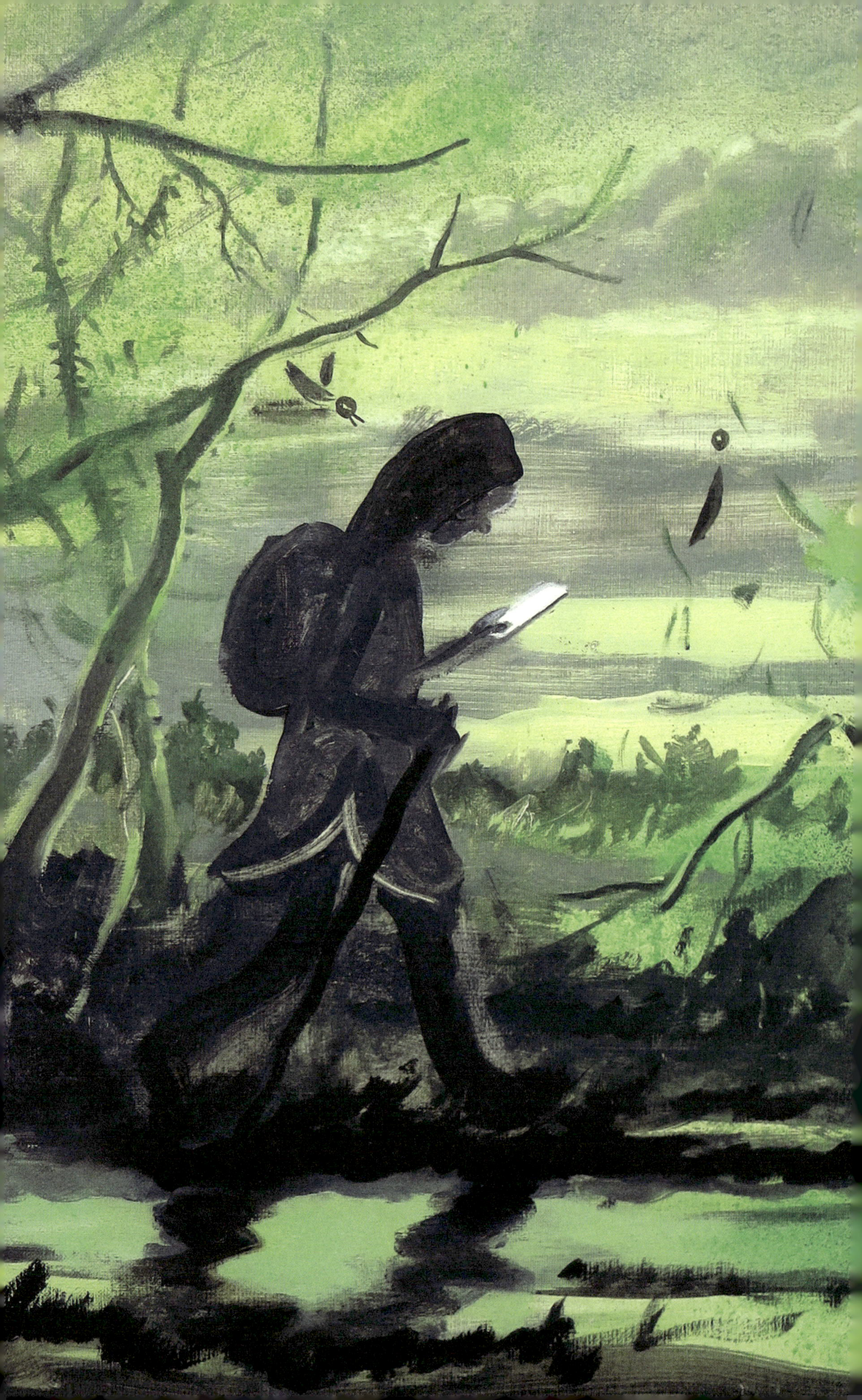

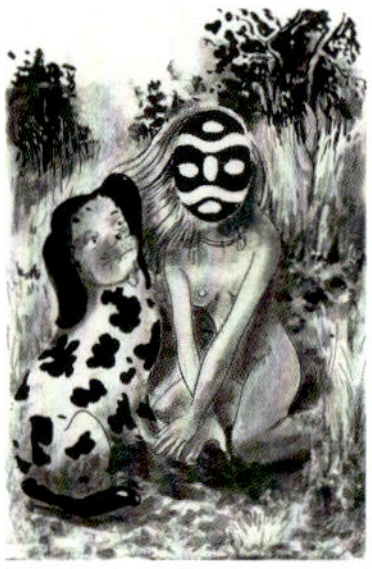

o.T.

2015, 40,5 × 27,5 cm
Kohle, Öl, Tusche und Pigment auf Papier/charcoal, oil, ink and pigment on paper

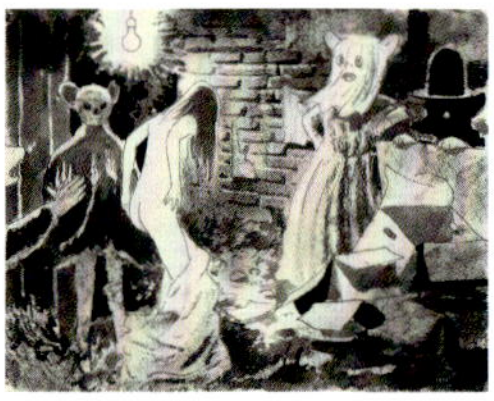

SHOW

2012, 21 × 29 cm
Kohle, Tusche und Pastell auf Papier/charcoal, ink and pastel on paper

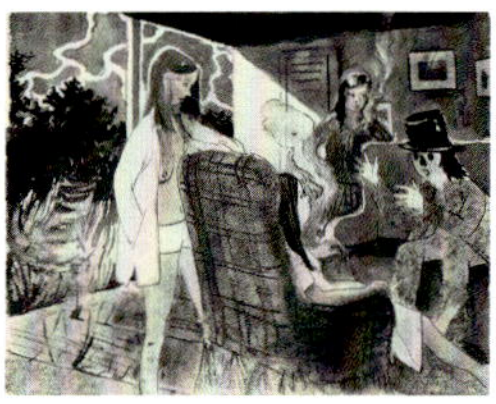

ERZÄHLER

2012, 21 × 29 cm
Kohle, Tusche und Pastell auf Papier/charcoal, ink and pastel on paper

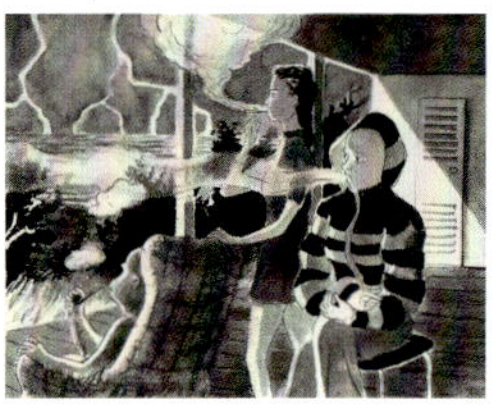

SOMMER

2012, 21 × 29 cm
Kohle, Tusche und Pastell auf Papier/charcoal, ink and pastel on paper

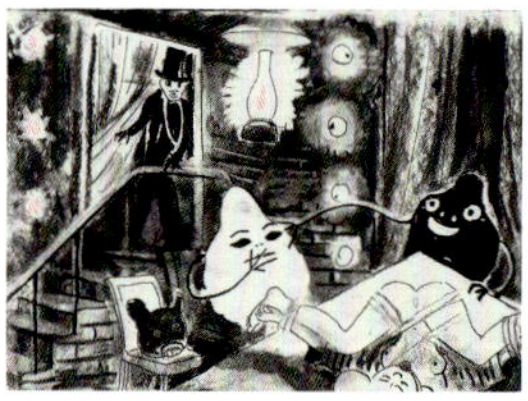

SHINJUKU

2014, 20,5 × 28,5 cm
Kohle, Tusche und Pastell auf Papier/charcoal, ink and pigment on paper

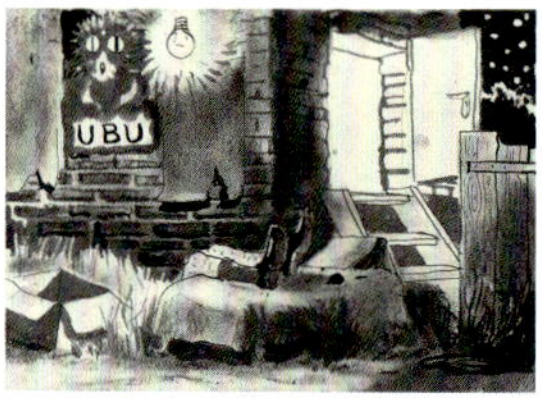

o.T.
(UBU)

2012, 21 × 29 cm
Kohle, Tusche und Pastell auf Papier/charcoal, ink and pastel on paper

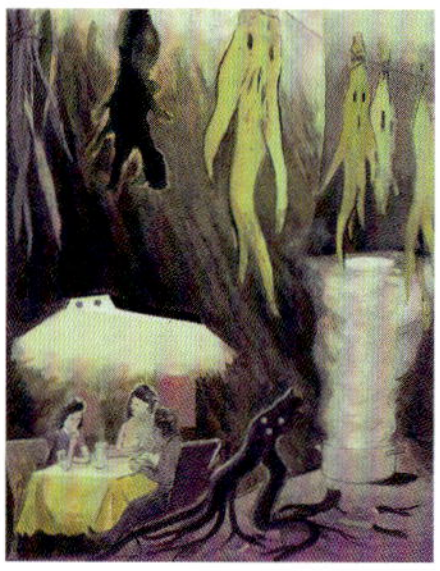

ESSENZ

2012, 50 × 40 cm
Öl auf Leinwand/oil on canvas

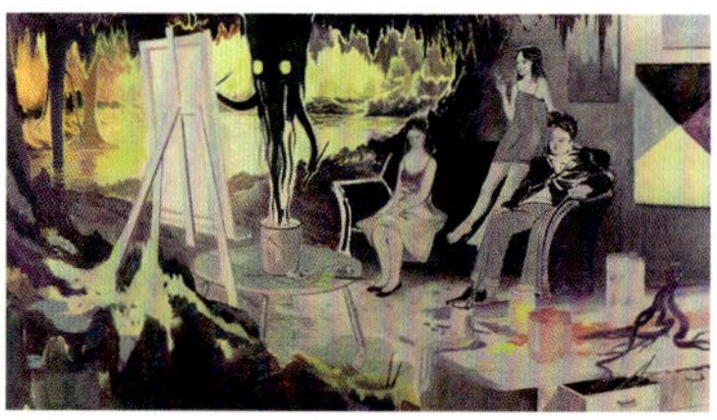

PATRON

2012, 150 × 250 cm
Öl auf Leinwand/oil on canvas

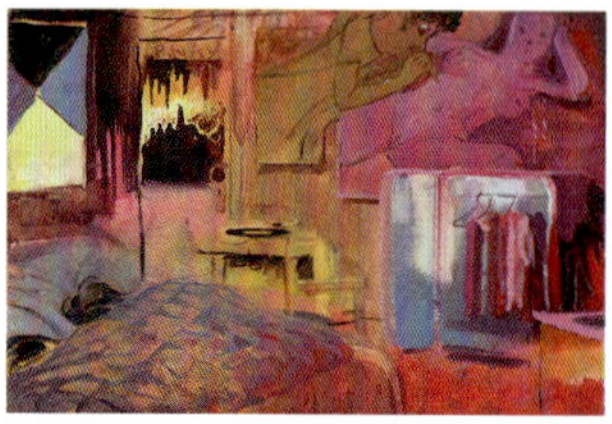

PINKYS RAUM

2012, 30 × 45 cm
Öl auf Leinwand/oil on canvas

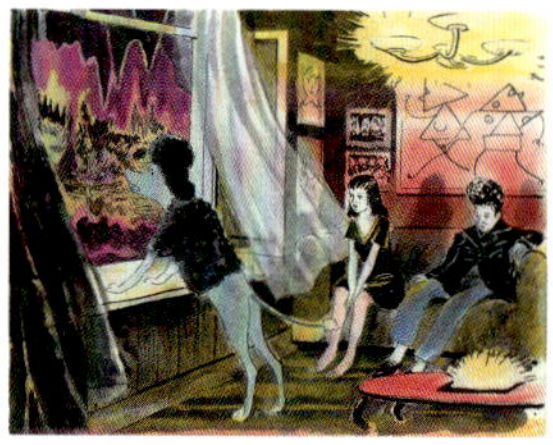

o.T.
(POODLE)

2012, 26 × 36 cm
Kohle, Pastell, Tusche auf Papier/charcoal, pastel, ink on paper

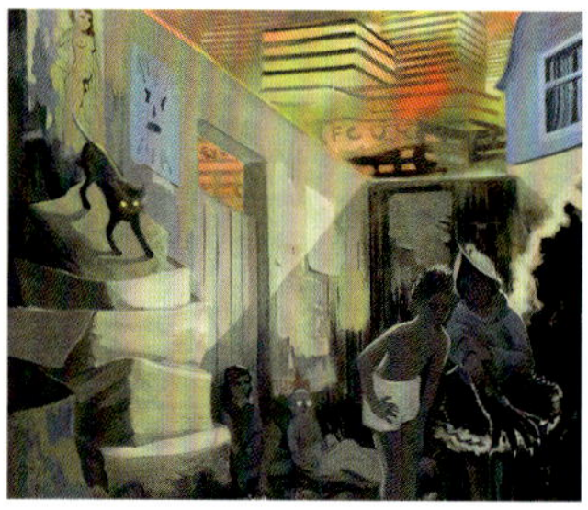

EYE FCUK

2011, 150 × 180 cm
Öl auf Leinwand/oil on canvas

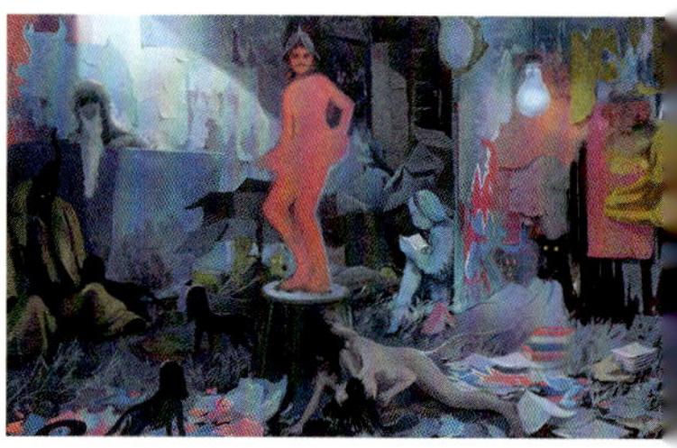

DIE NACHTWACHE

2011, 250 × 400 cm
Öl auf Leinwand/oil on canvas

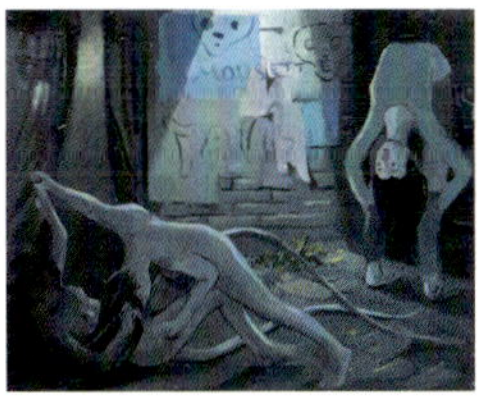

MOUSETTE

2012, 24 × 30 cm
Öl auf Leinwand/oil on canvas

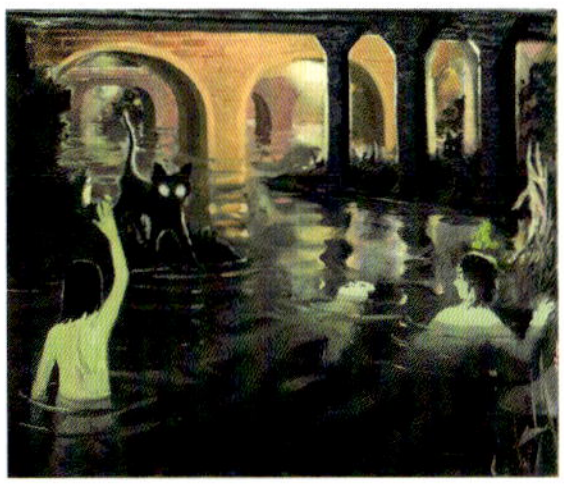

DELPHI

2011, 40 × 50 cm
Öl auf Leinwand/oil on canvas

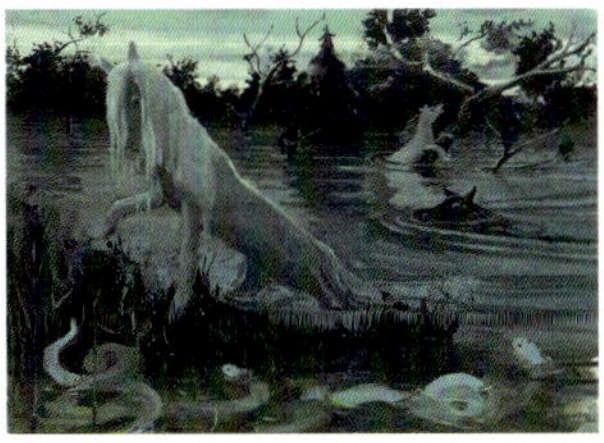

ALBIS

2013, 49 × 70 cm
Öl auf Leinwand/oil on canvas

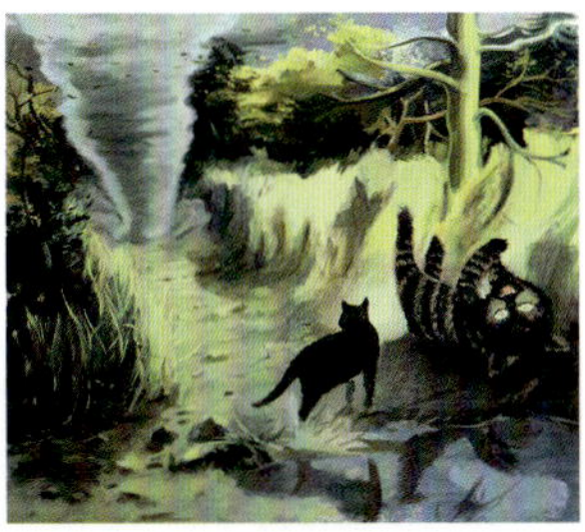

SPIRO

2012, 70 × 80 cm
Öl auf Leinwand/oil on canvas

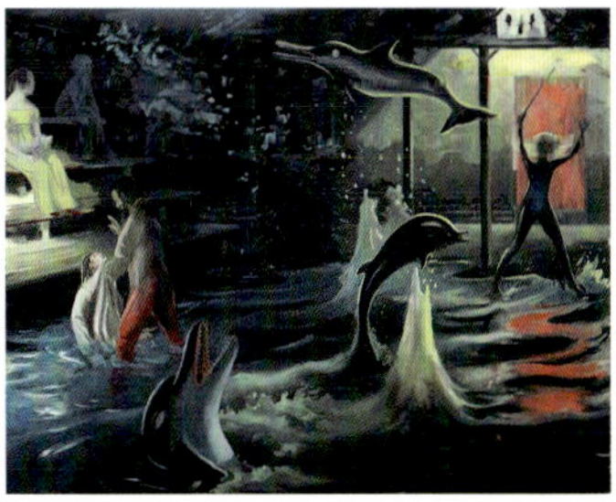

BROD

2012, 190 × 240 cm
Öl auf Leinwand/oil on canvas

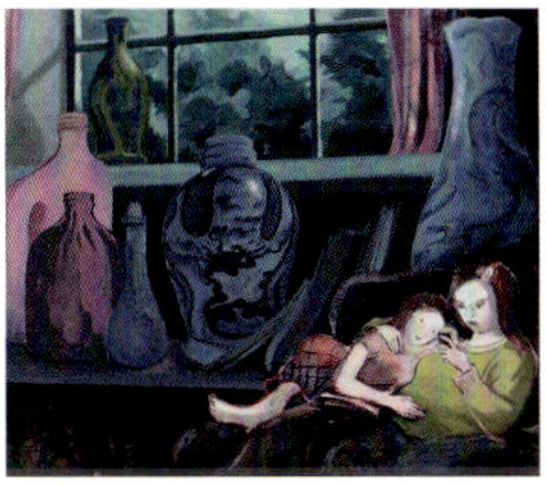

MING

2012, 60 × 70 cm
Öl auf Leinwand/oil on canvas

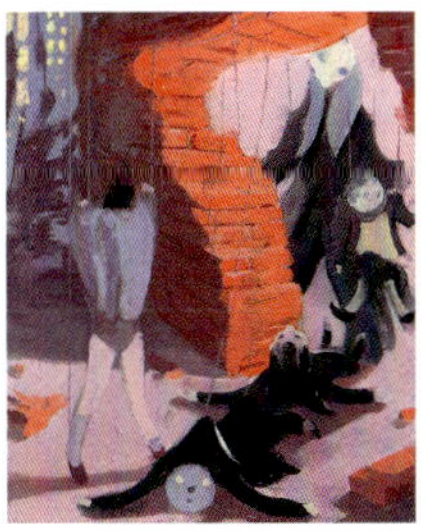

SAVOY

2011, 30 × 24 cm
Öl auf Leinwand/oil on canvas

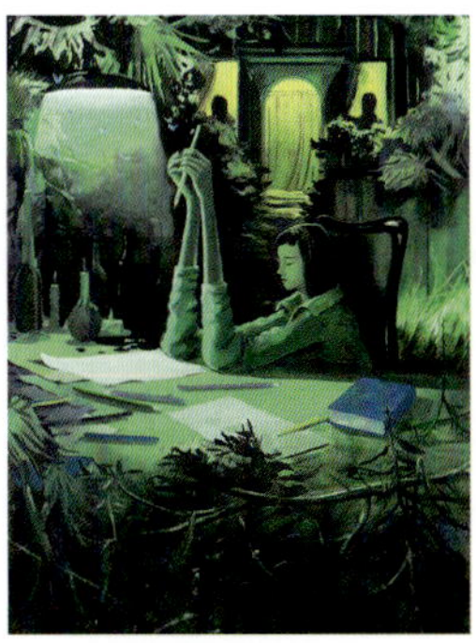

HELIA

2013, 200 × 150 cm
Öl auf Leinwand/oil on canvas

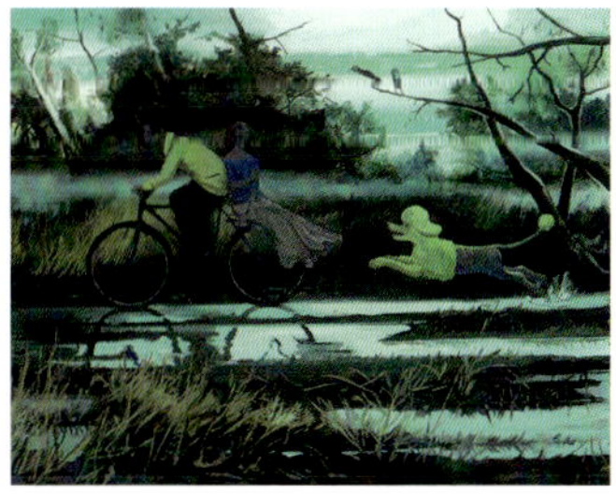

WATAMAN

2013, 150 × 180 cm
Öl auf Leinwand/oil on canvas

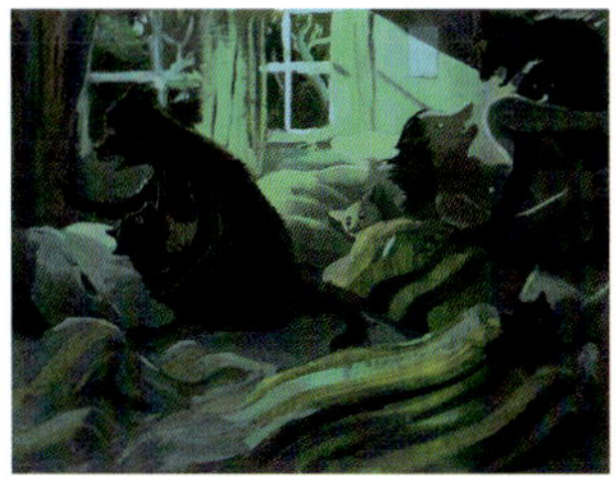

SAVAGES

2013, 60 × 80 cm
Öl auf Leinwand/oil on canvas

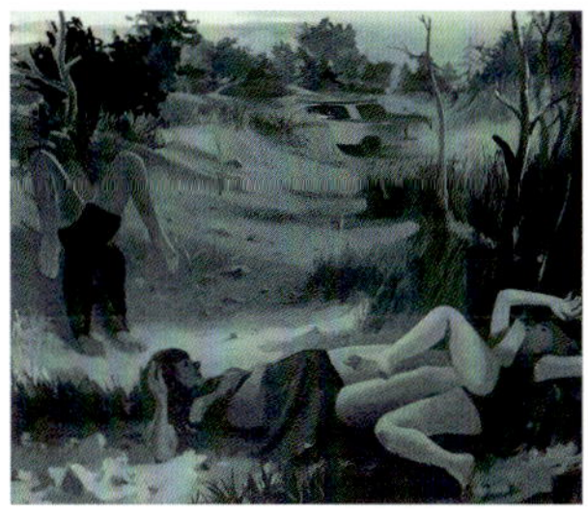

LONG ISLAND SOUND

2011, 150 × 180 cm
Öl auf Leinwand/oil on canvas

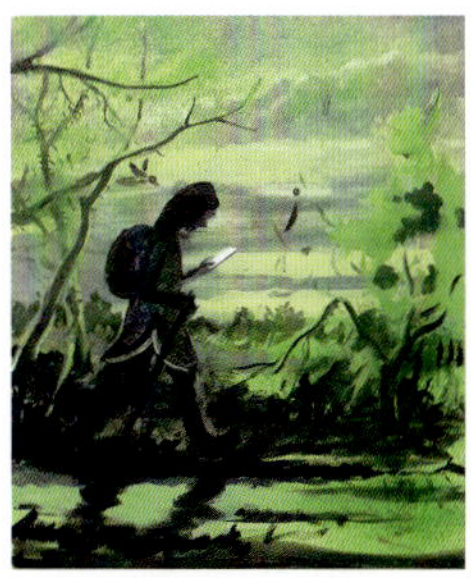

PILGRIM

2014, 60 × 50 cm
Öl auf Leinwand/oil on canvas

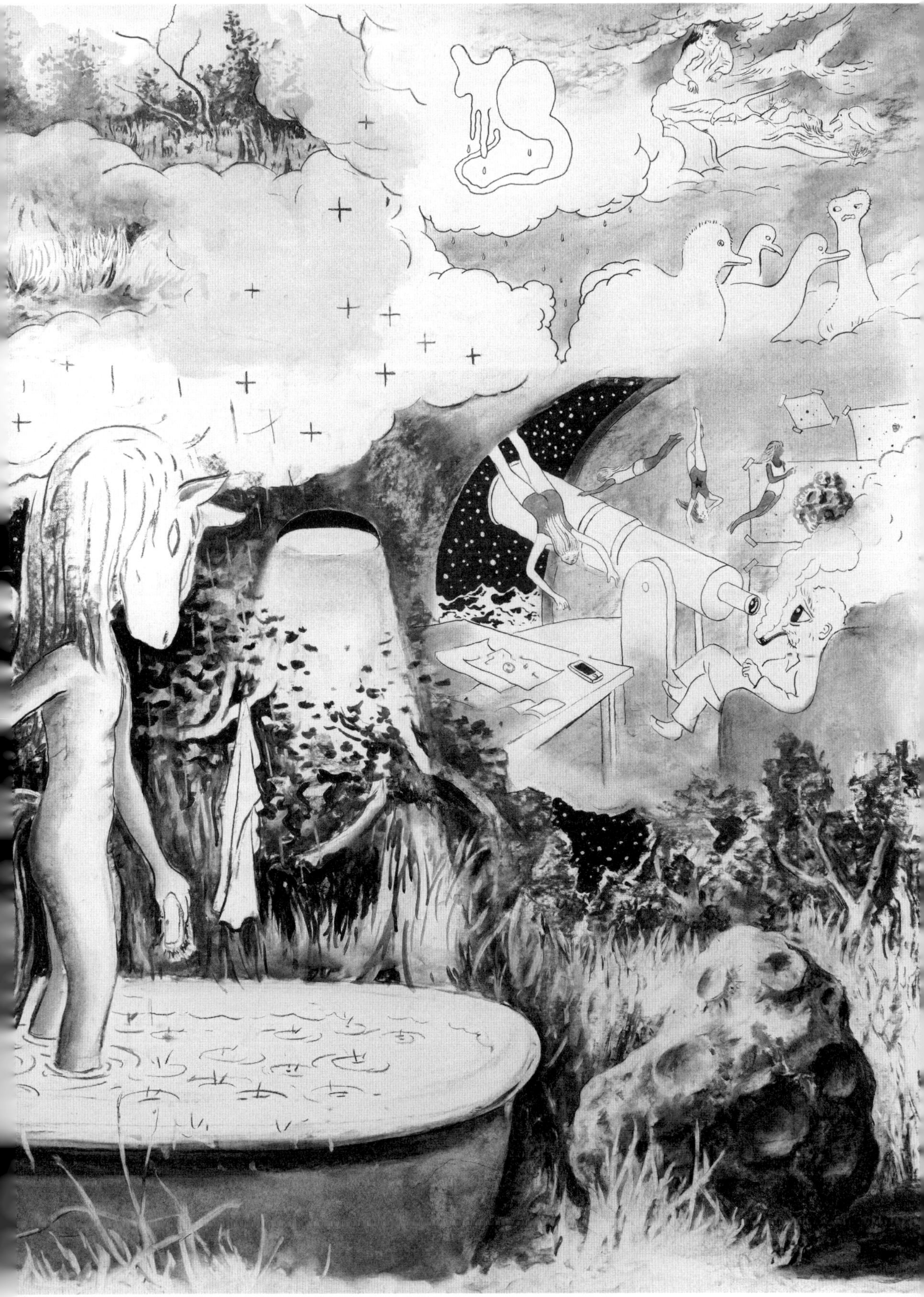

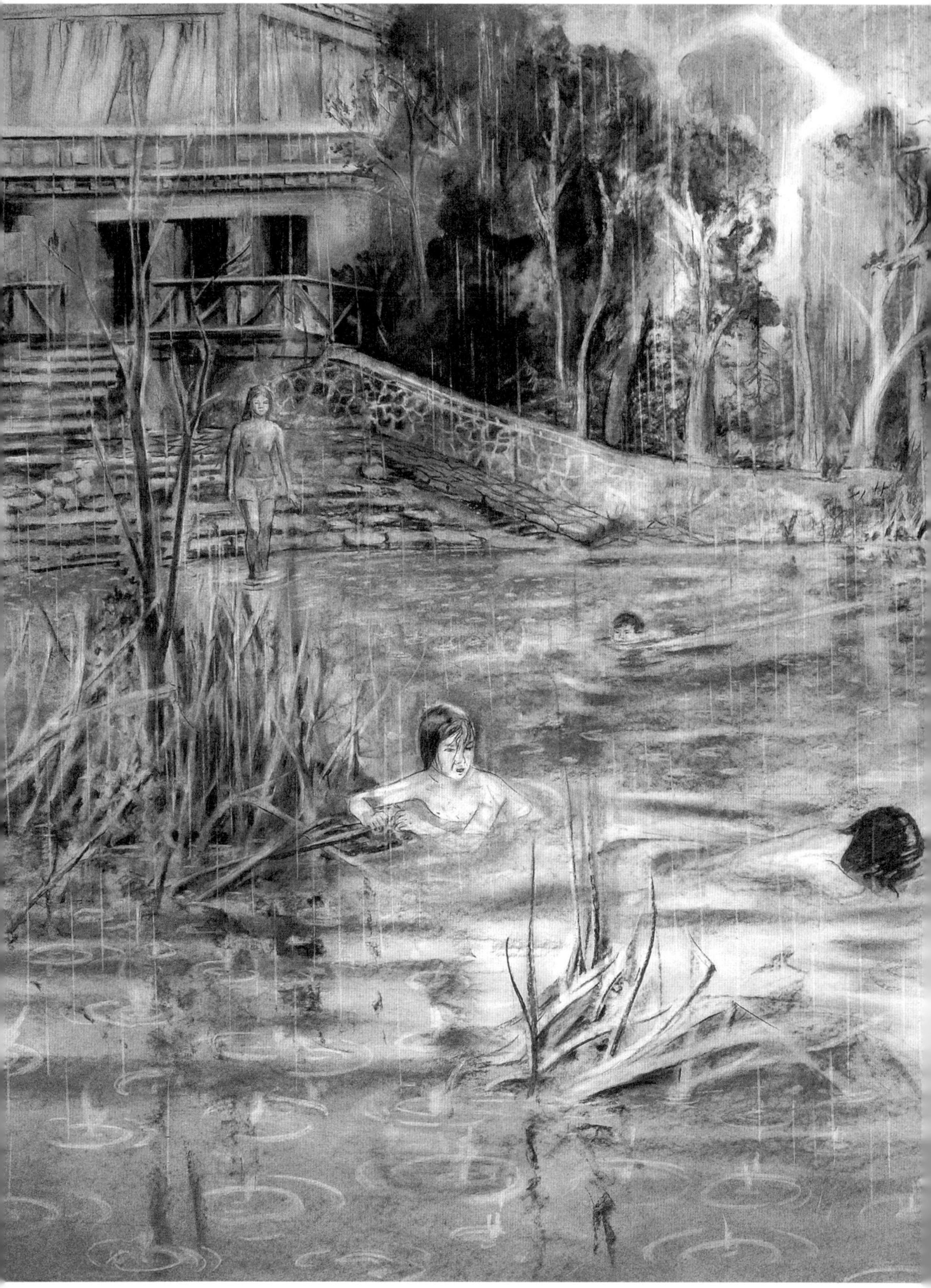

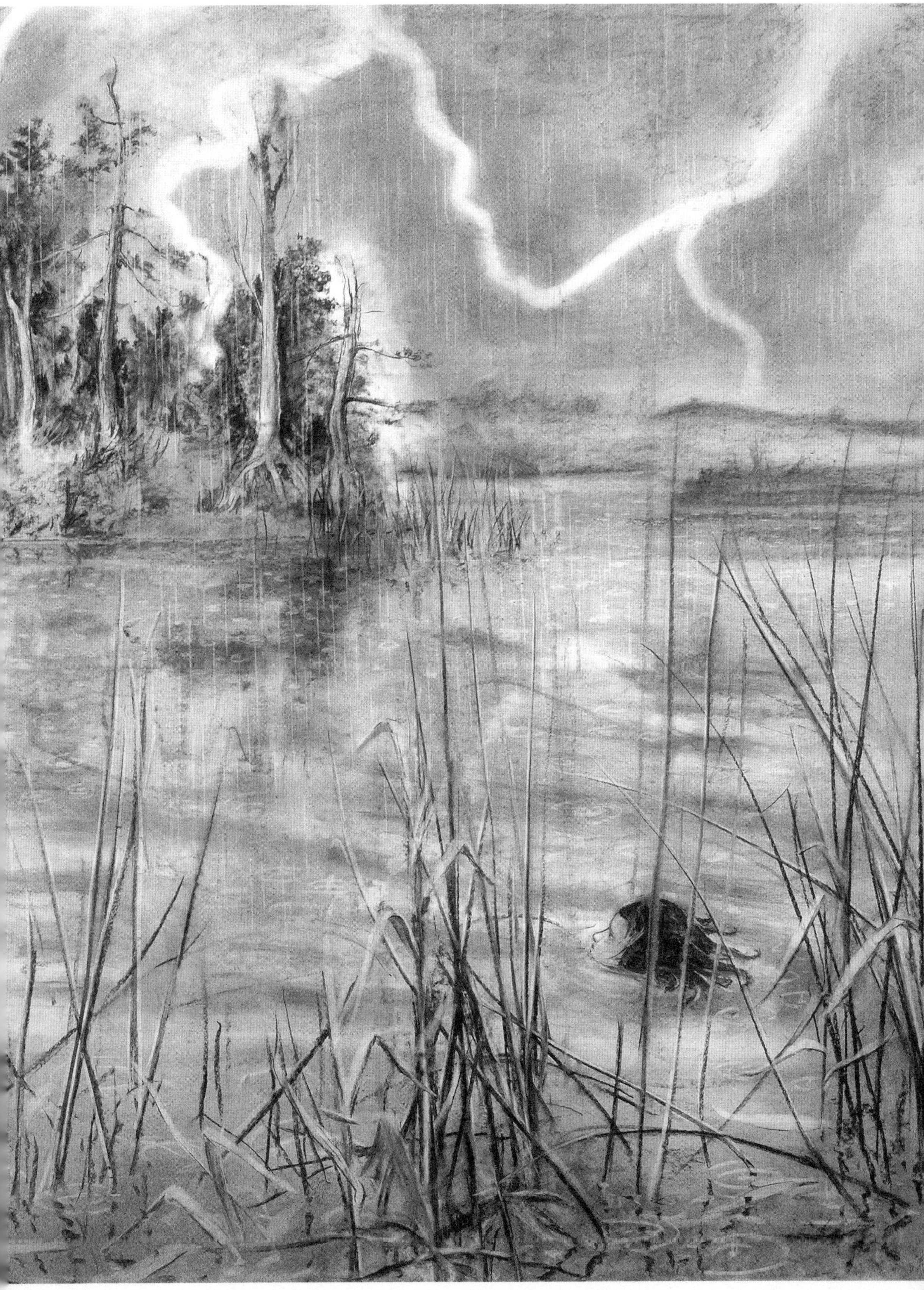

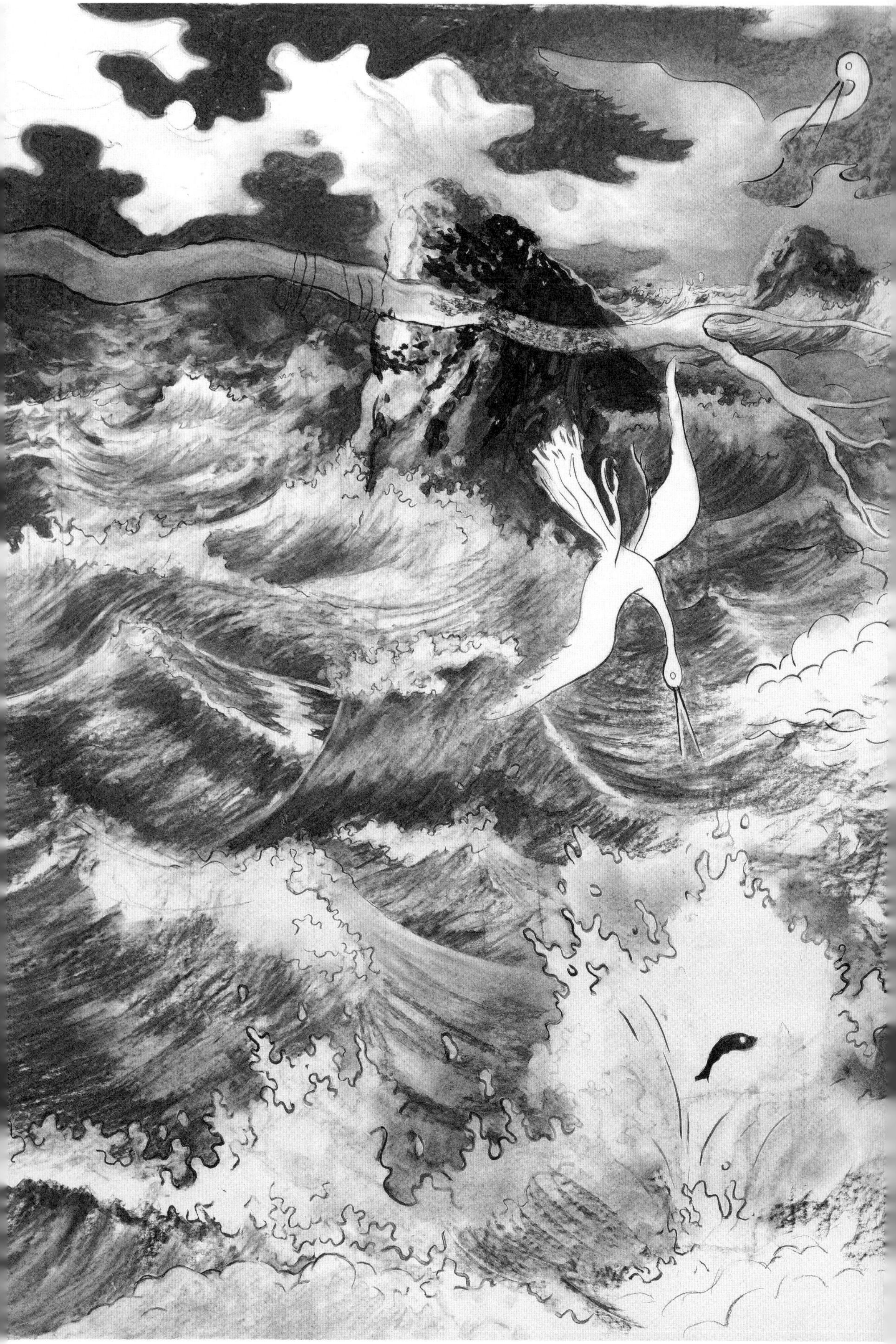

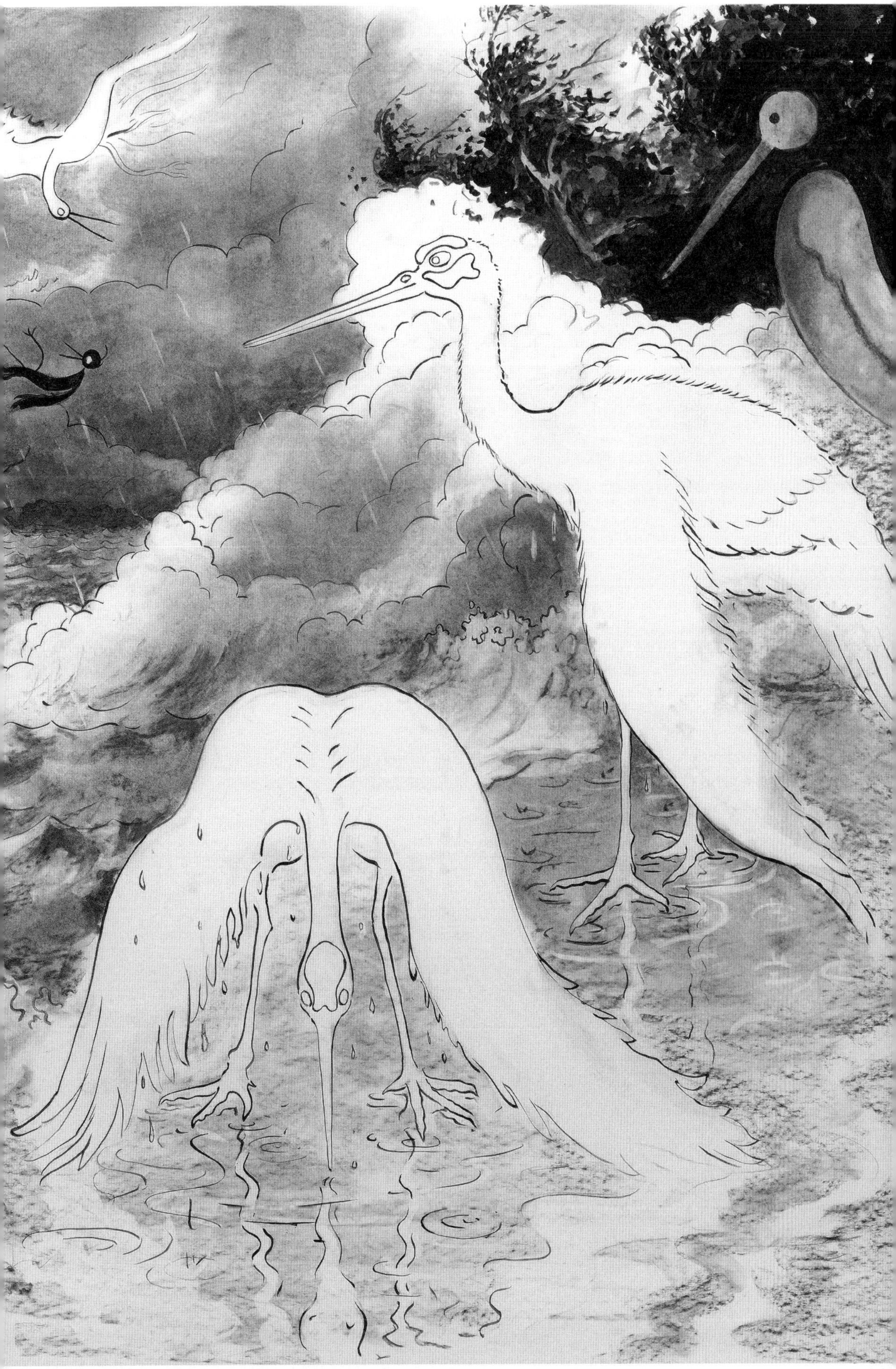

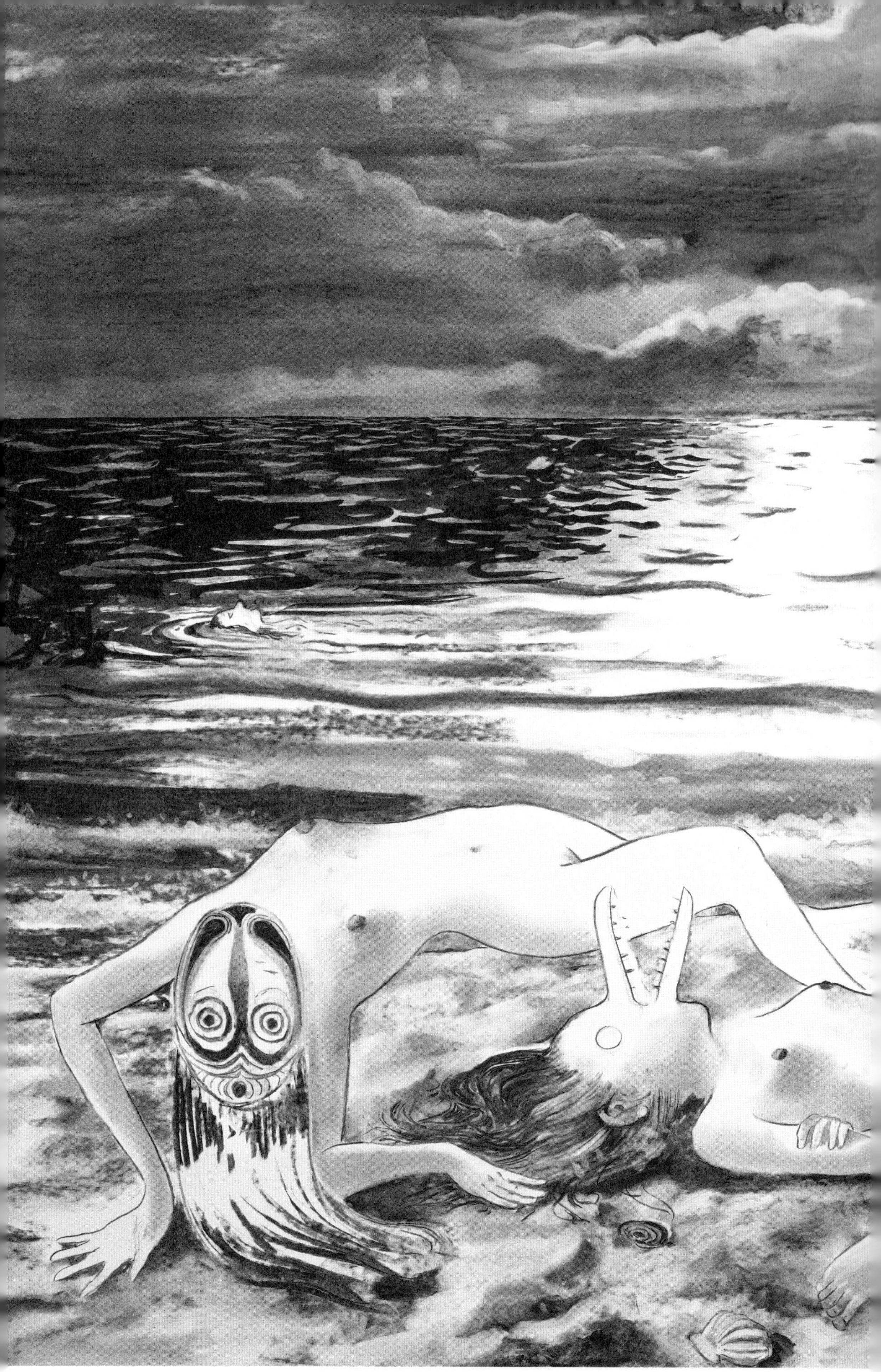

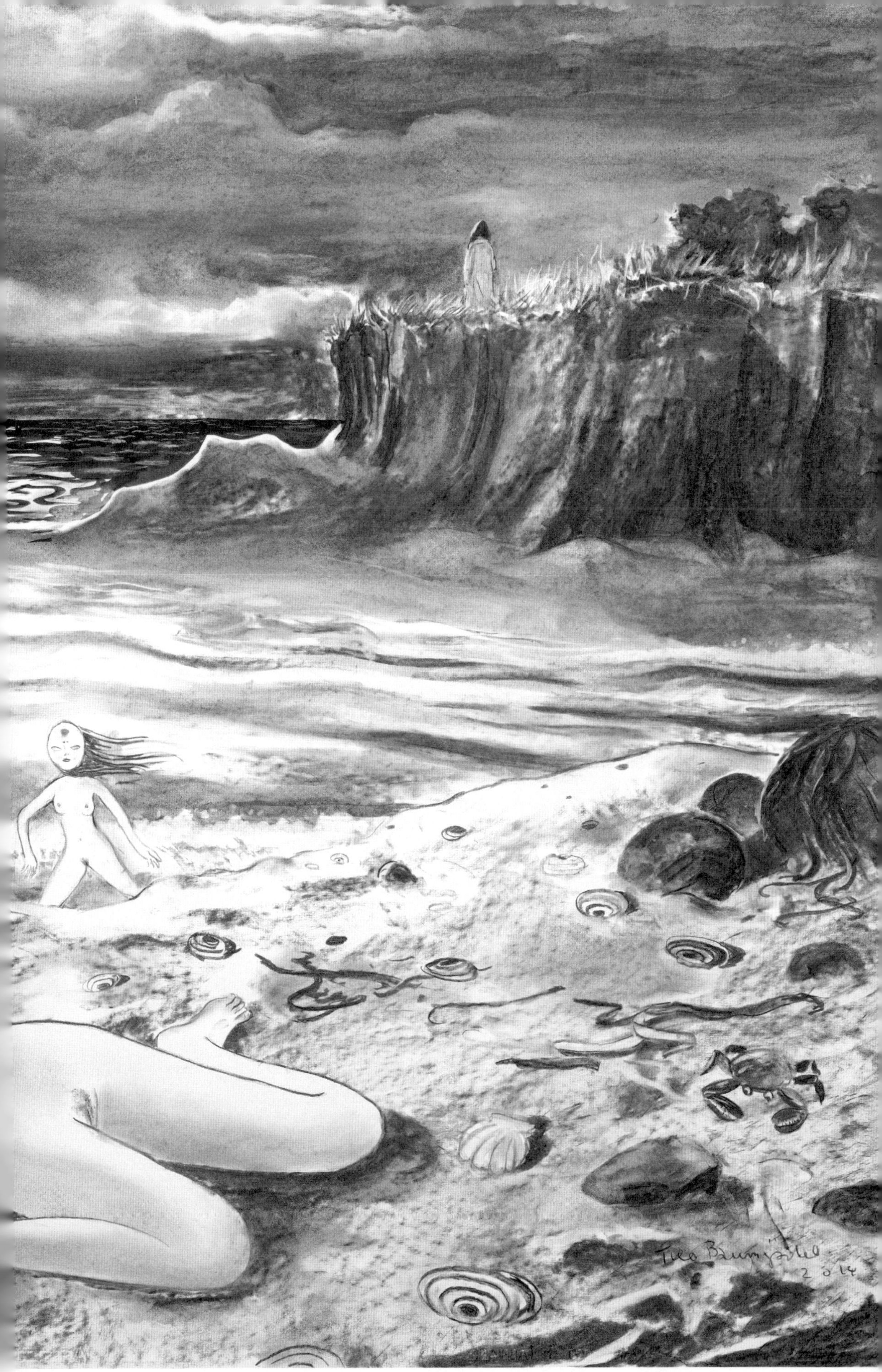
2014

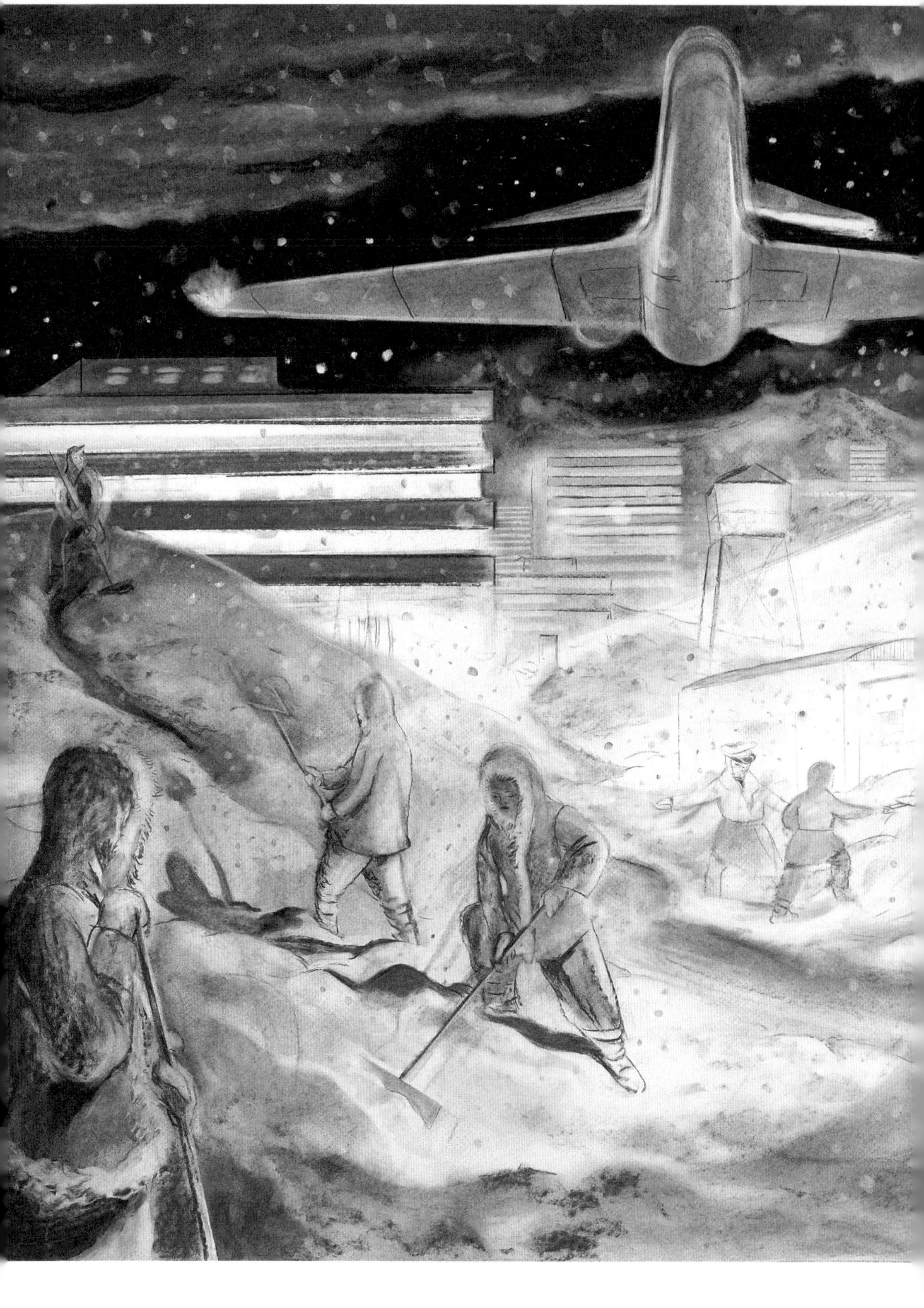

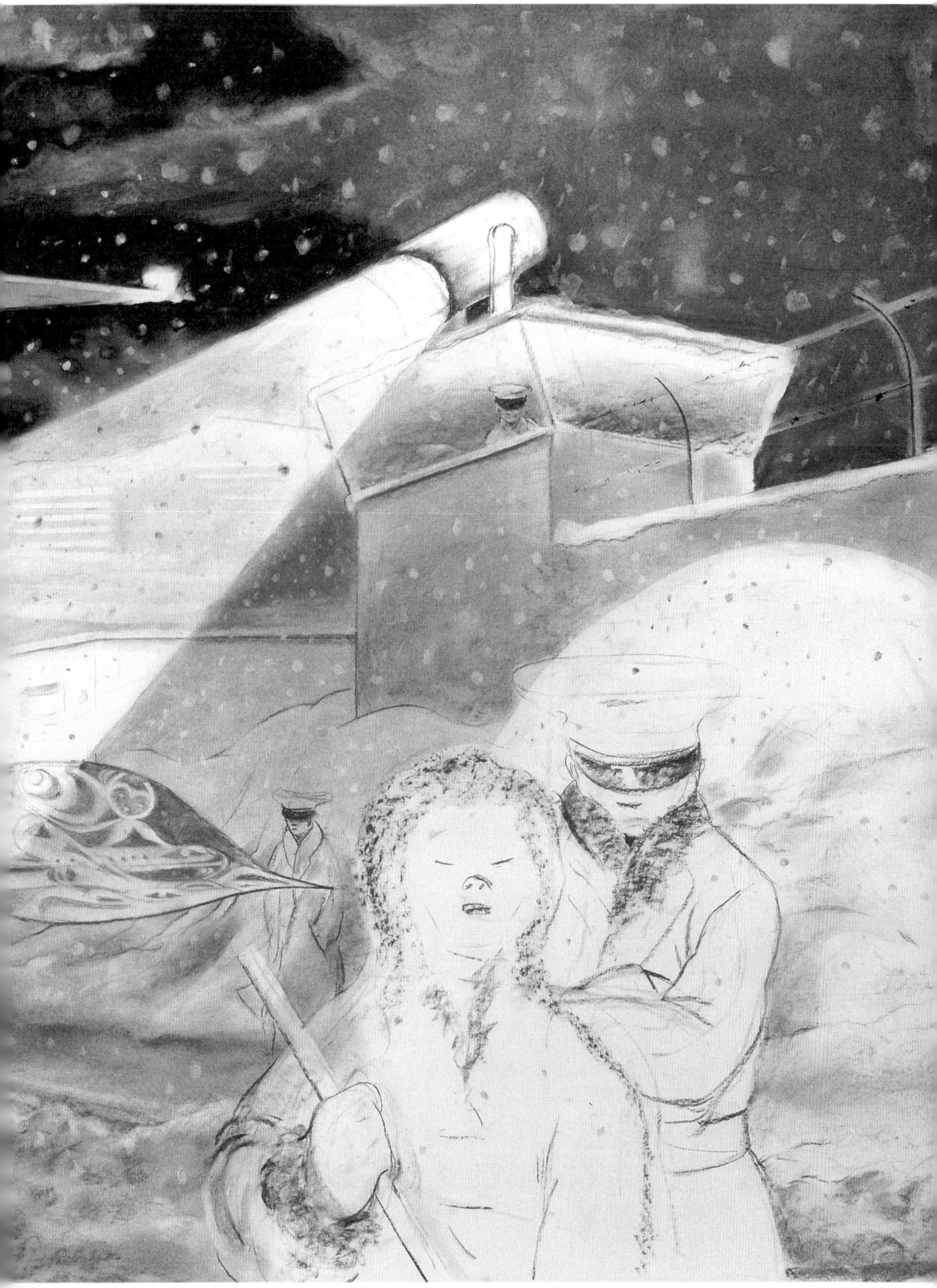

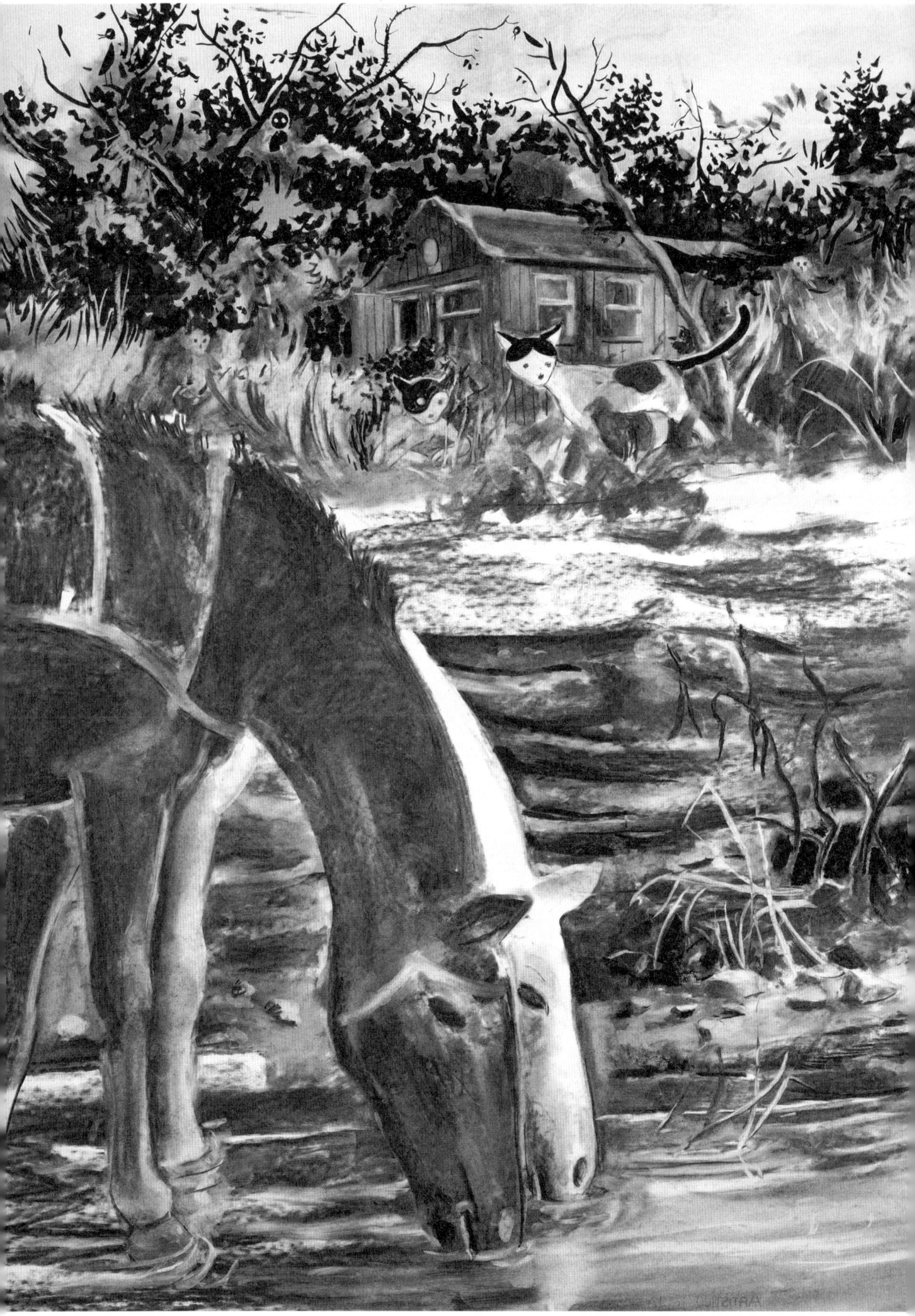

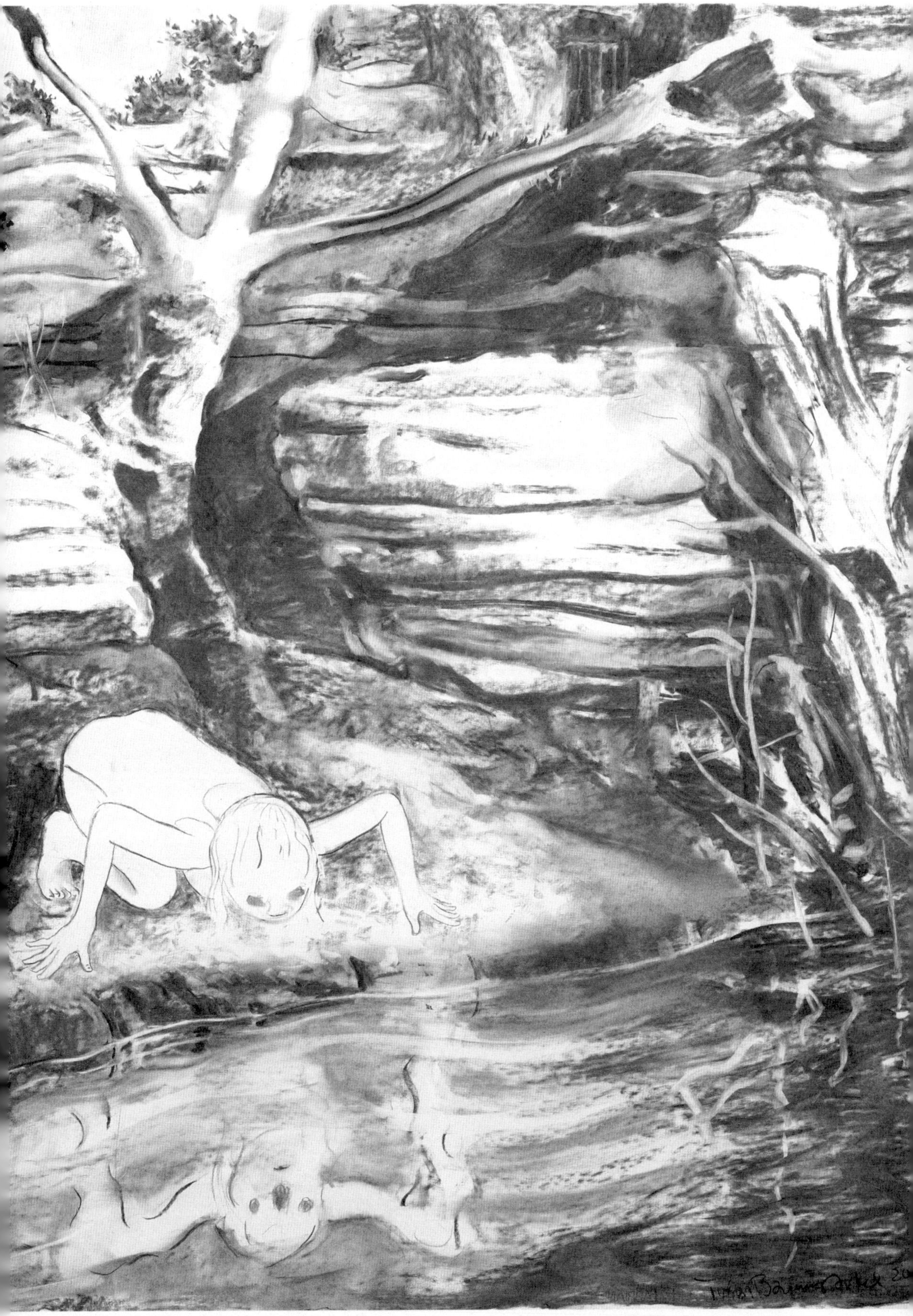

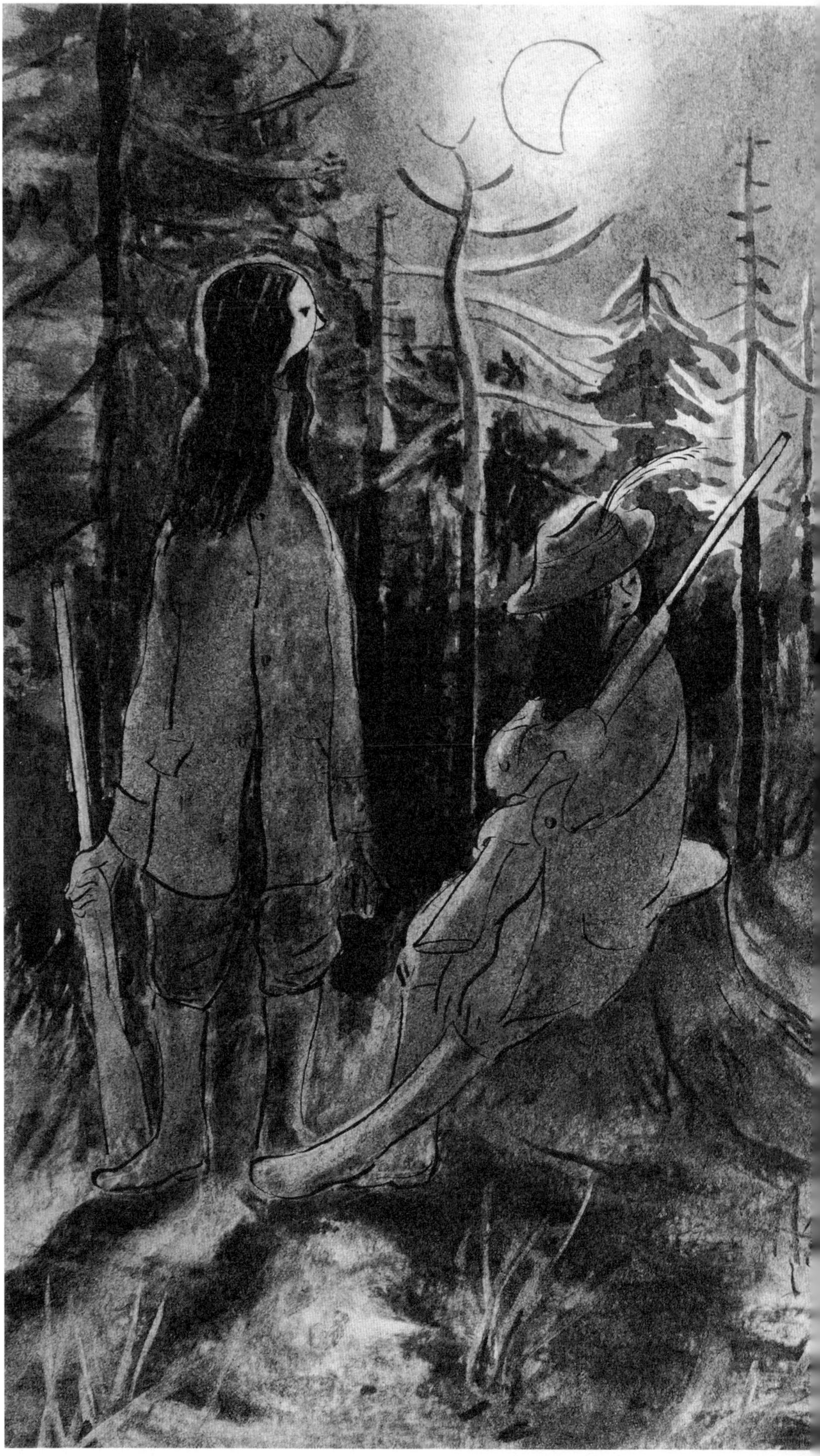

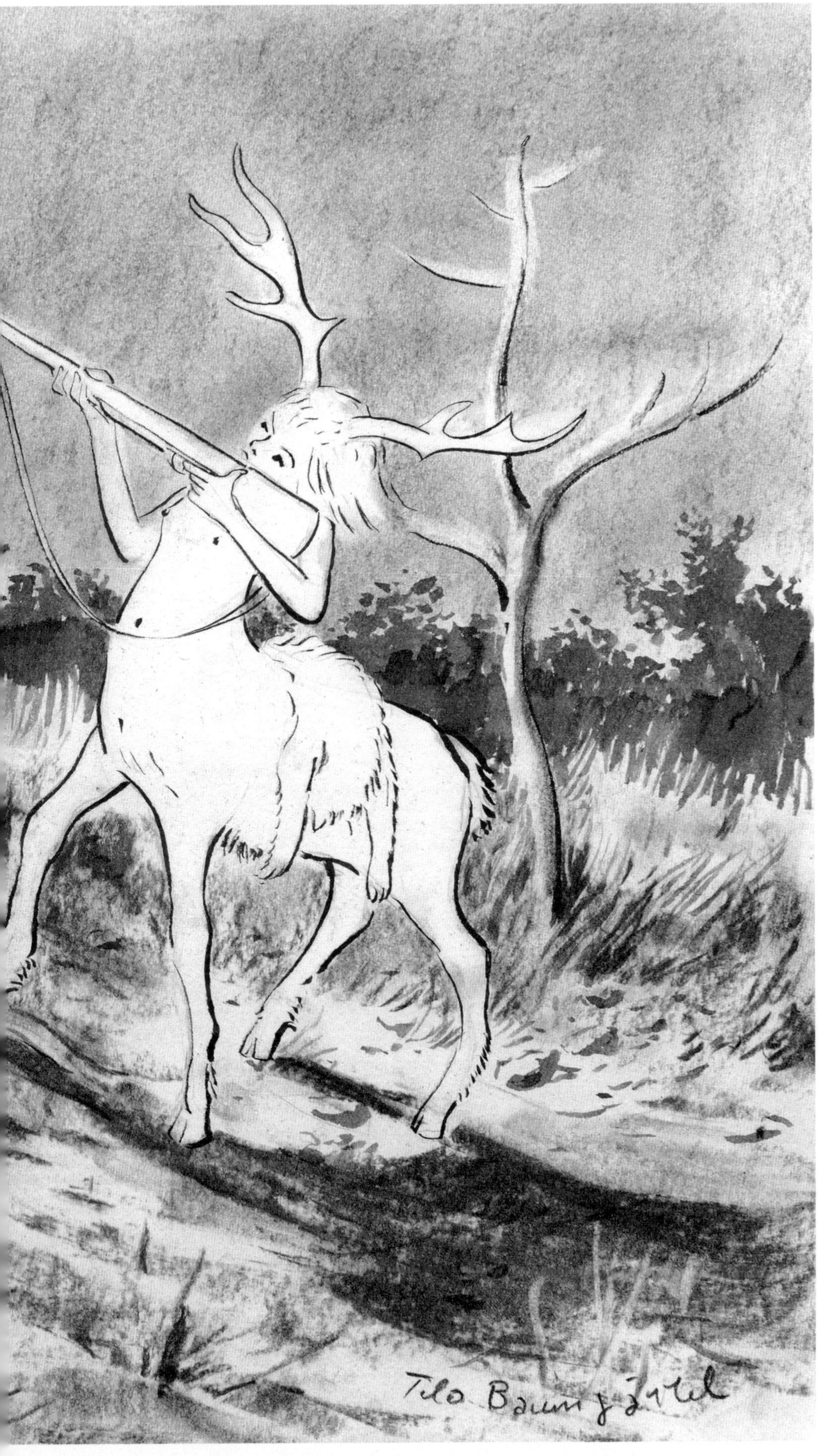
Tilo Baumgärtel

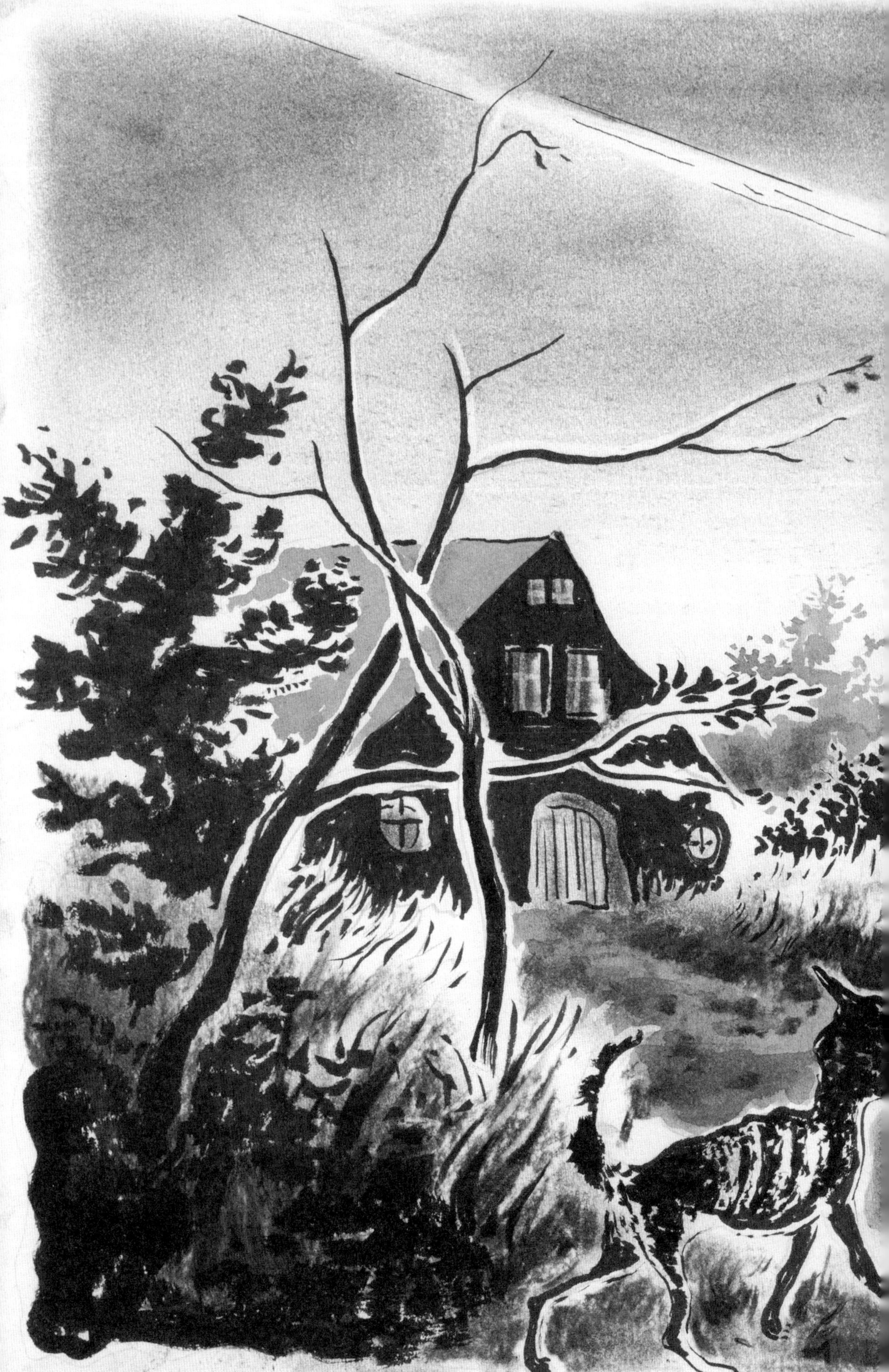

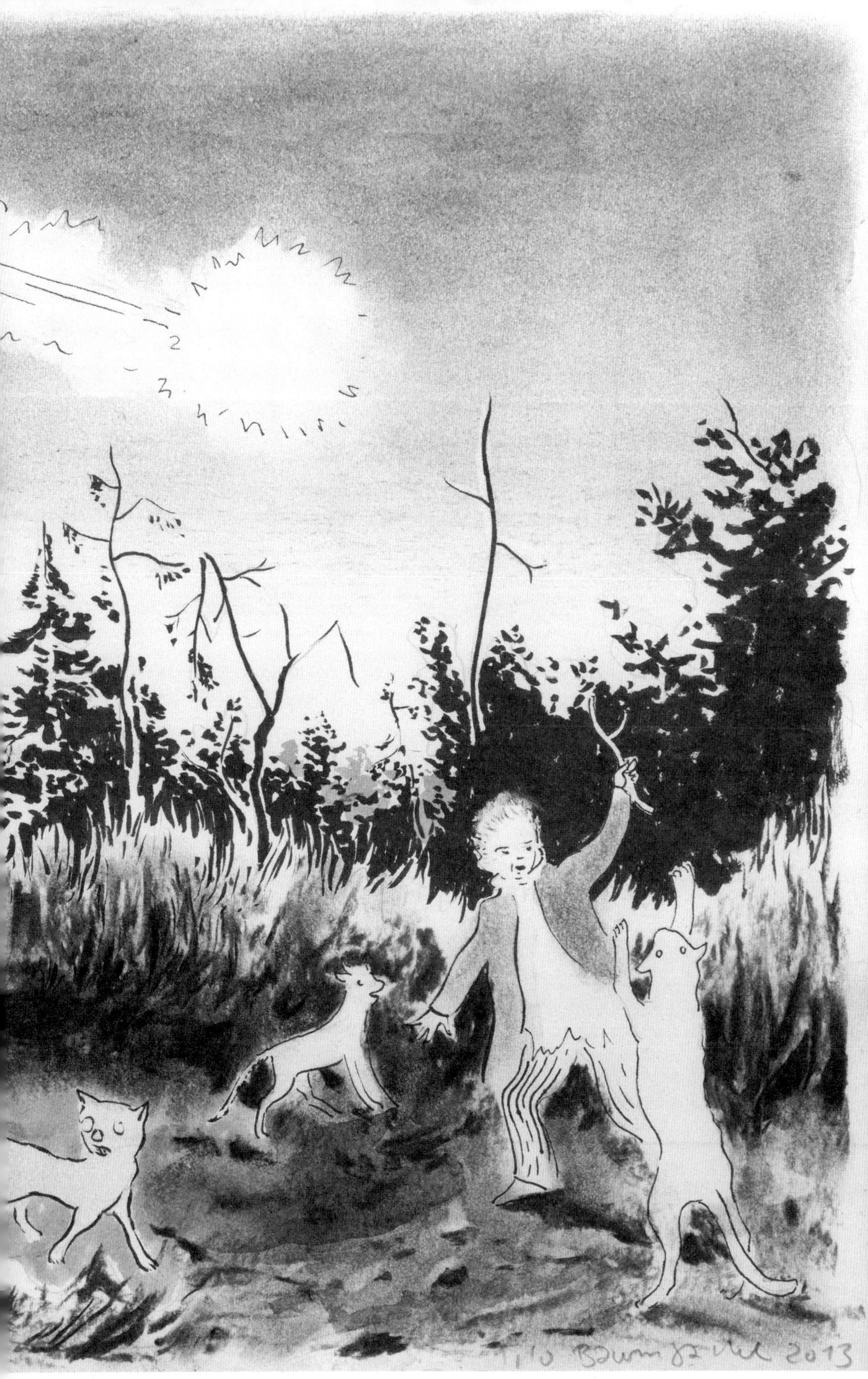

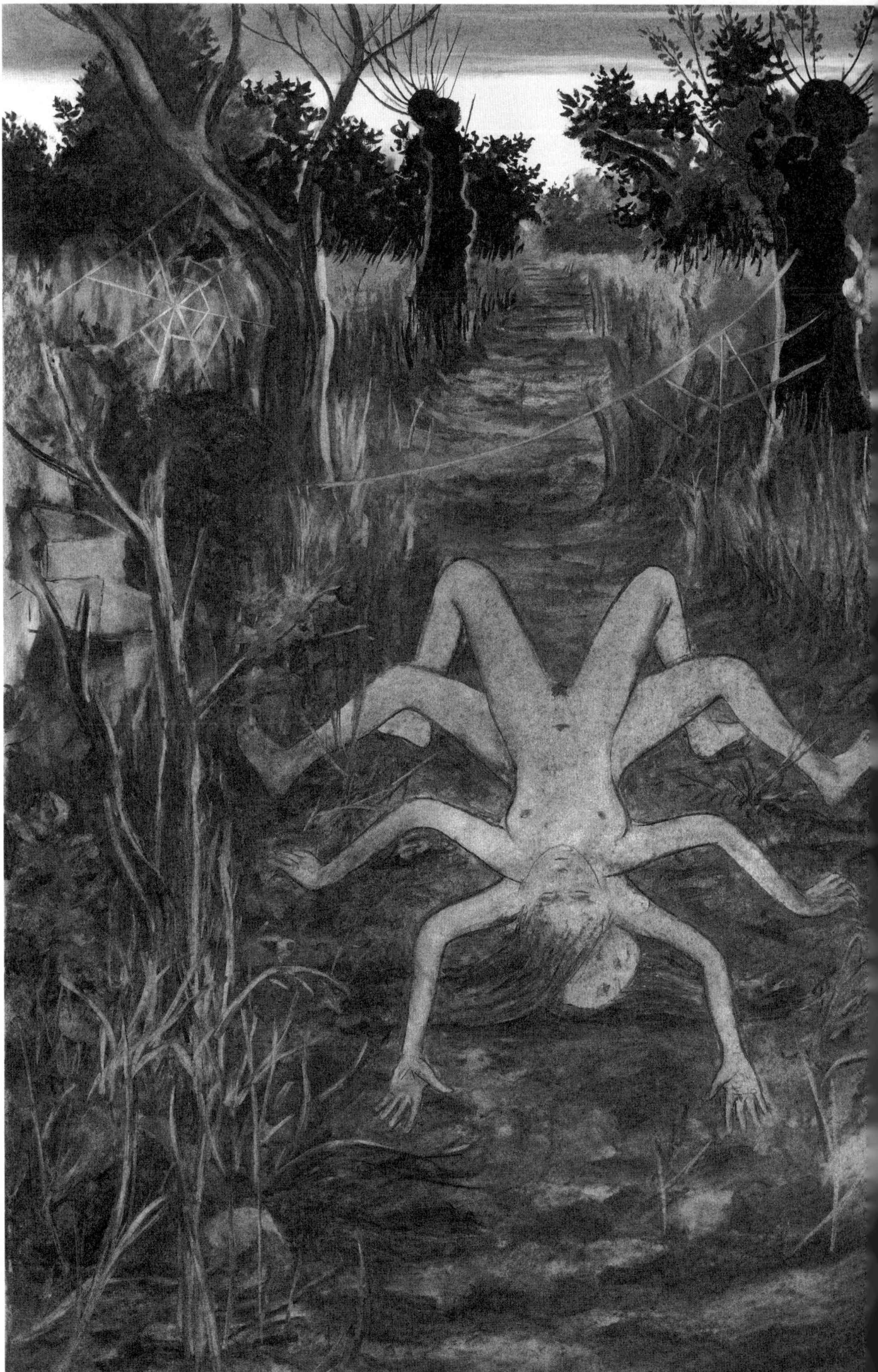

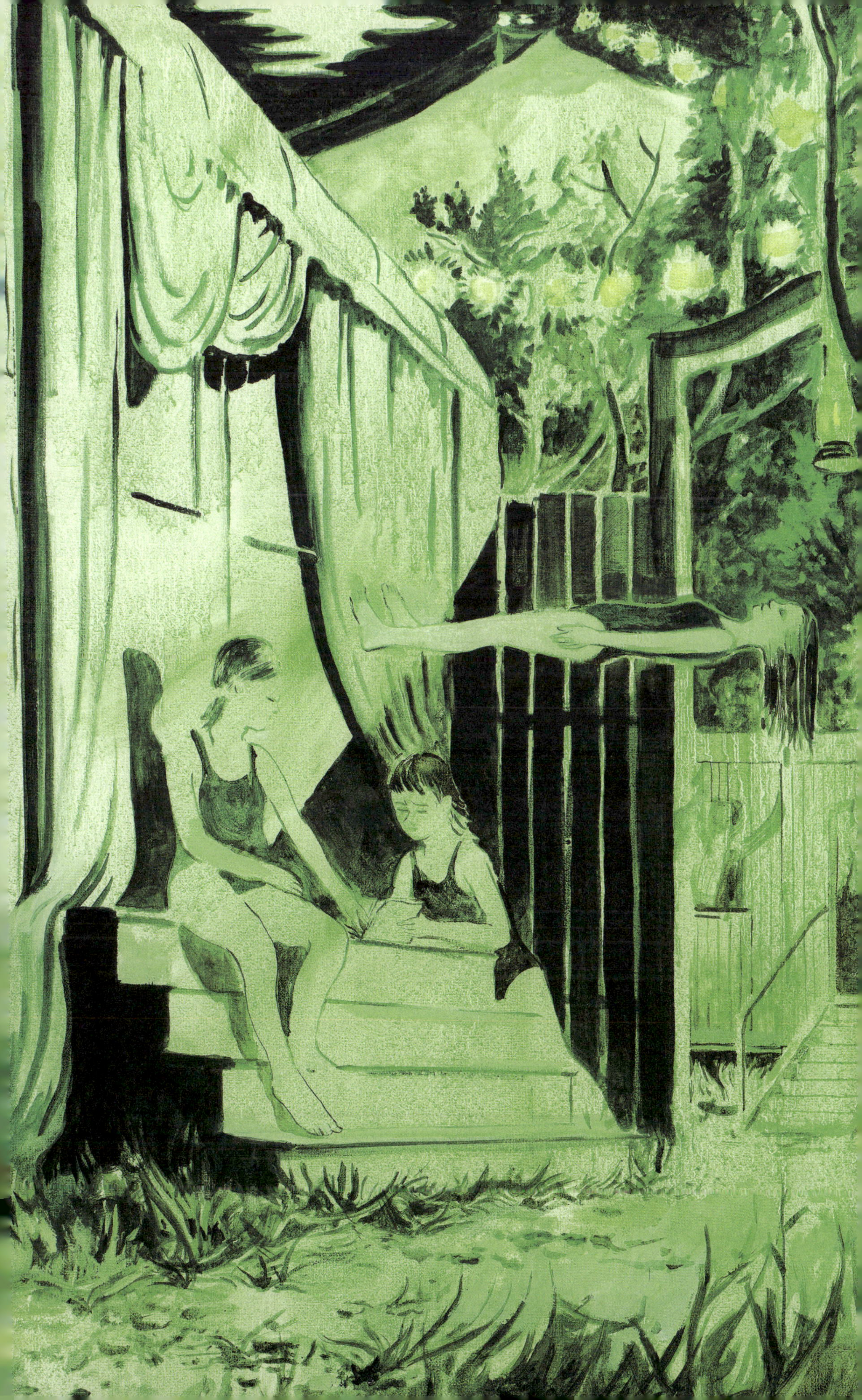

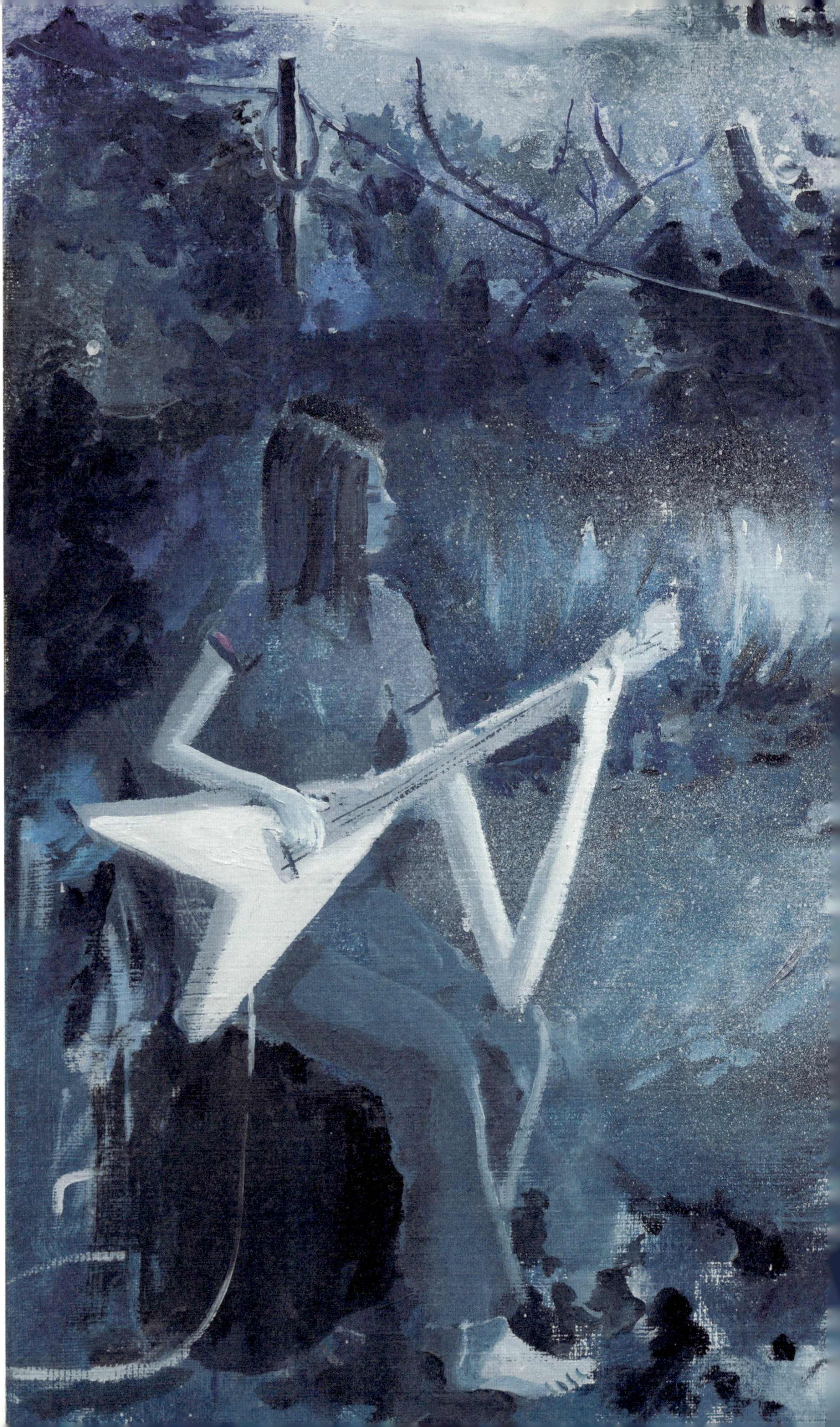

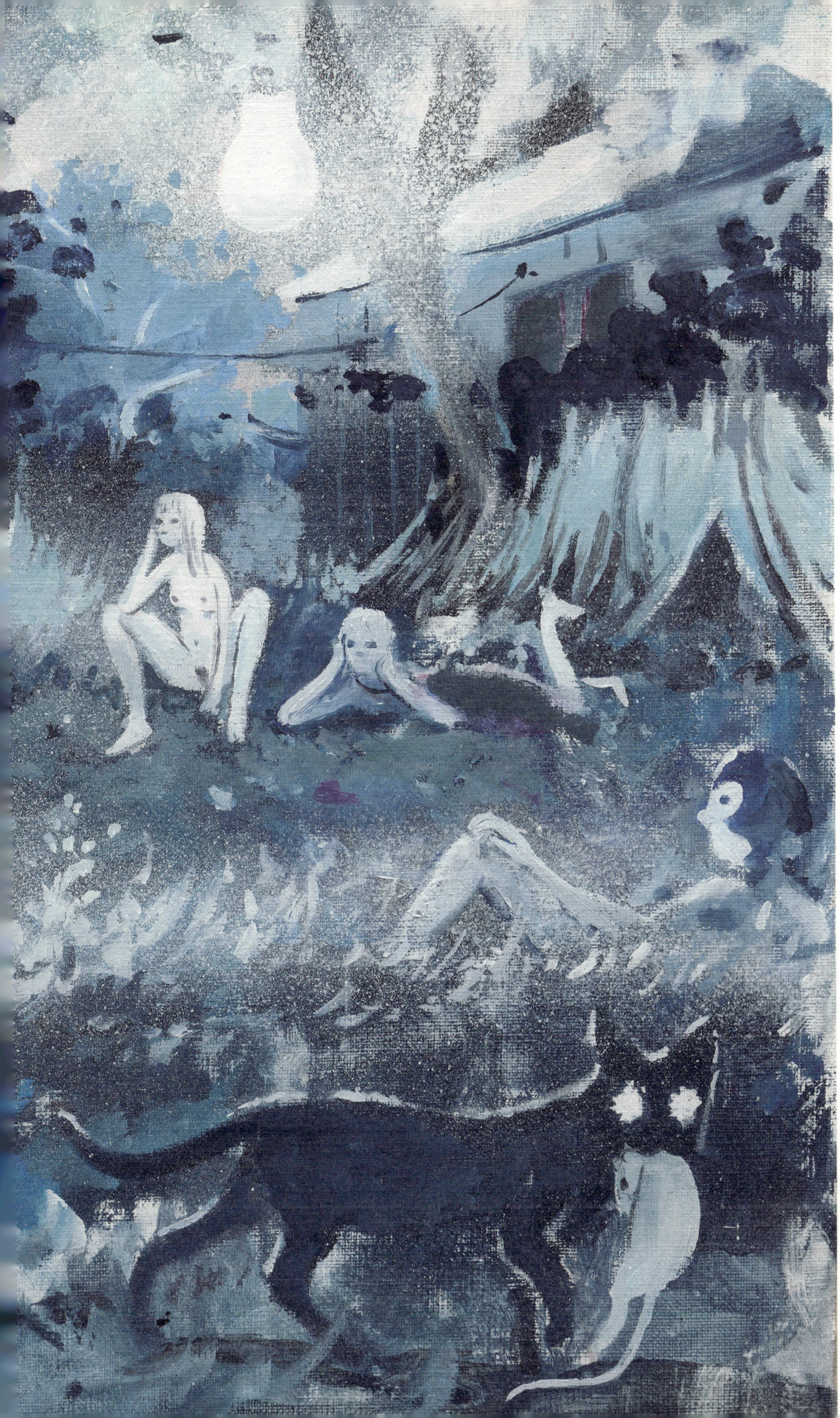

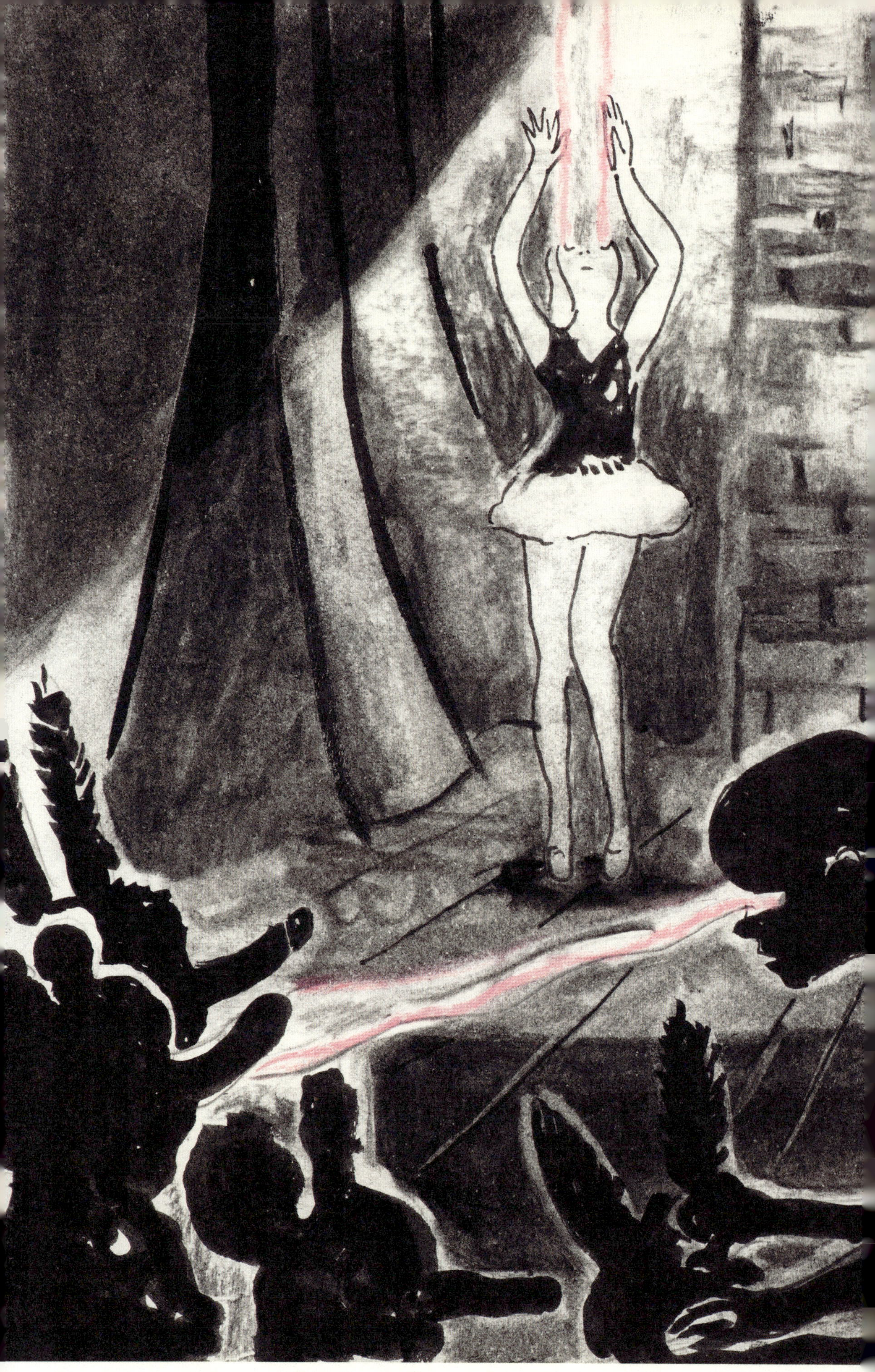

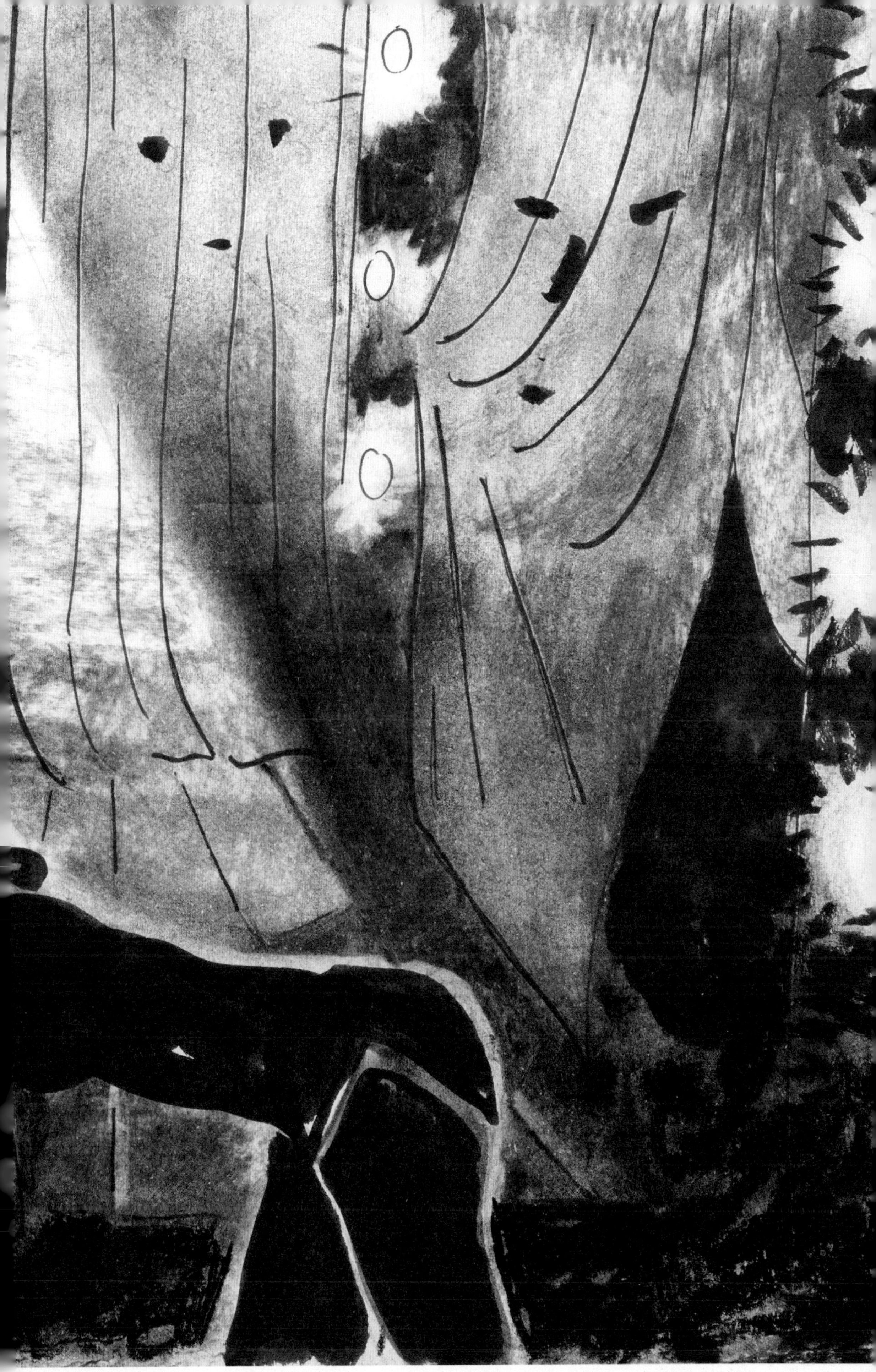

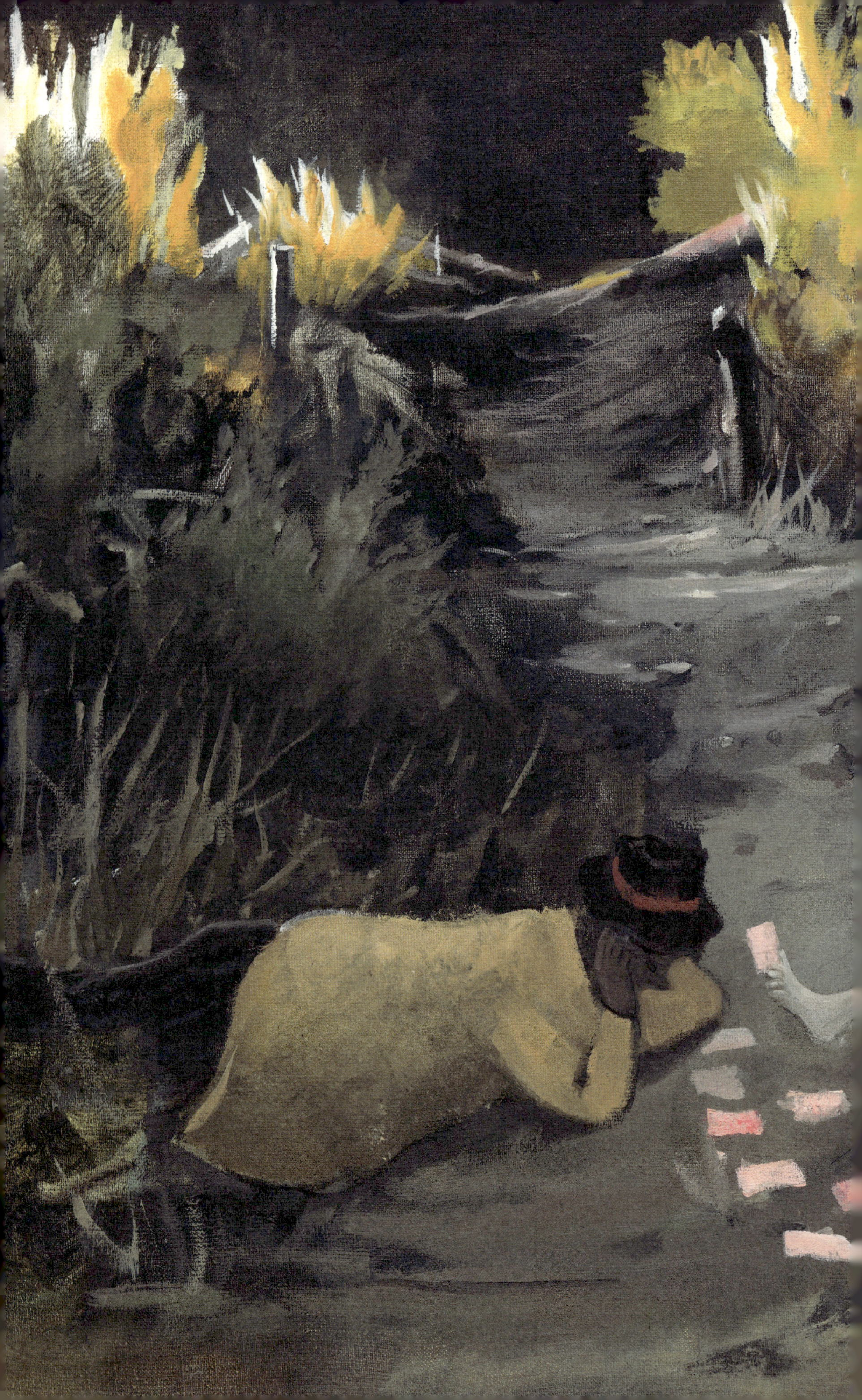

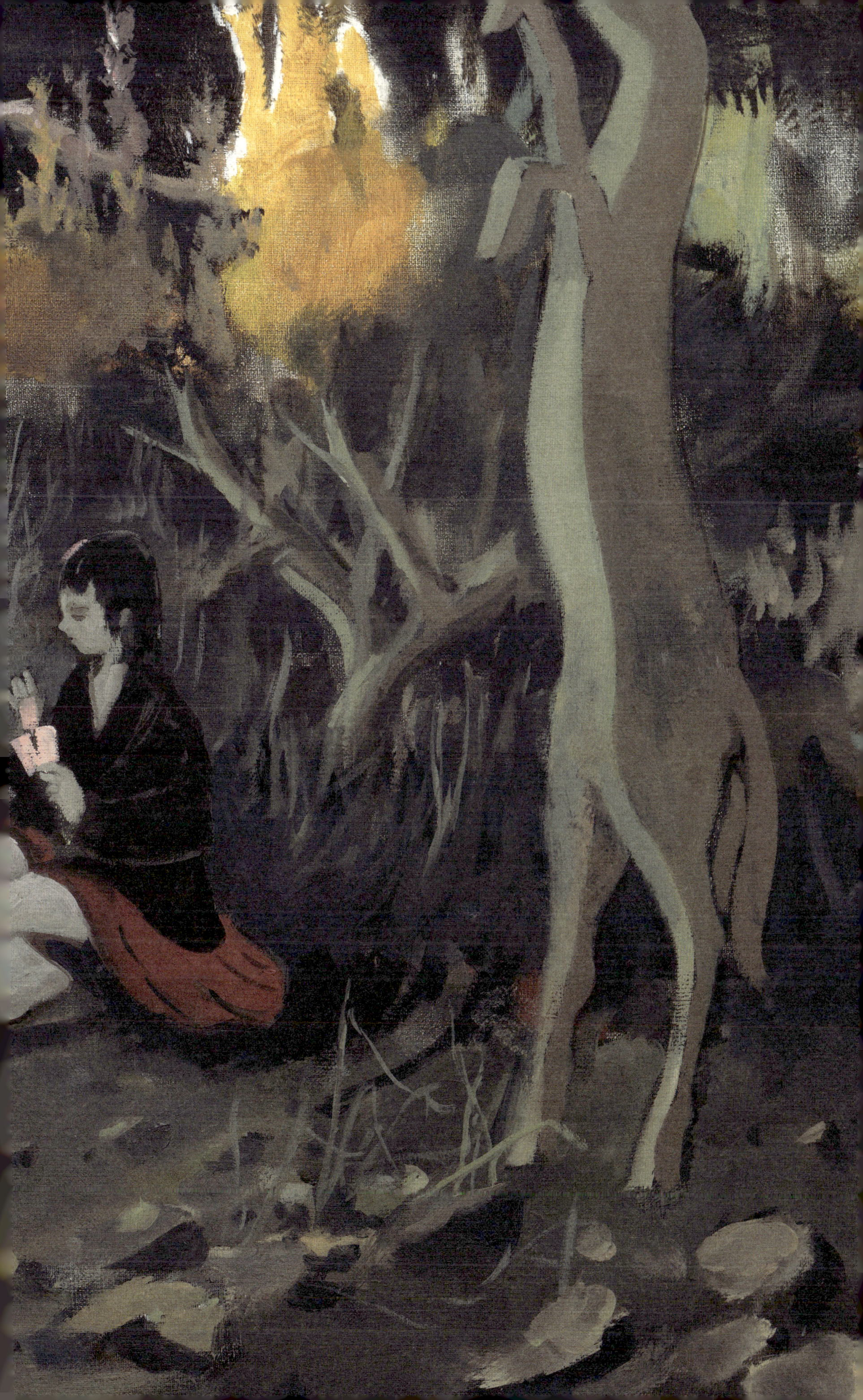

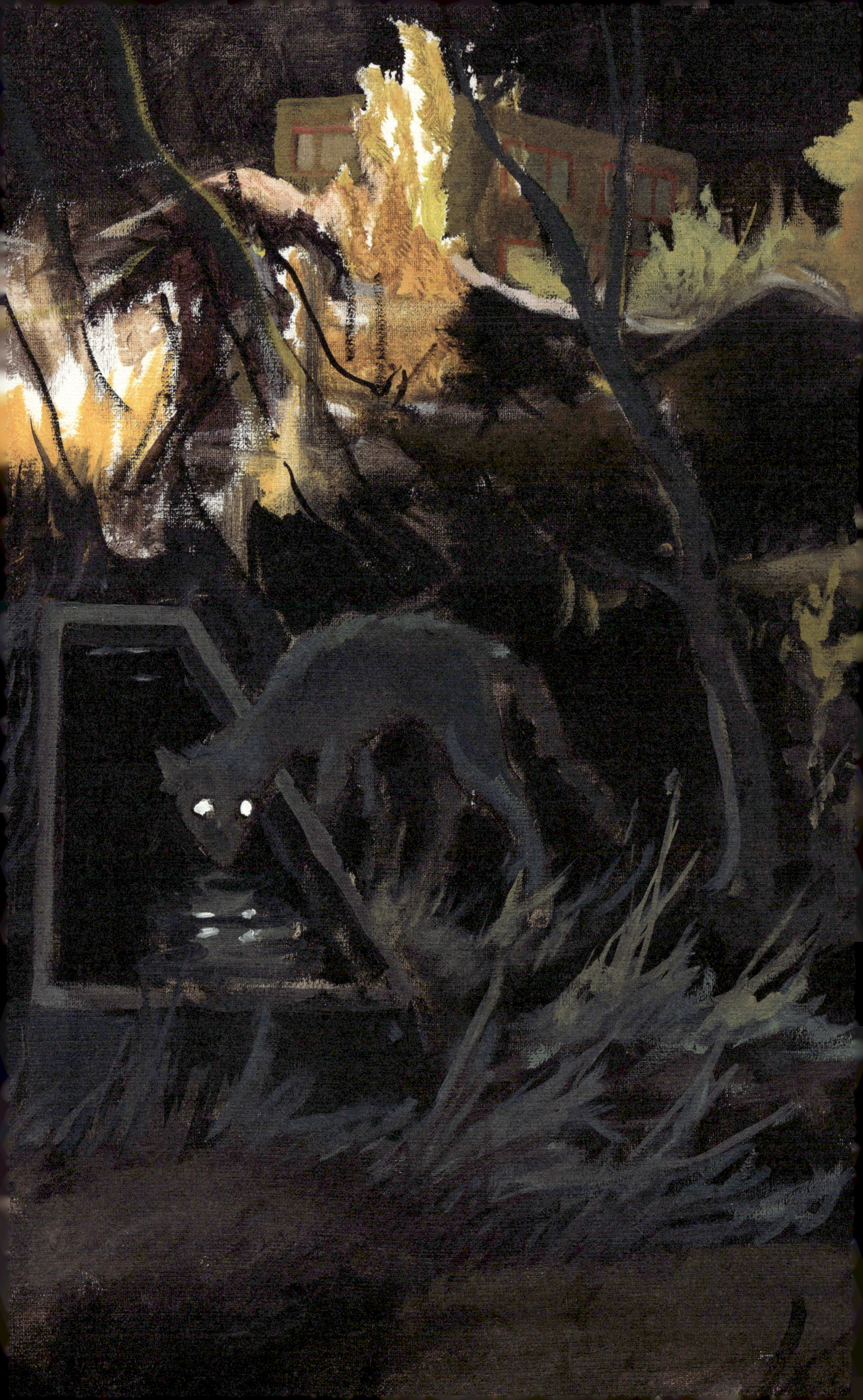

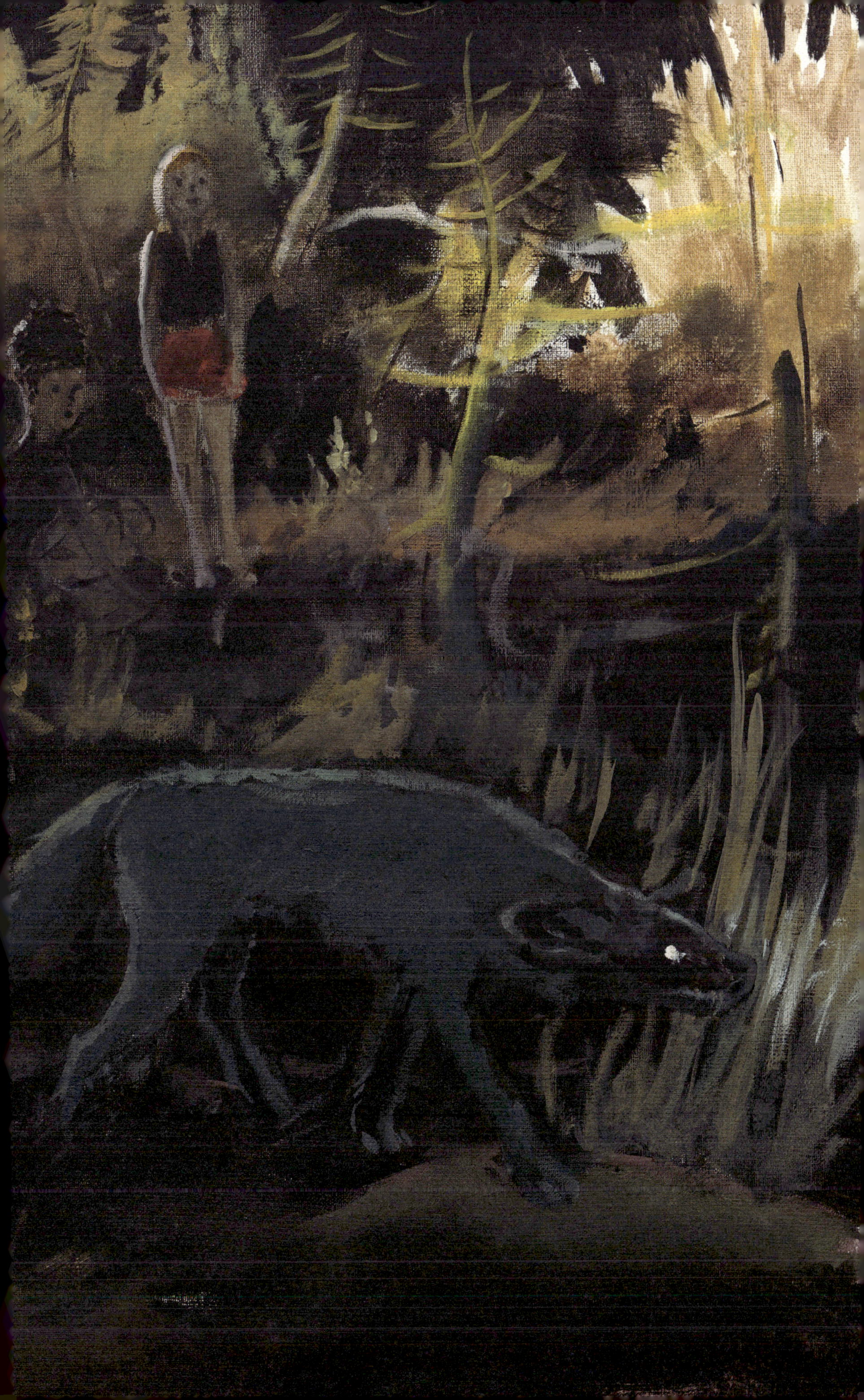

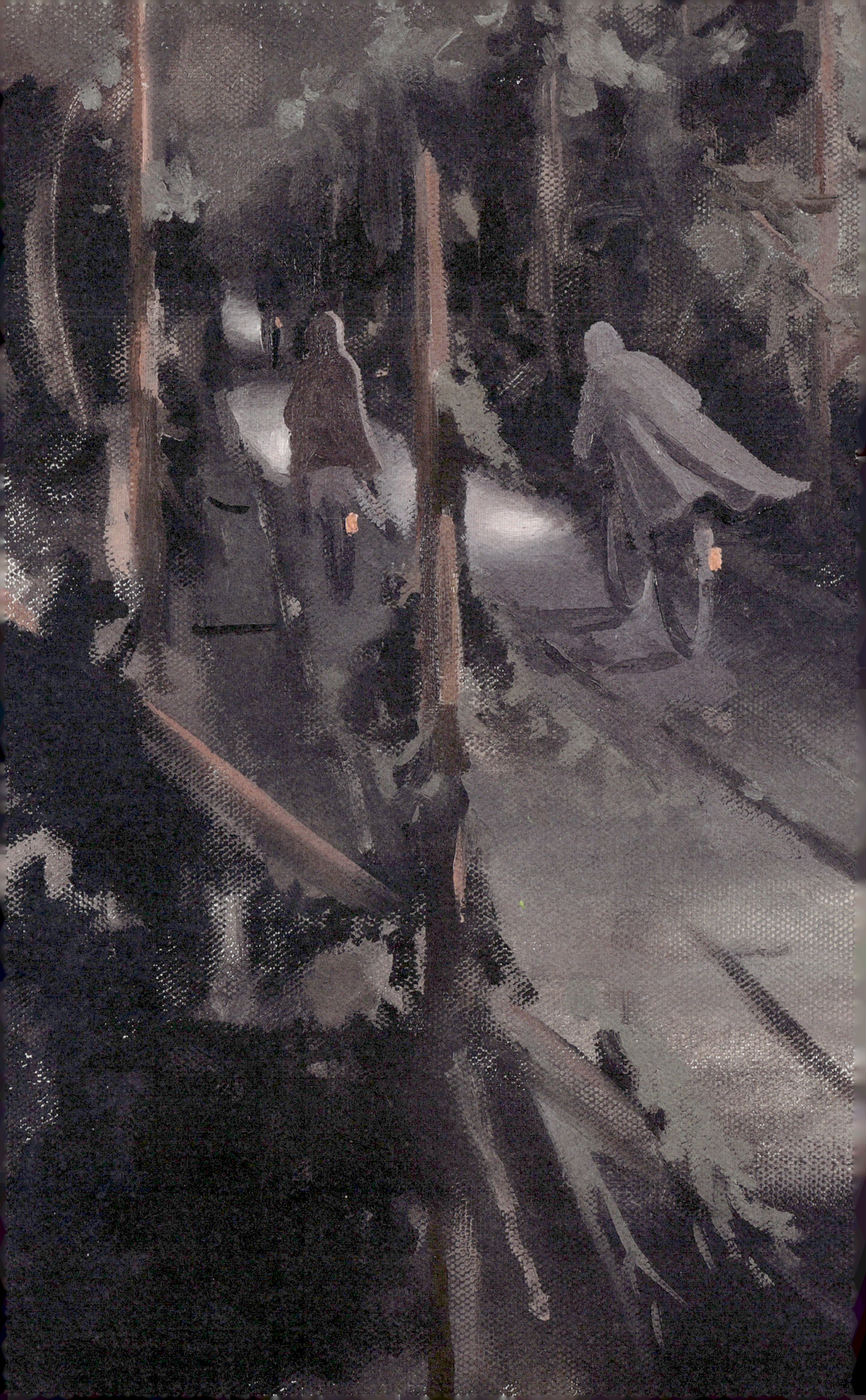

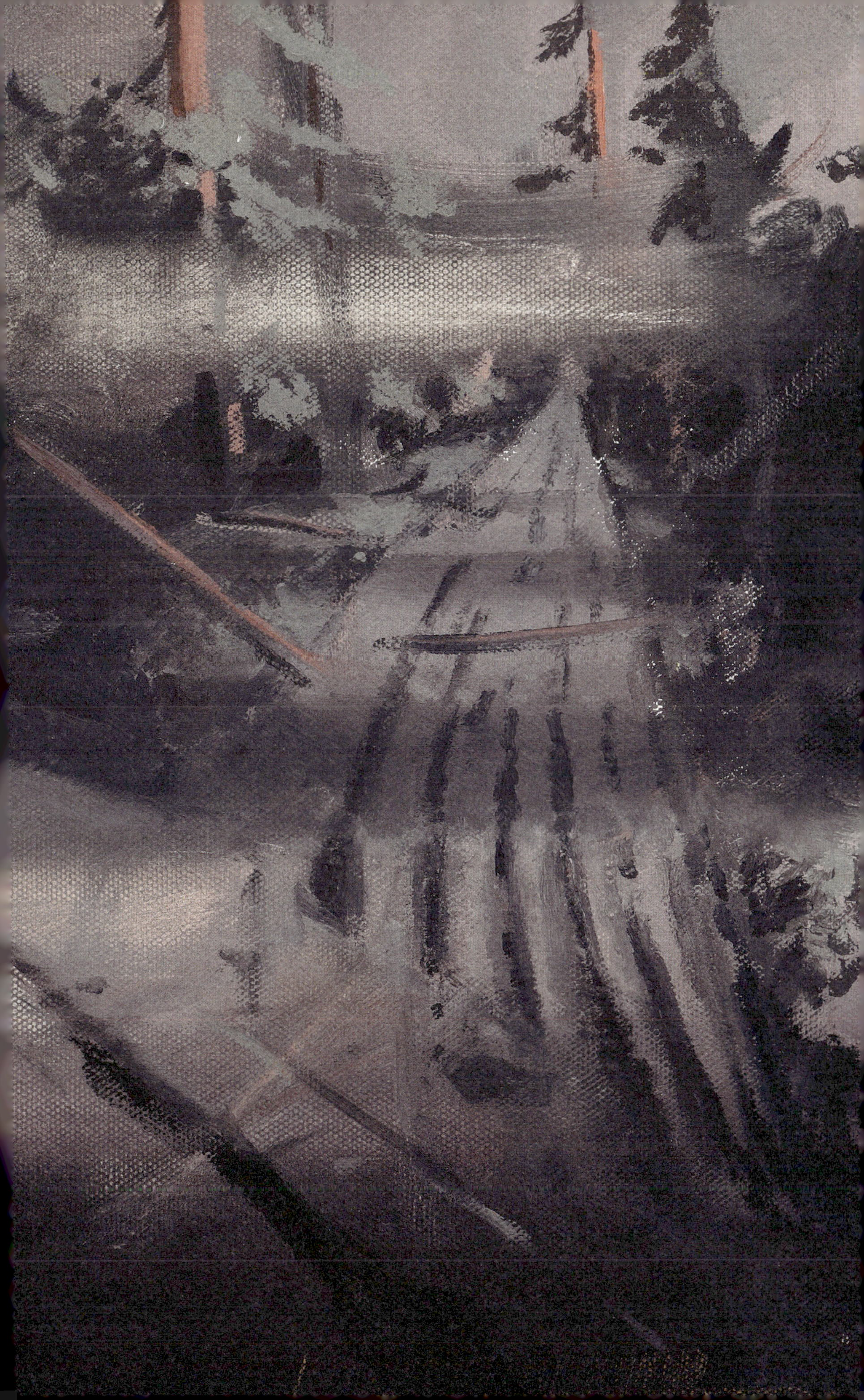

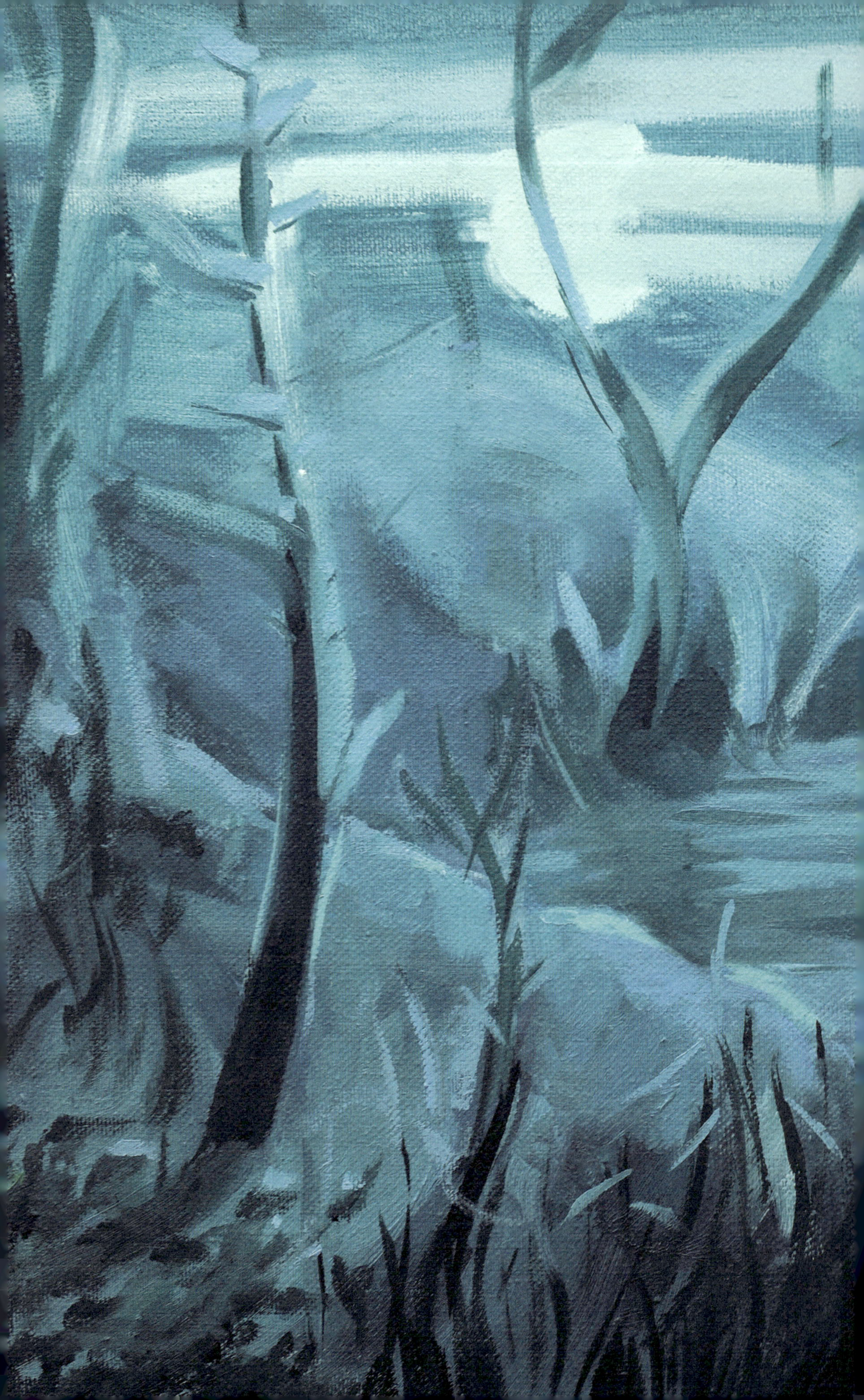

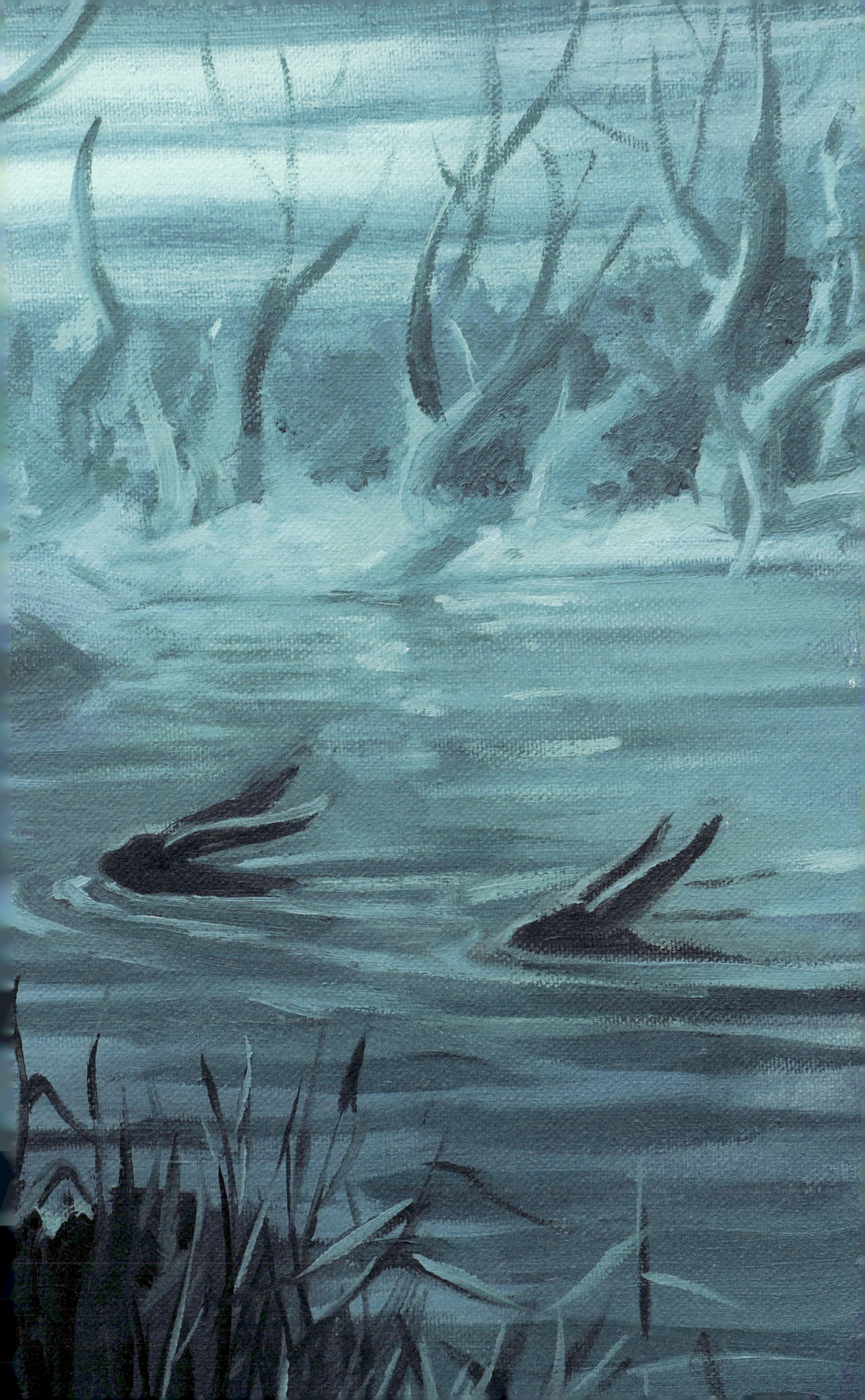

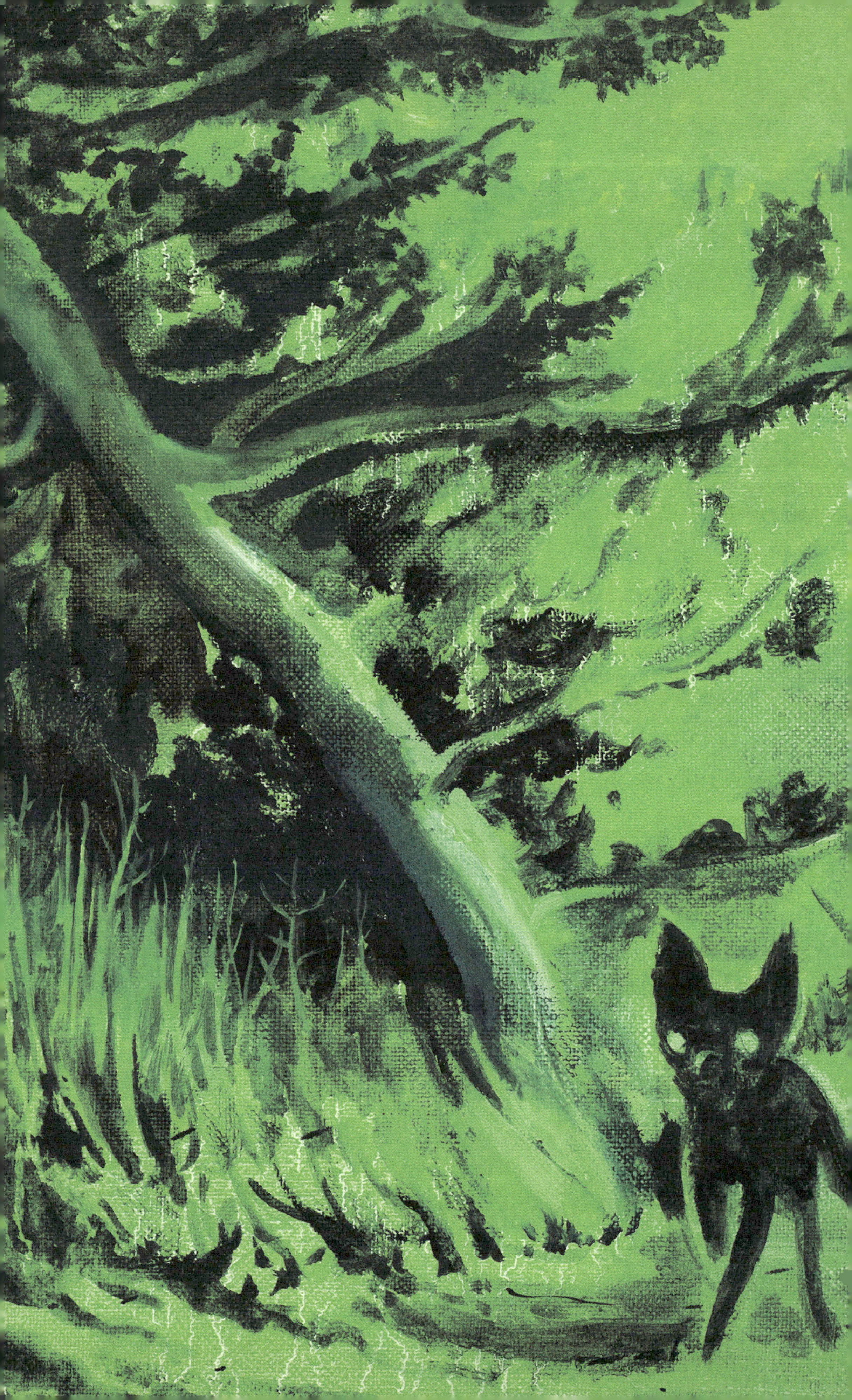

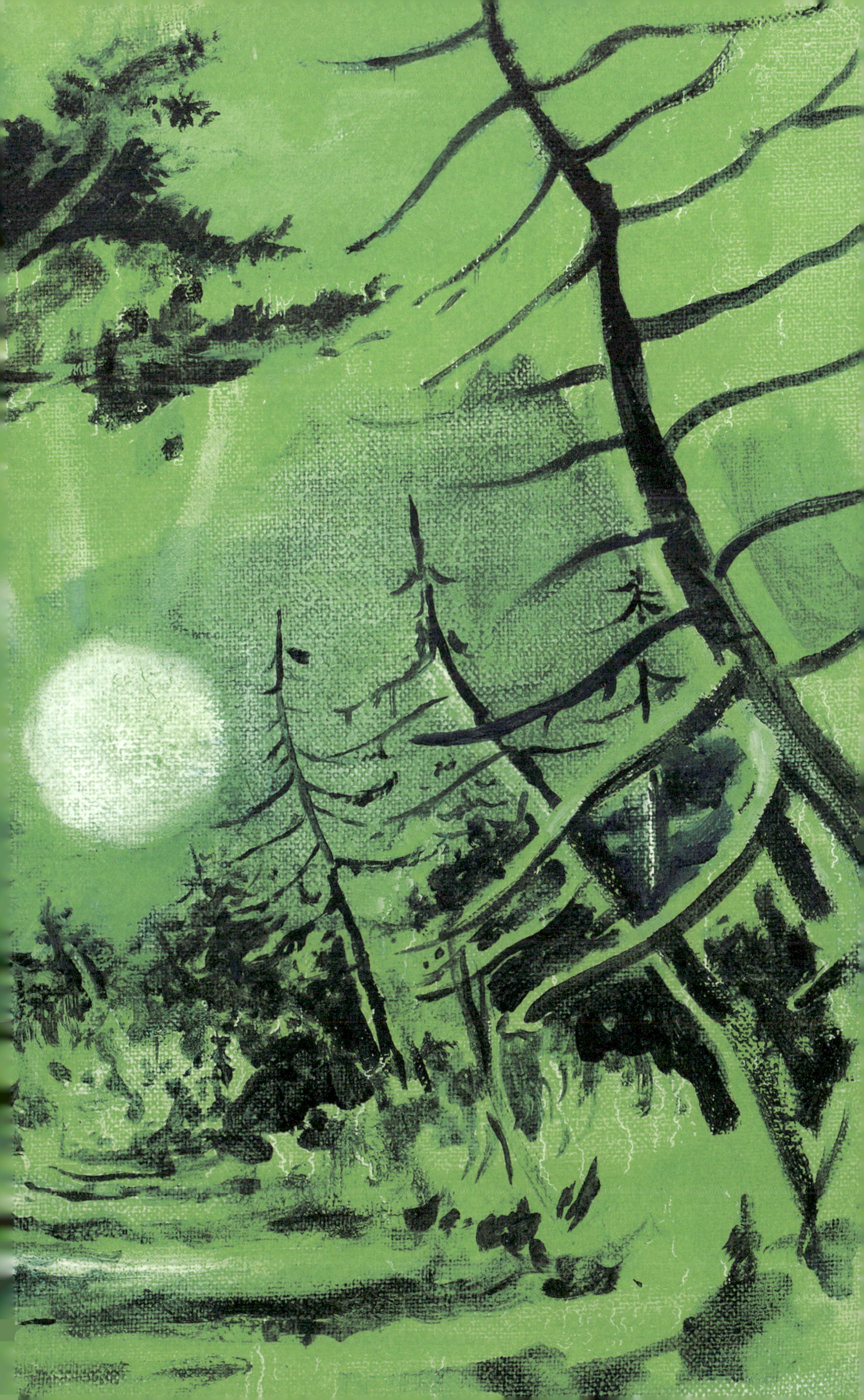

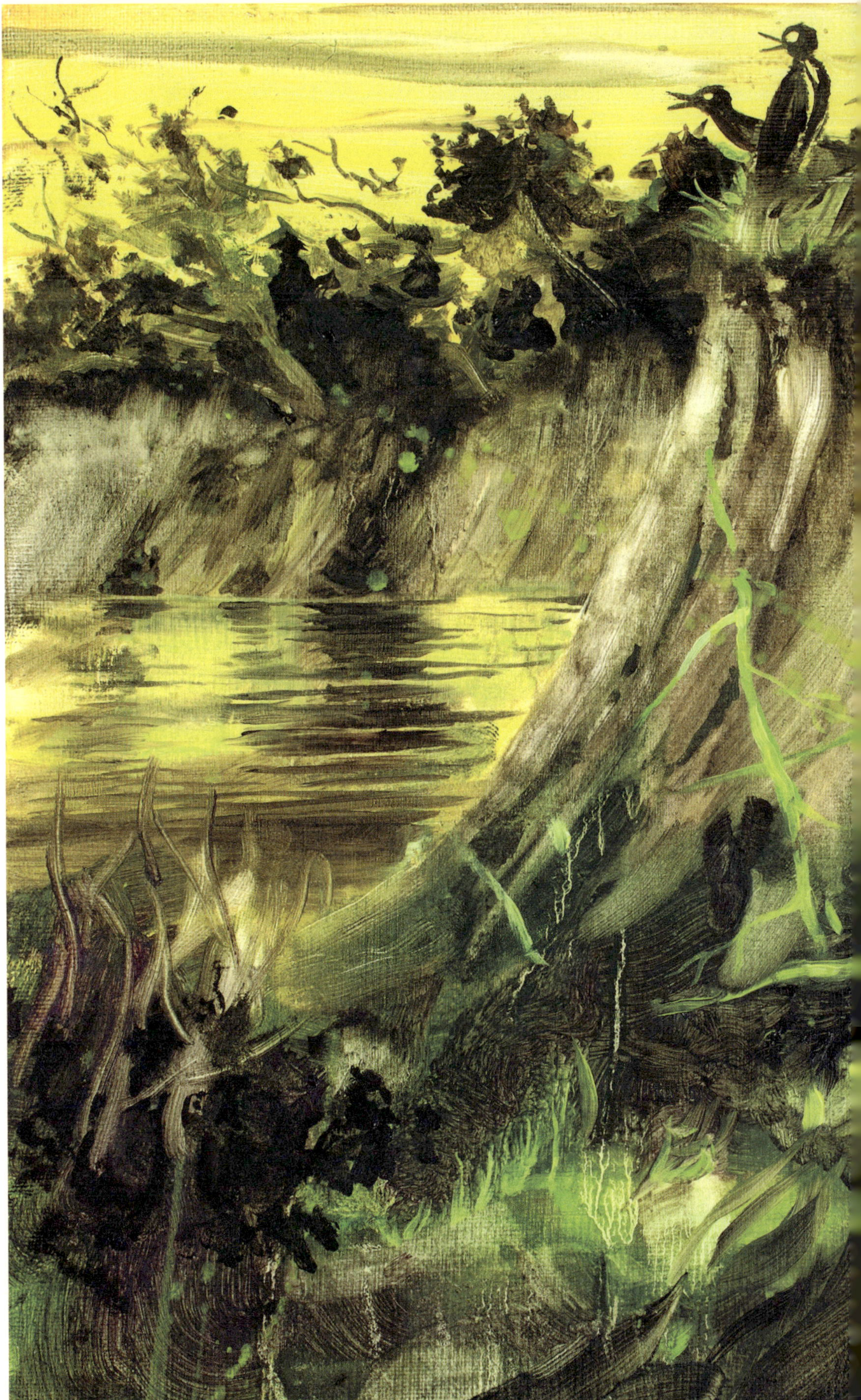

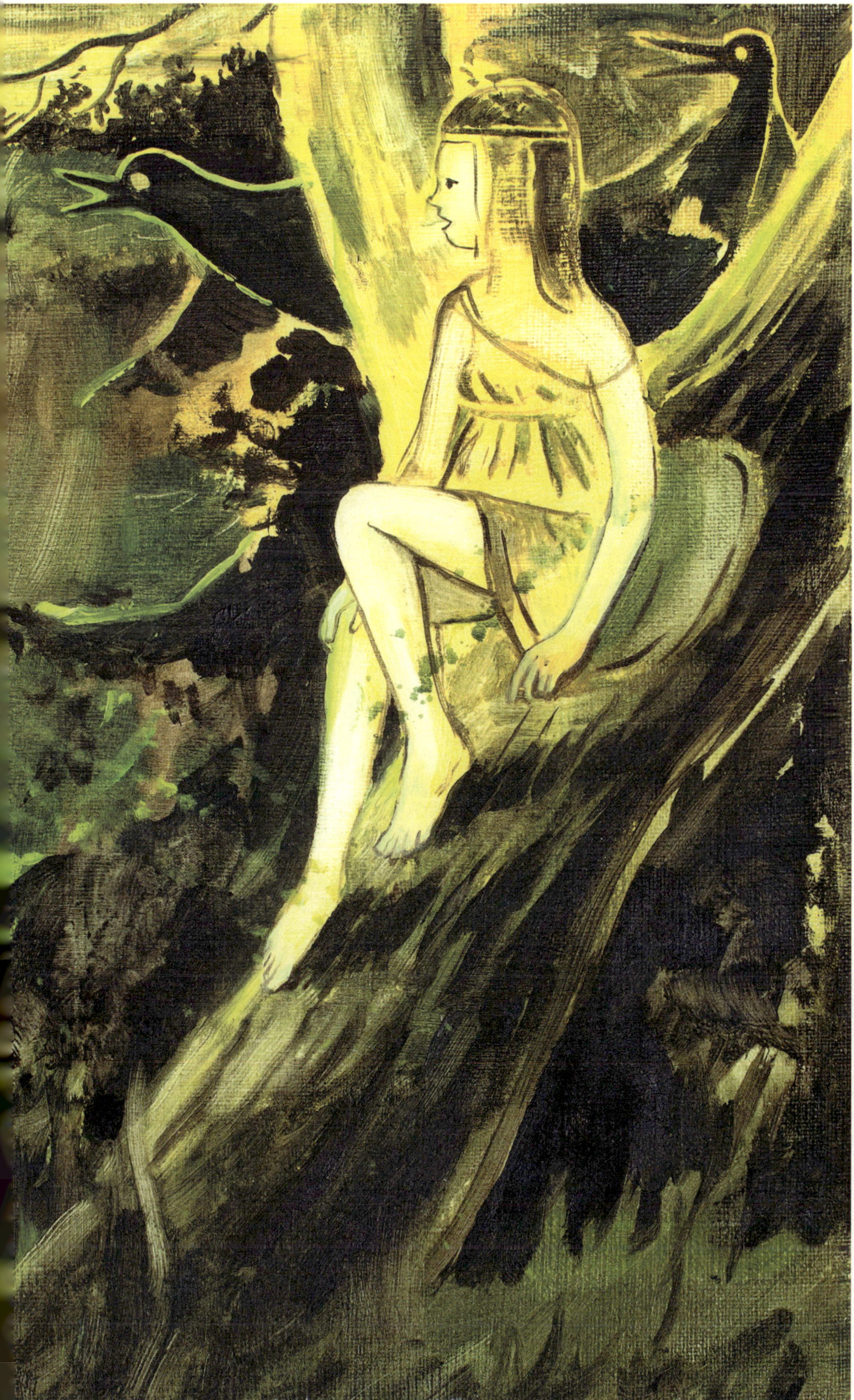

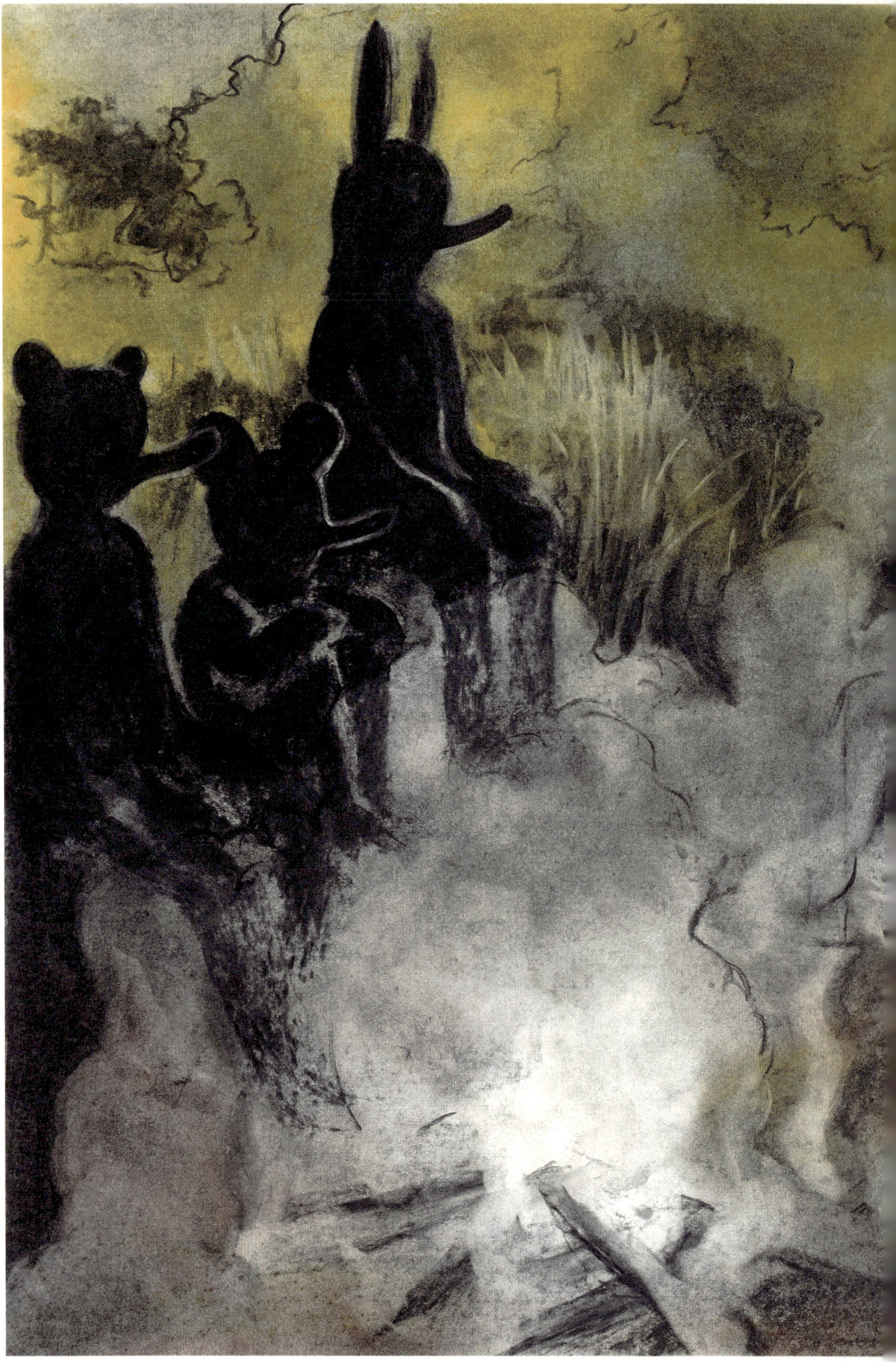

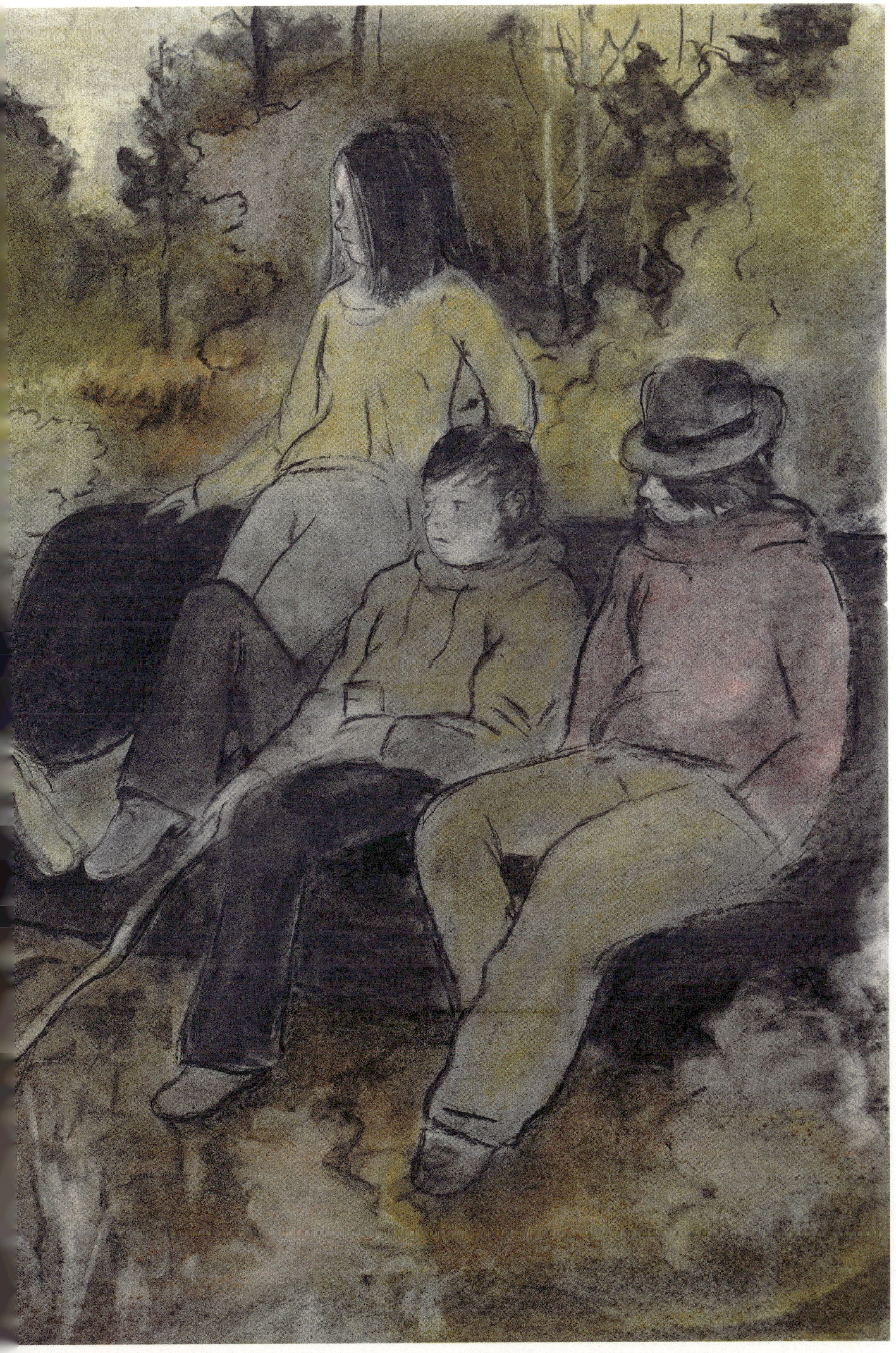

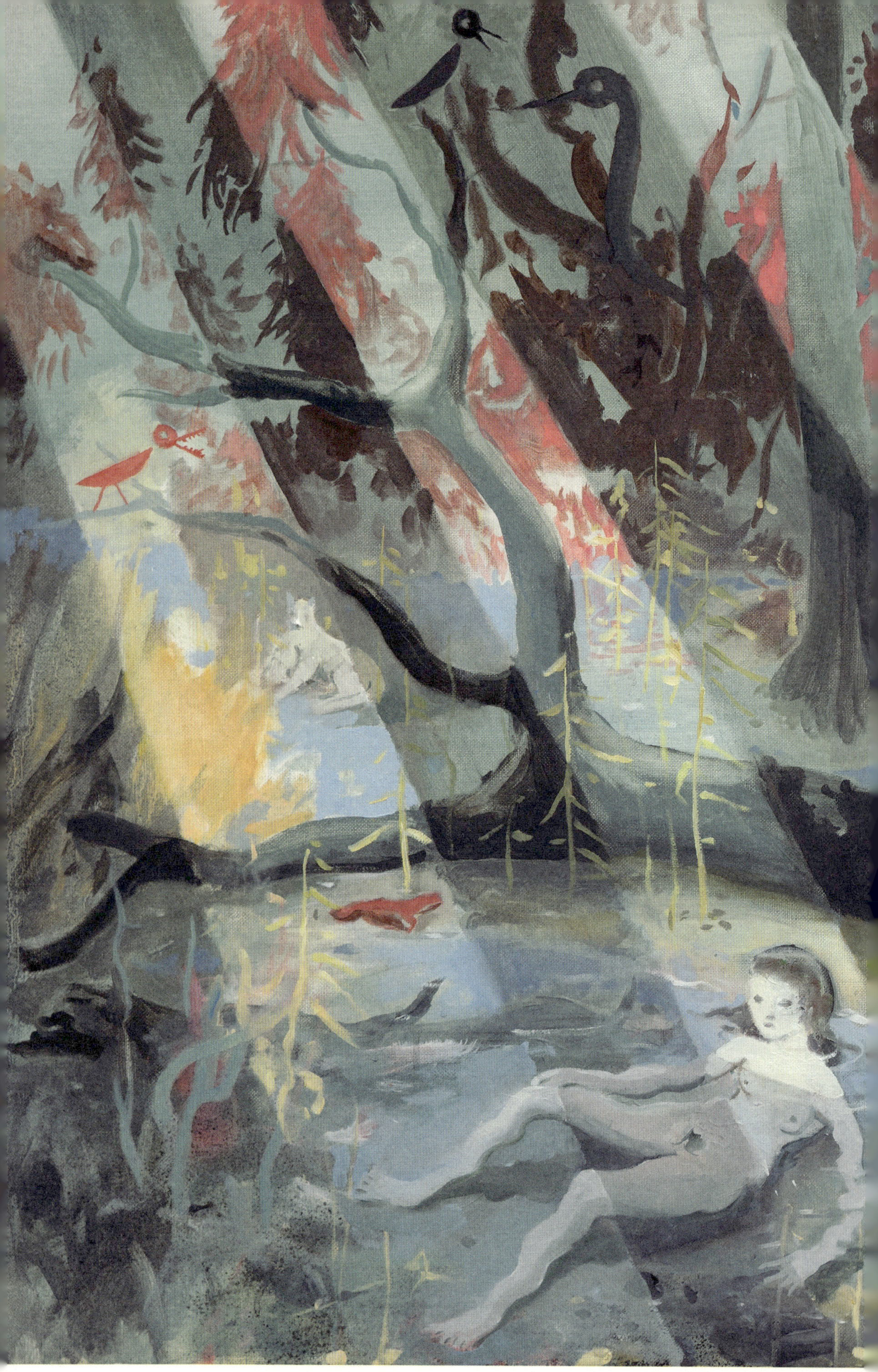

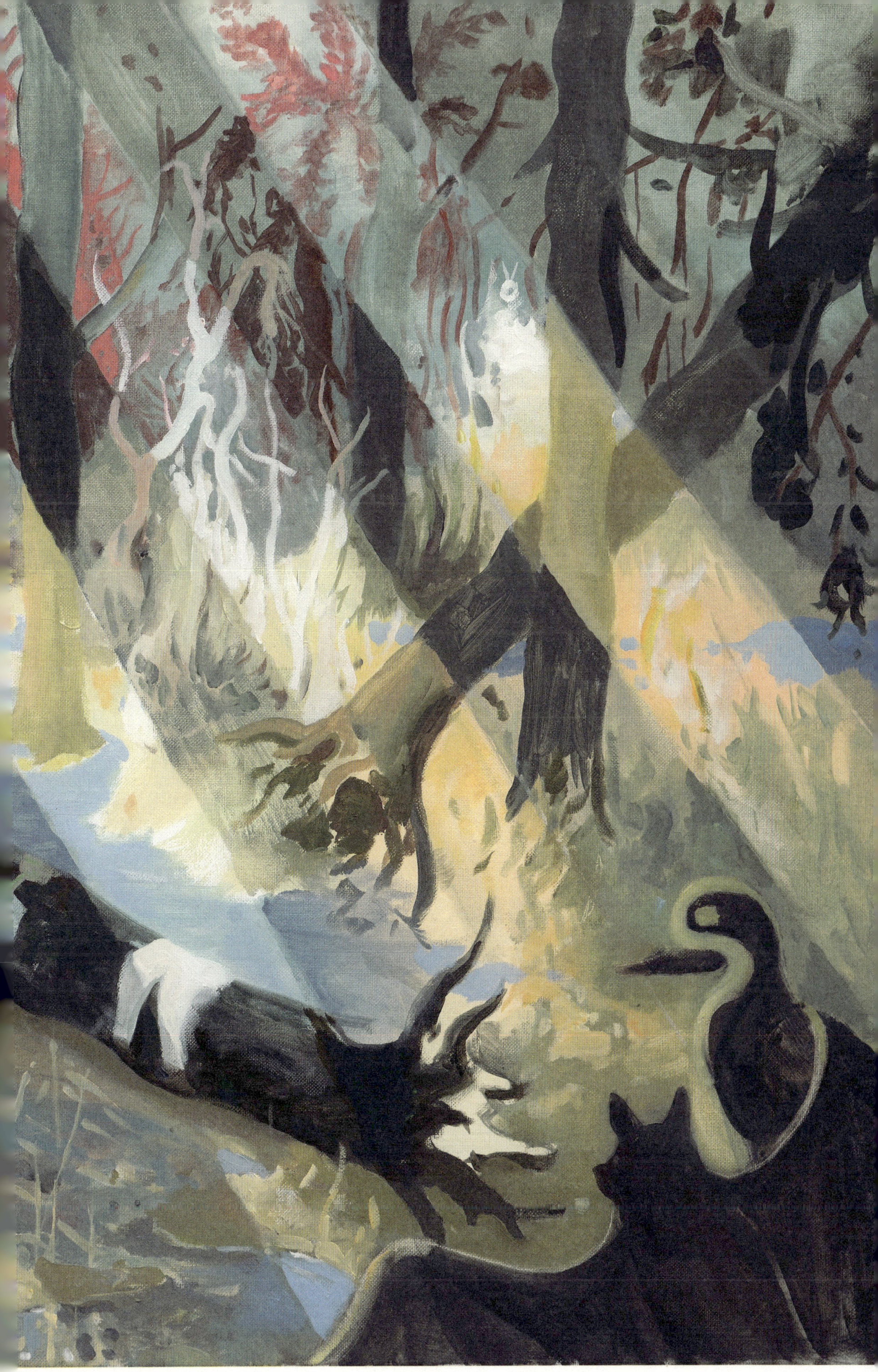

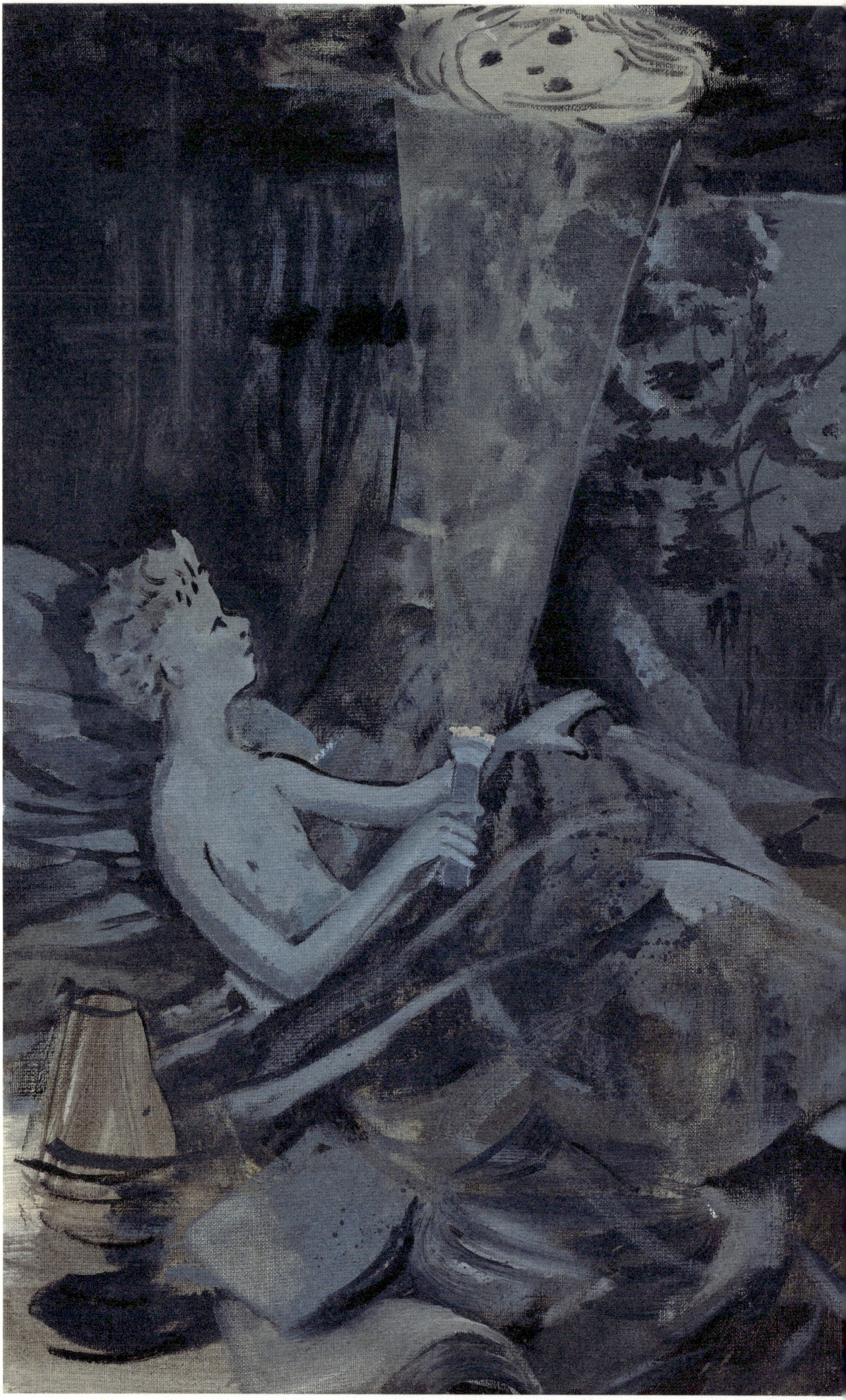

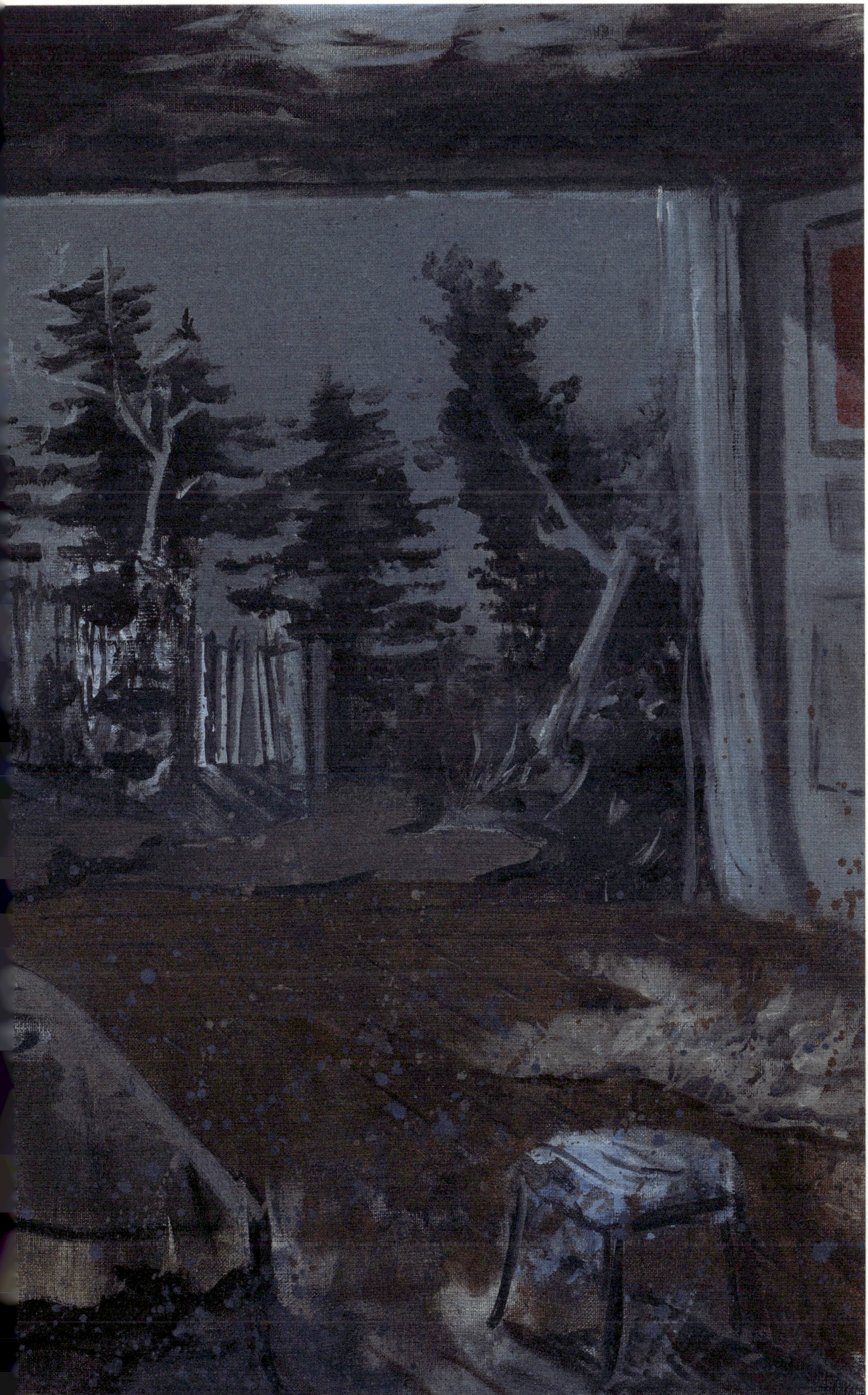

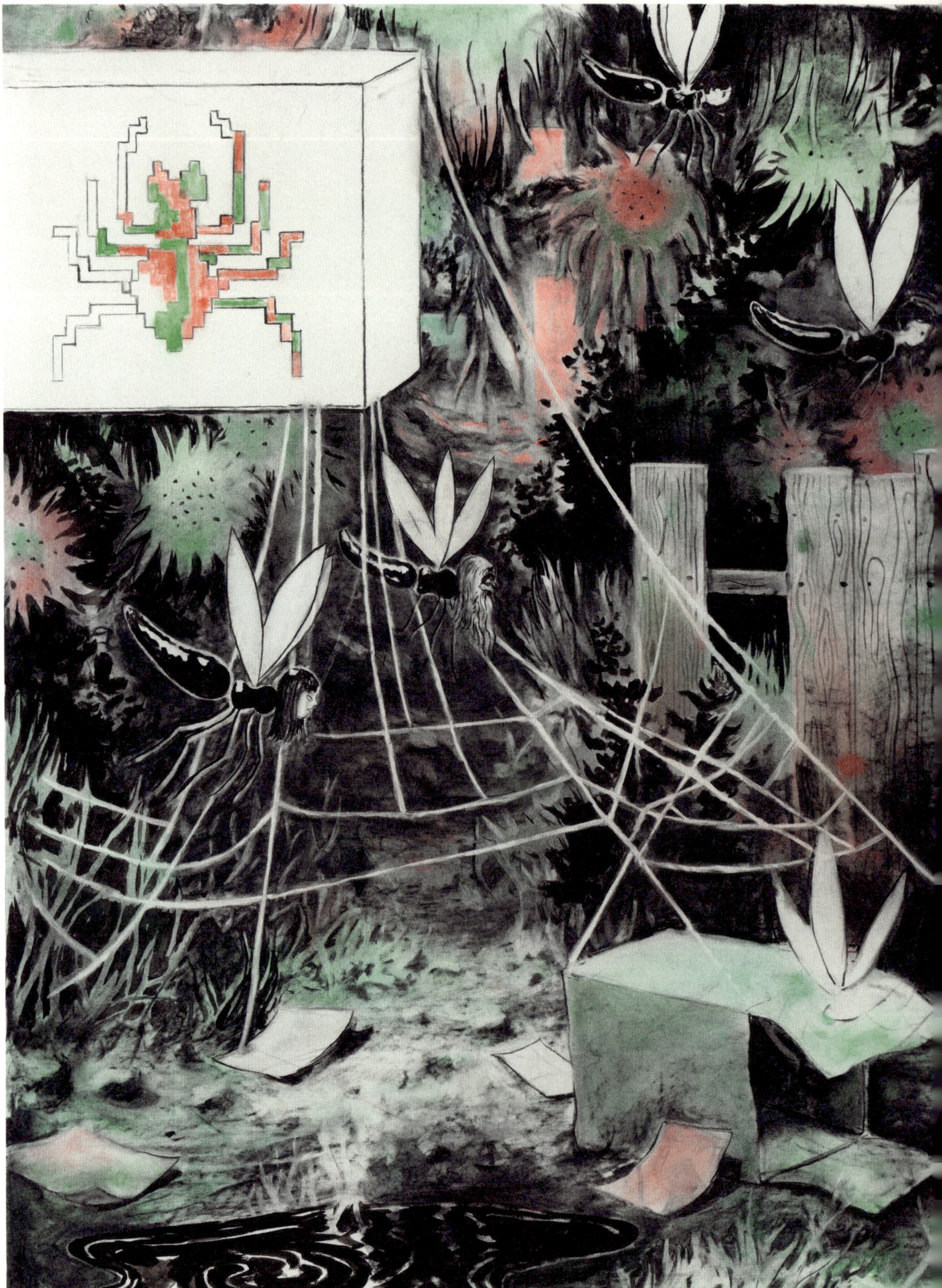

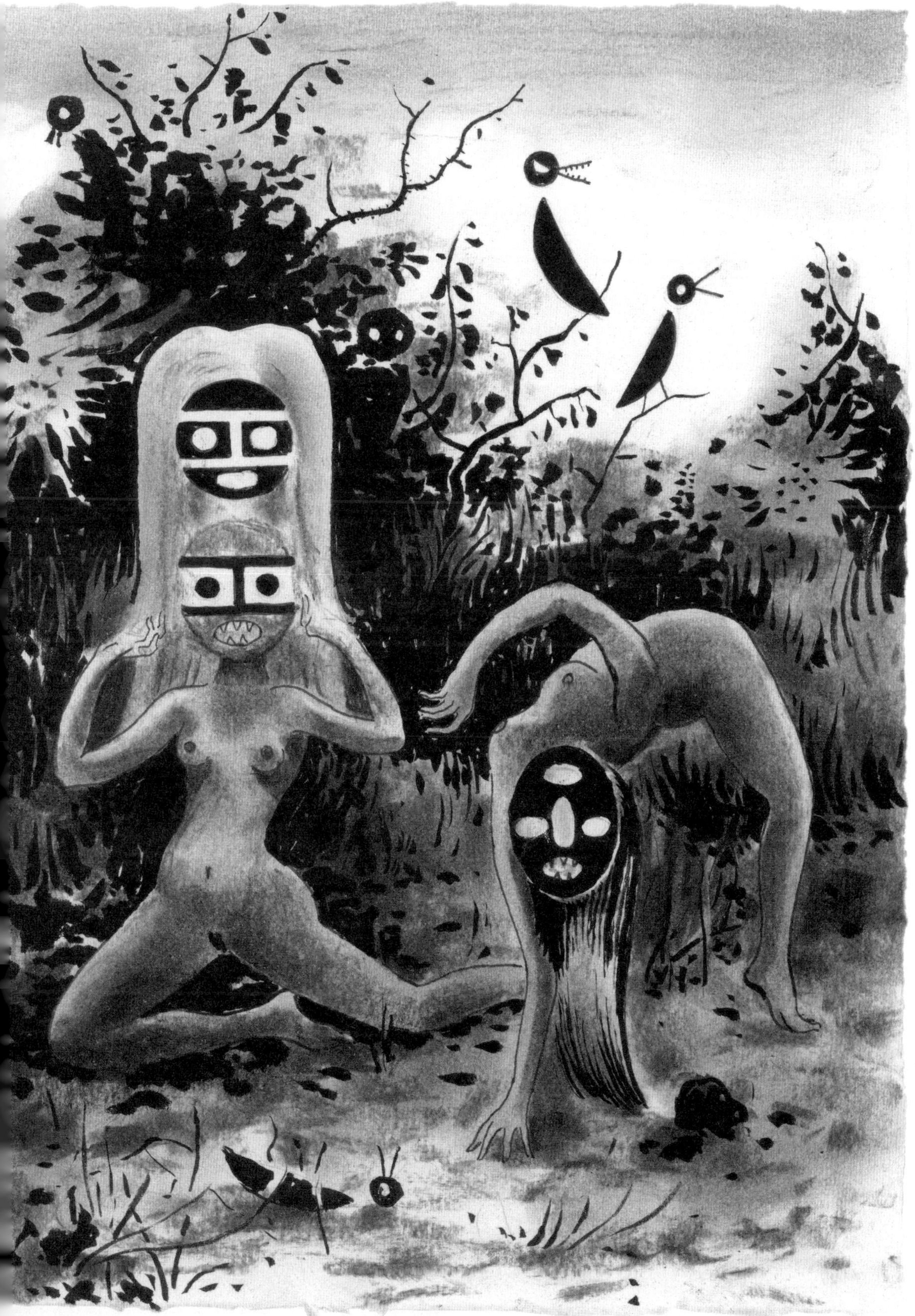

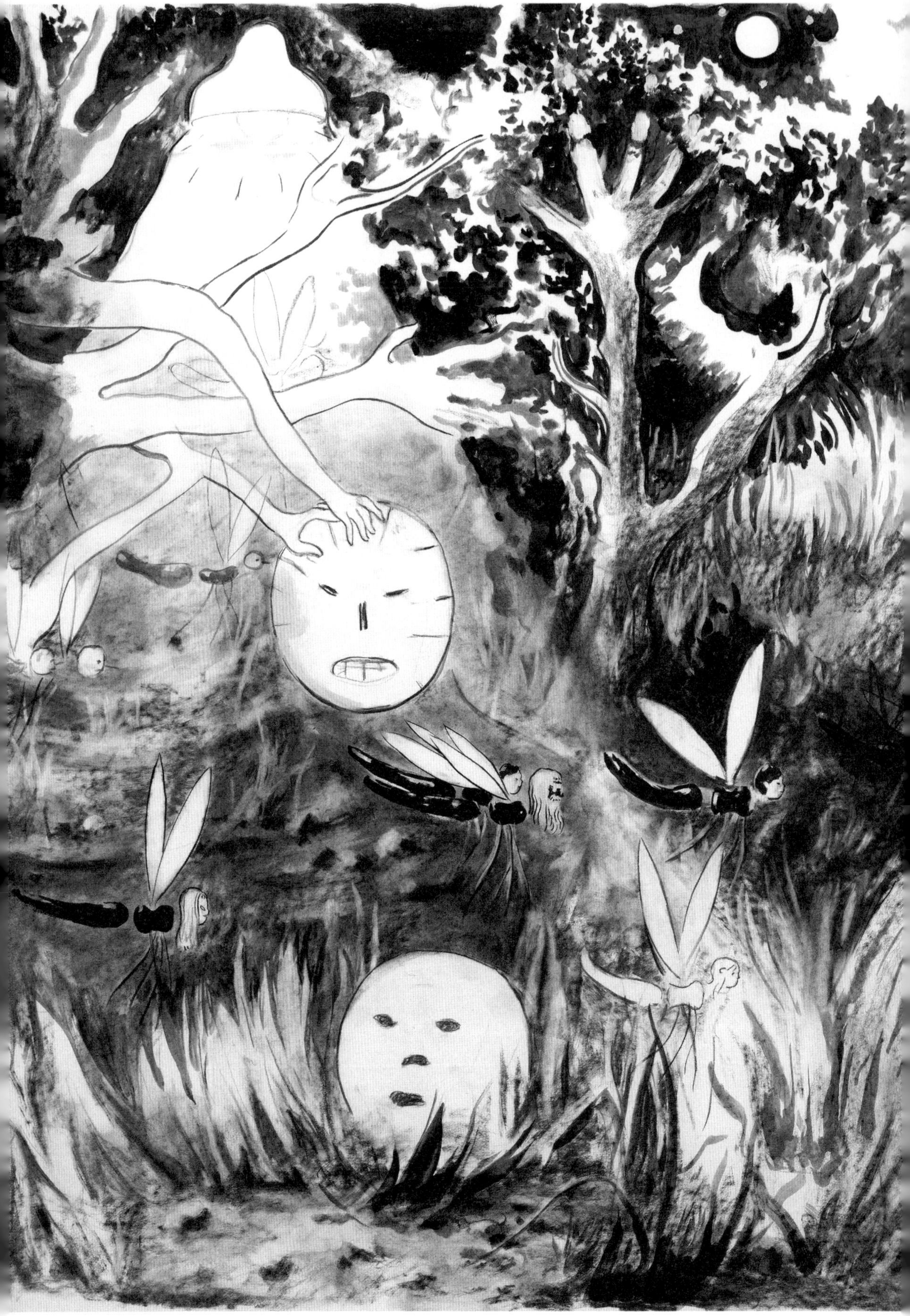

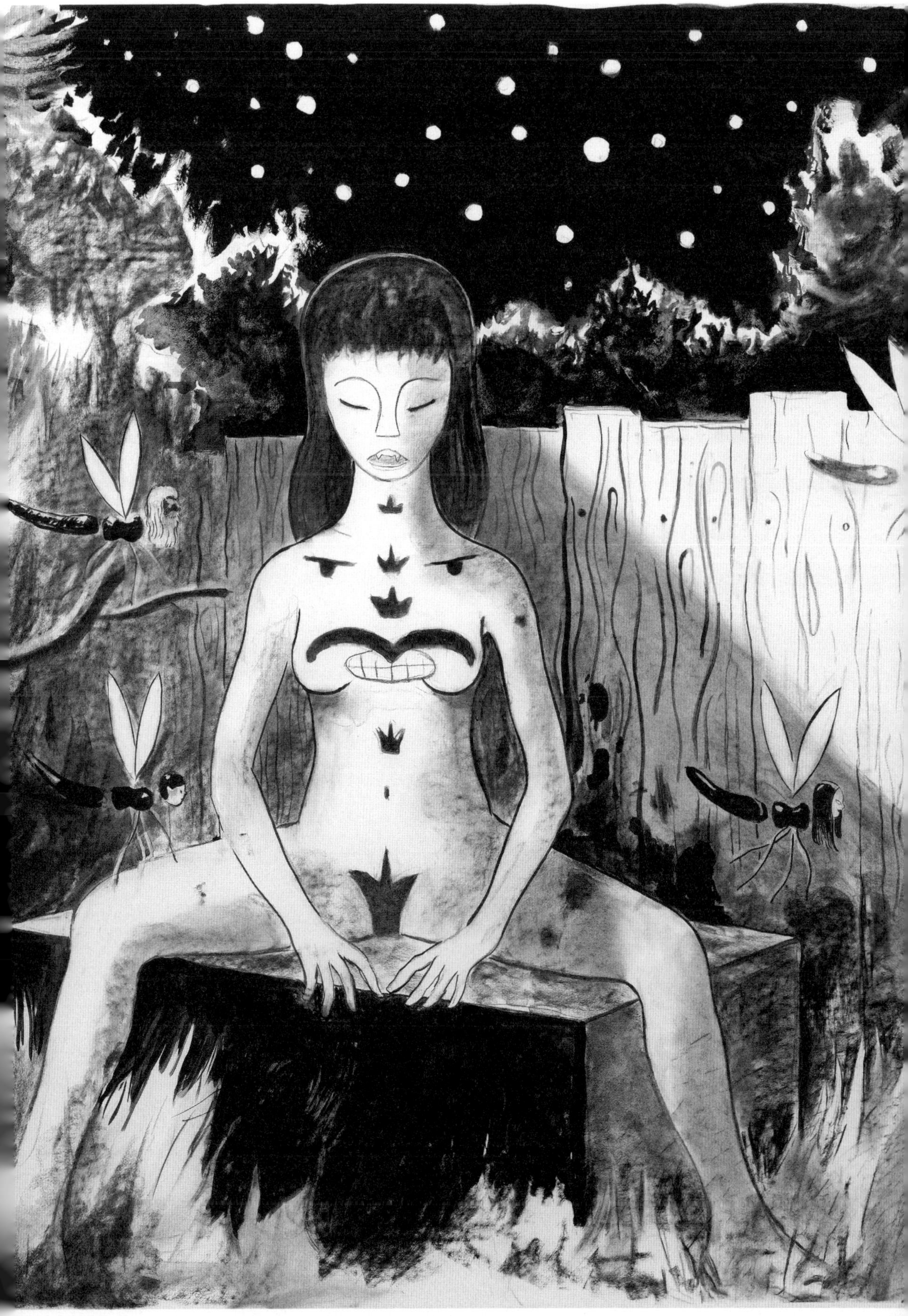

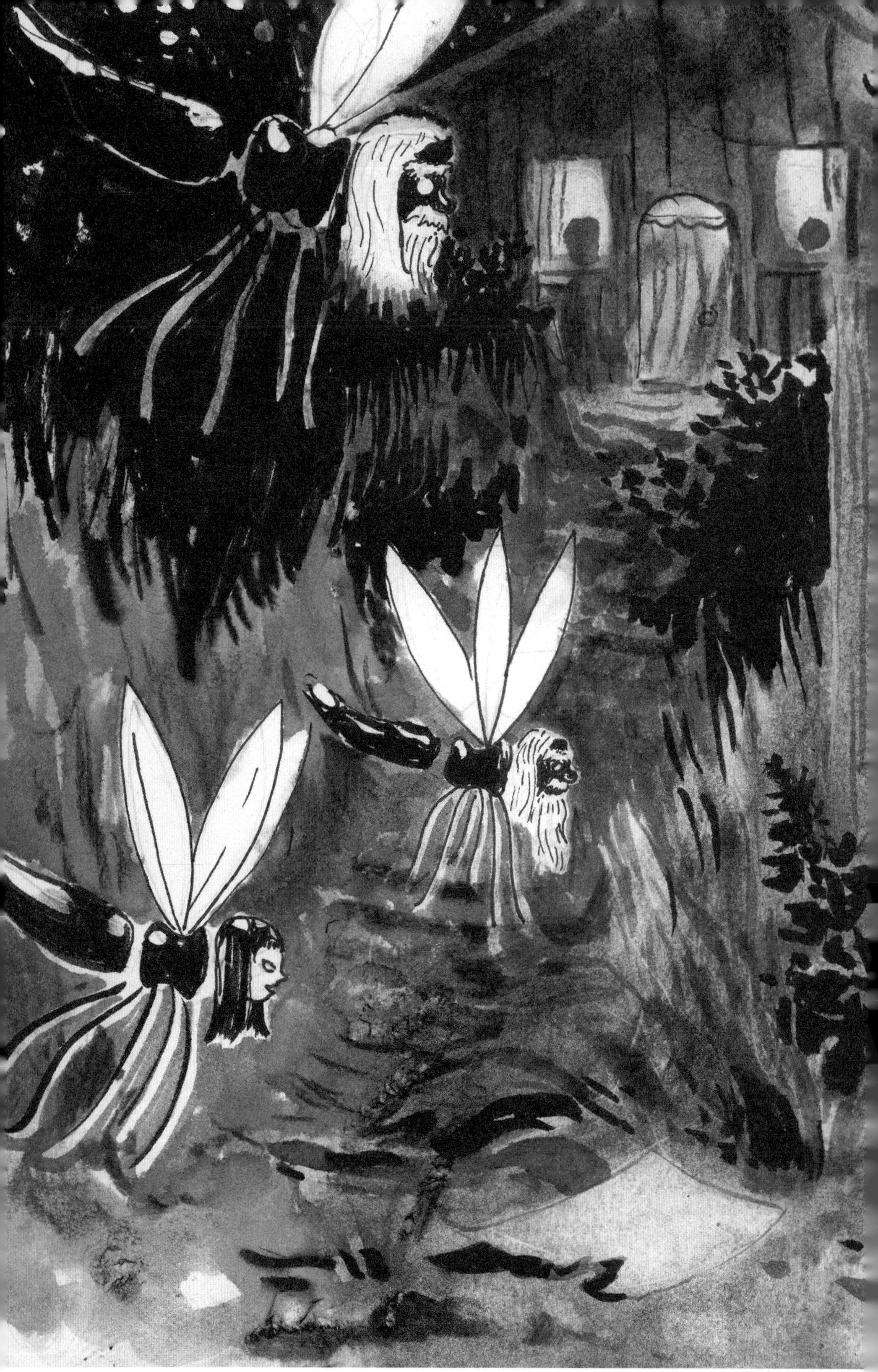

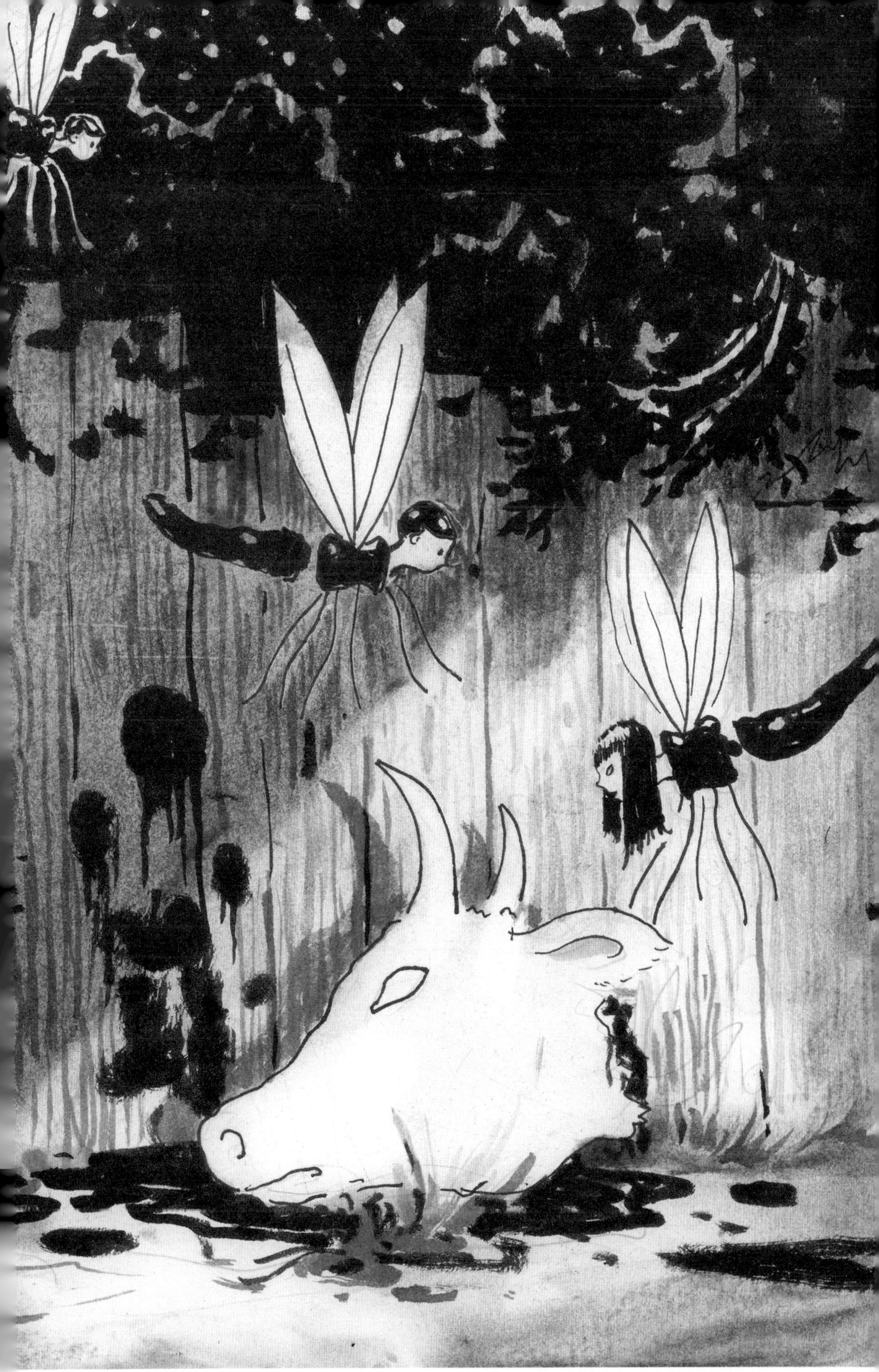

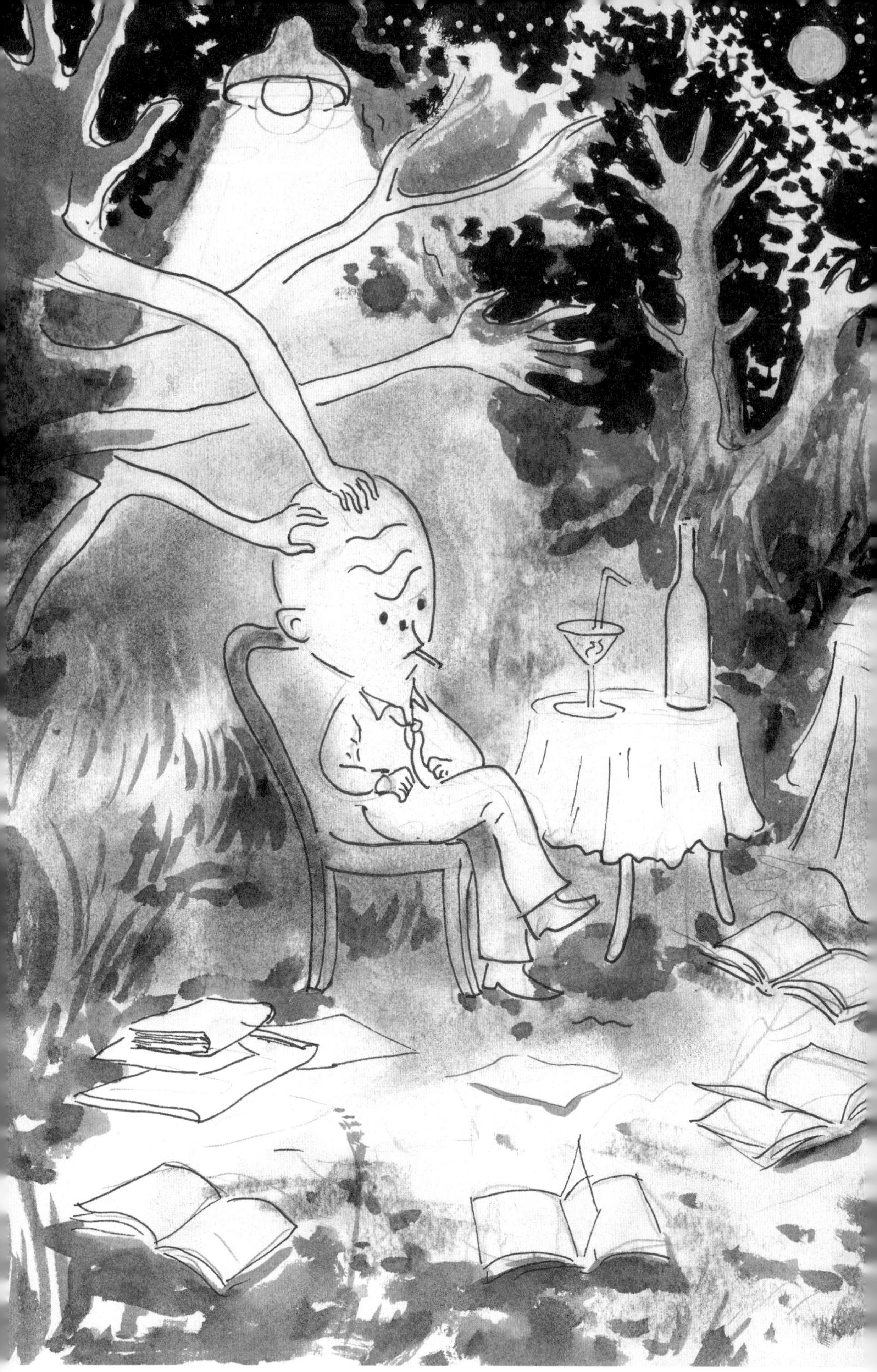

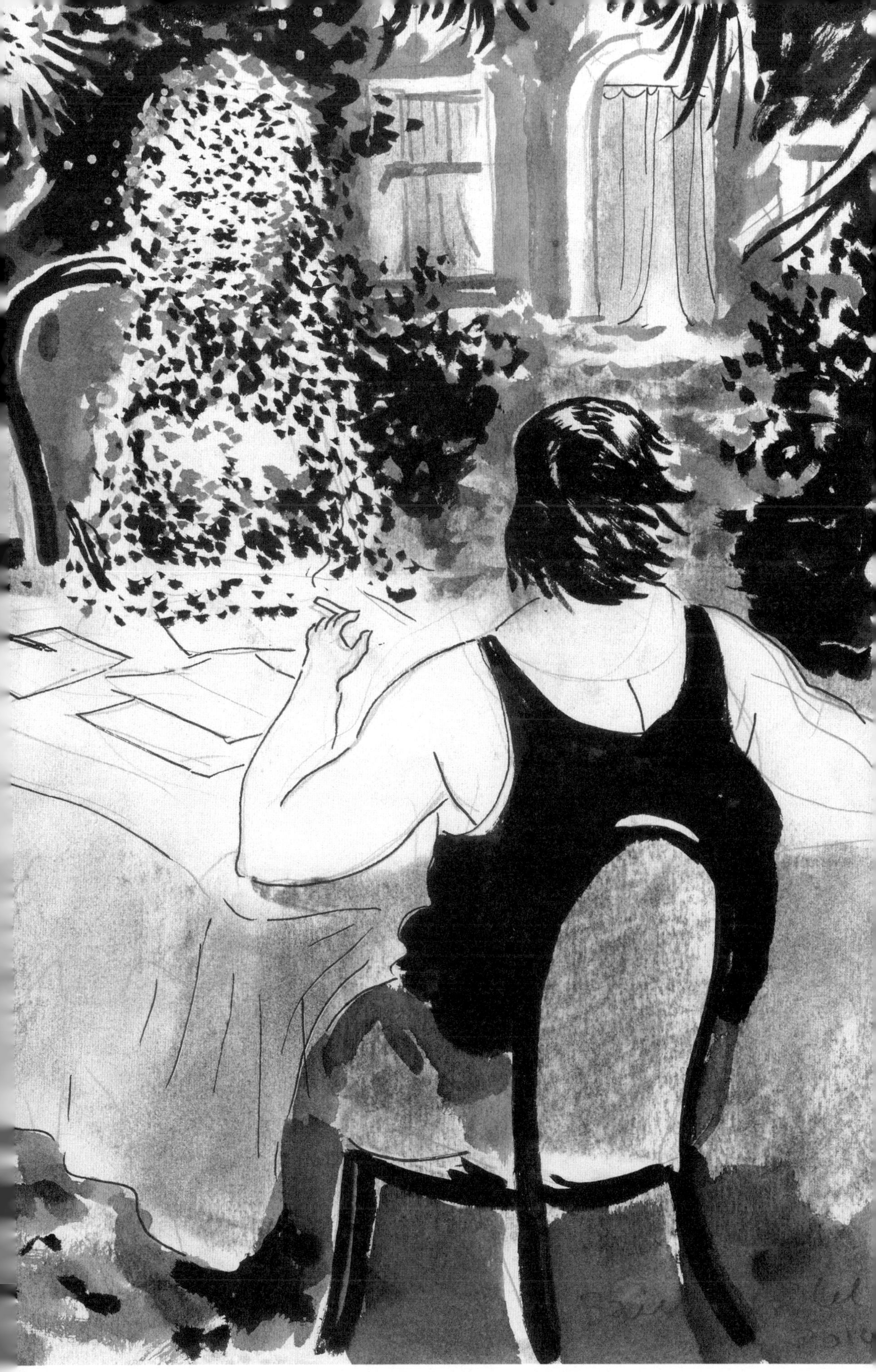

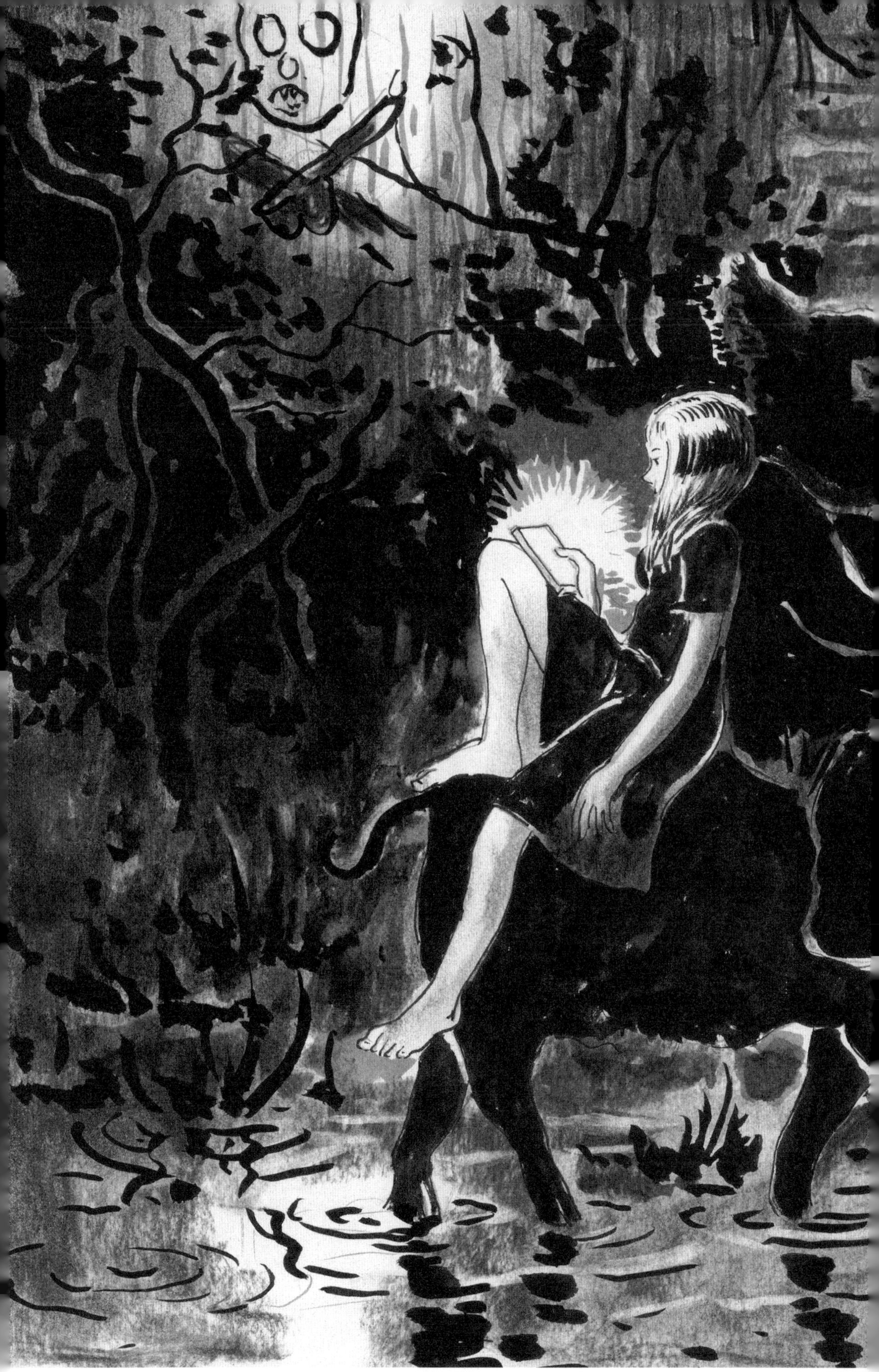

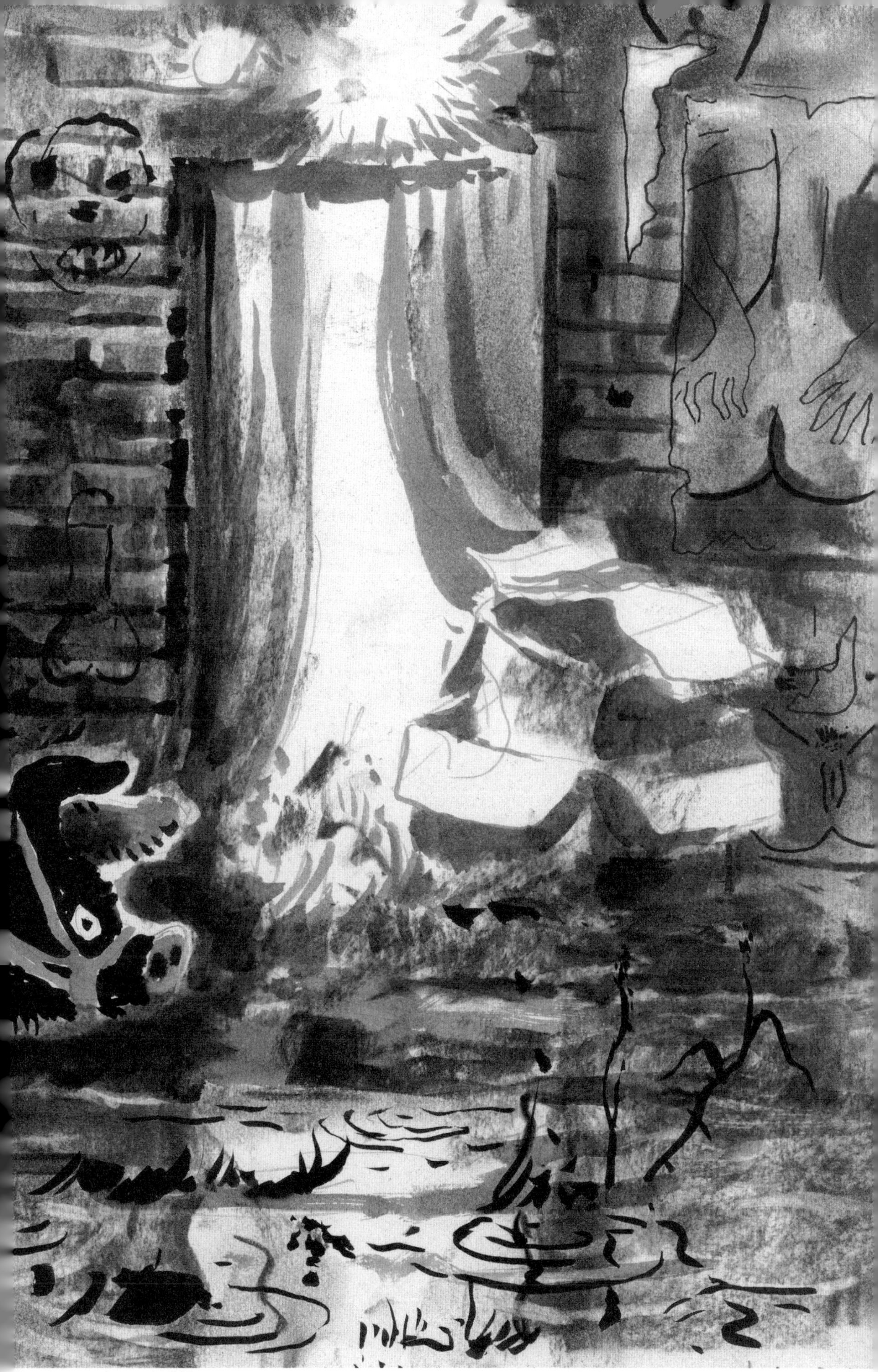

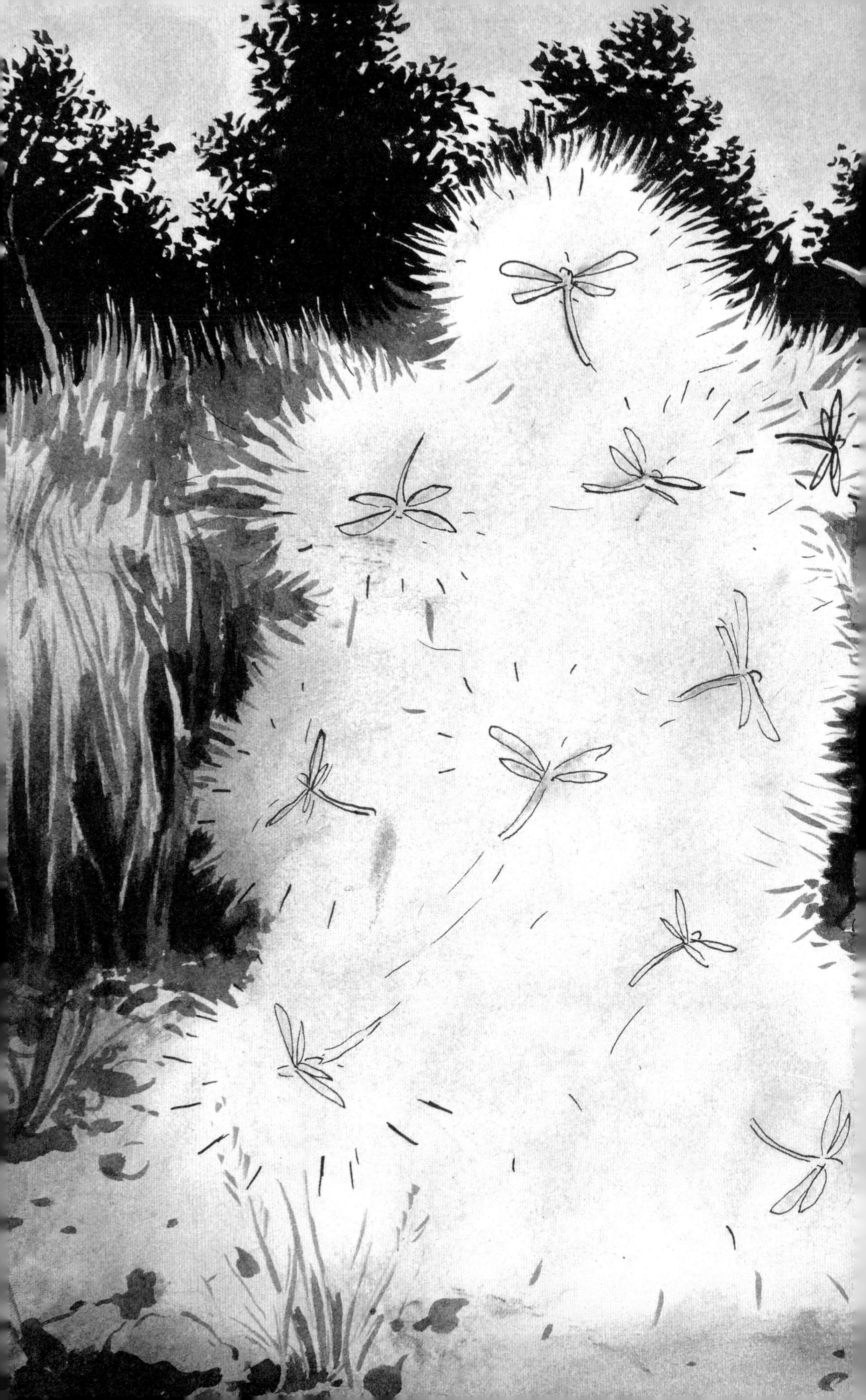

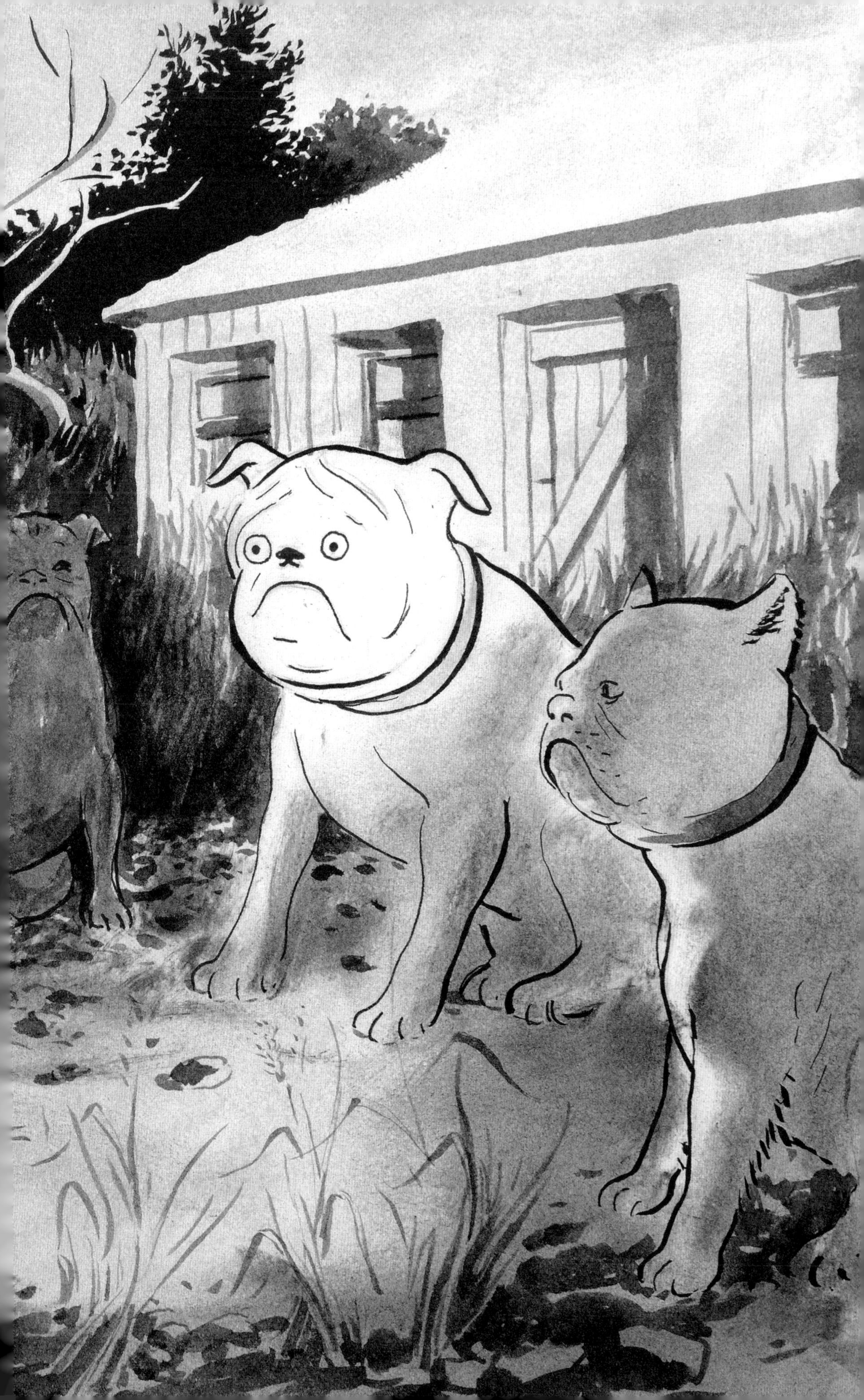

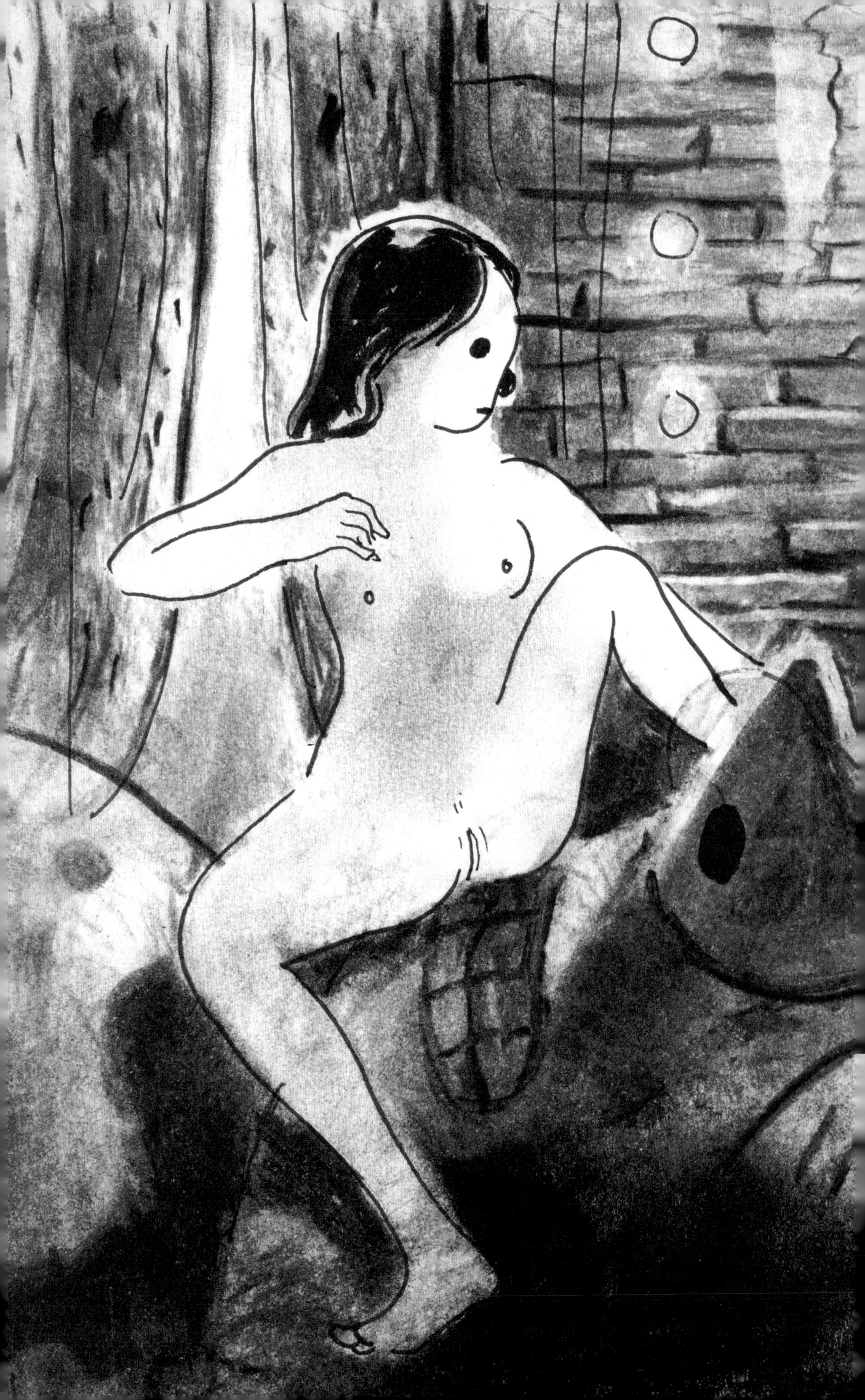

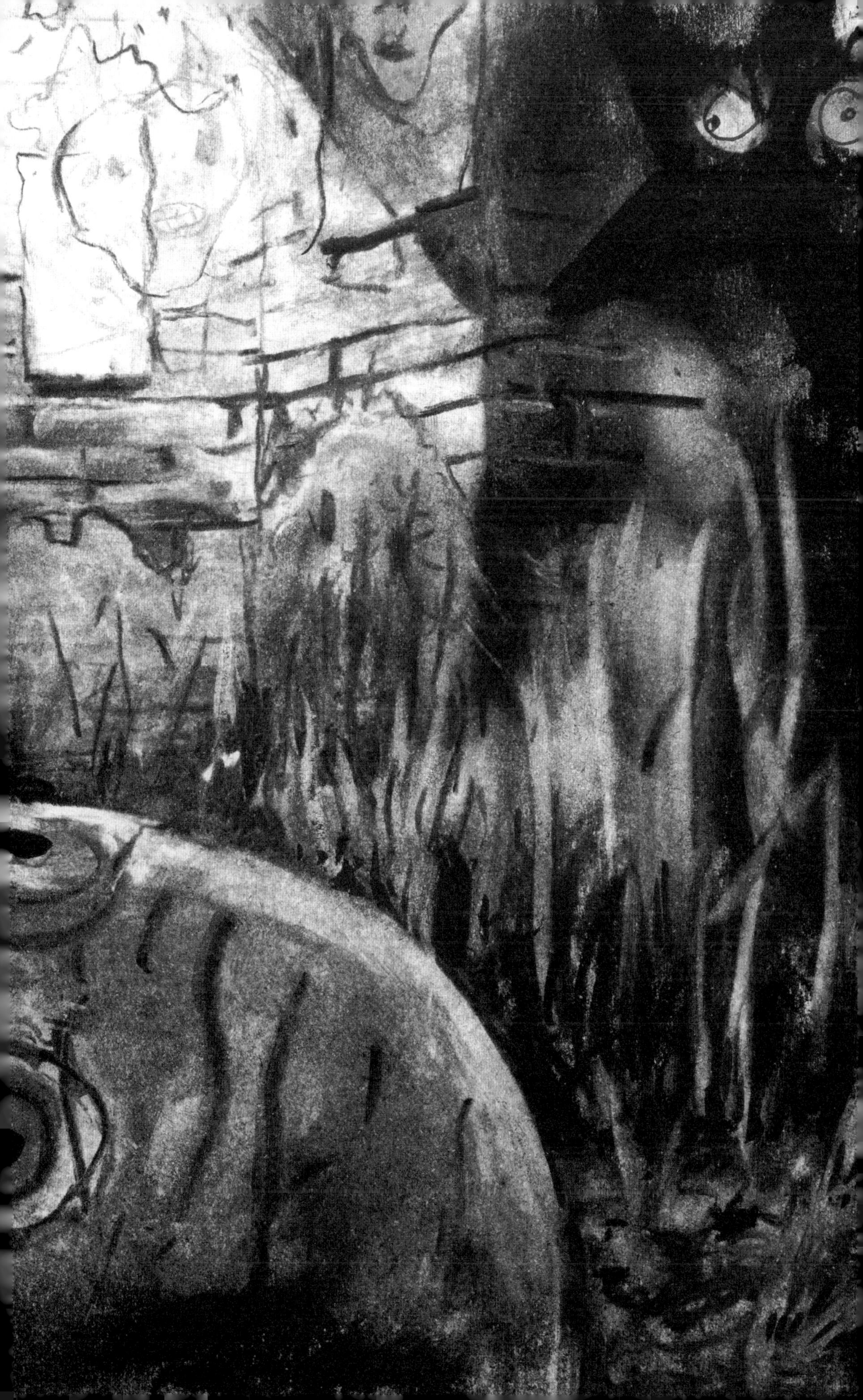

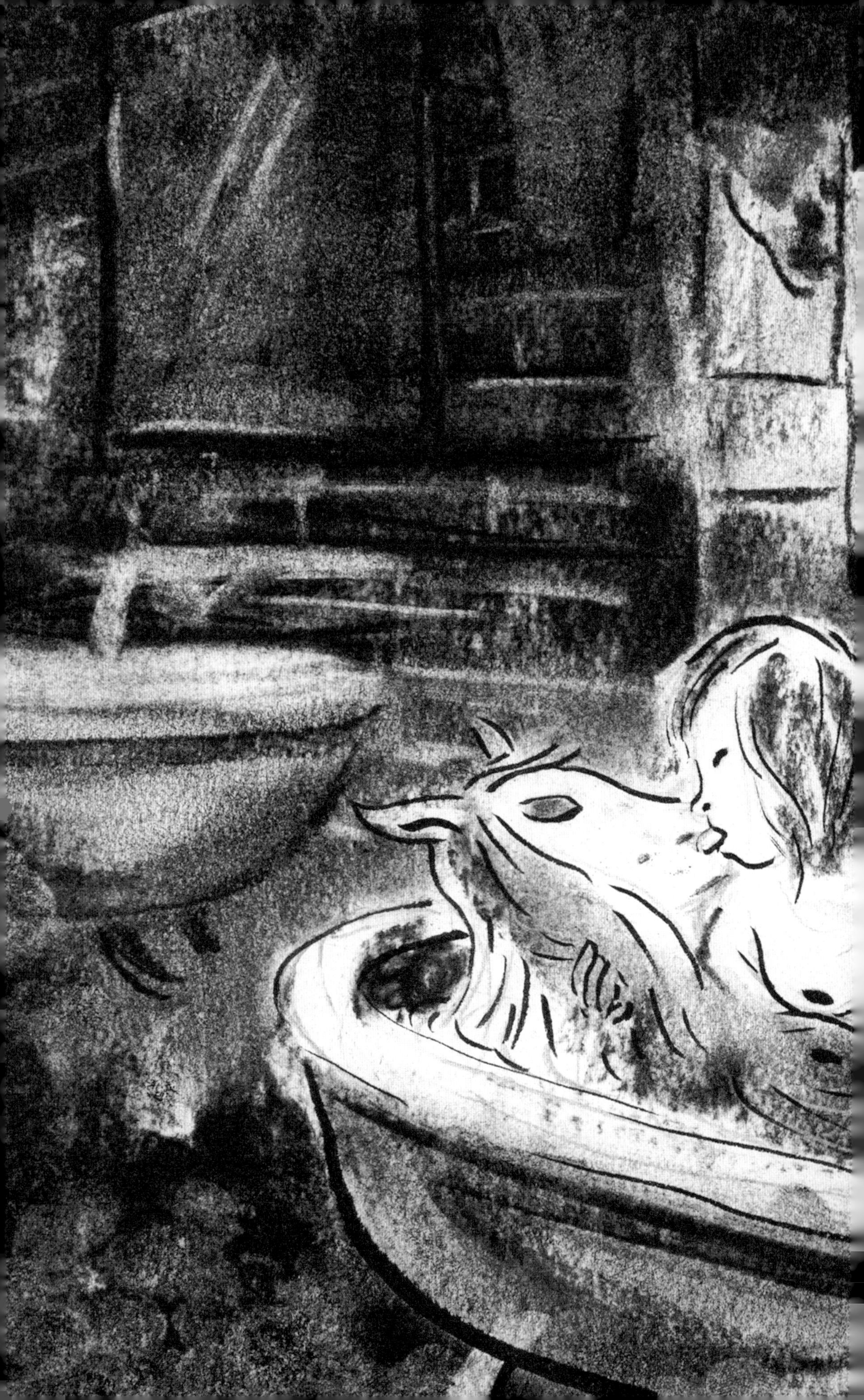

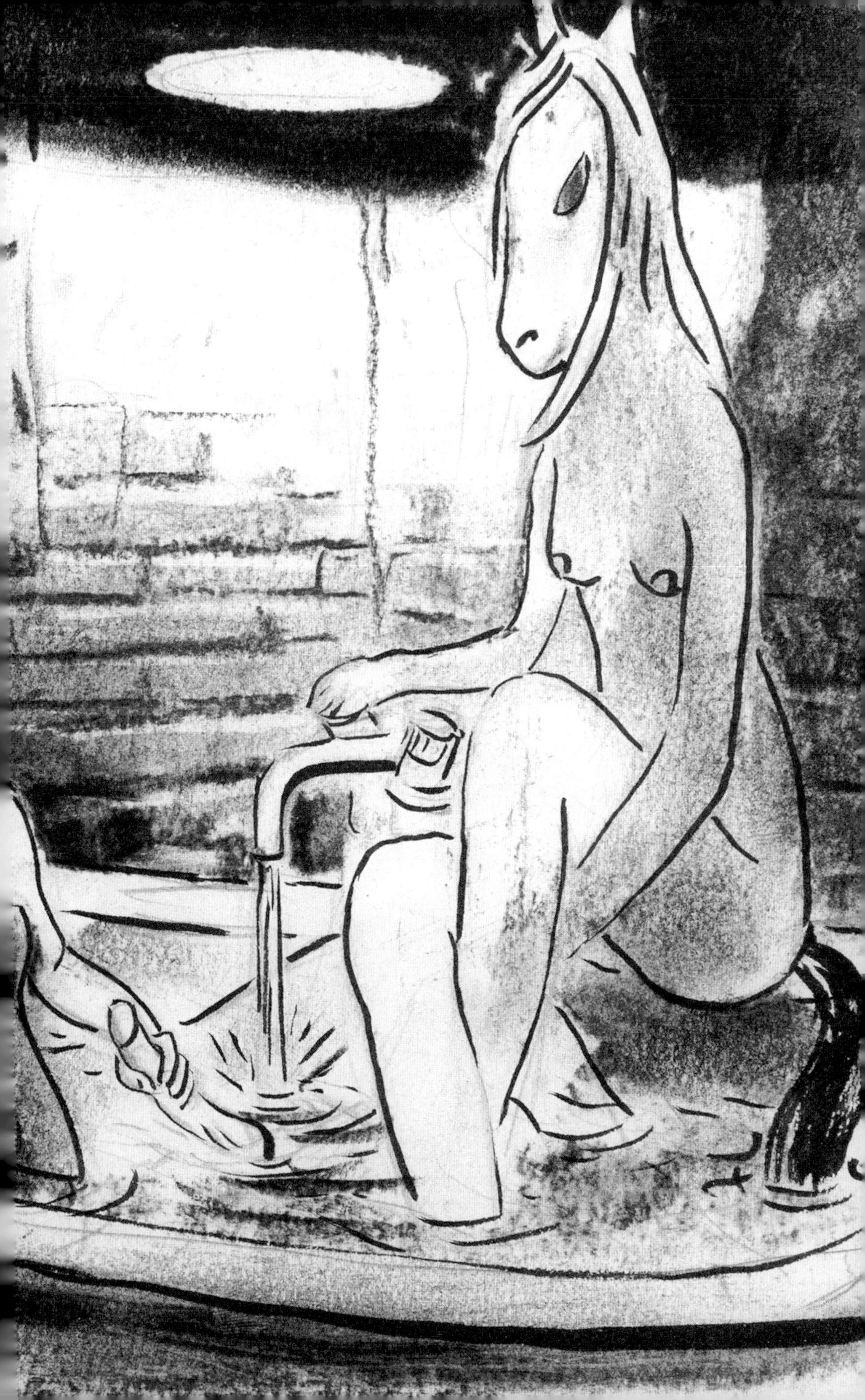

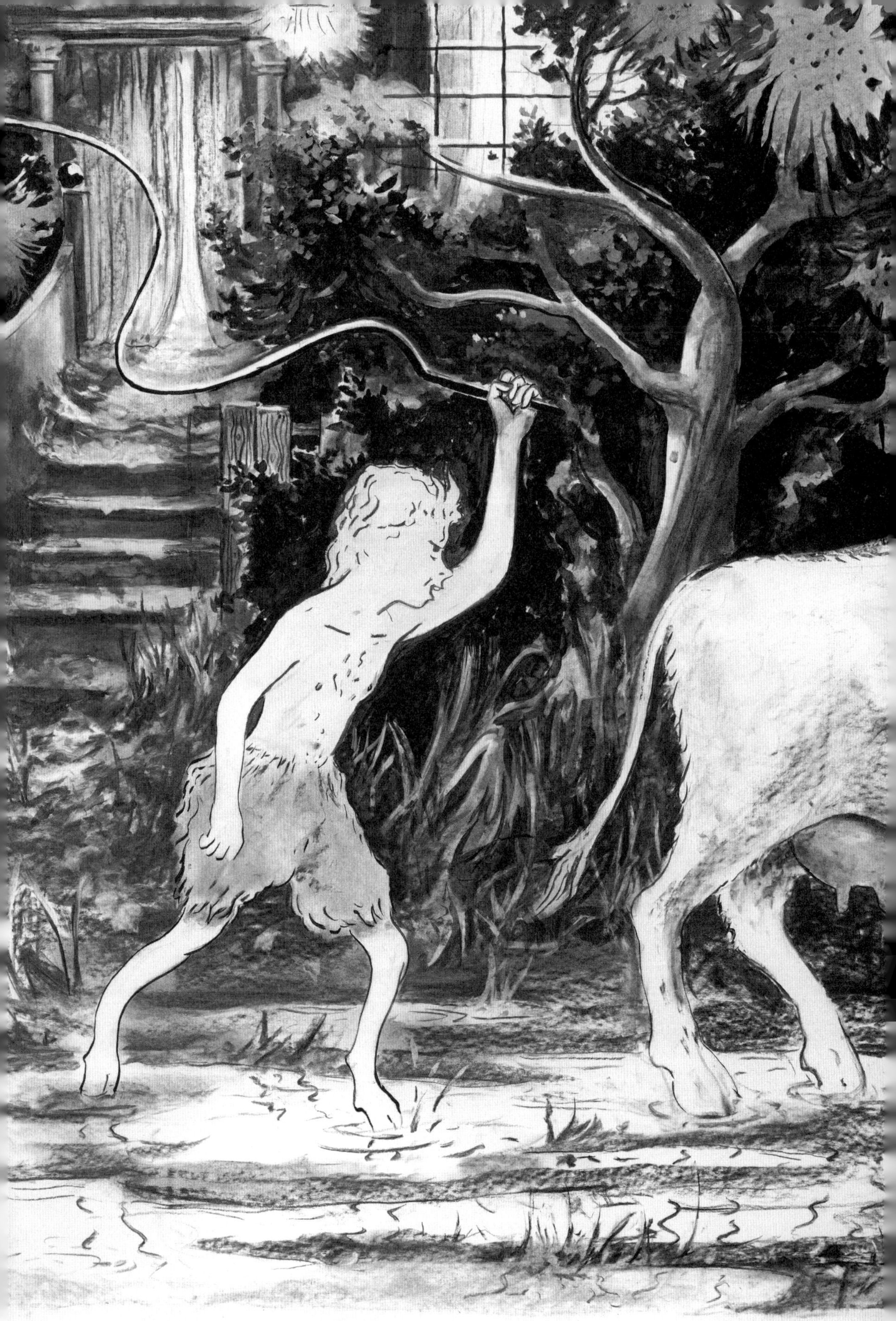

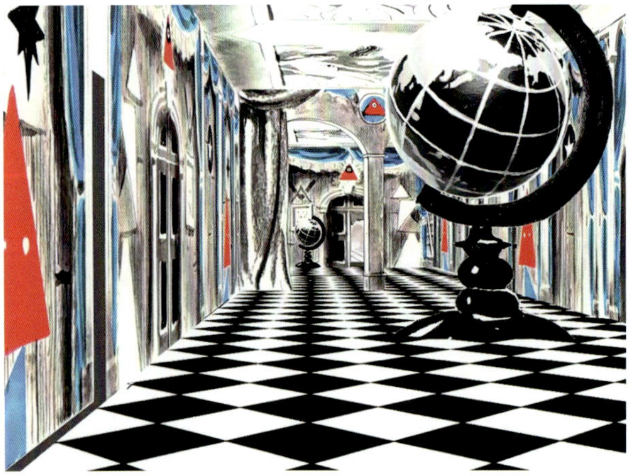
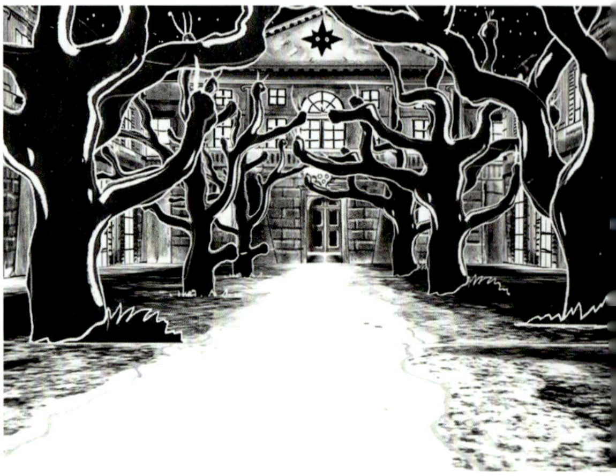
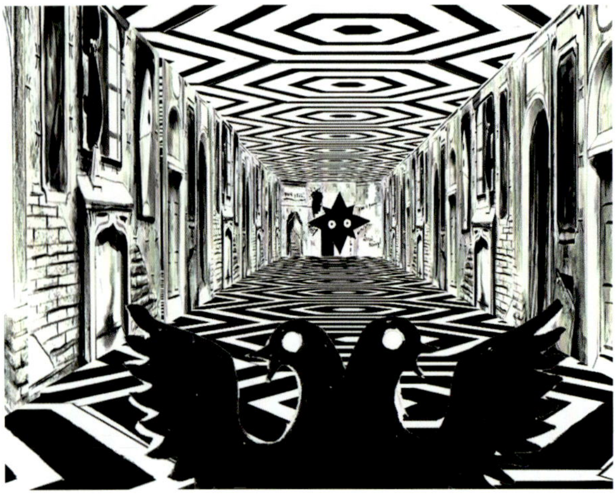
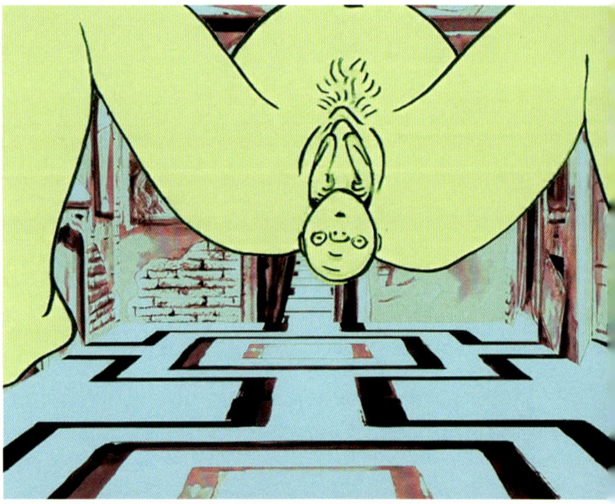
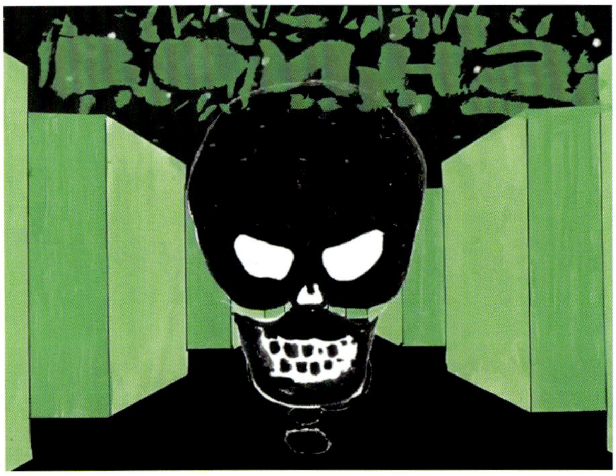
война
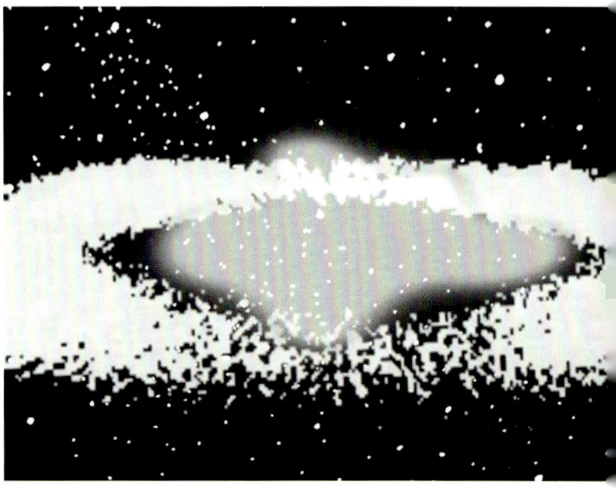
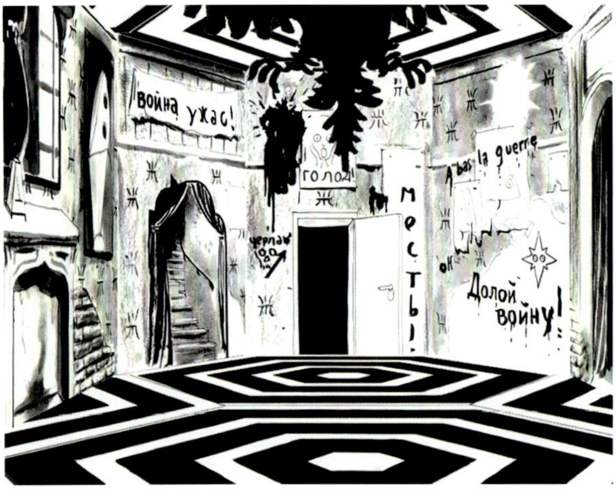
война ужас!
голод!
A bas la guerre
месть!
Долой войну!
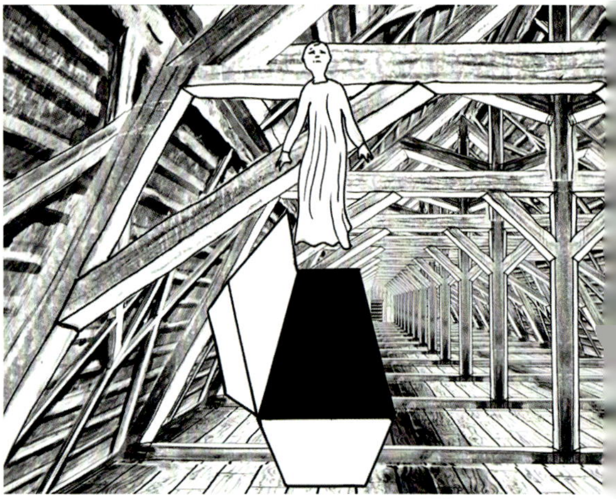

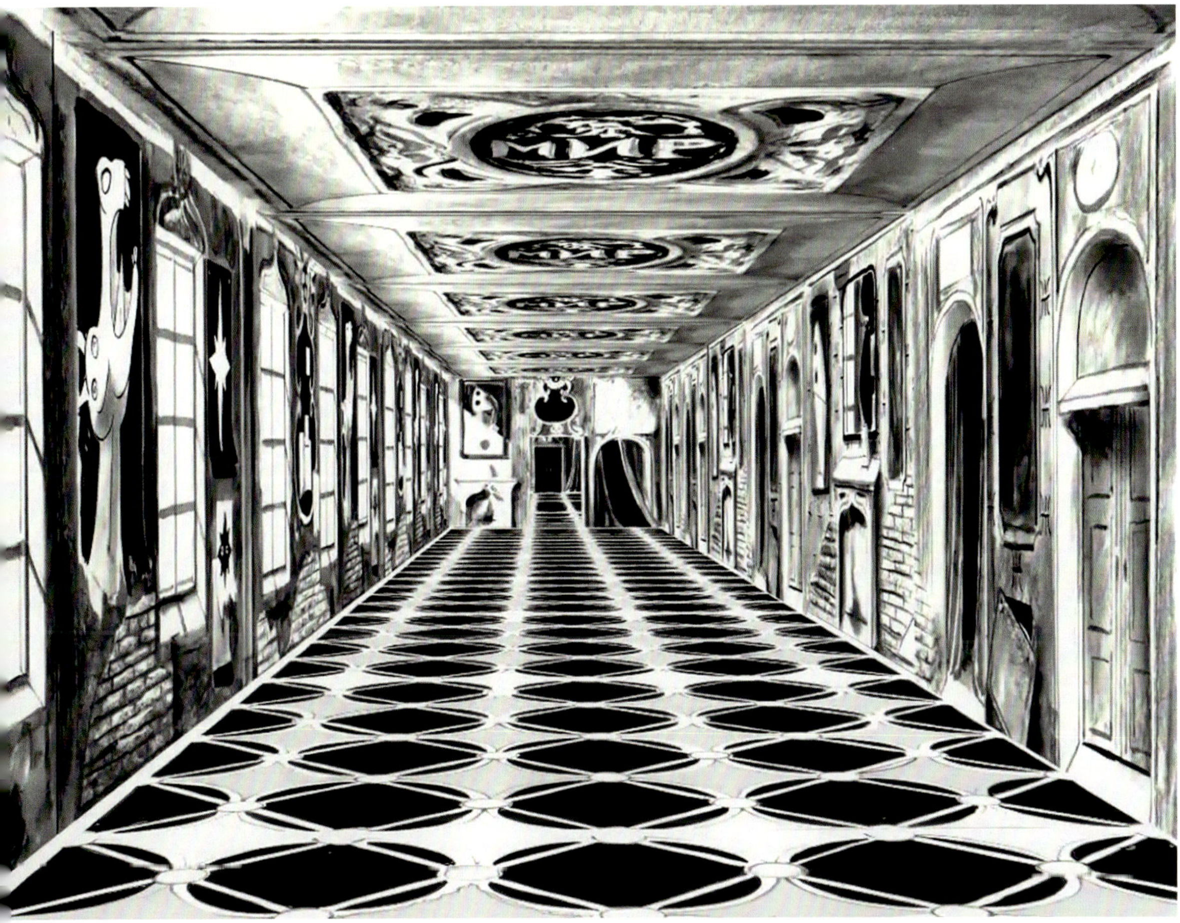
МИР

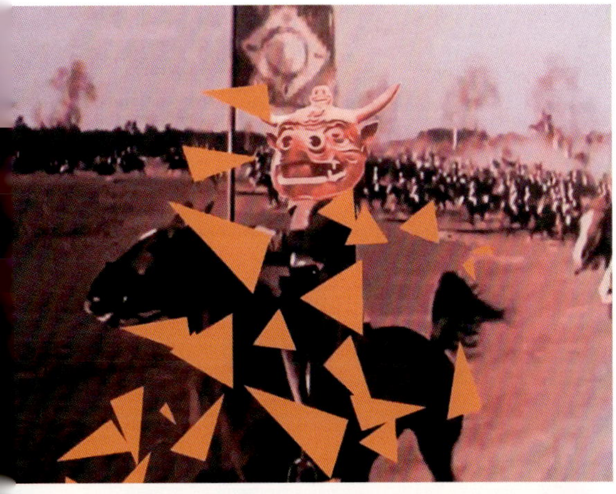

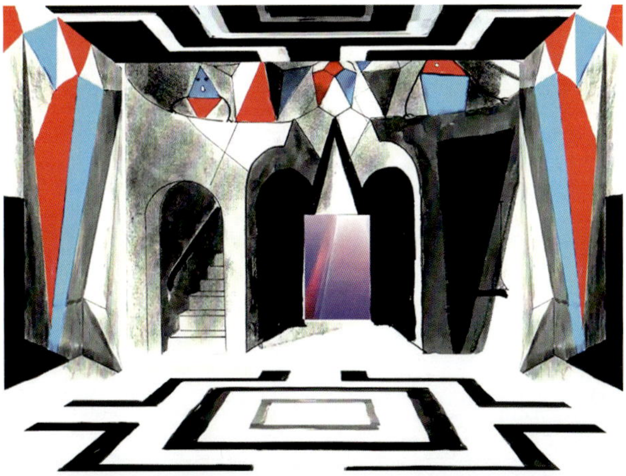

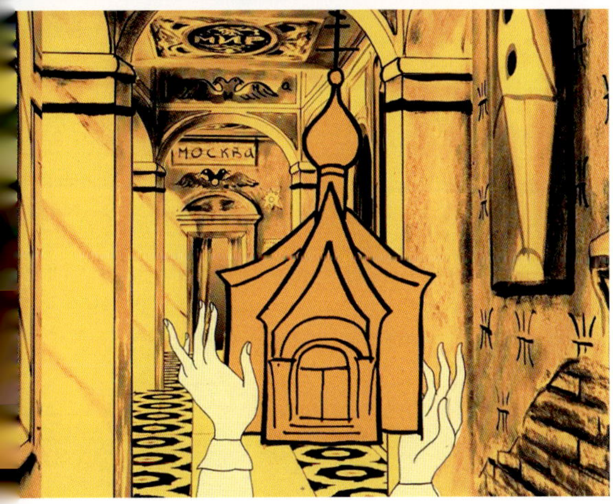
МИР
МОСКВА

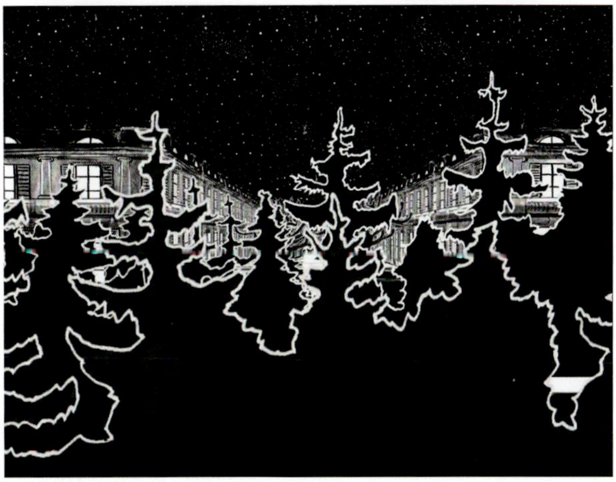

KRIEG UND FRIEDEN

(Video für Theater / video for theater), 30 min

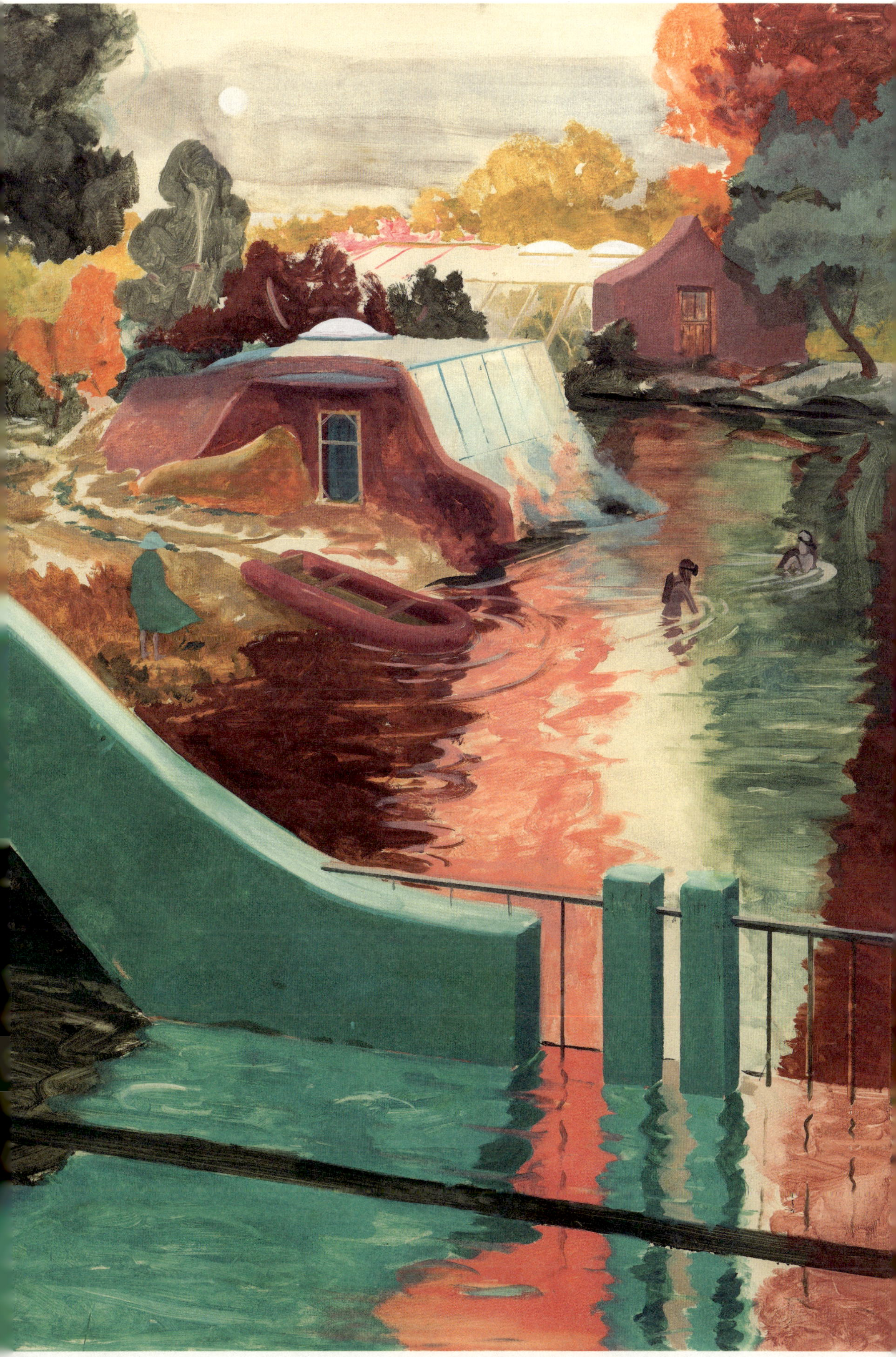

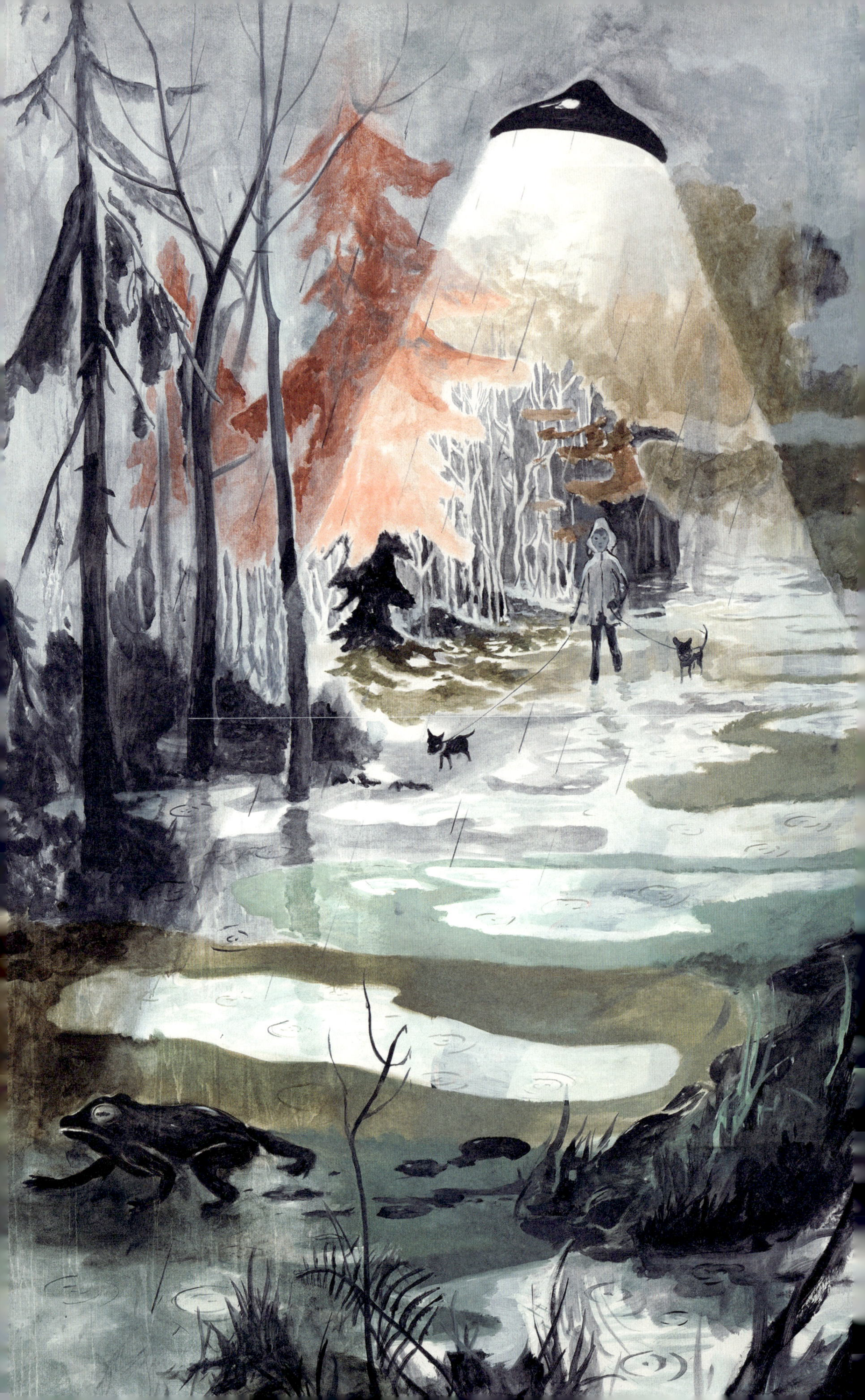

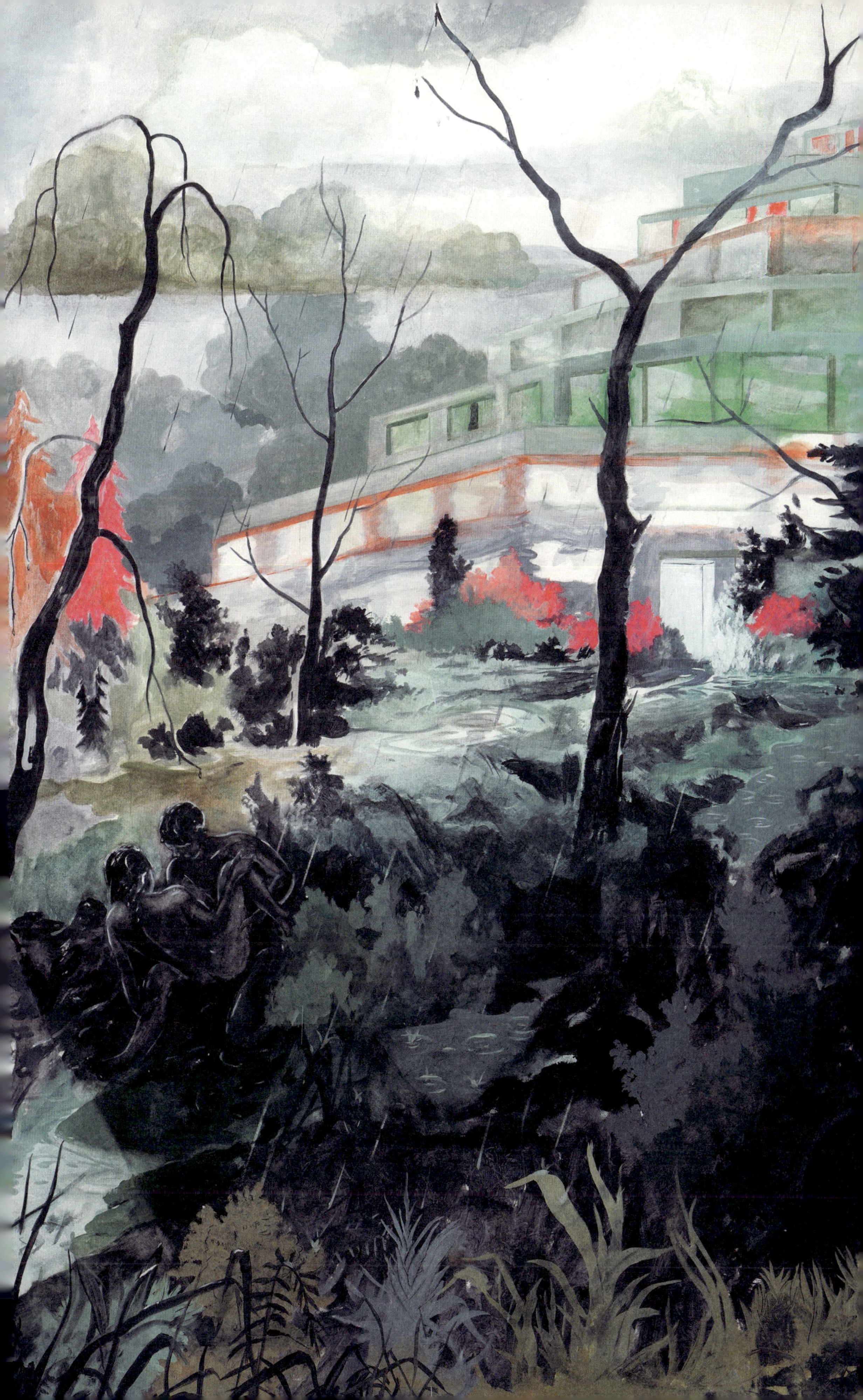

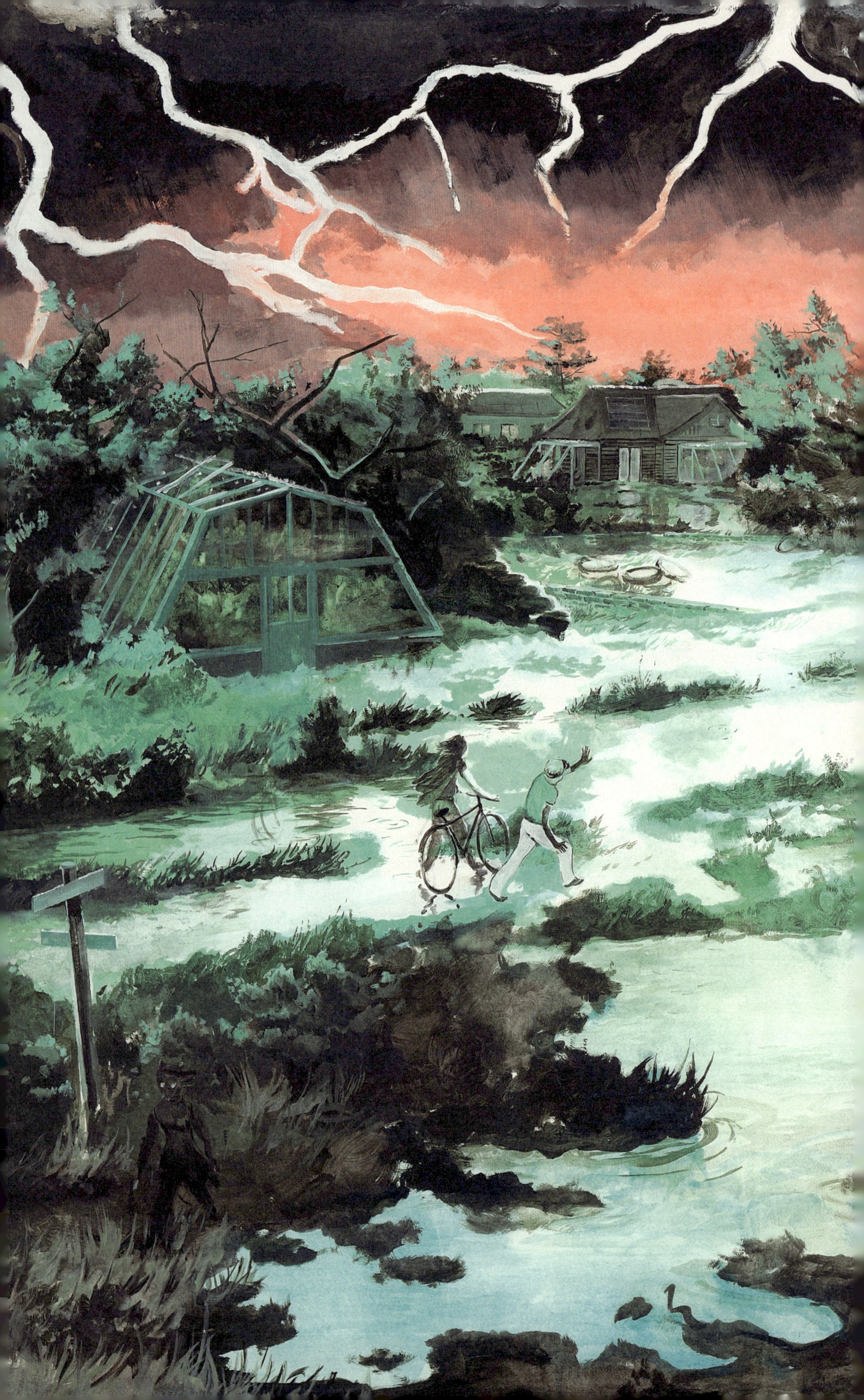

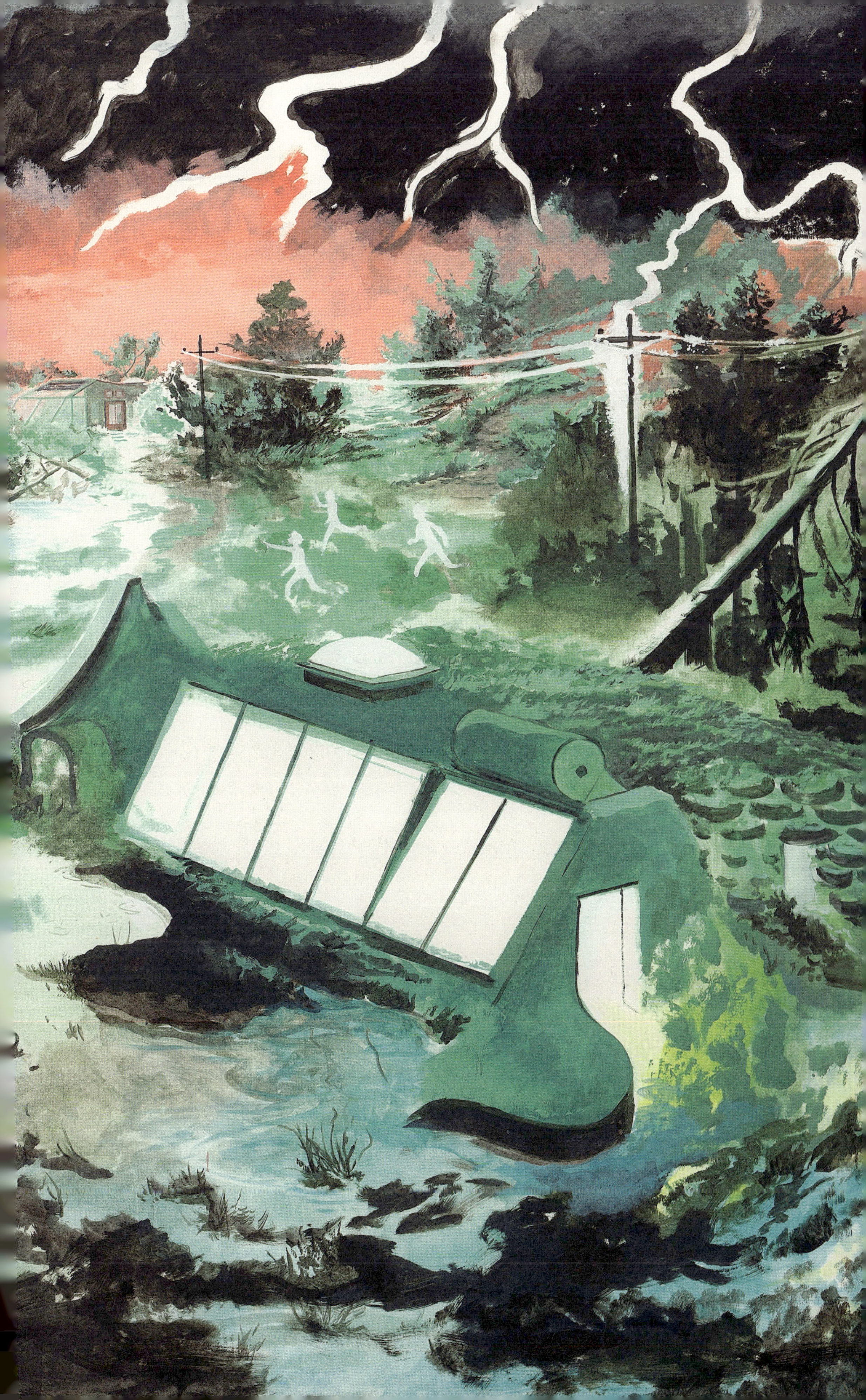

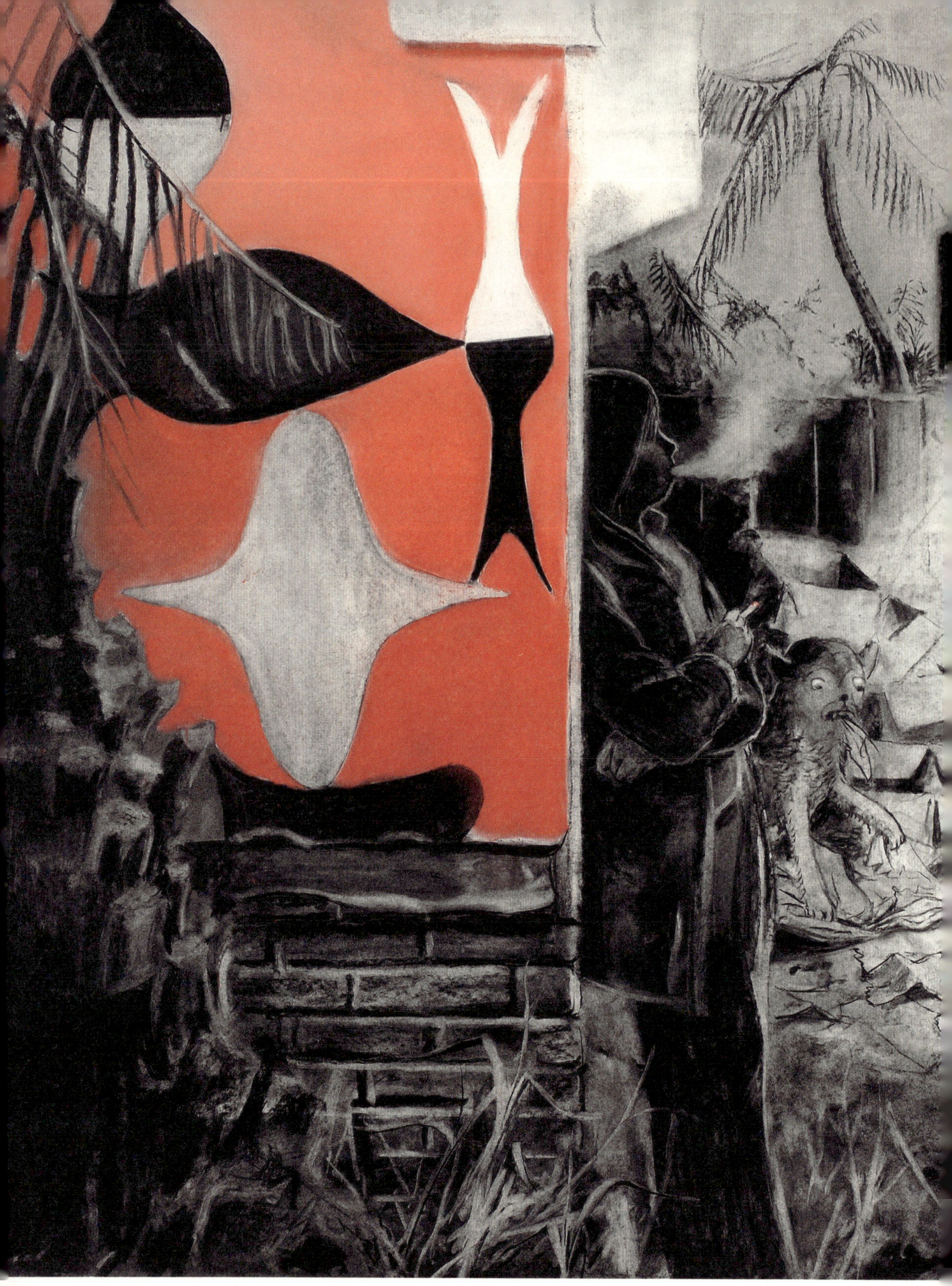

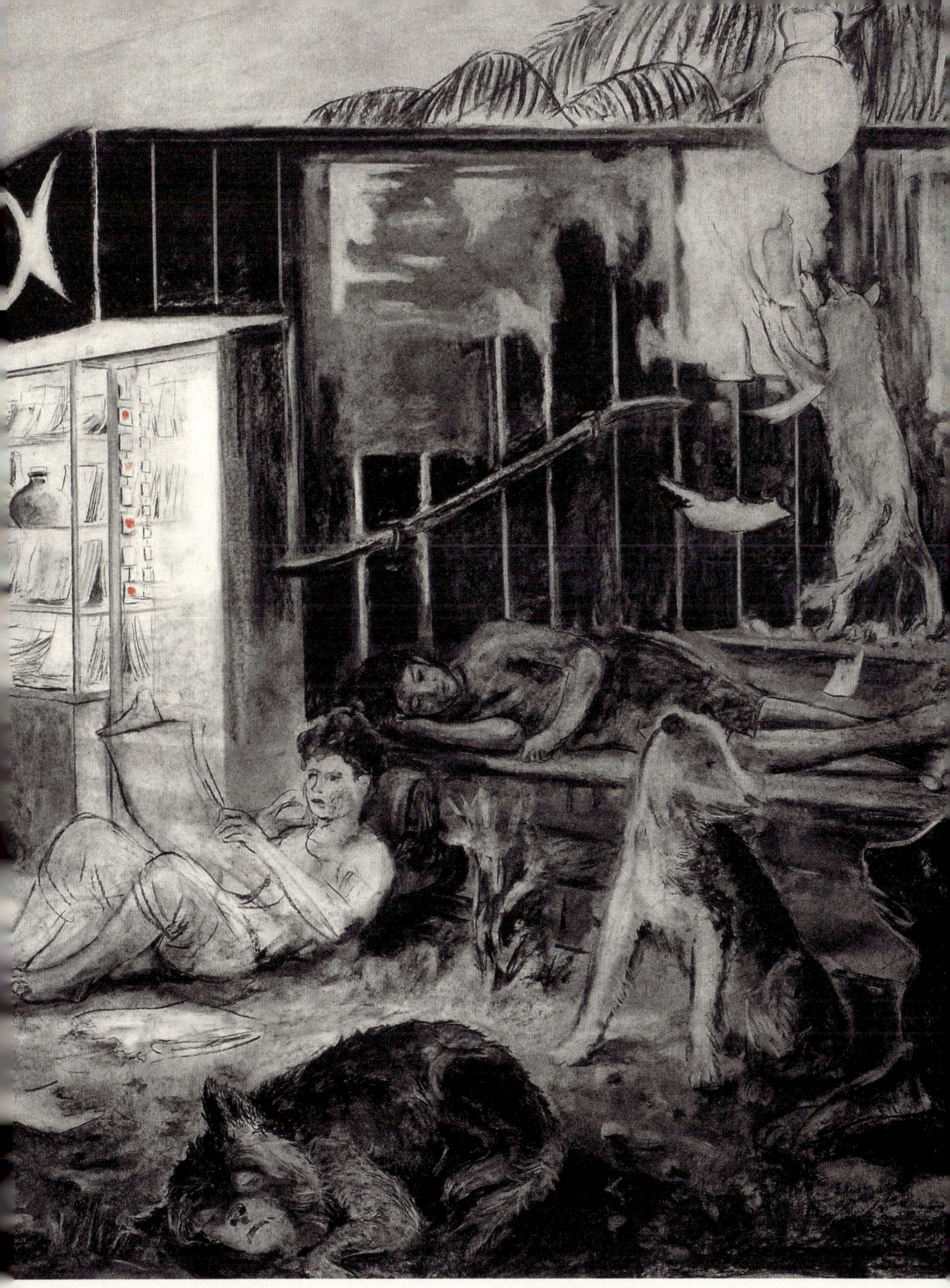

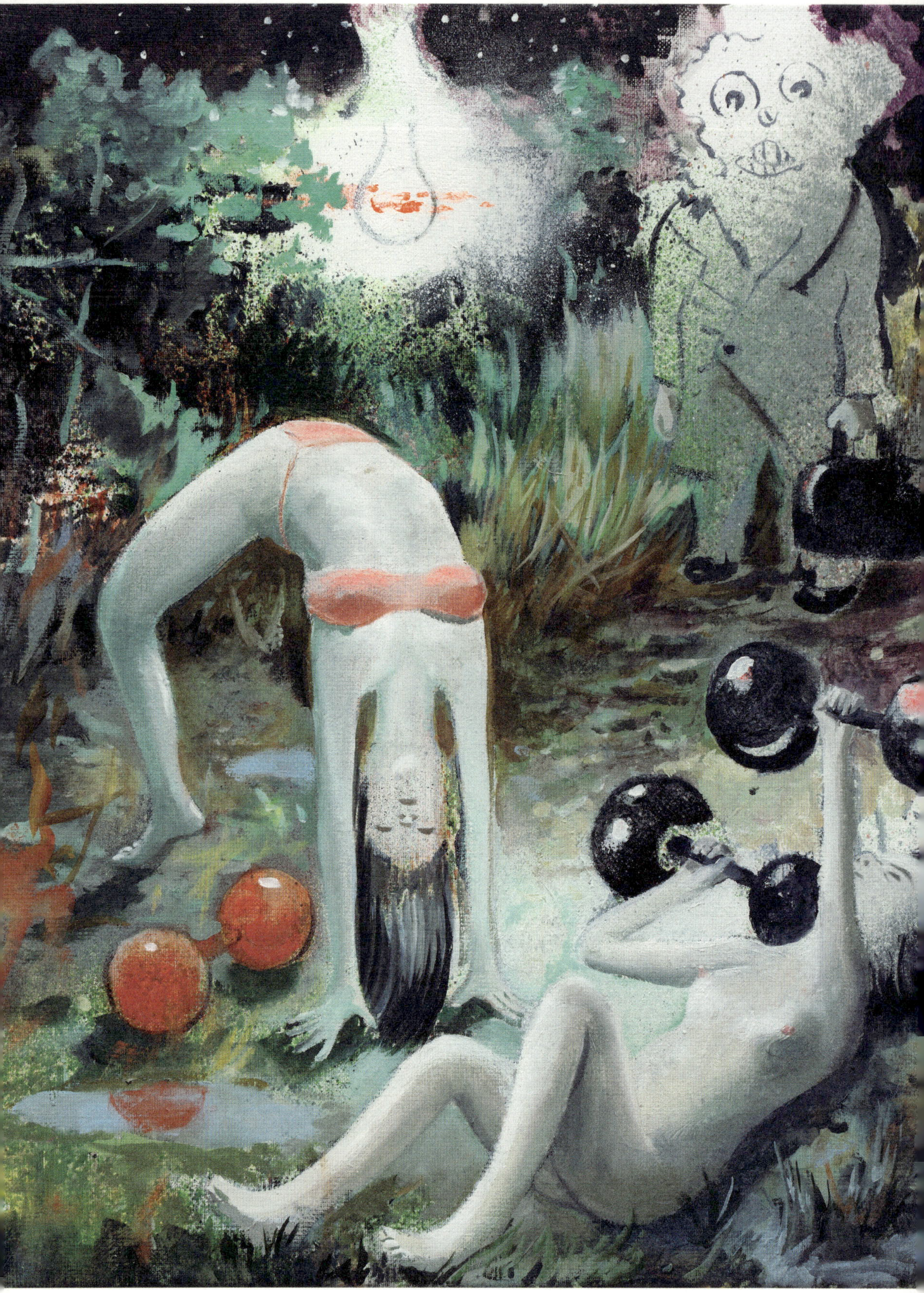

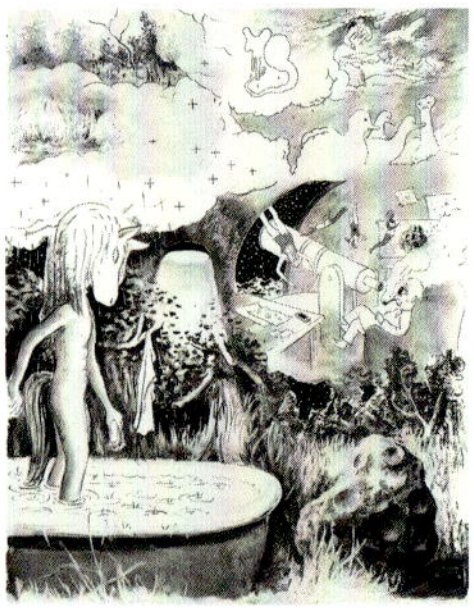

EQUUS

2015, 140 × 100 cm
Kohle, Tusche auf Papier/
charcoal, ink on paper

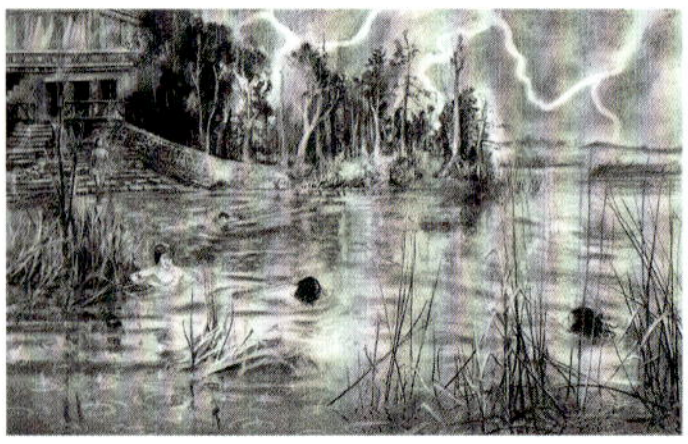

DIE INSEL

2009, 125 × 200 cm
Kohle auf Papier/ charcoal on paper

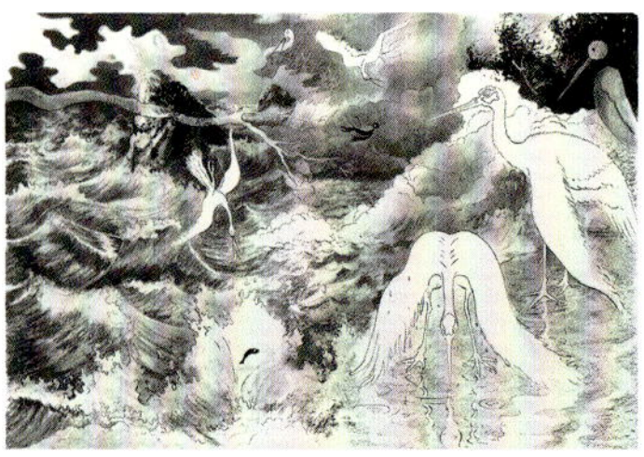

WILLEN + WELLEN

2015, 140 × 220 cm
Kohle, Tusche, Öl und Pigment
auf Papier/ charcoal, ink, oil and
pigment on paper

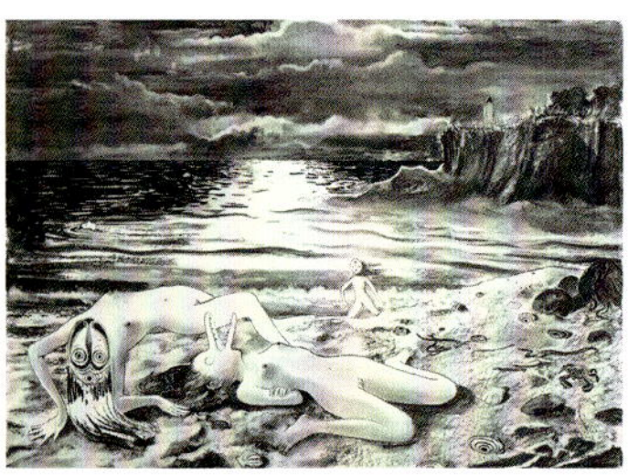

FAR AWAY

2014, 140 × 220 cm
Kohle auf Papier/ charcoal on paper

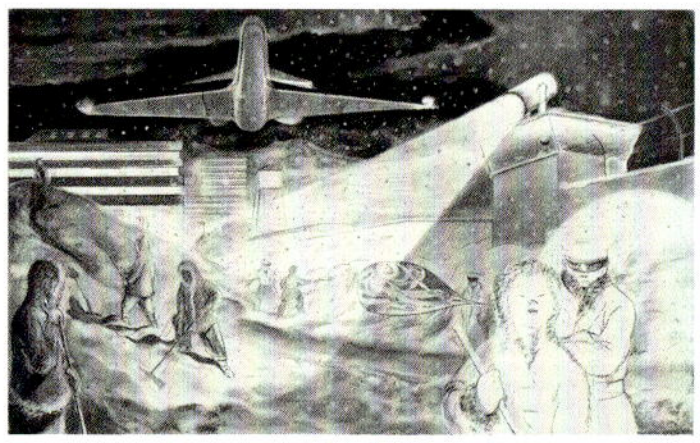

SCHEINWERFER

2009, 120 × 200 cm
Kohle auf Papier/ charcoal on paper

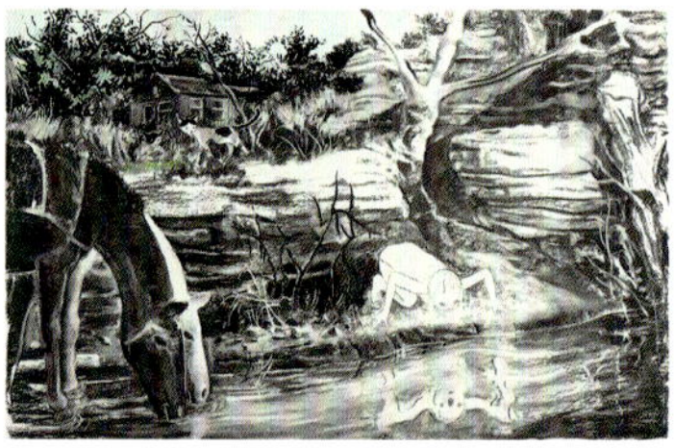

MIRROR

2014, 140 × 220 cm
Kohle auf Papier/ charcoal on paper

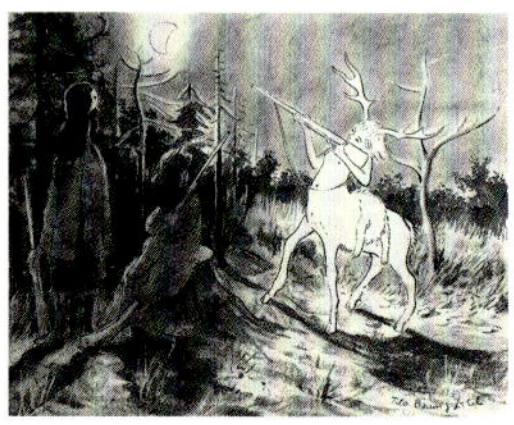

o.T.
(JAGD)

2009, 30 × 42 cm
Kohle auf Papier/ charcoal on paper

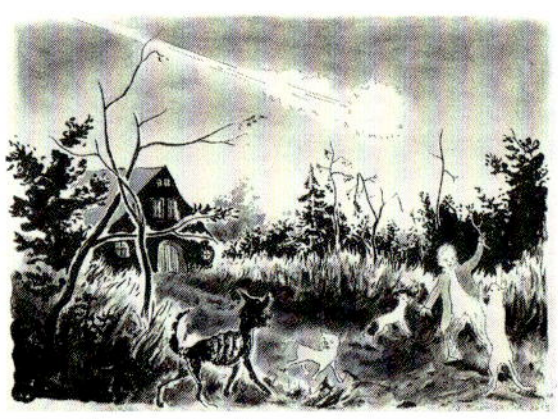

o.T.

2012, 30 × 42 cm
Kohle, Tusche und Pastell auf Papier/
charcoal, ink and pastel on paper

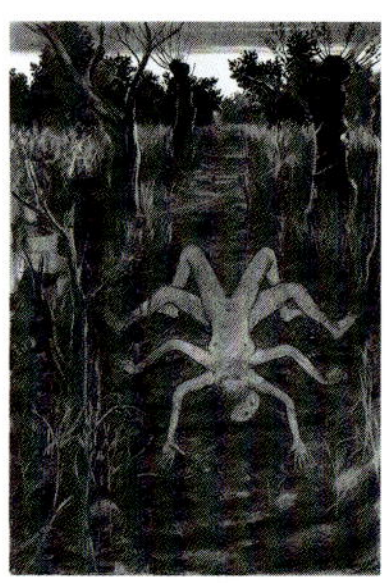

ARACHNE

2010, 100 × 70 cm
Kohle, Tusche, Pastell auf Papier/
charcoal, ink, pastel on paper

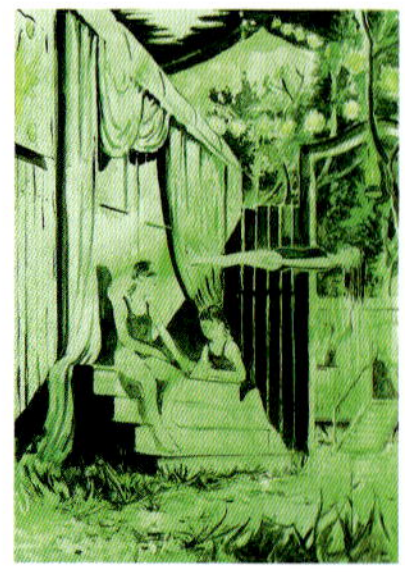

DER PFAD

2013, 70 × 50 cm
Öl auf Leinwand/oil on canvas

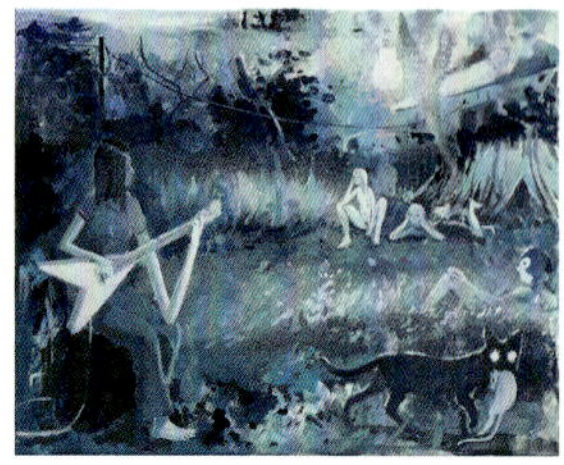

o.T.
(GITARRE)

2014, 40 × 50 cm
Öl auf Leinwand/oil on canvas

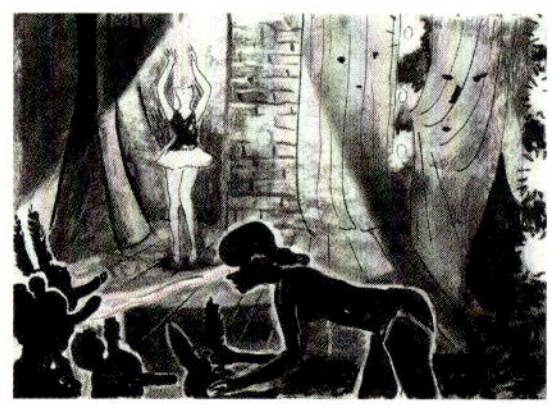

PRISCILLA

2012, 21 × 29 cm
Kohle, Tusche und Pastell auf Papier/
charcoal, ink and pastel on paper

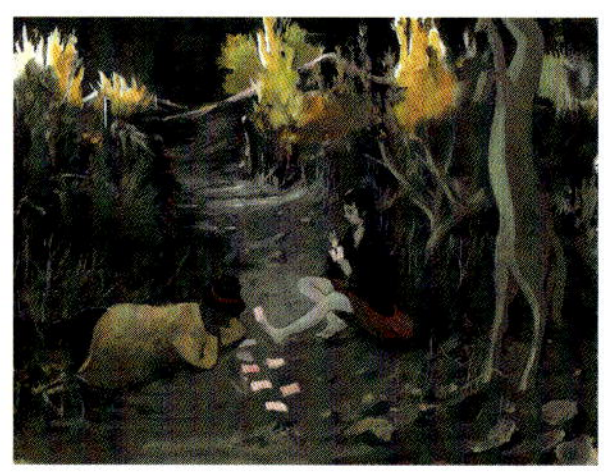

SPIEL DES LEBENS

2014, 60 × 80 cm
Öl auf Leinwand/oil on canvas

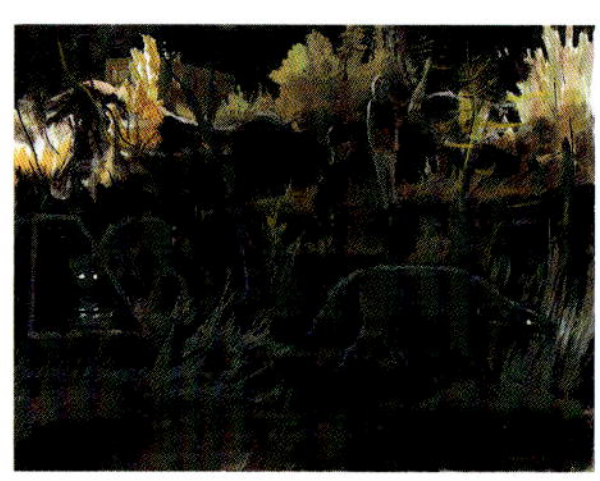

PALFAN

2014, 60 × 80 cm
Öl auf Leinwand/oil on canvas

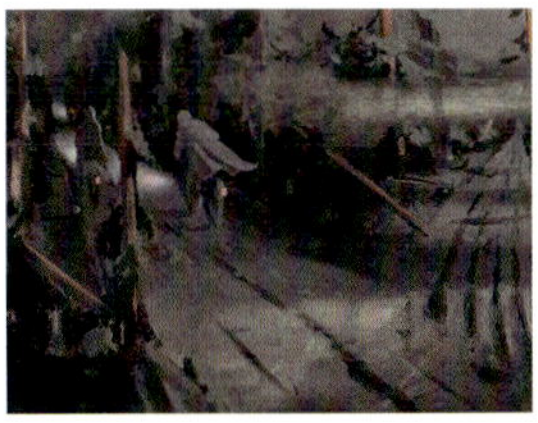

WOODWAY

2009, 30 × 40 cm
Öl auf Leinwand/oil on canvas

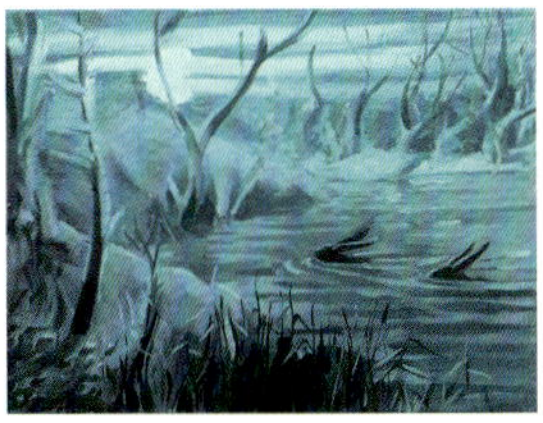

NOCTURNE

2011, 30 × 40 cm
Öl auf Leinwand/oil on canvas

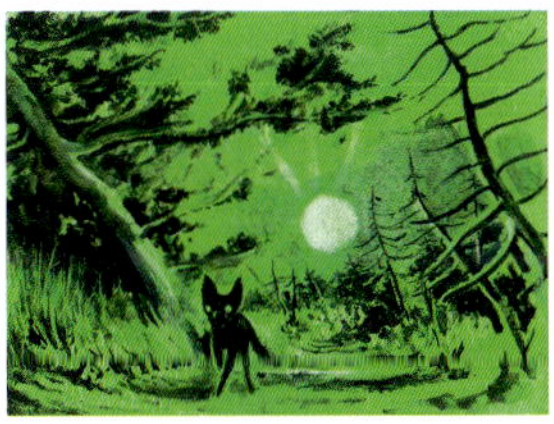

VULPI

2013, 33 × 45 cm
Öl auf Leinwand/oil on canvas

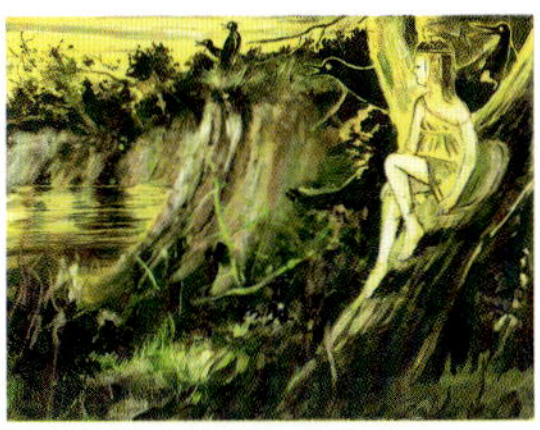

GESANG

2012, 30 × 40 cm
Öl auf Leinwand/oil on canvas

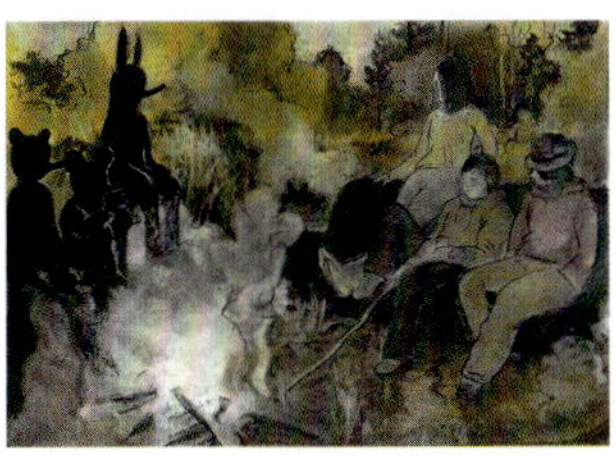

GIALLO

2010, 70 × 100 cm
Kohle, Tusche und Pastell auf Papier/
charcoal, ink and pastel on paper

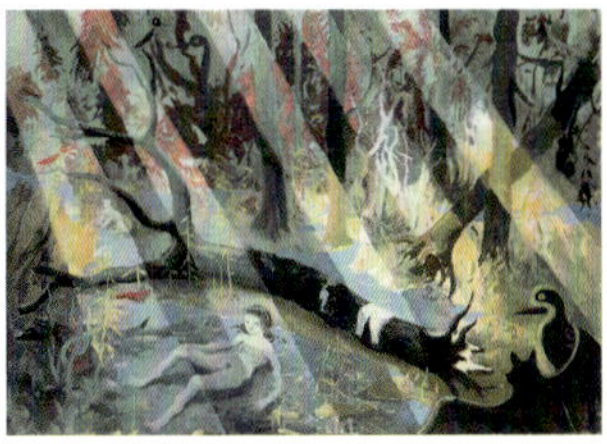

o.T.

2015, 70 × 100 cm
Öl auf Leinwand/oil on canvas

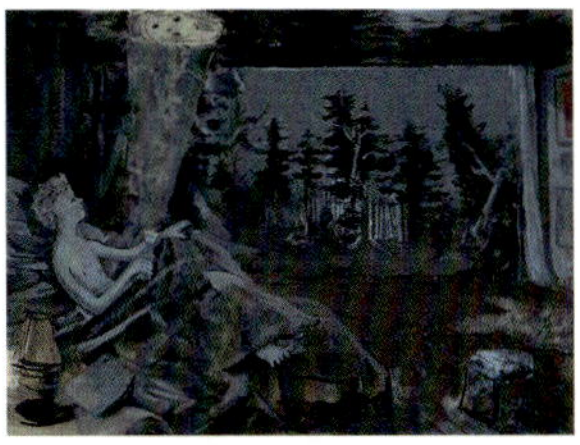

SONDBERG

2014, 60 × 80 cm
Öl auf Leinwand/oil on canvas

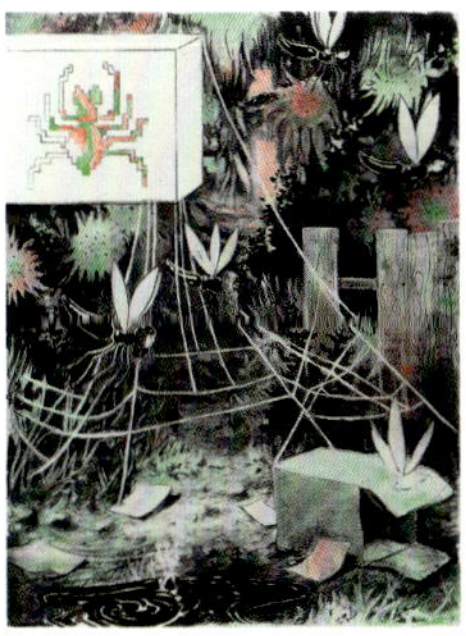

SPINNENSTRASSE

2015, 140 × 100 cm
Kohle, Tusche auf Papier/
charcoal, ink on paper

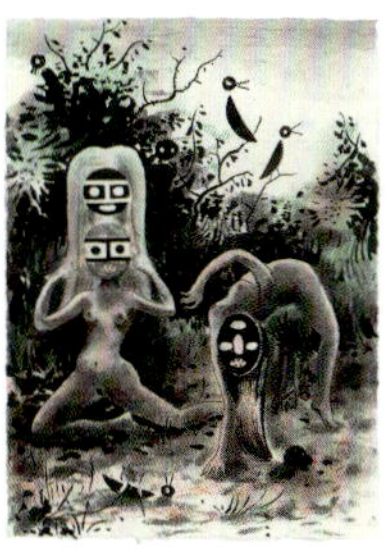

o.T.

2015, 29 × 21 cm
Kohle, Tusche und Pastell auf Papier/
charcoal, ink and pastel on paper

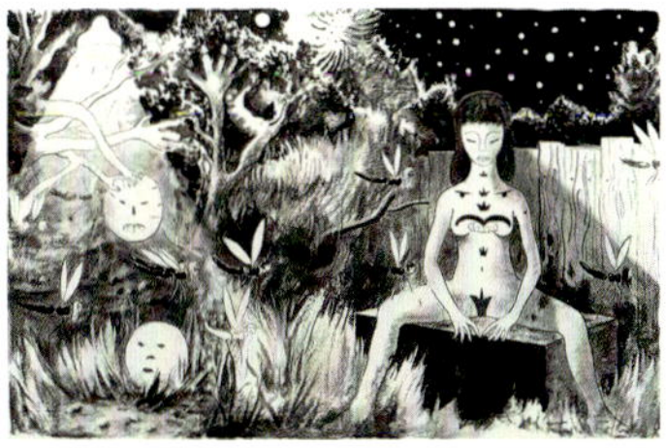

NACHTSCHWÄRMER

2015, 140 × 220 cm
Kohle, Tusche auf Papier/
charcoal, ink on paper

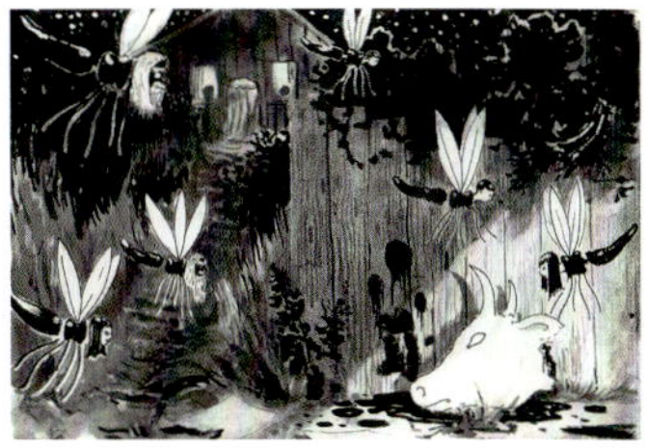

CORRIDA

2015, 140 × 220 cm
Kohle, Tusche auf Papier/
charcoal, ink on paper

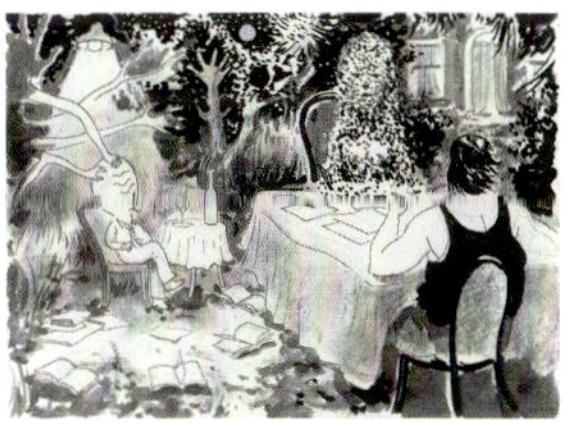

o.T.

2015, 30 × 42 cm
Kohle, Tusche und Pastell auf Papier/
charcoal, ink and pastel on paper

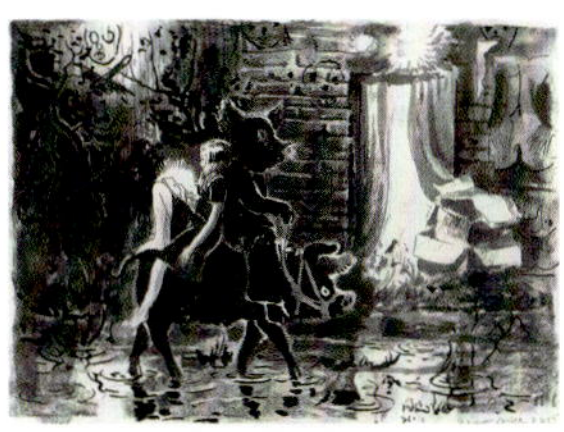

o.T.

2015, 30 × 42 cm
Kohle, Tusche und Pastell auf Papier/
charcoal, ink and pastel on paper

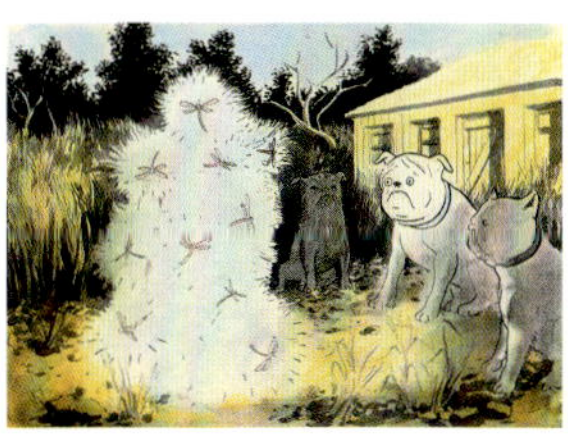

o.T.
(BOXER)

2010, 30 × 42 cm
Kohle, Pastell auf Papier/
charcoal, pastel on paper

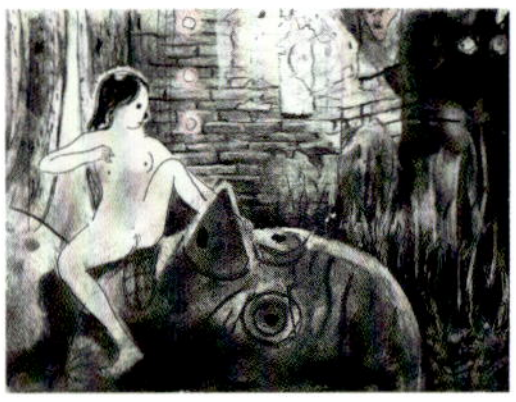

GAUCHO

2014, 20,5 × 28,5 cm
Kohle, Tusche und Pigment auf Papier/charcoal, ink and pigment on paper

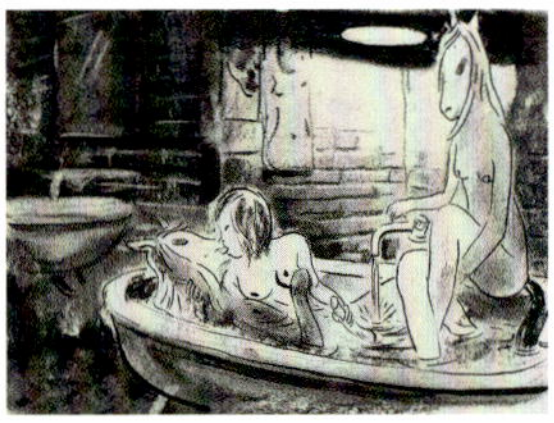

o.T.

2015, 28 × 40 cm
Kohle, Tusche und Pastell auf Papier/charcoal, ink and pastel on paper

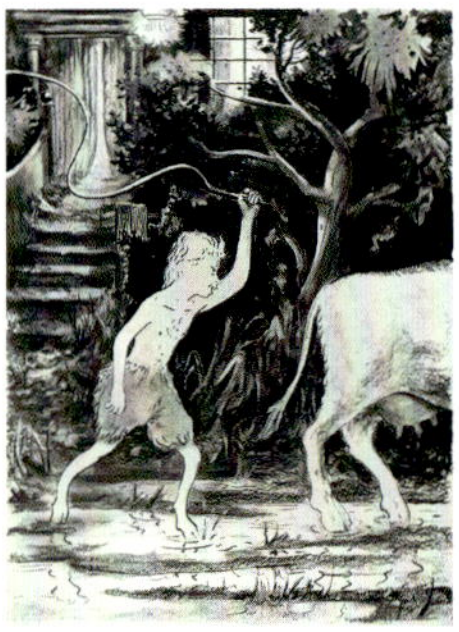

SATYR

2015, 140 × 100 cm
Kohle, Tusche, Öl und Pigment auf Papier/charcoal, ink, oil and pigment on paper

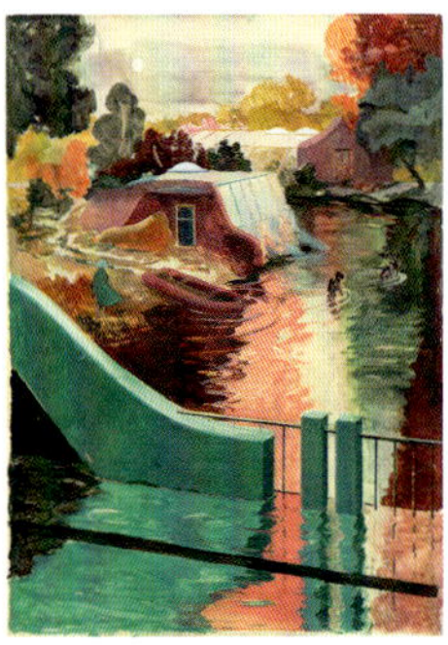

MEKONG

2014, 218 × 160 cm
Öl auf Papier/ oil on paper

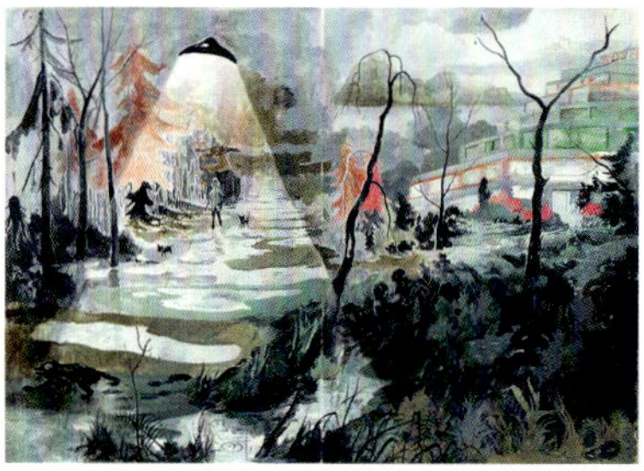

DER GRÜNGRAUE TAG

2014, 280 × 395 cm
Öl auf Papier/oil on paper

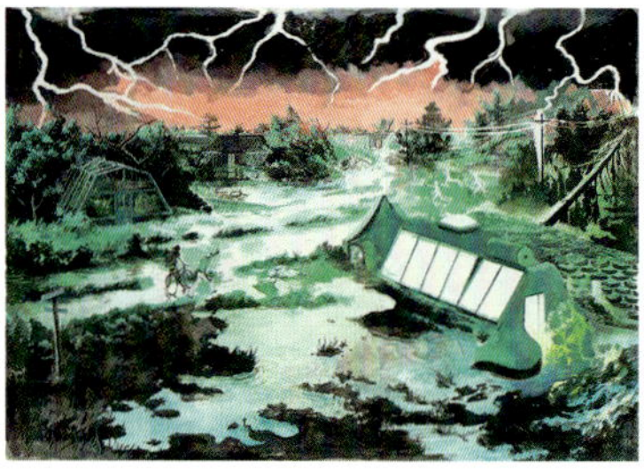

TERRA

2014, 218 × 305 cm
Öl auf Papier/oil on paper

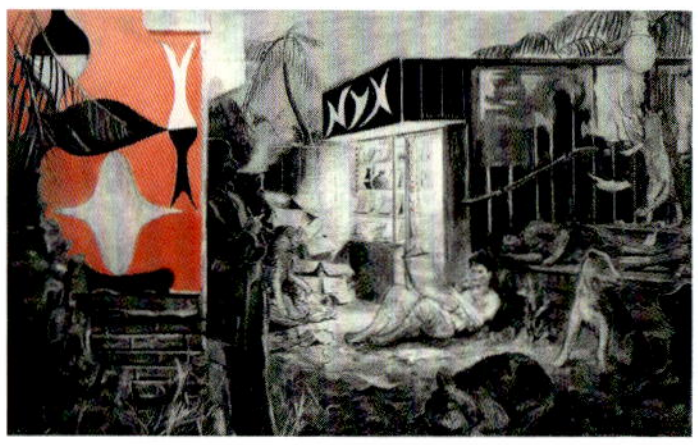

NYX

2009, 125 × 200 cm
Kohle, Tusche und Pastell auf Papier/charcoal, ink and pastel on paper

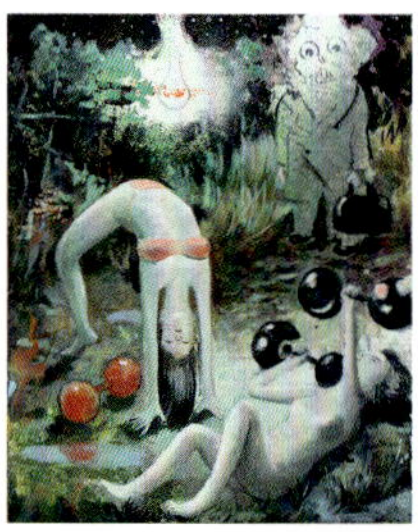

GOGO

2014, 50 × 40 cm
Öl auf Leinwand/oil on canvas

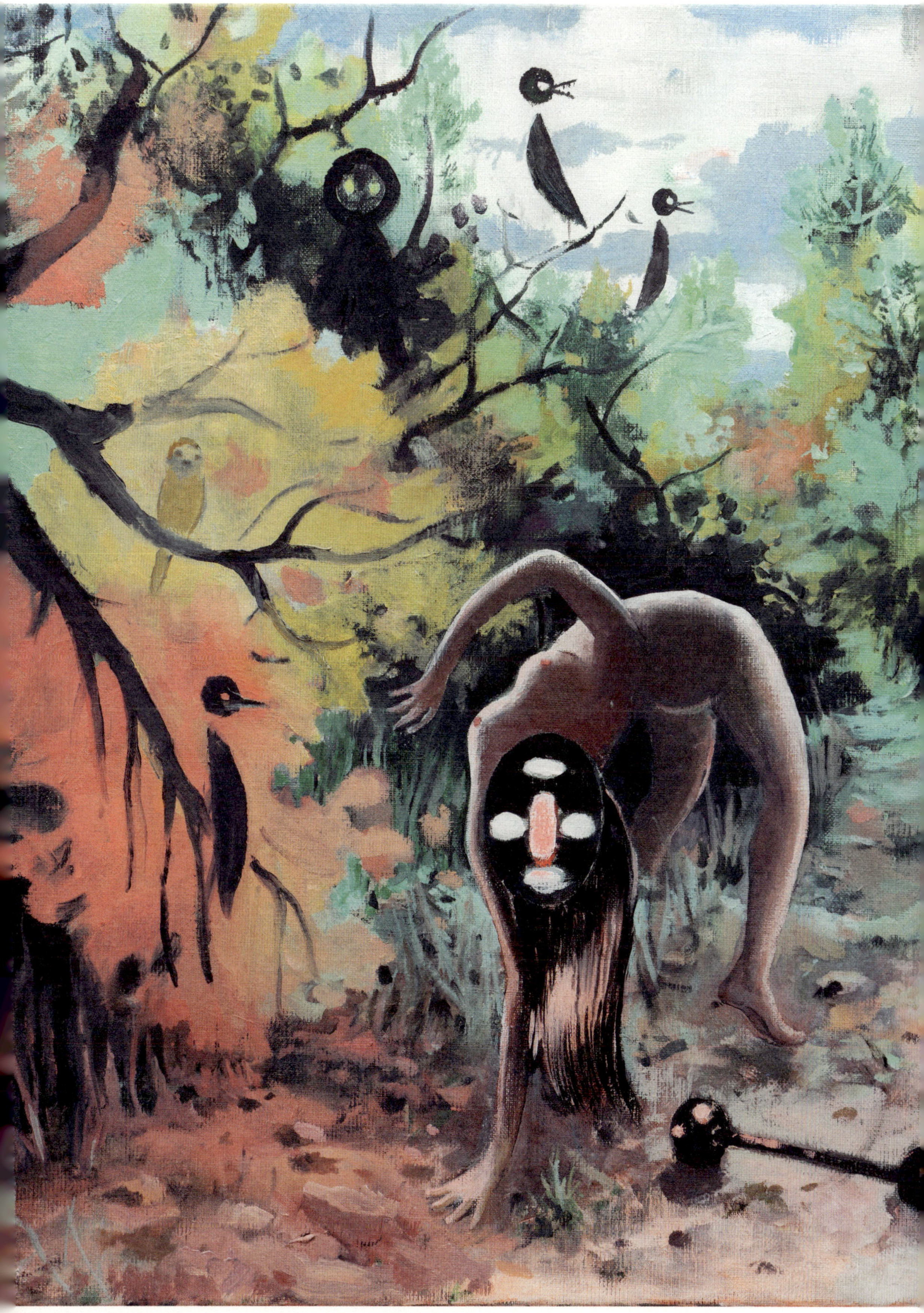

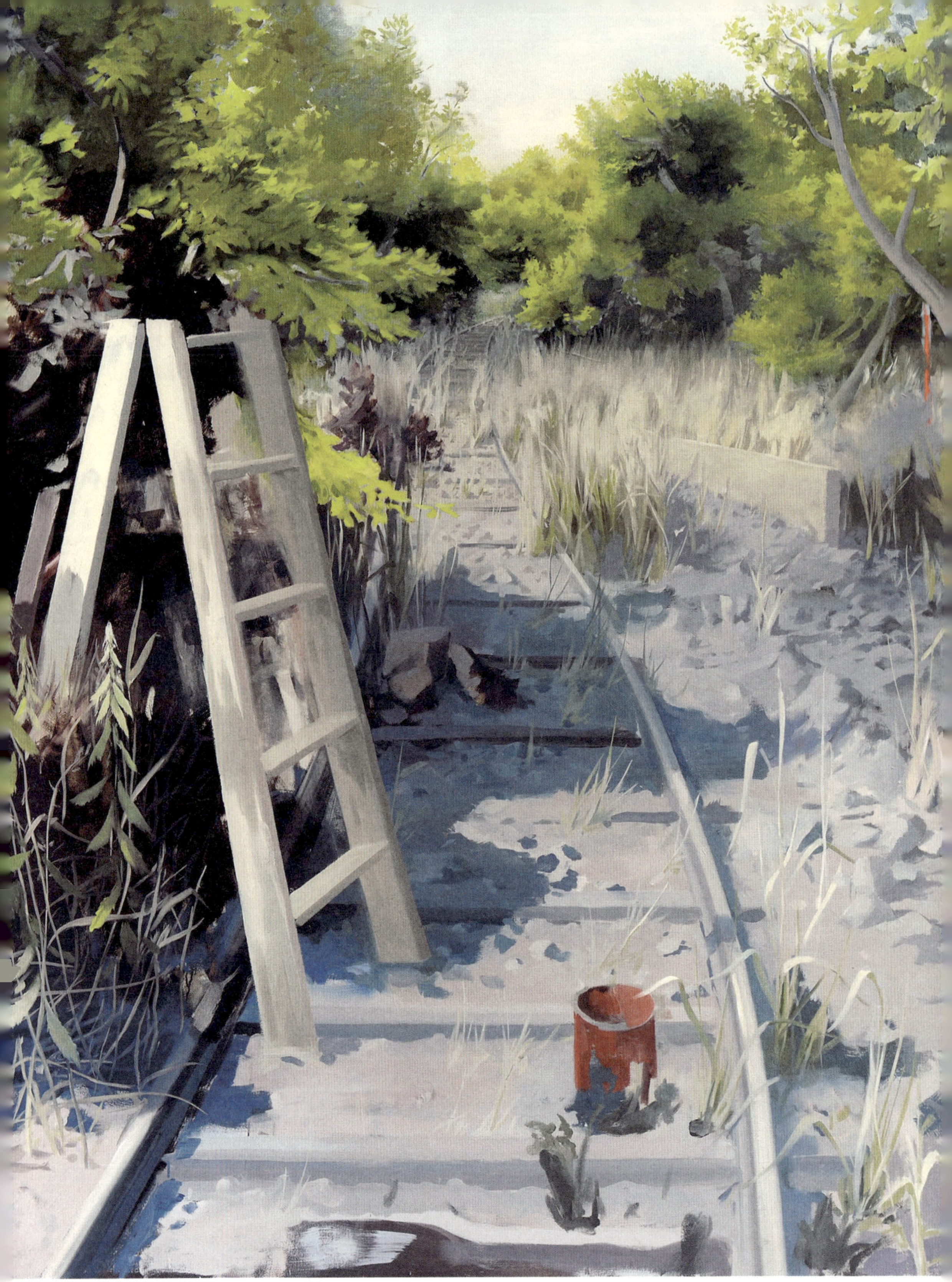

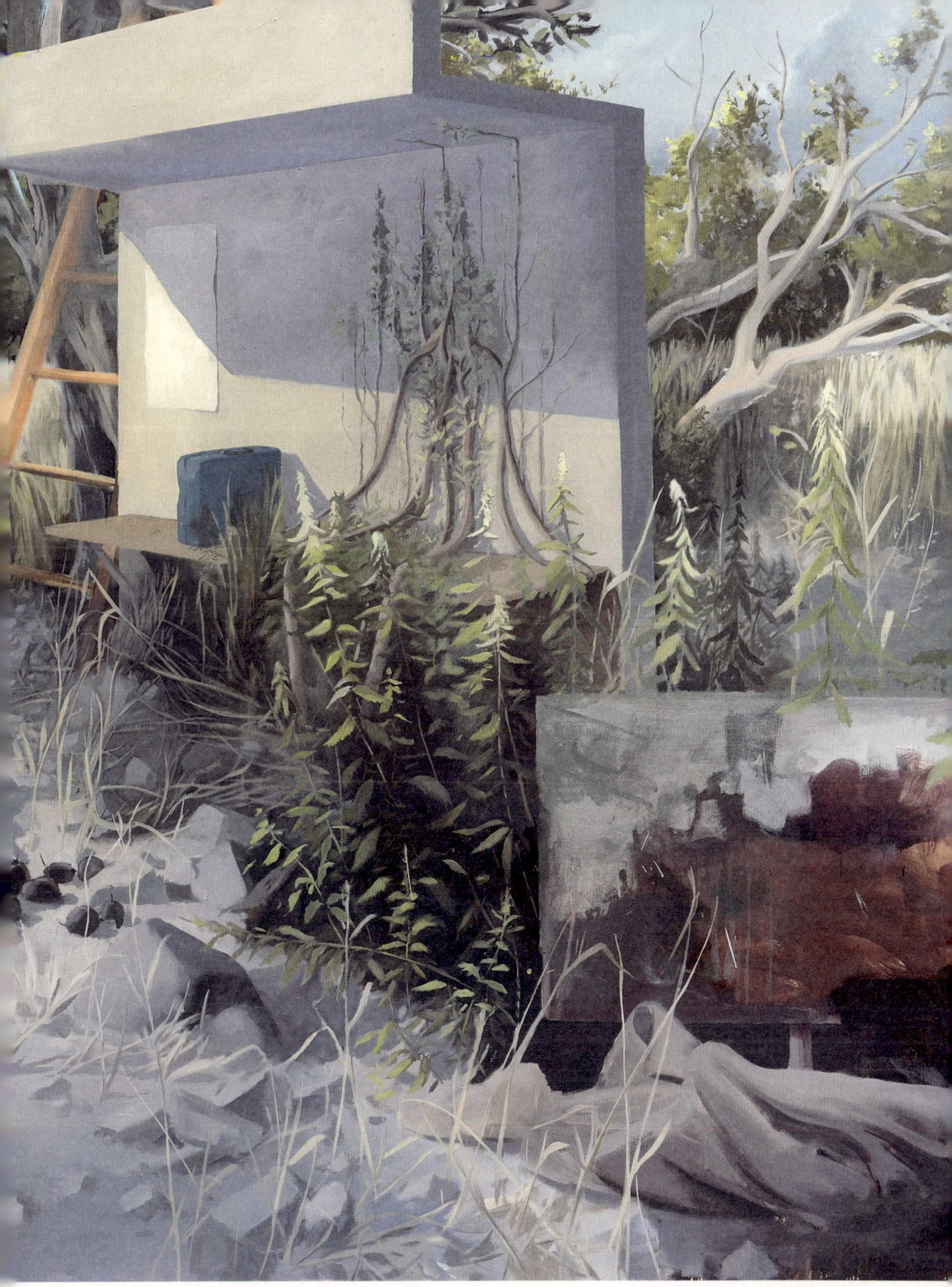

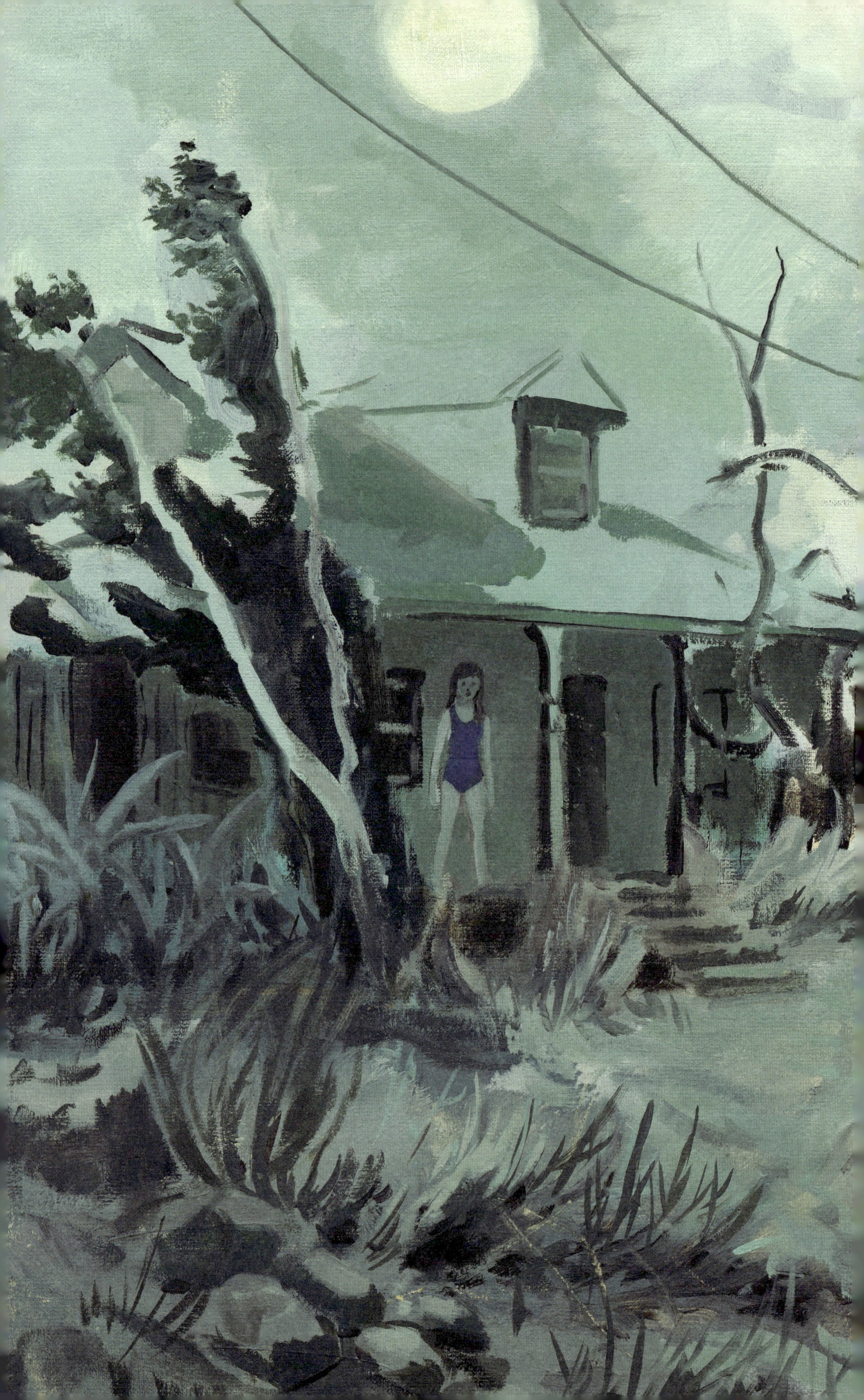

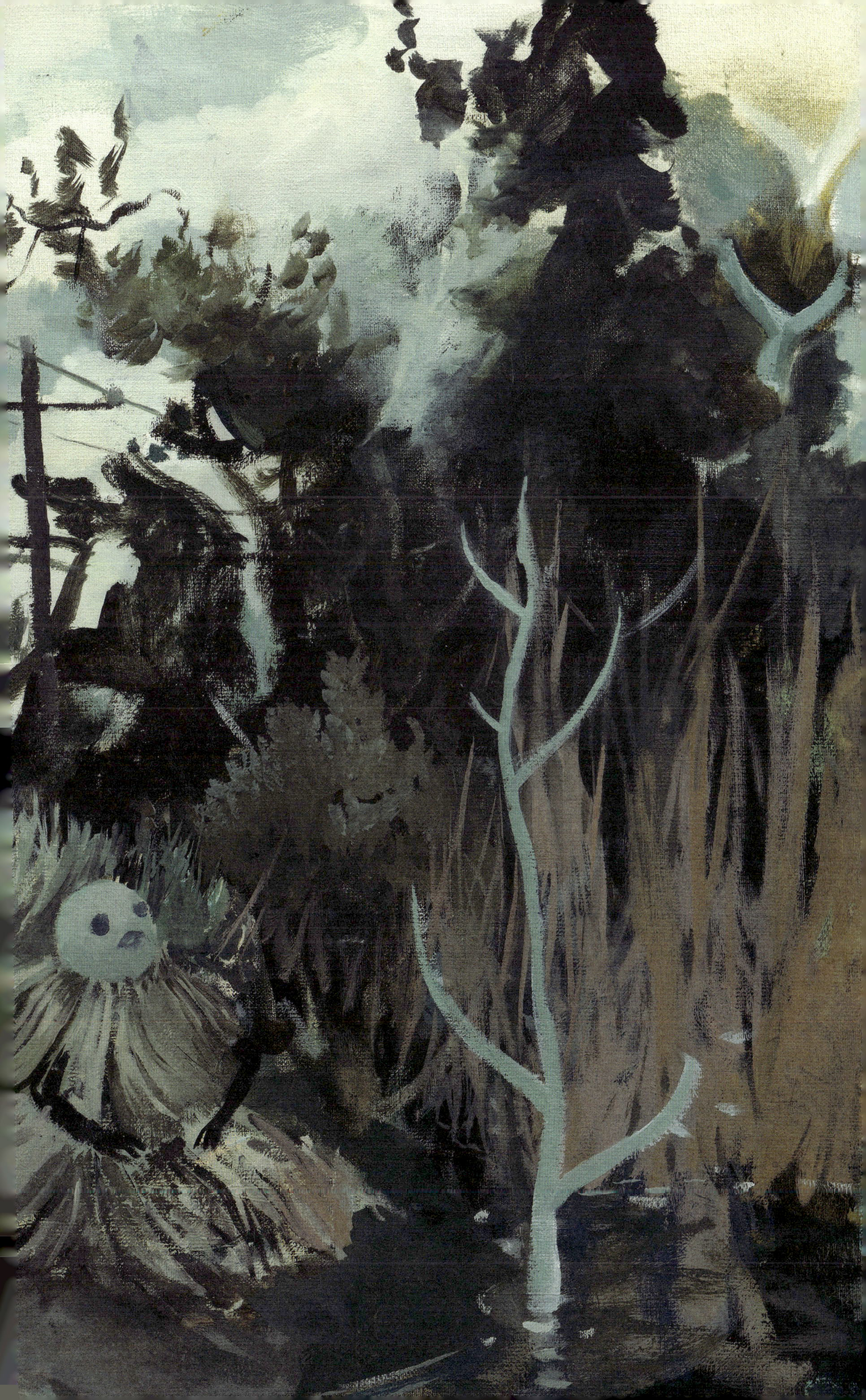

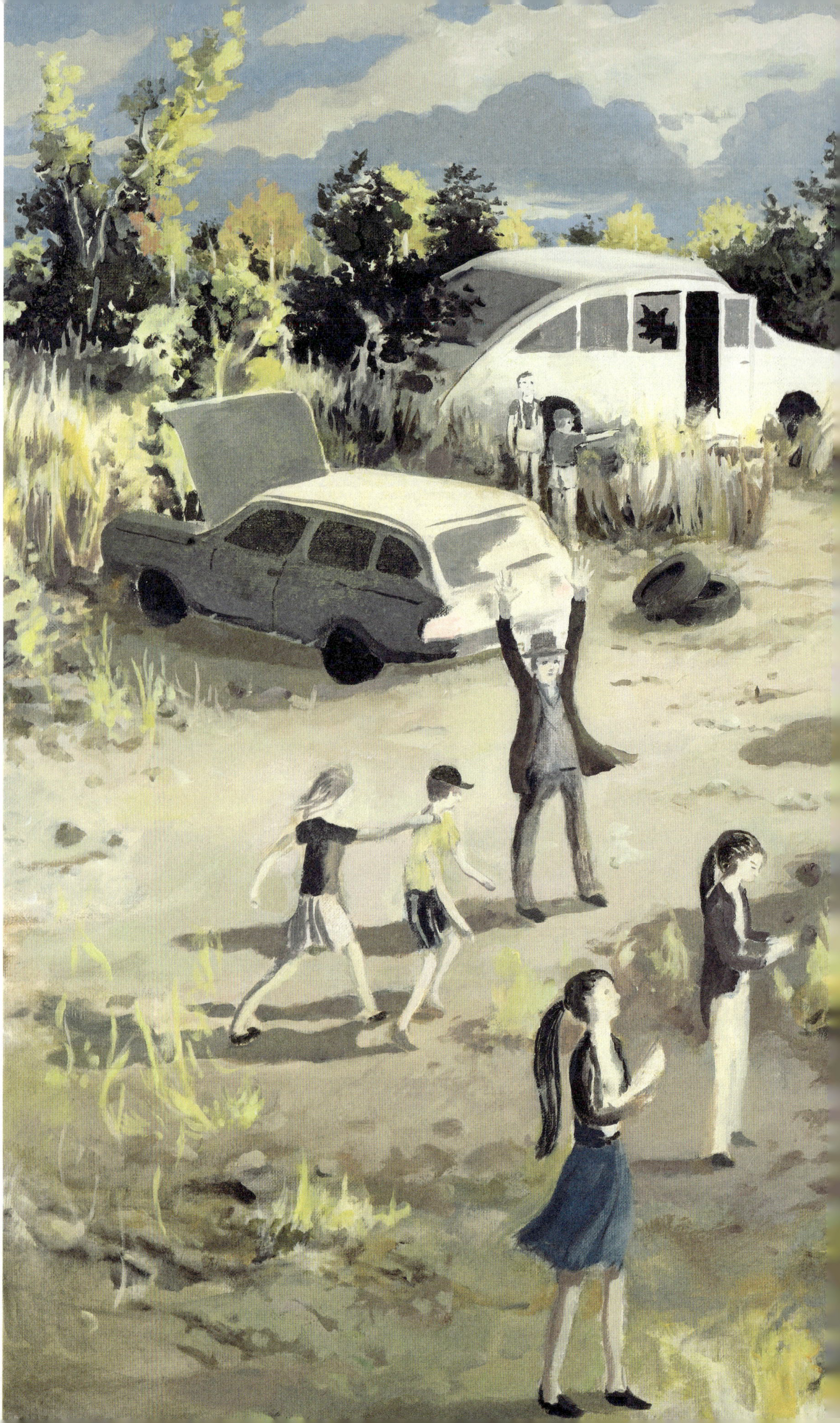

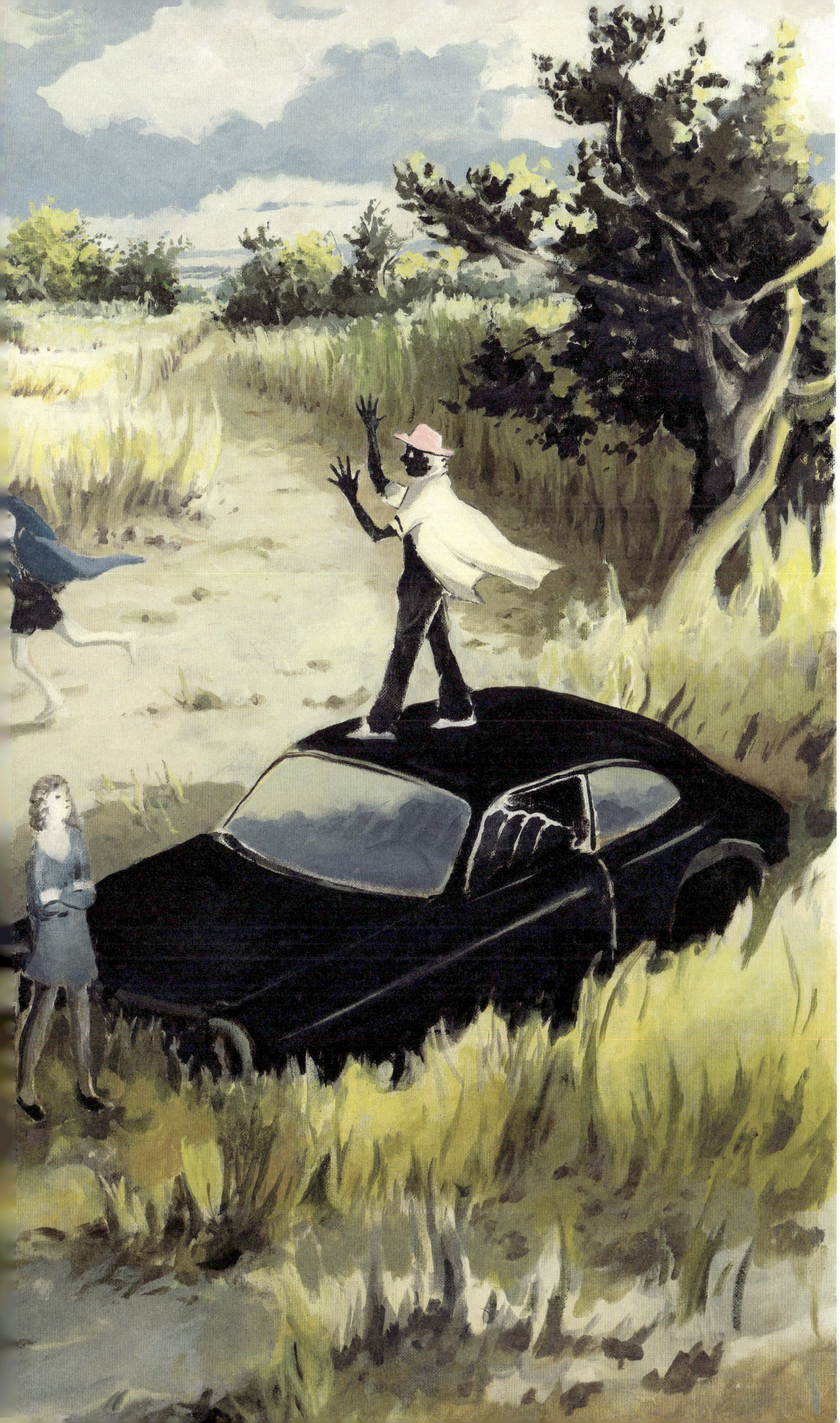

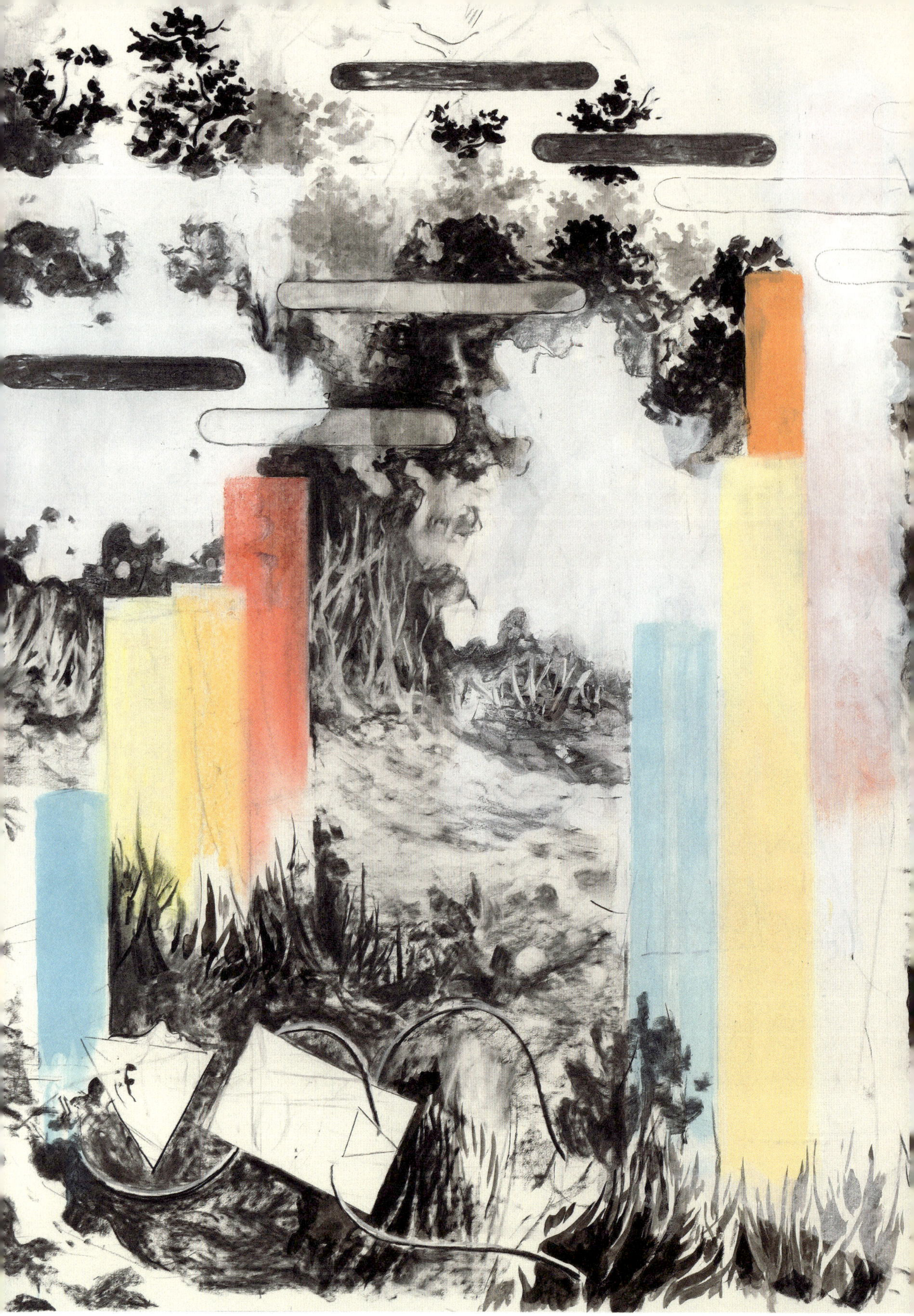

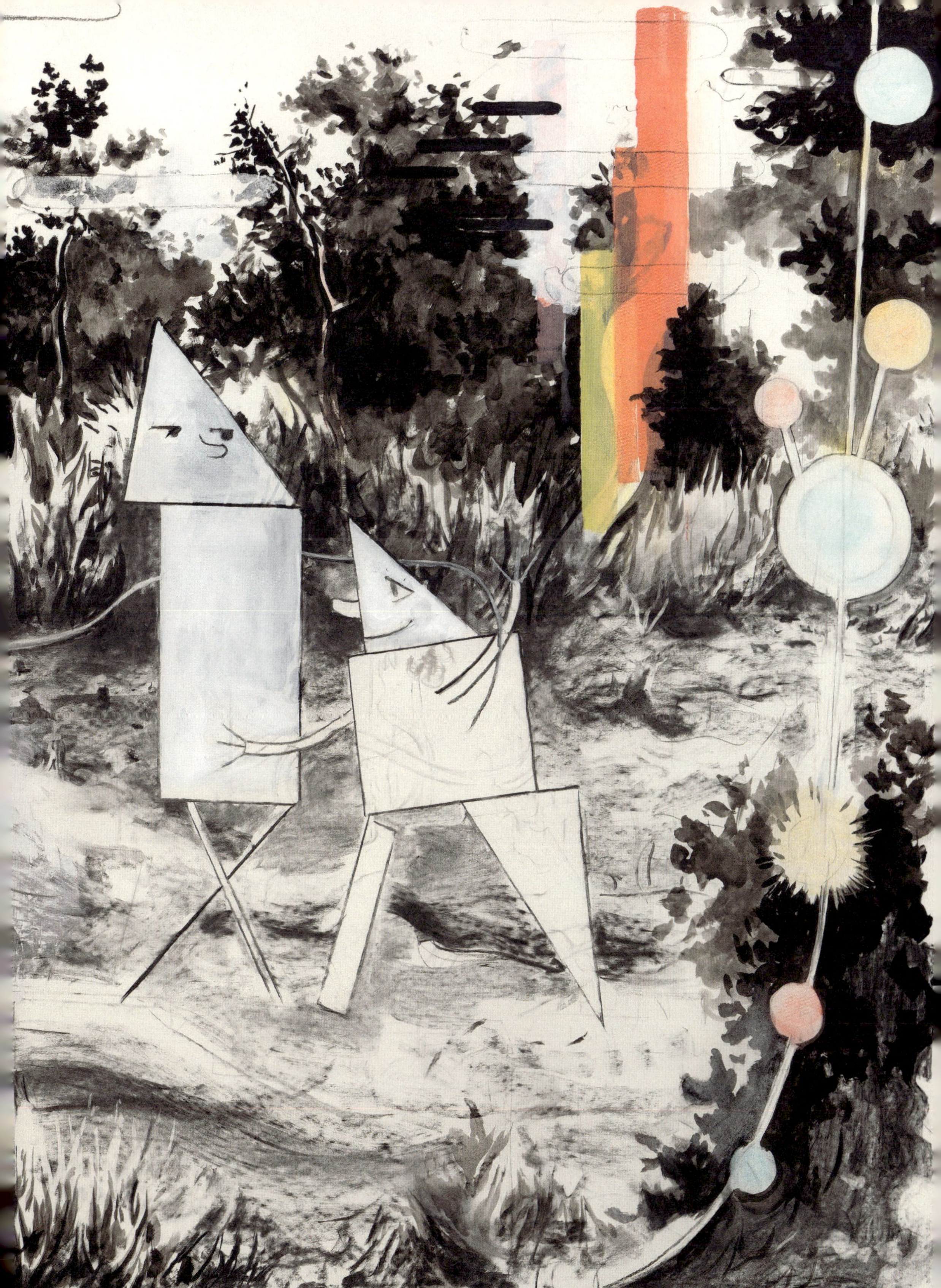

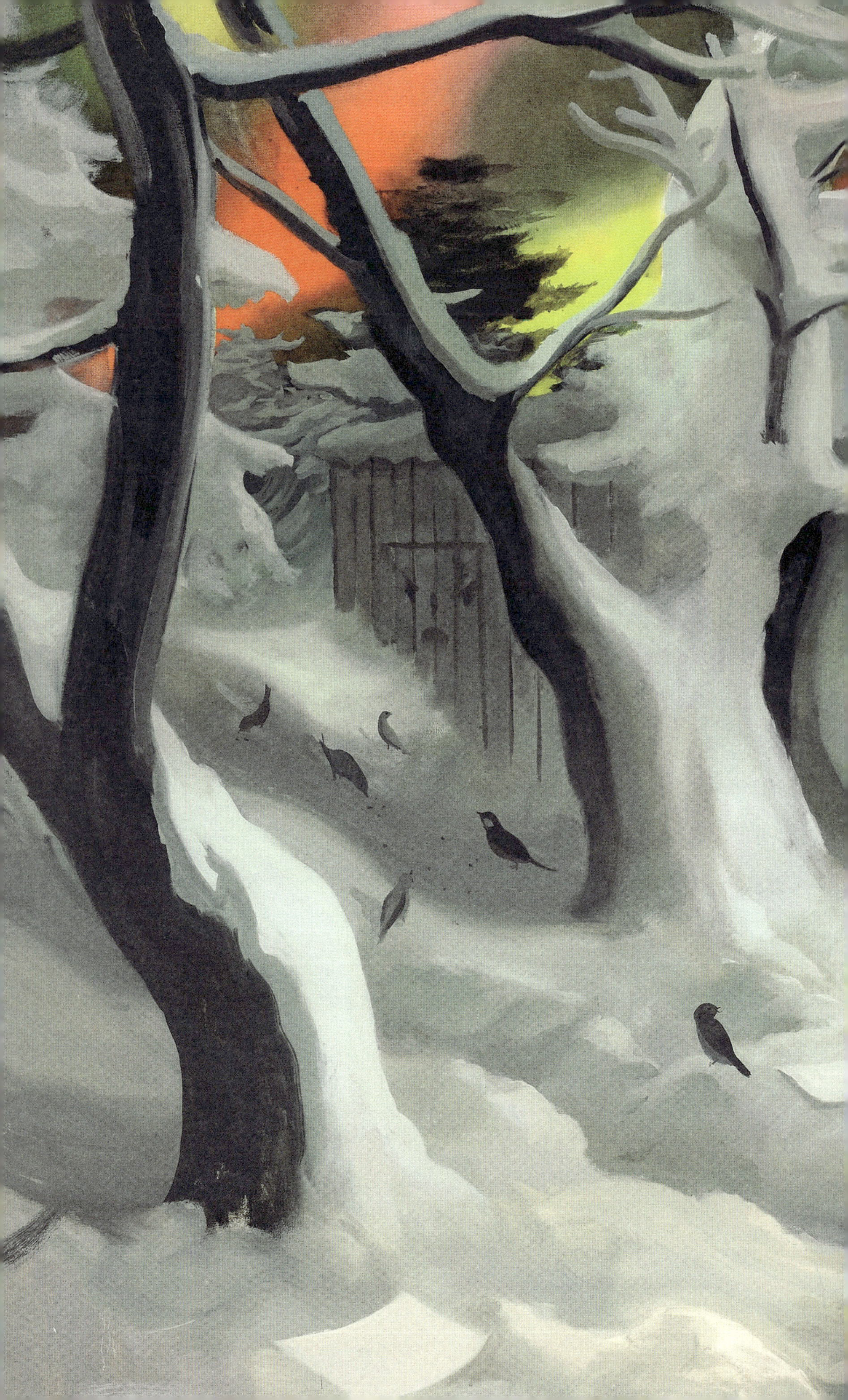

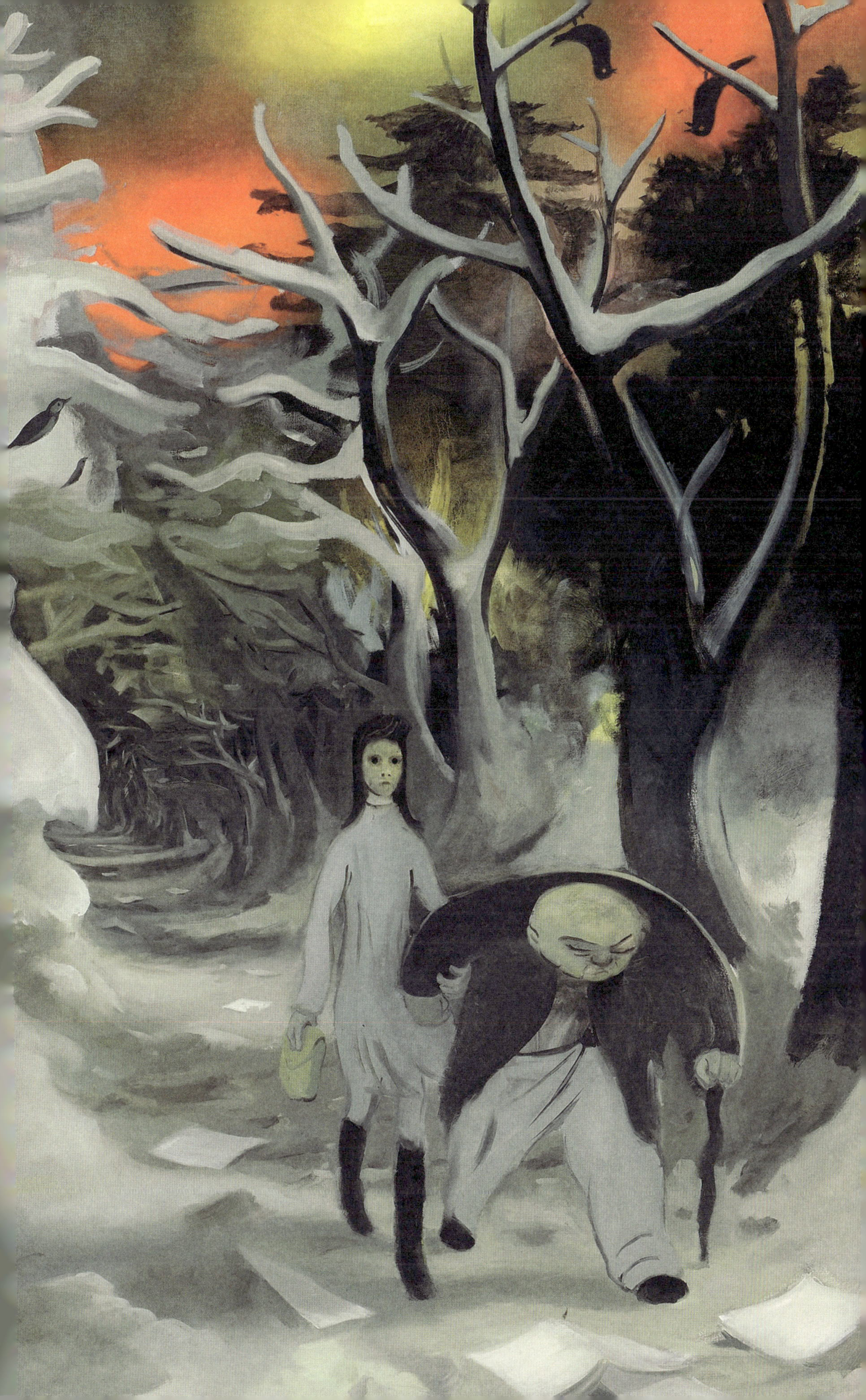

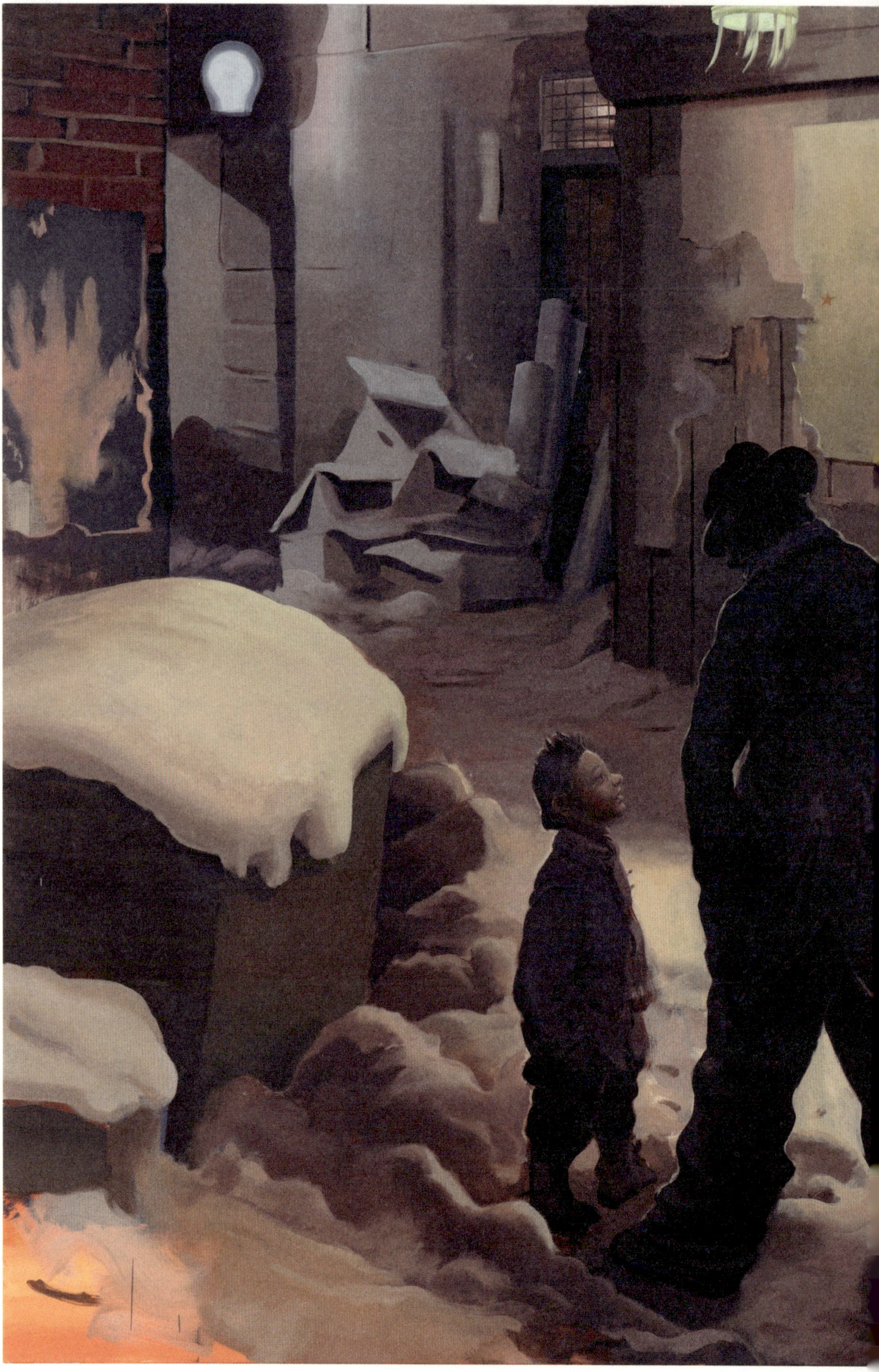

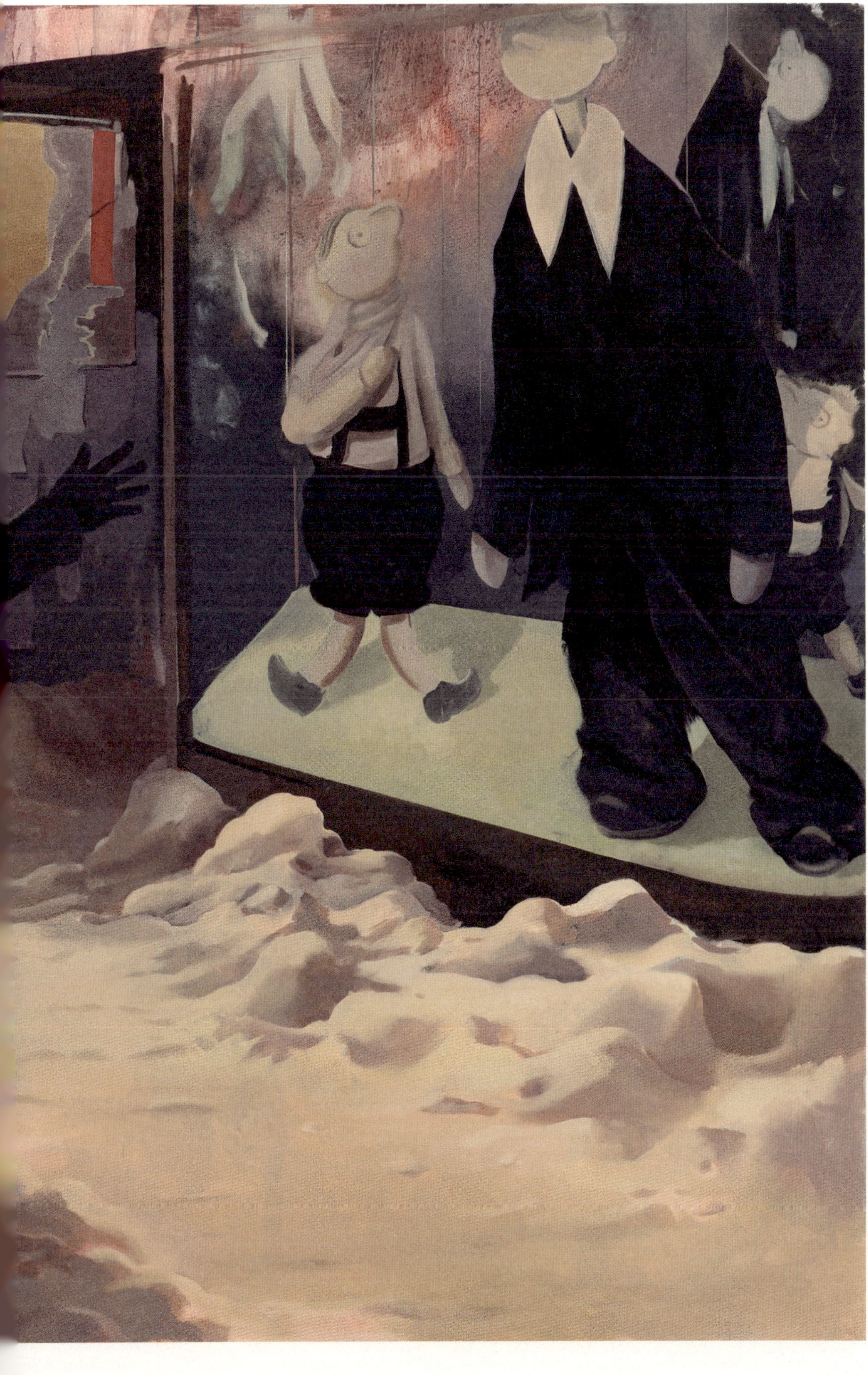

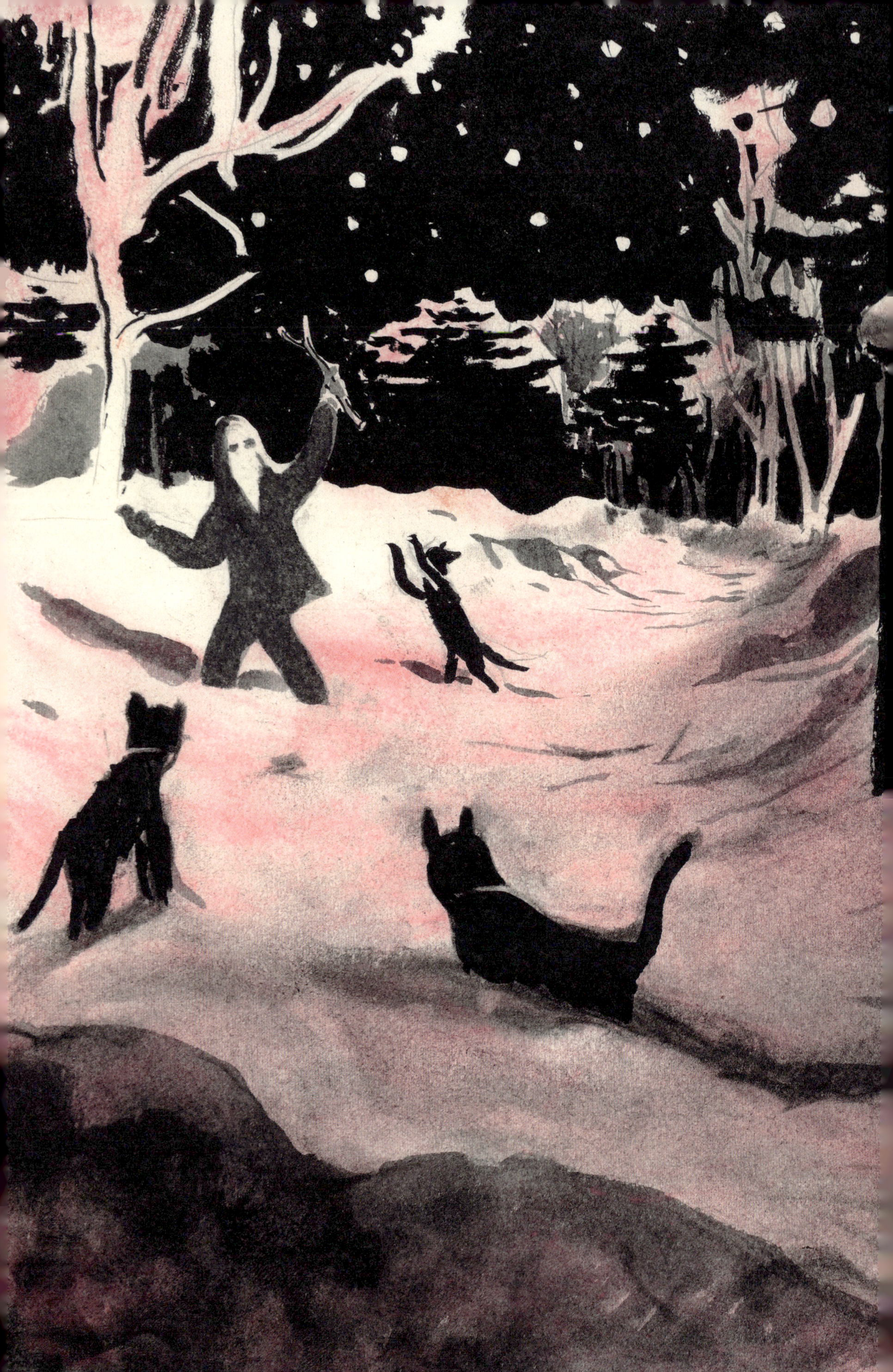

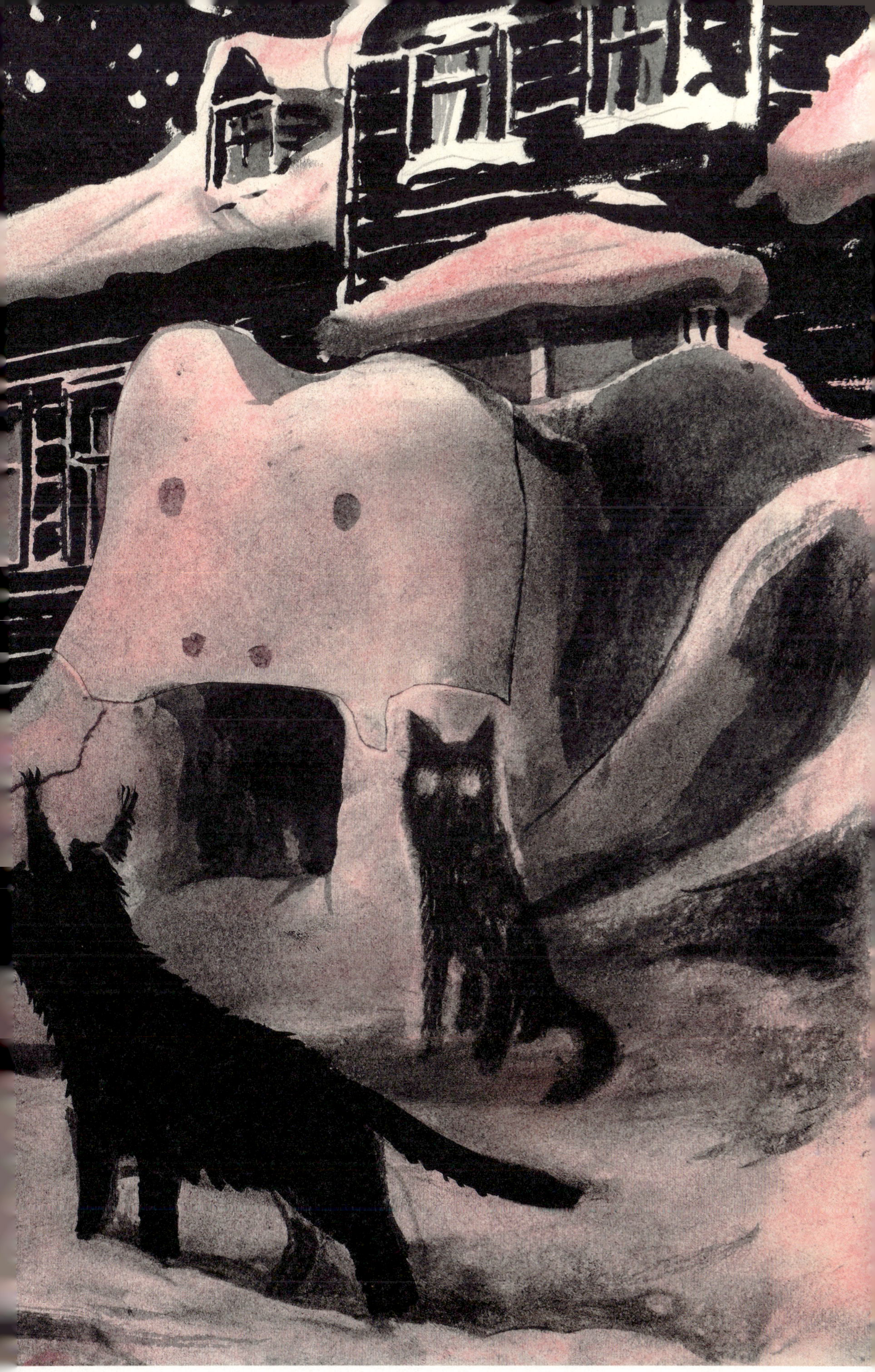

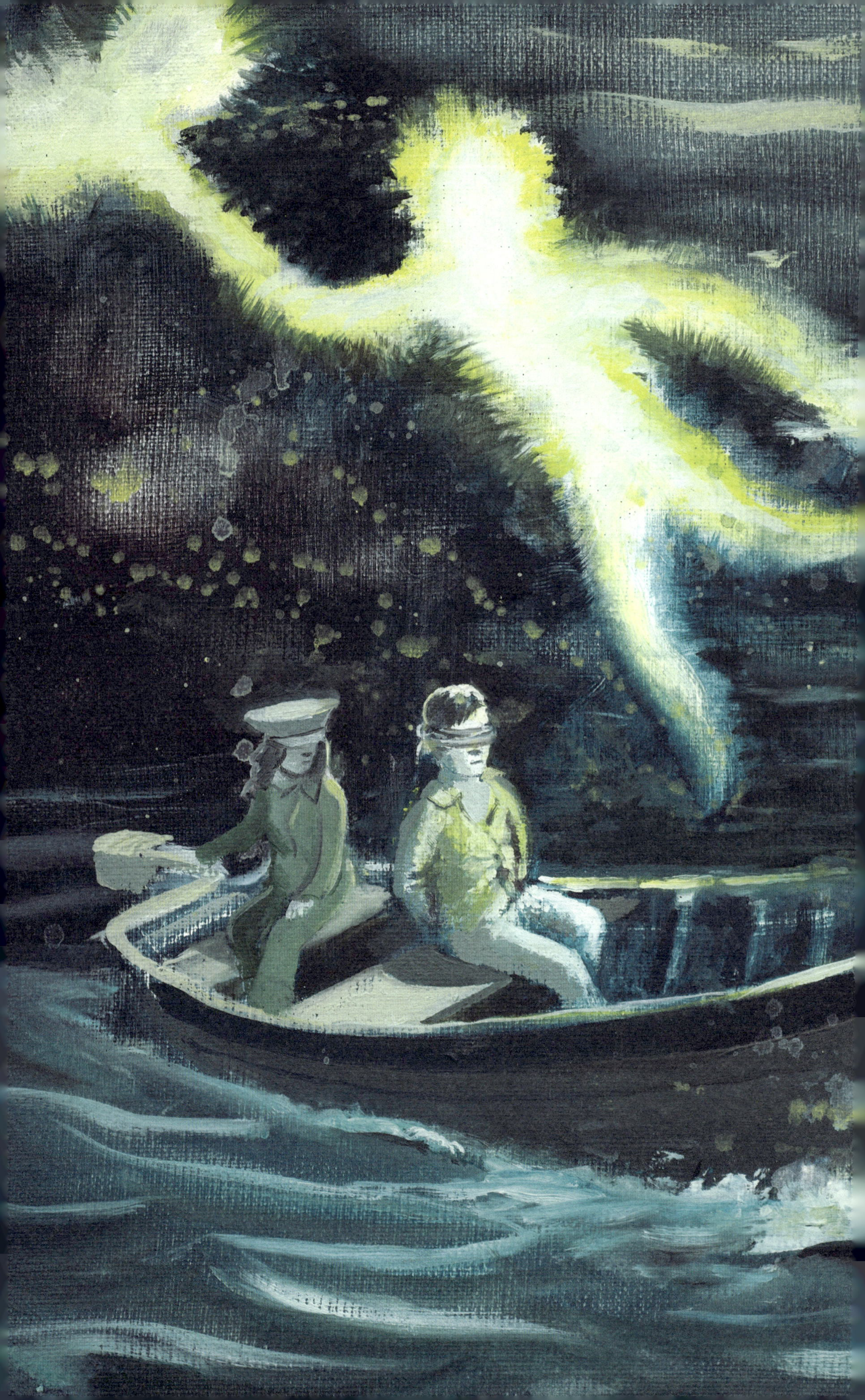

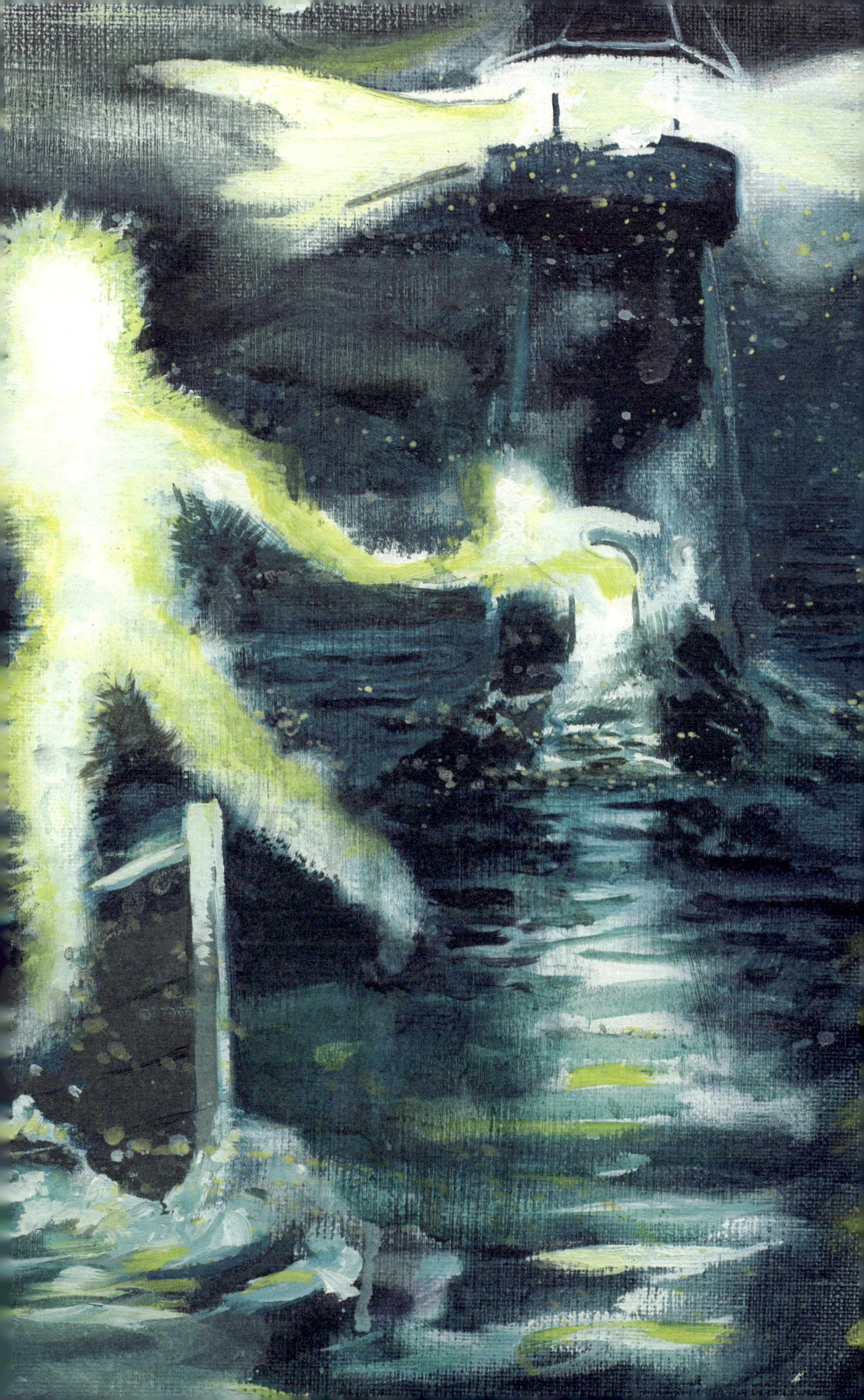

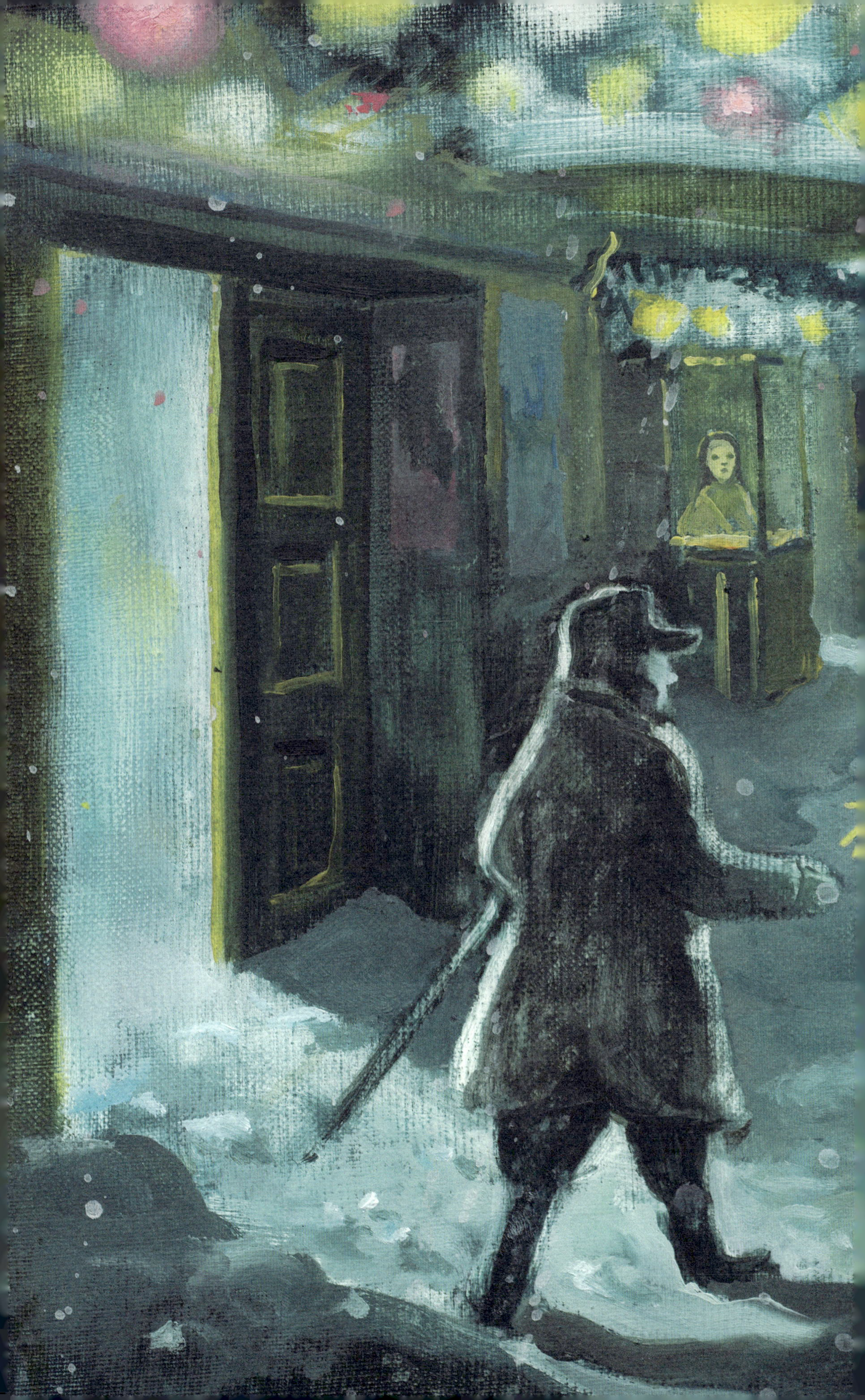

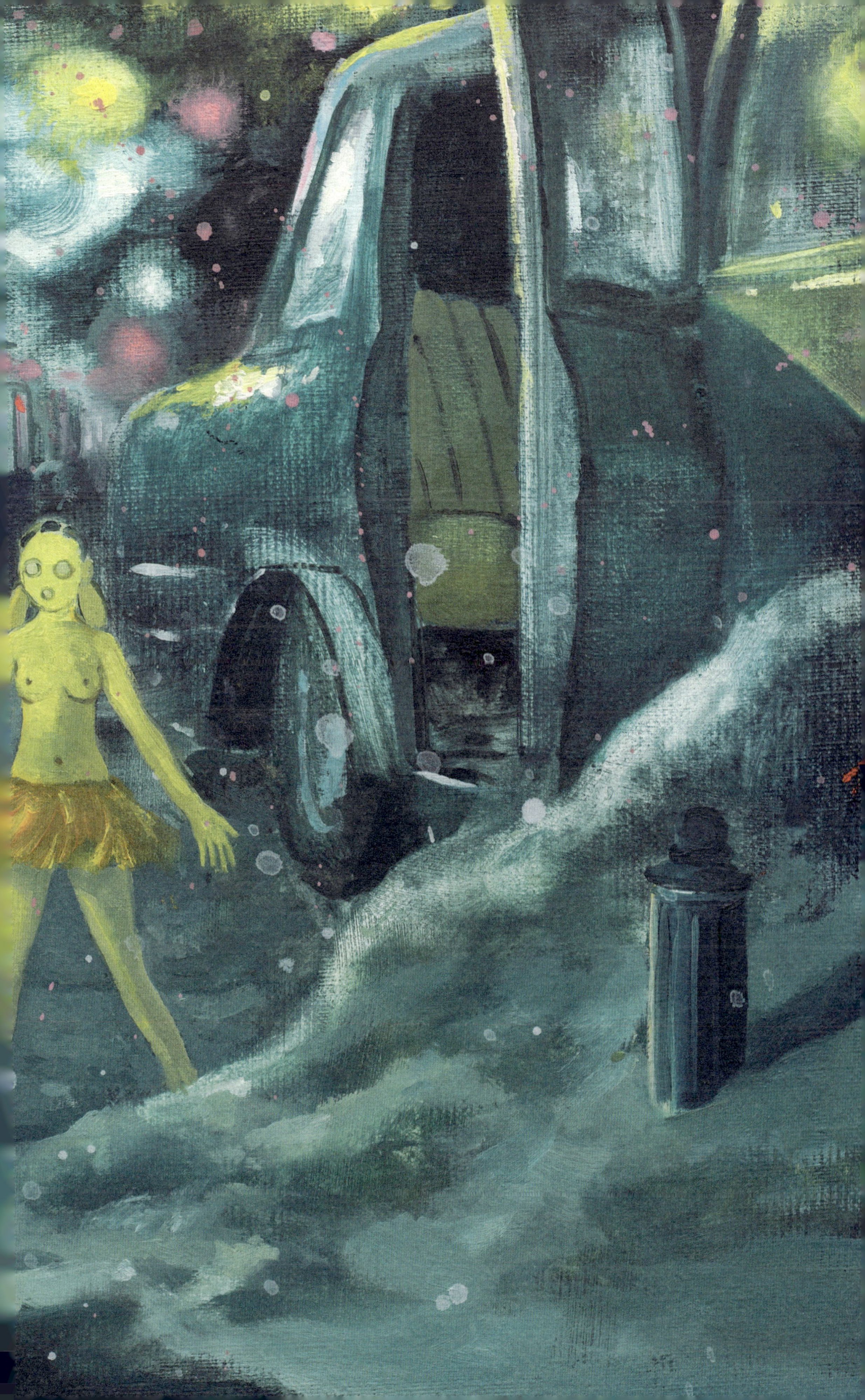

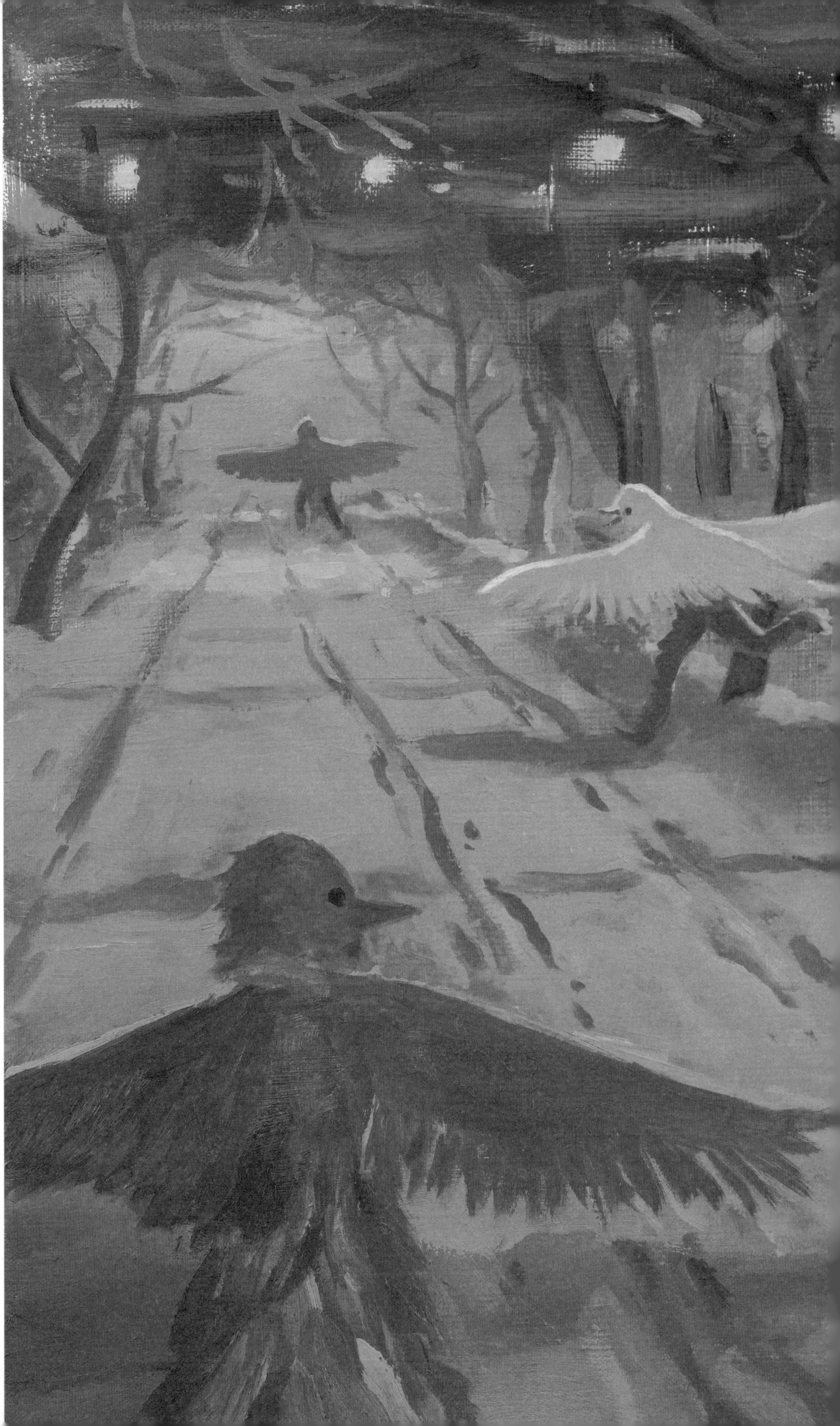

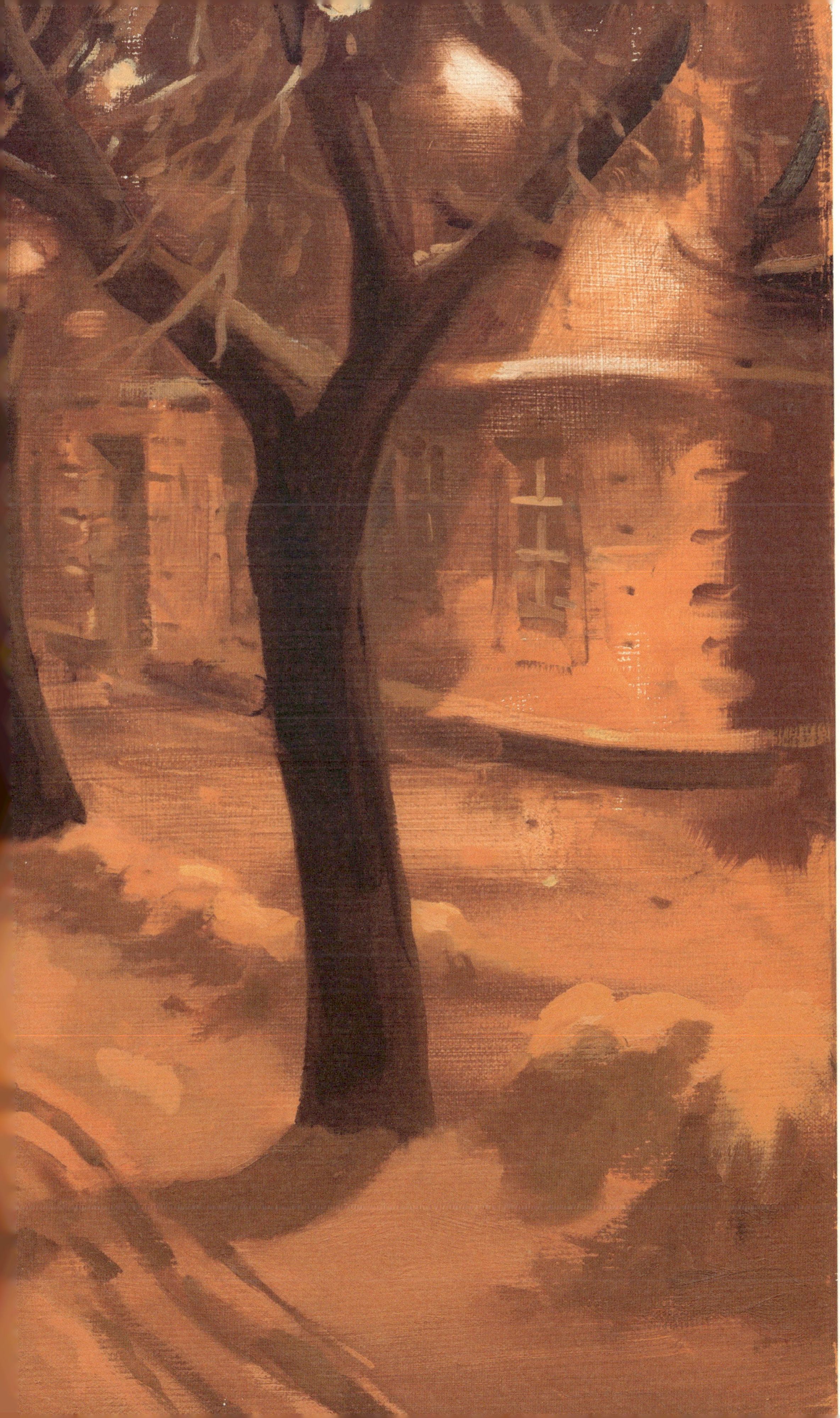

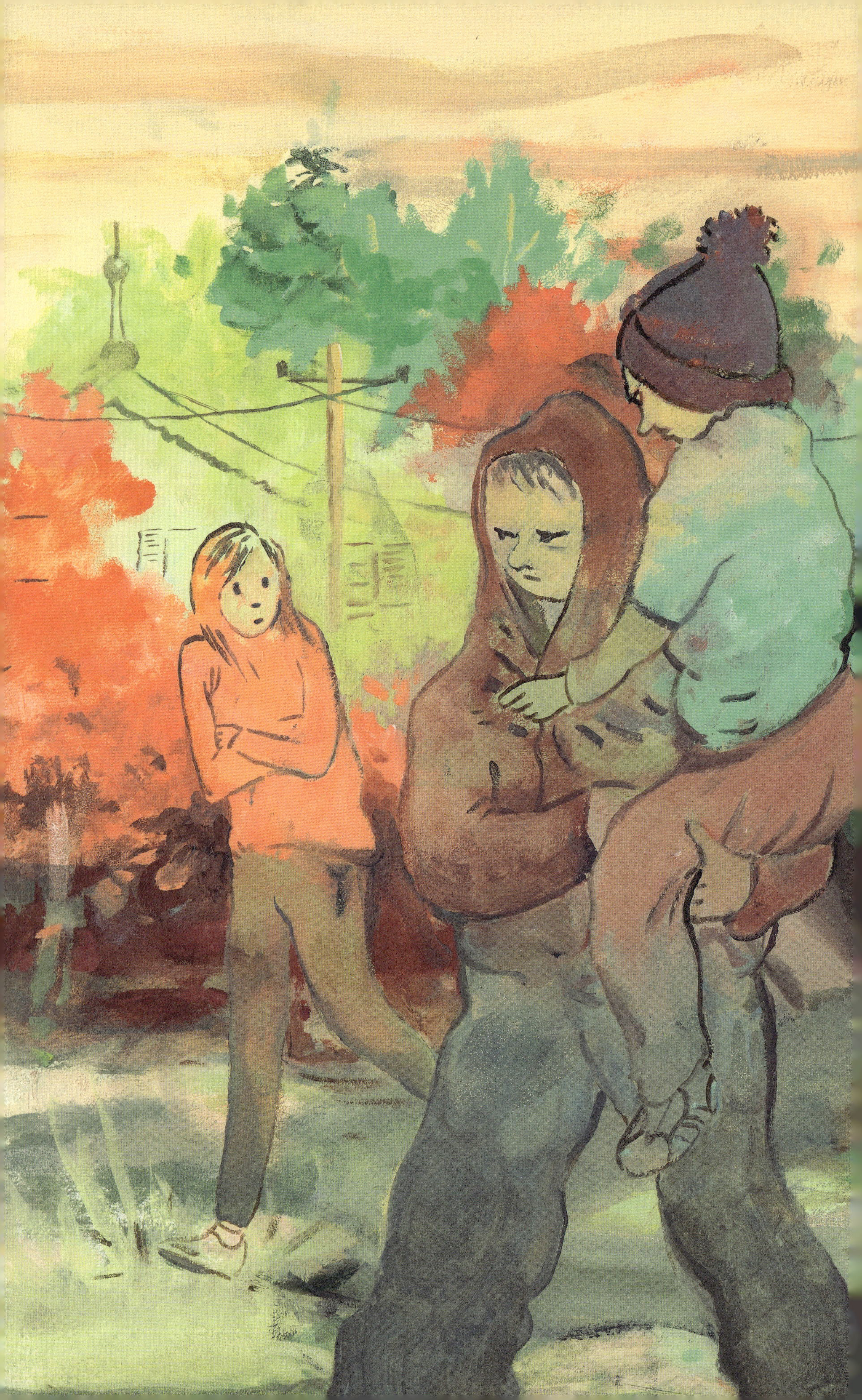

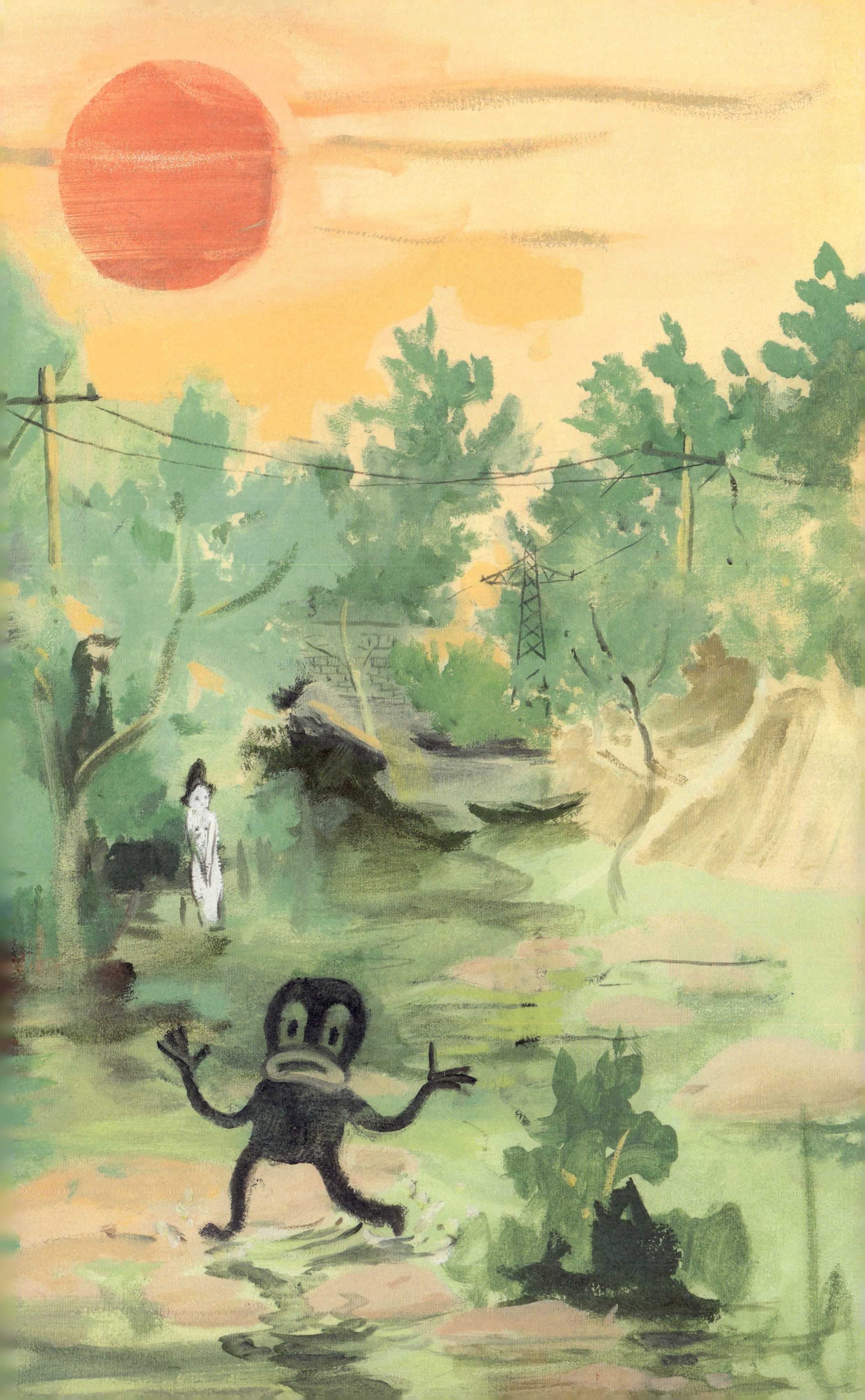

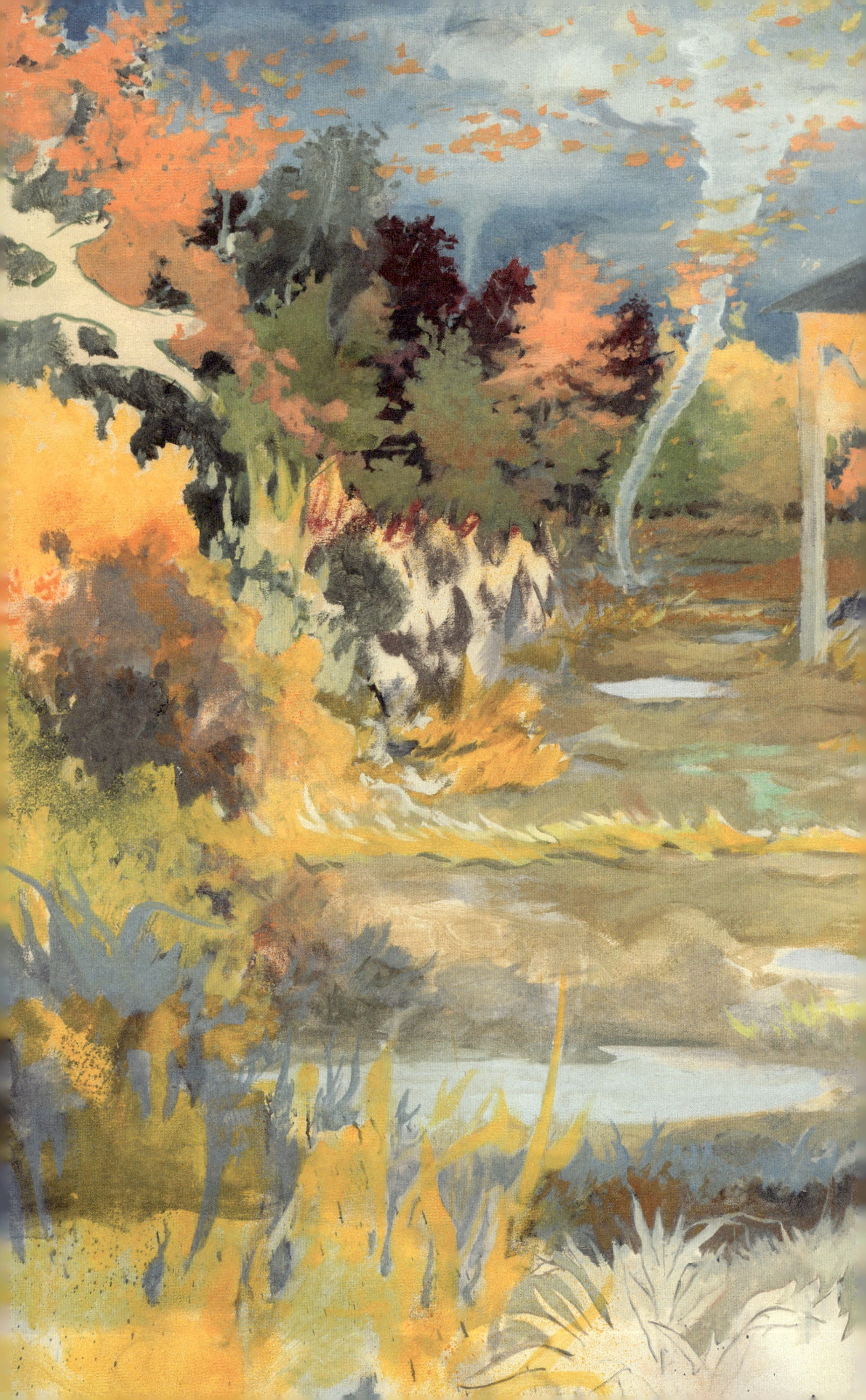

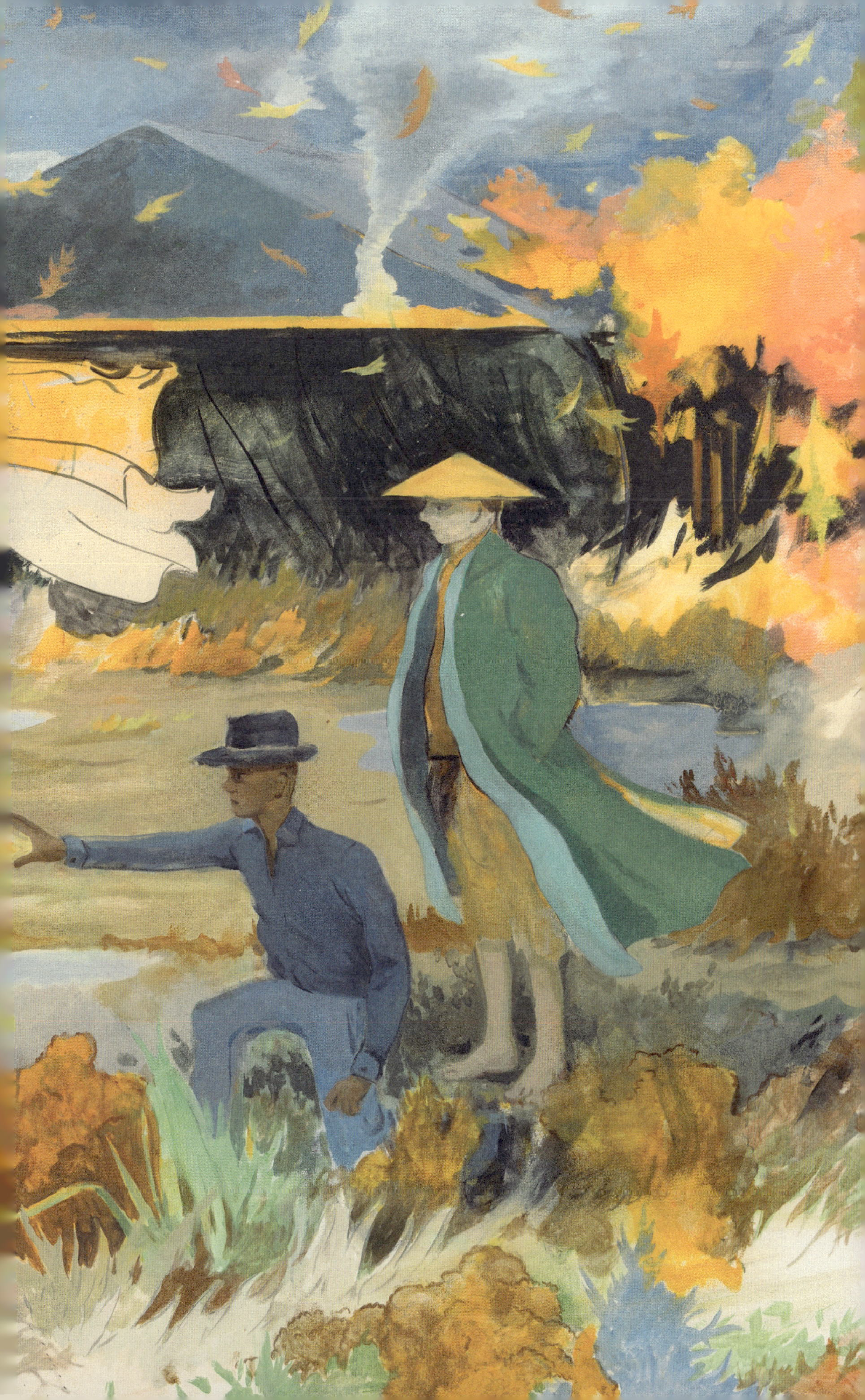

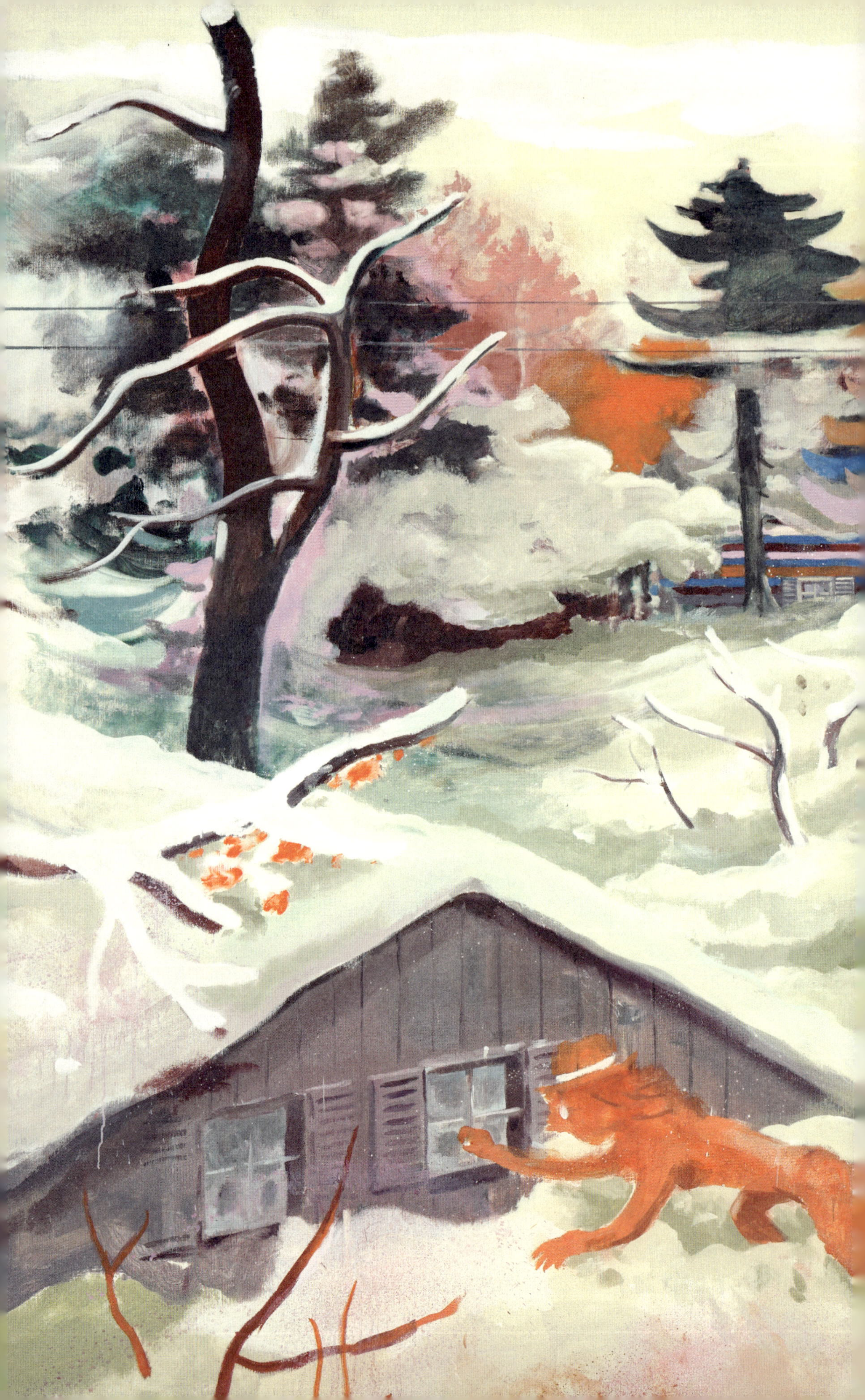

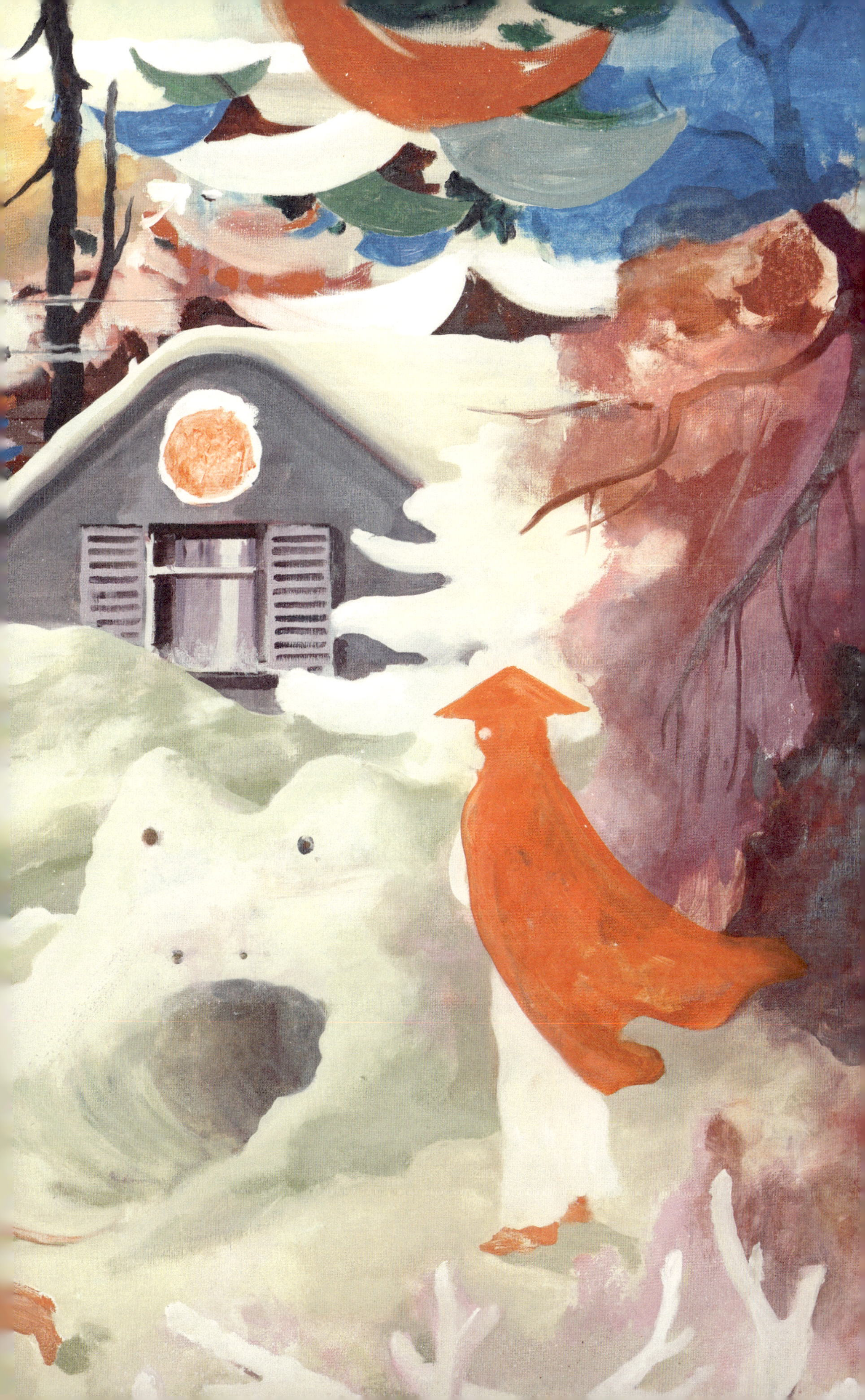

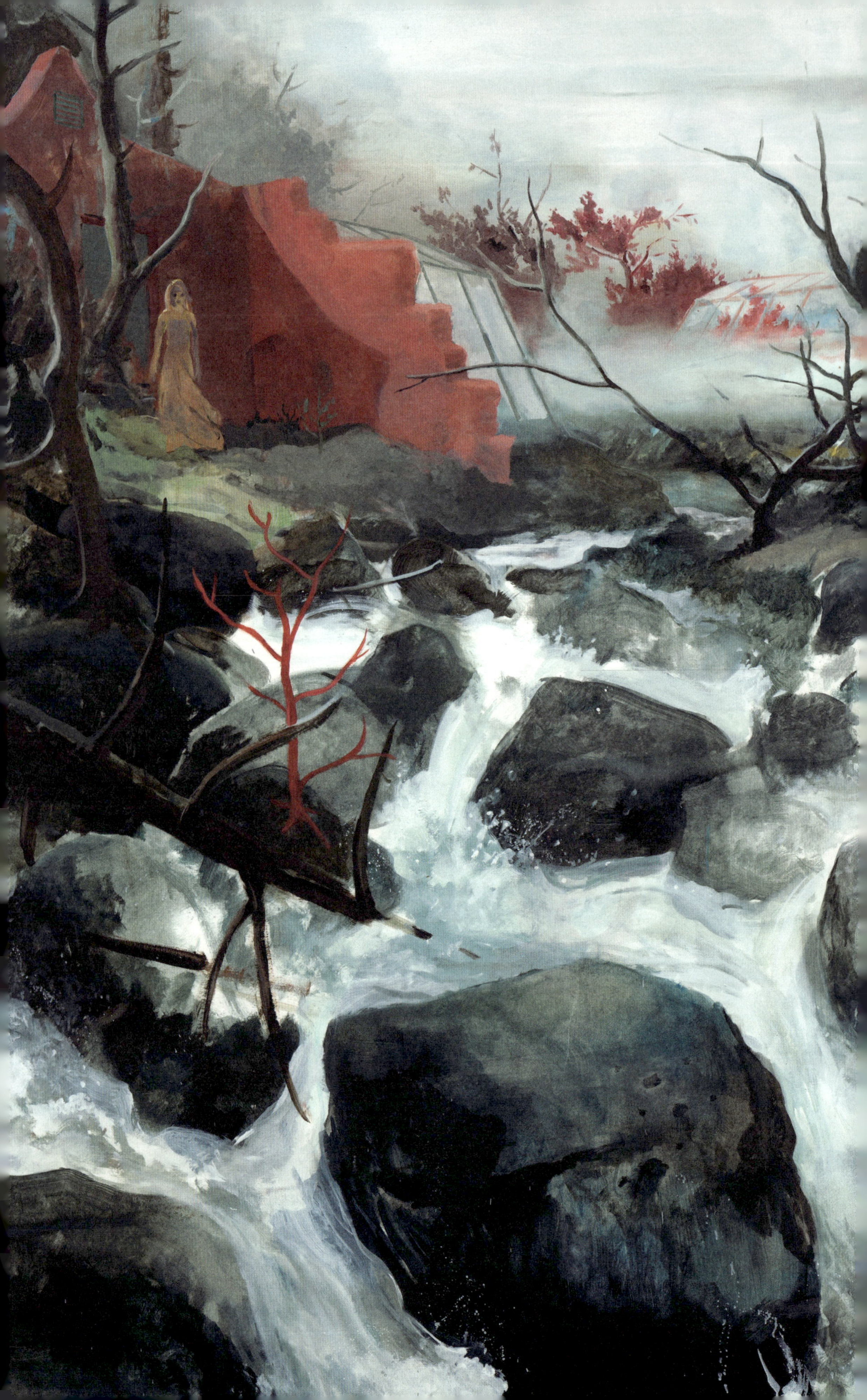

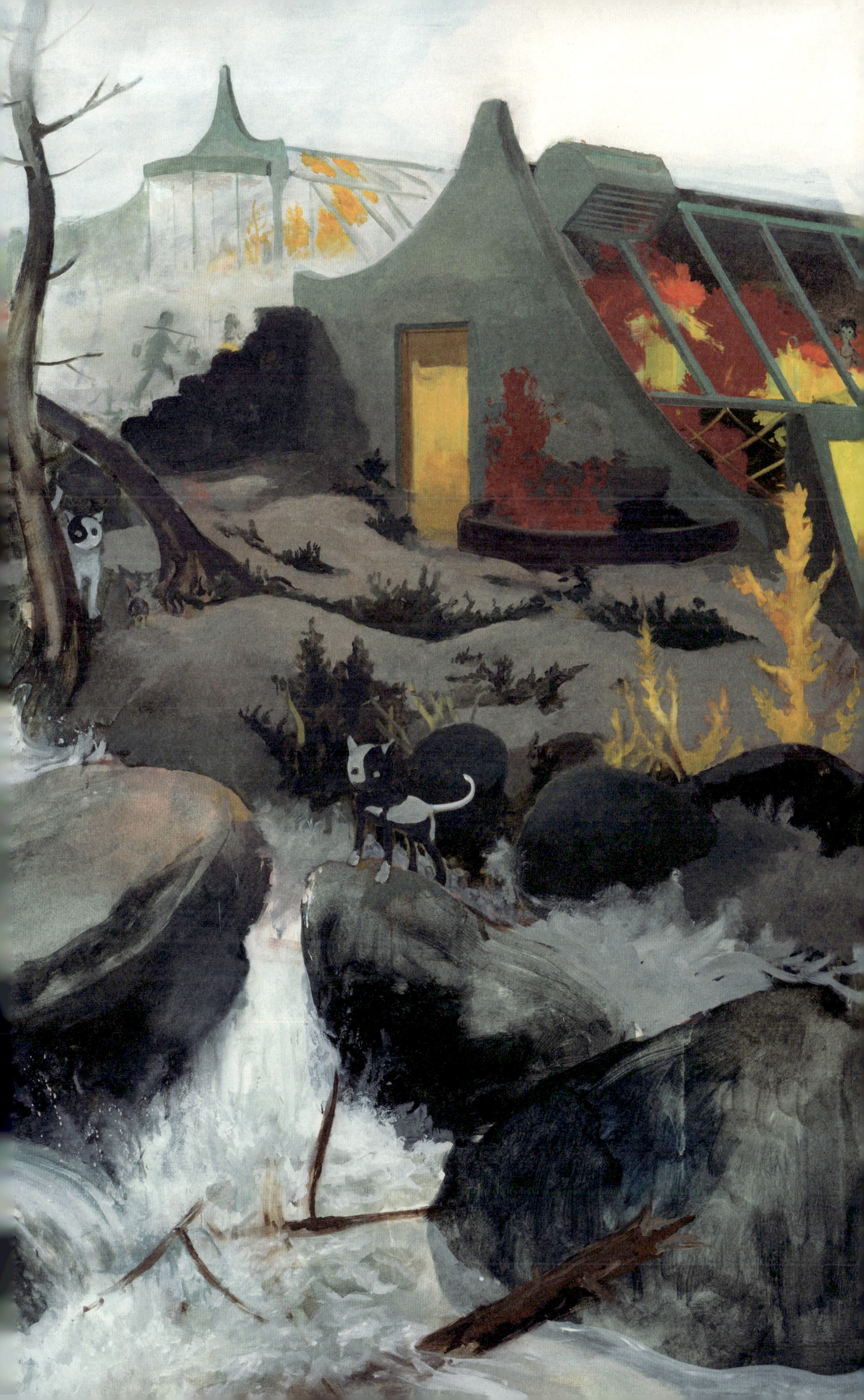

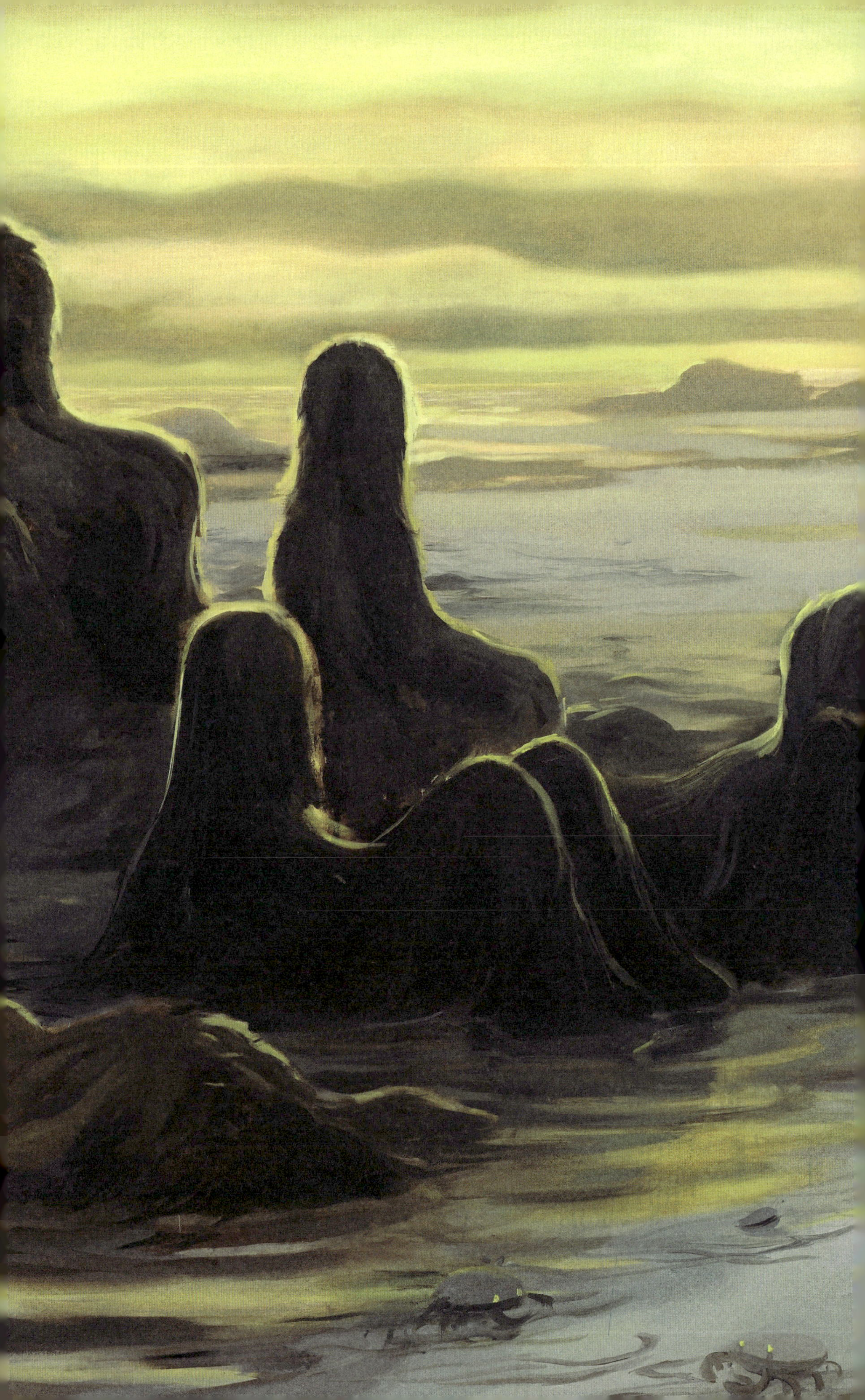

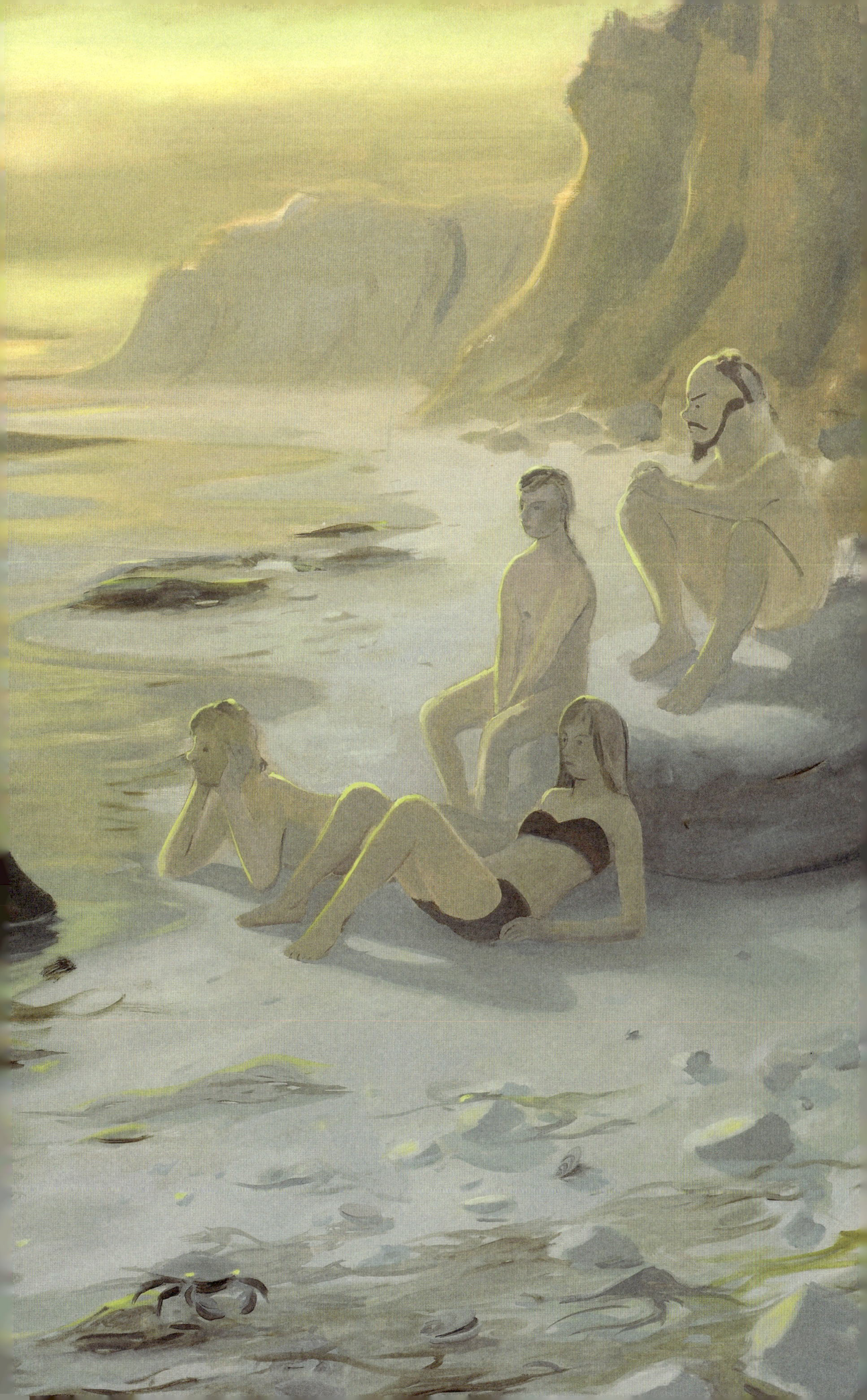

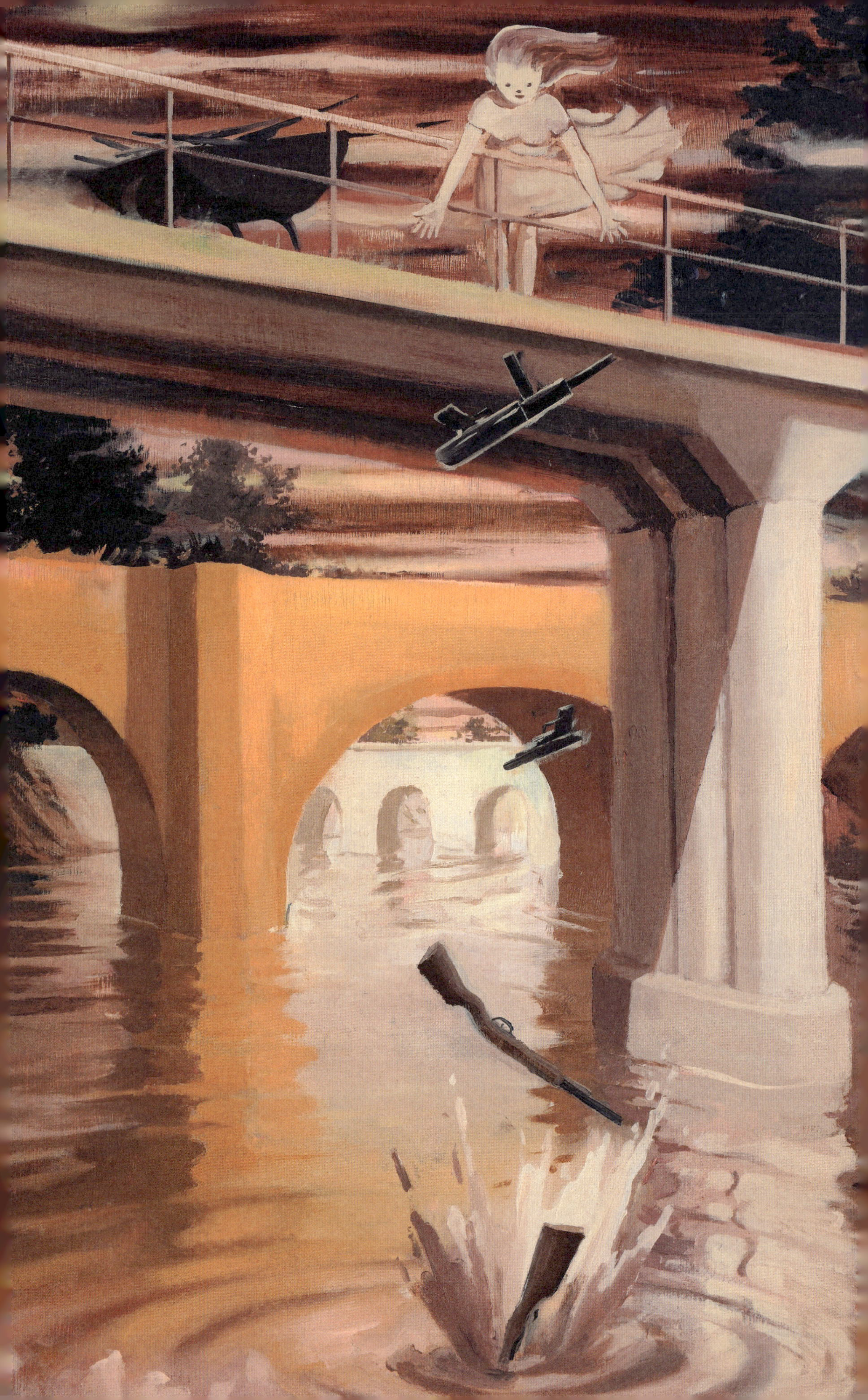

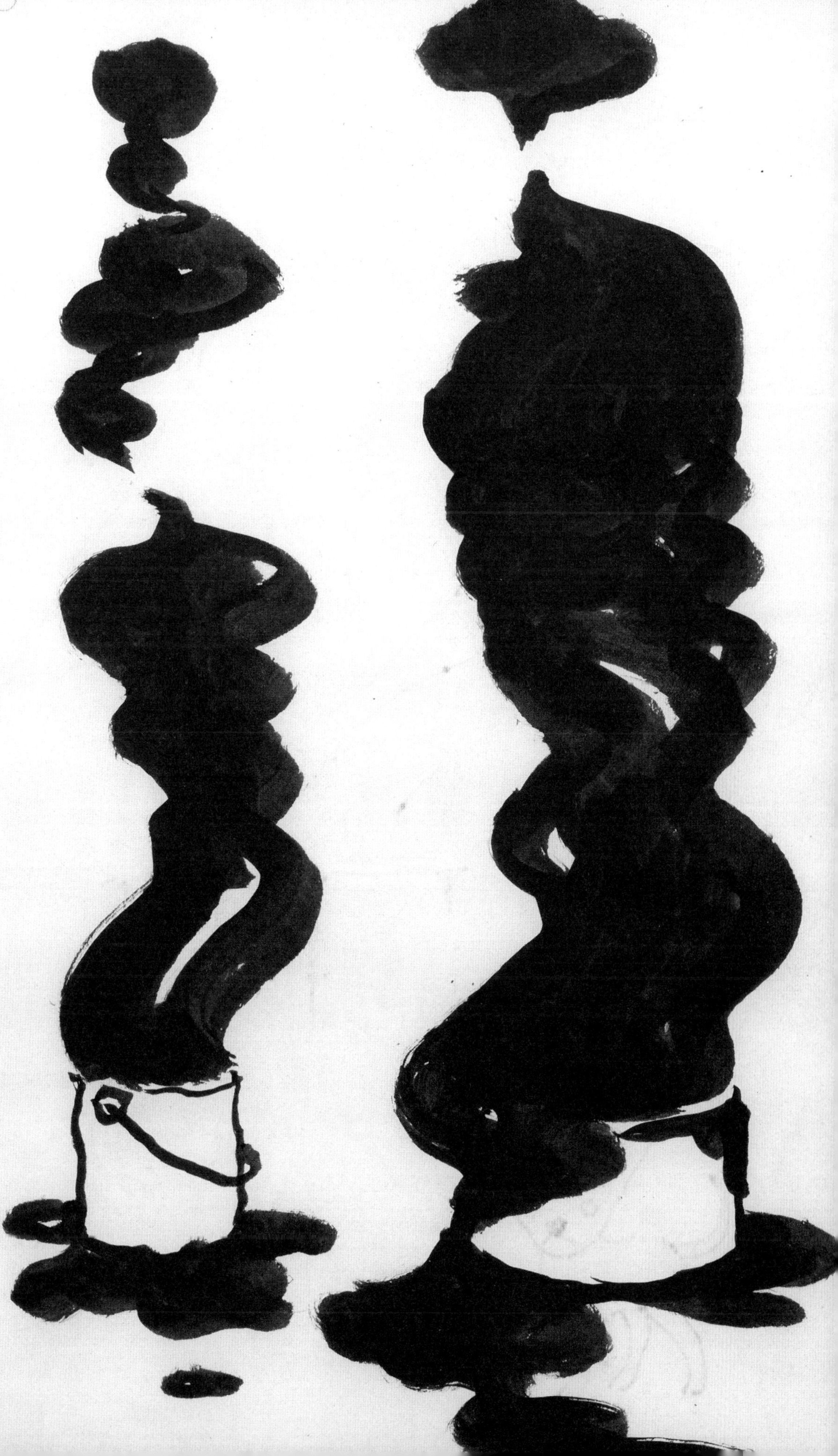

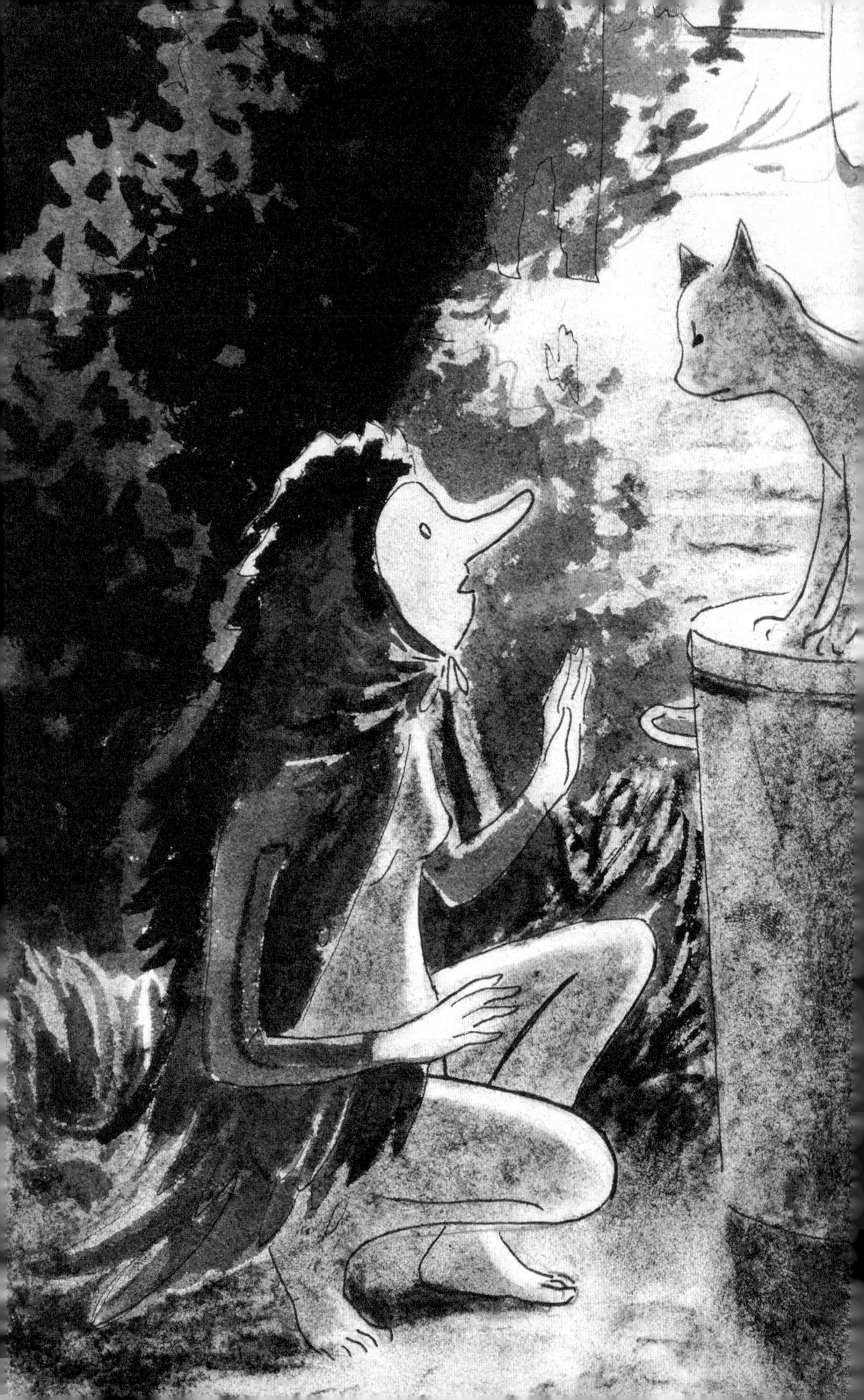

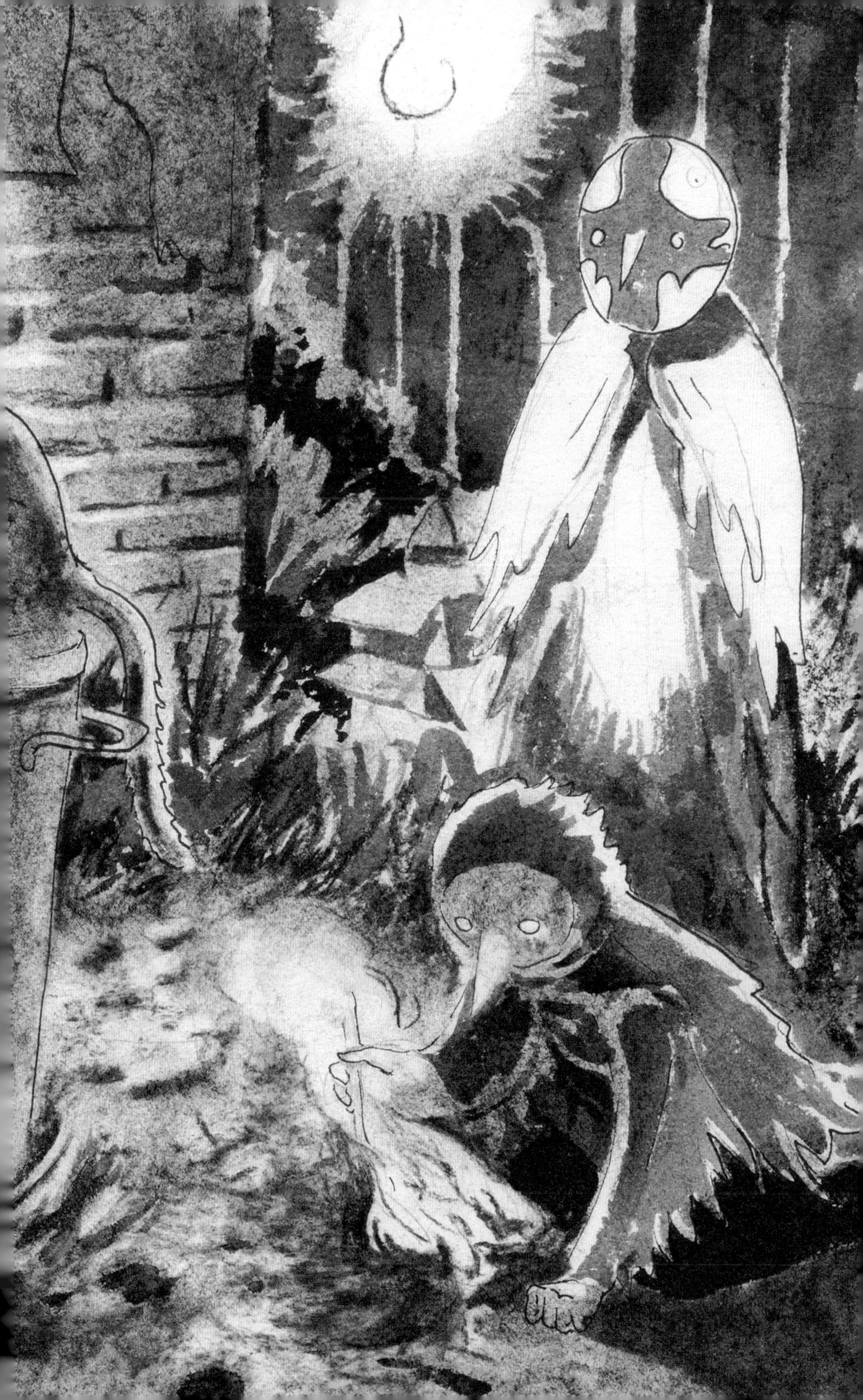

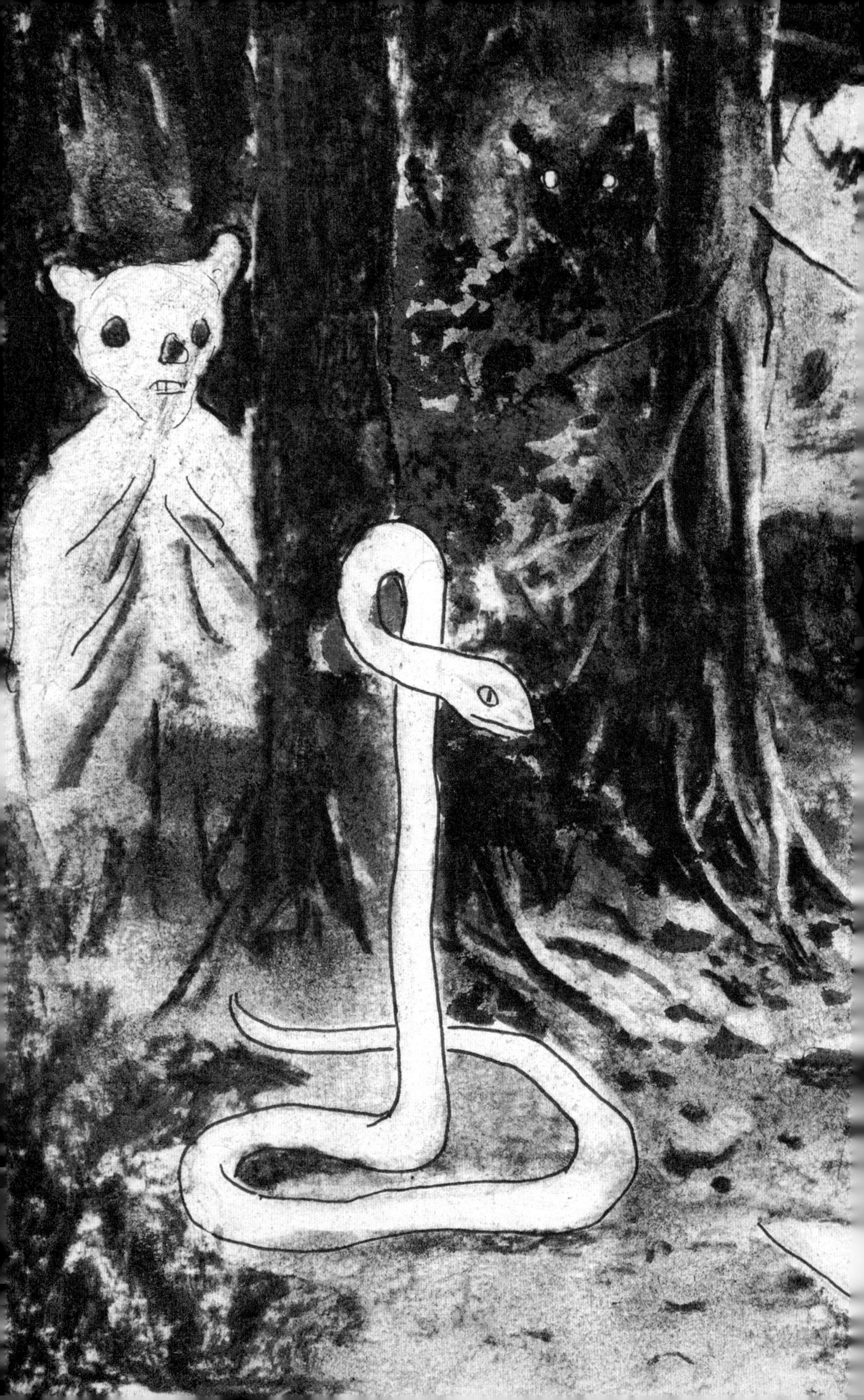

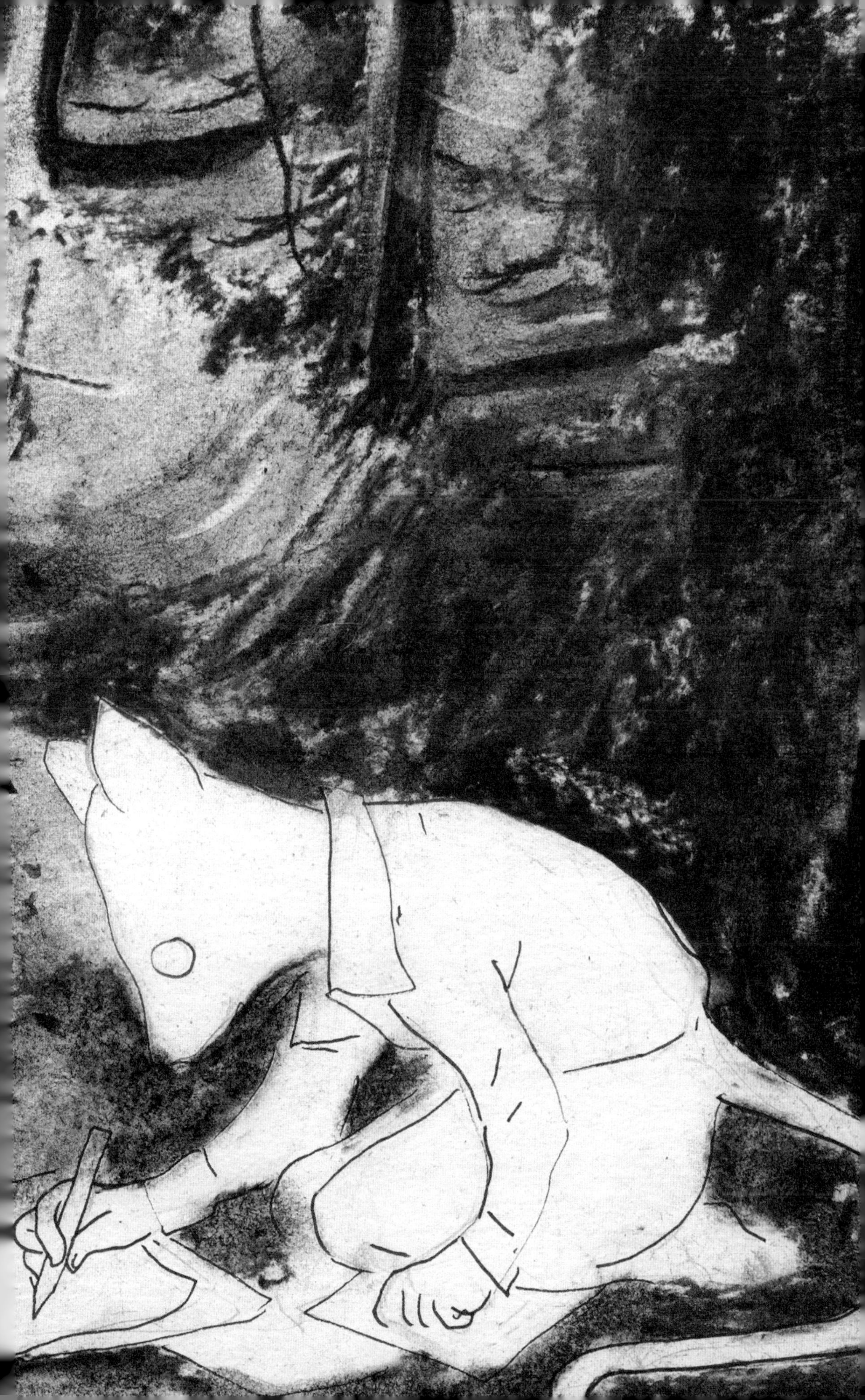

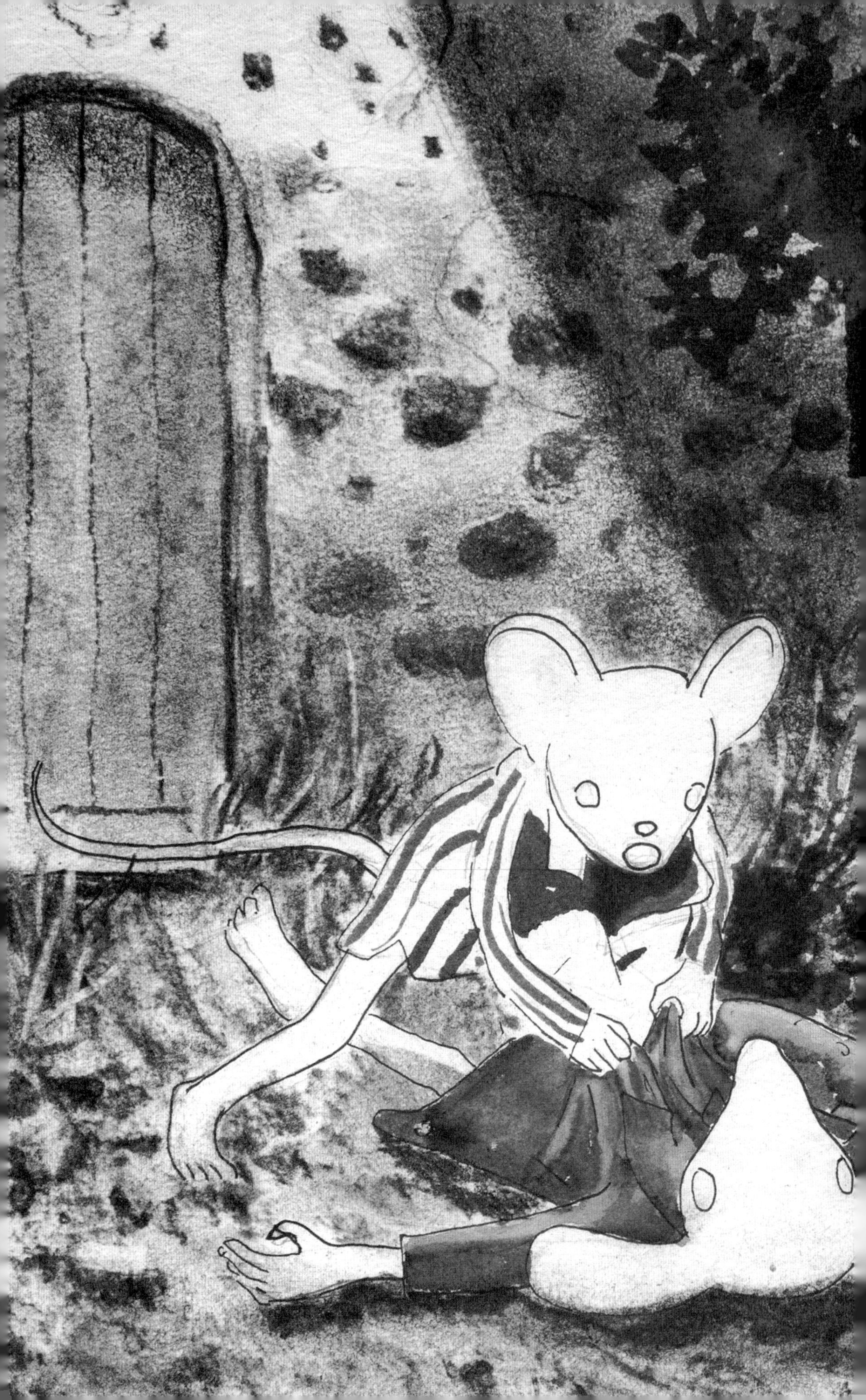

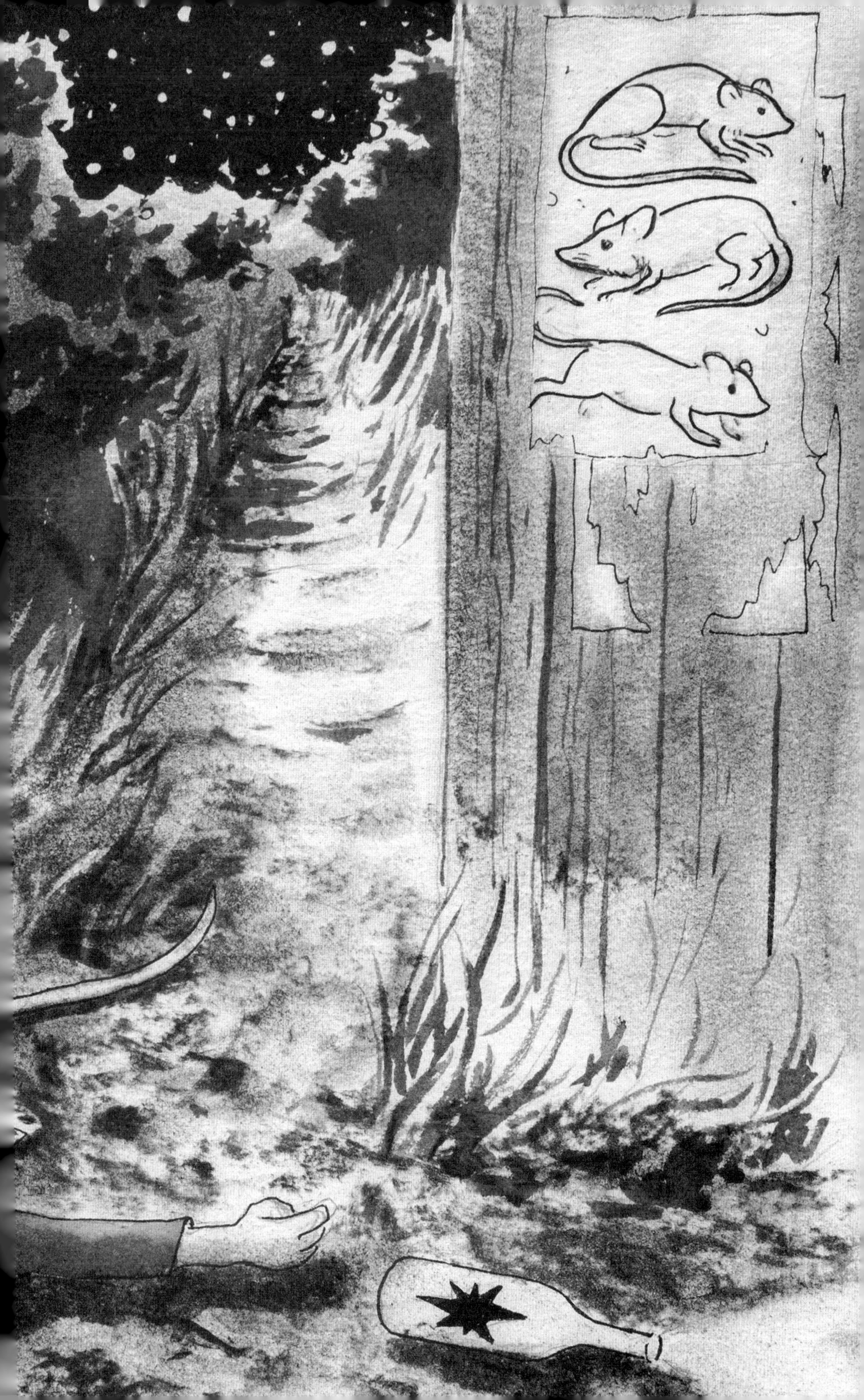

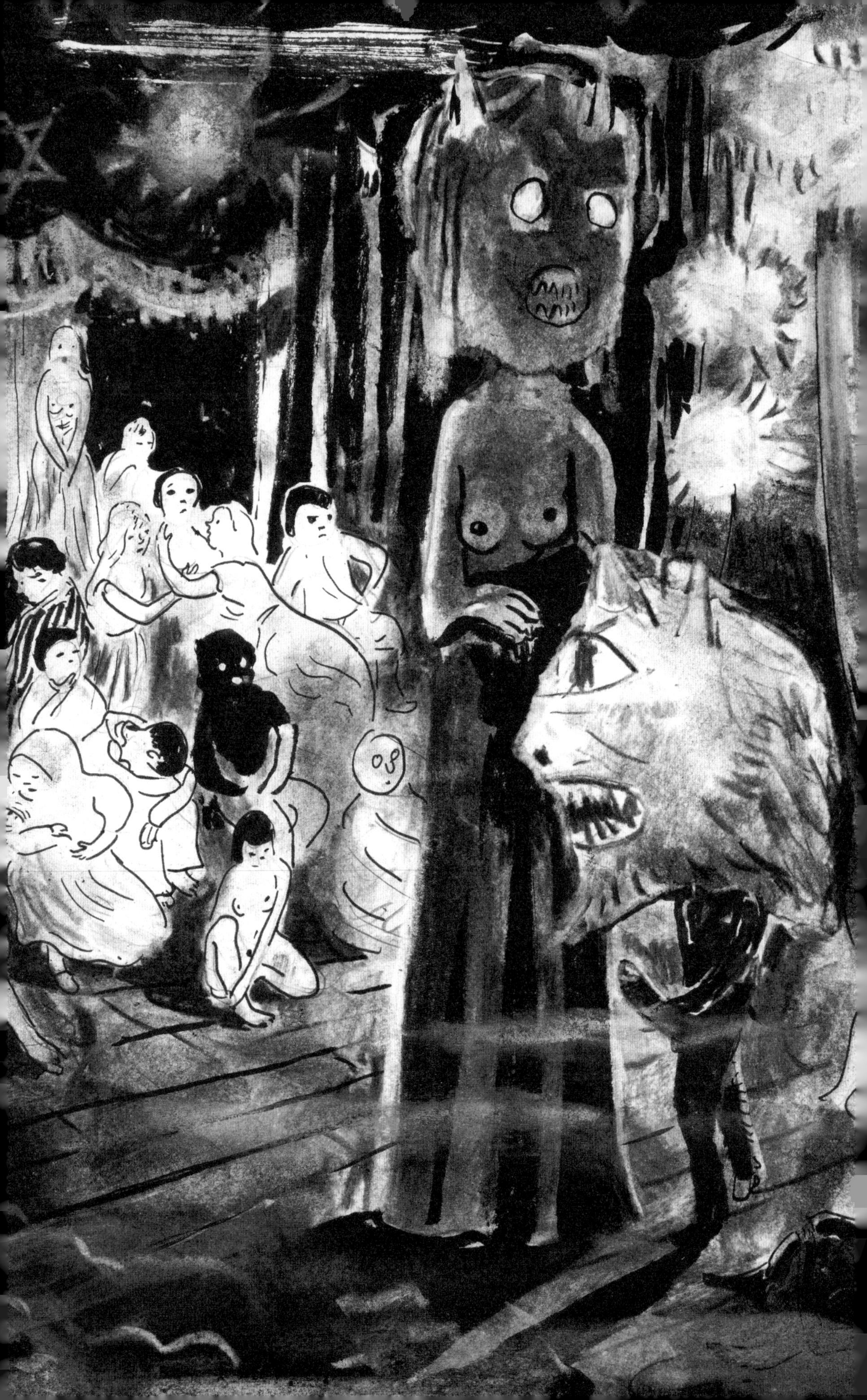

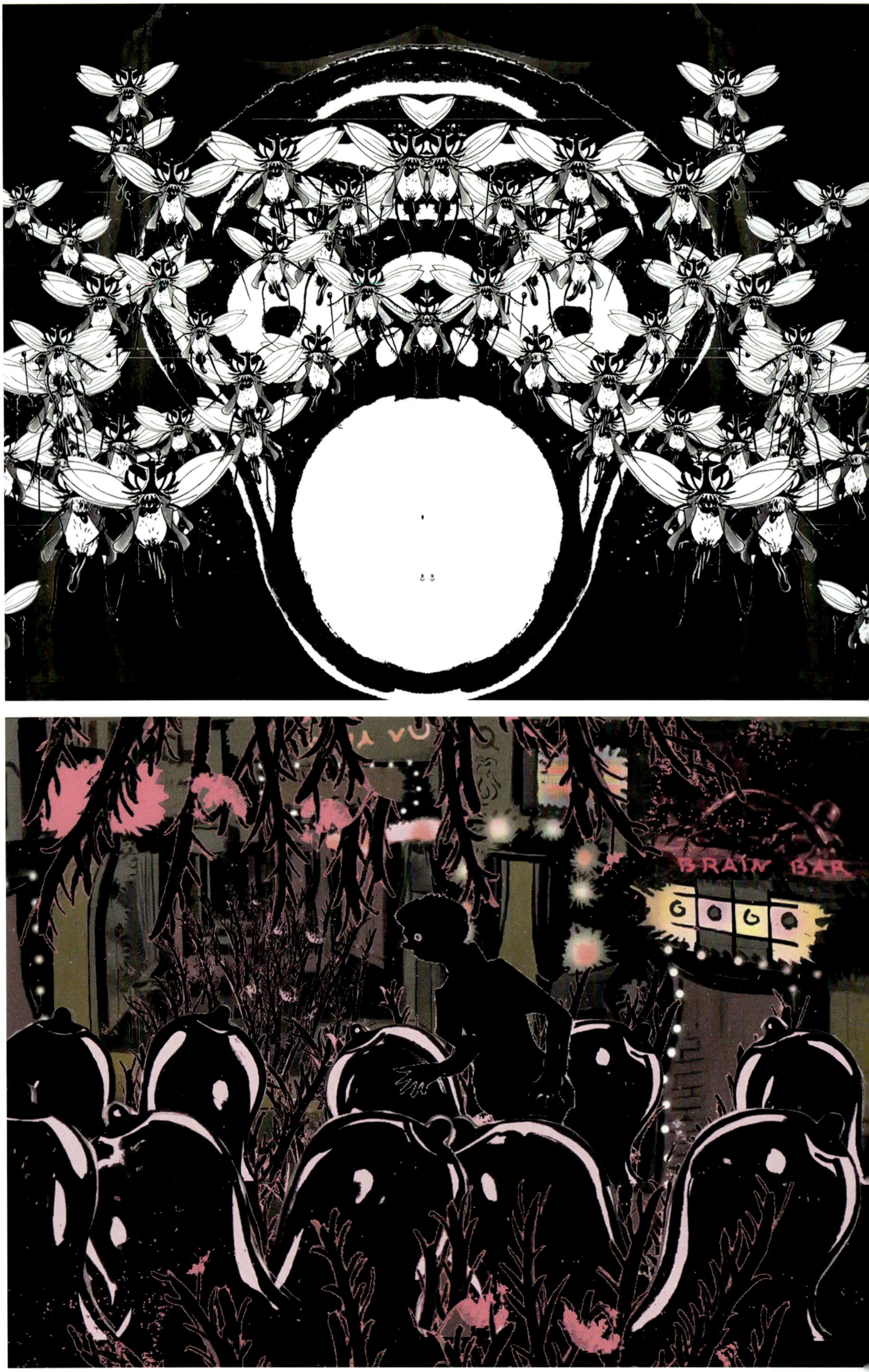
BRAIN BAR
GOGO

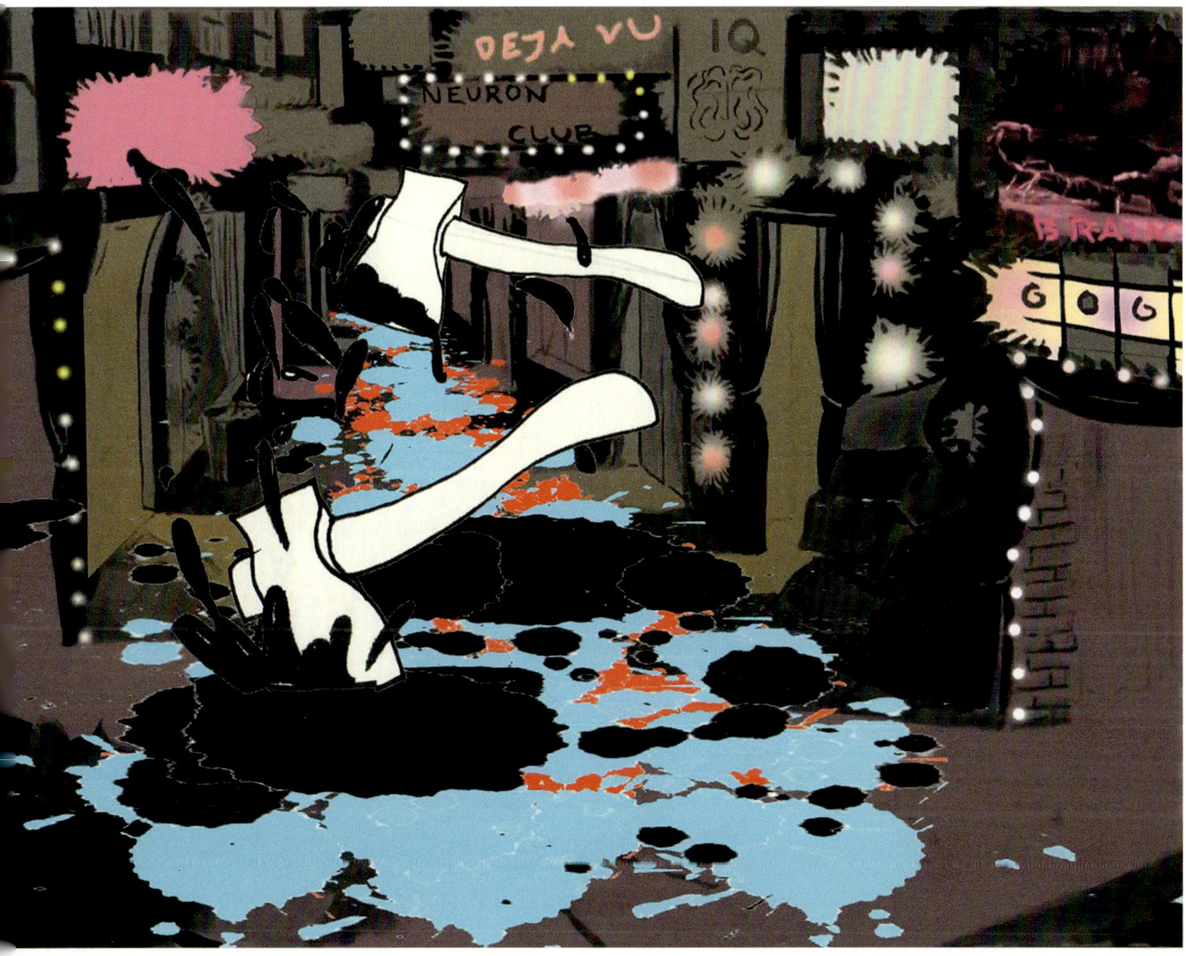
DEJA VU
NEURON CLUB
IQ

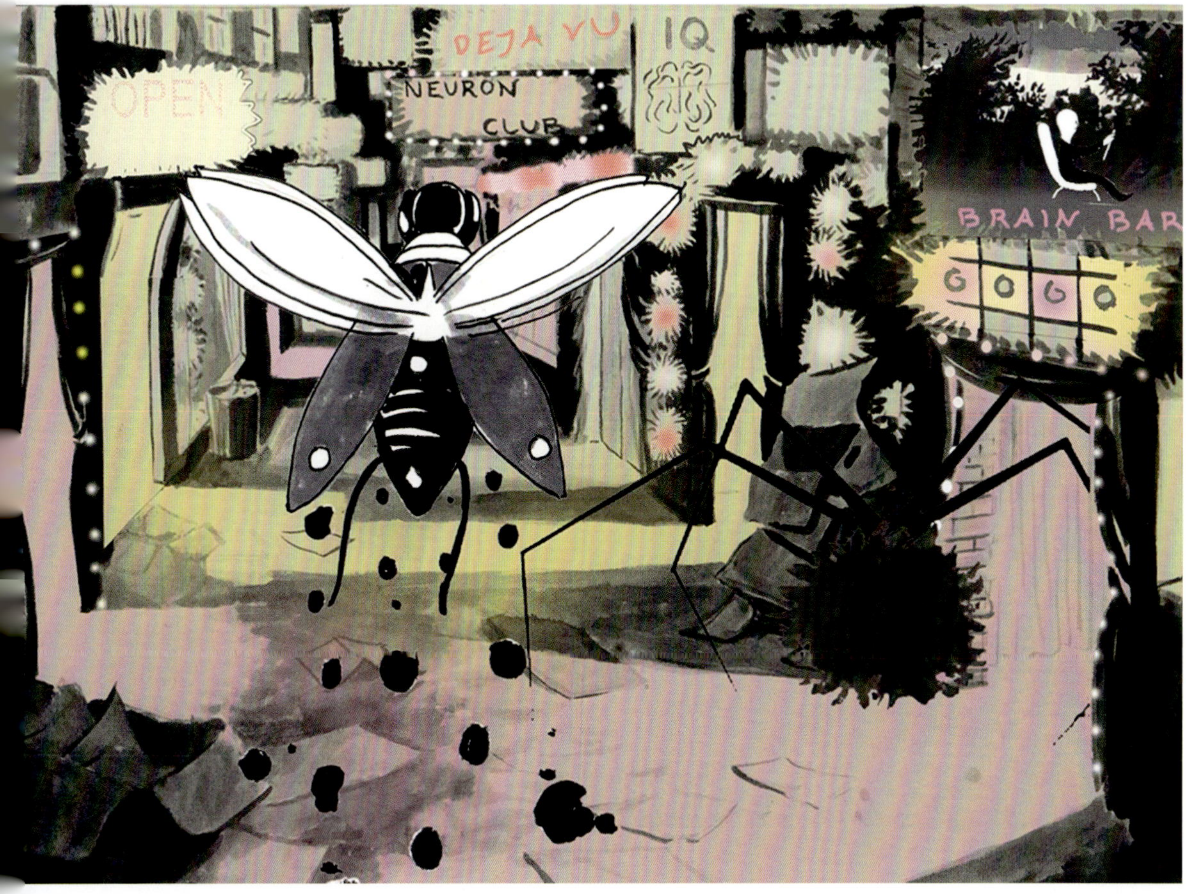
DEJA VU
OPEN
NEURON CLUB
IQ
BRAIN BAR
GOGO

DER TRINKER

(Video für Theater / video for theater), 30 min

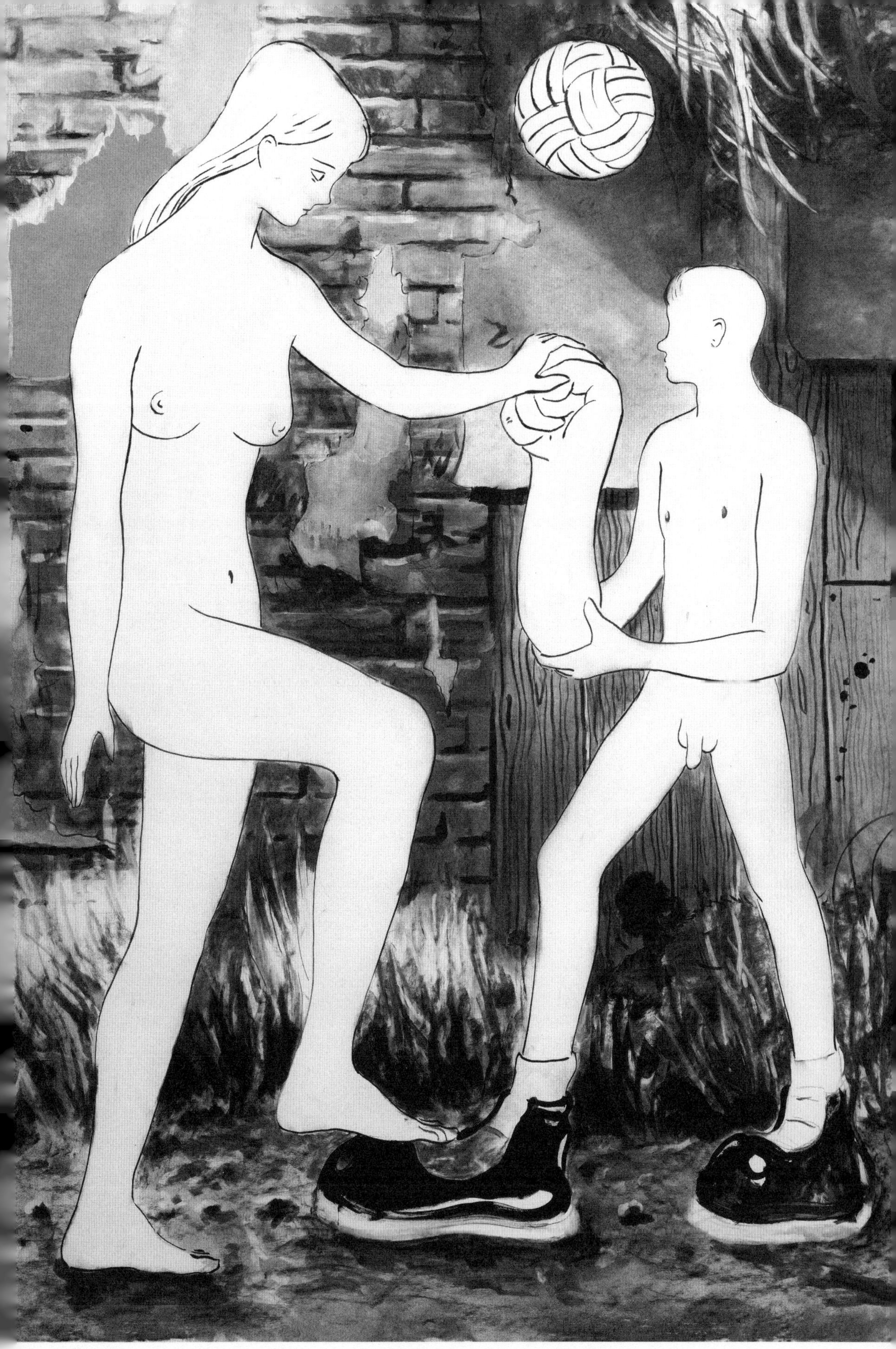

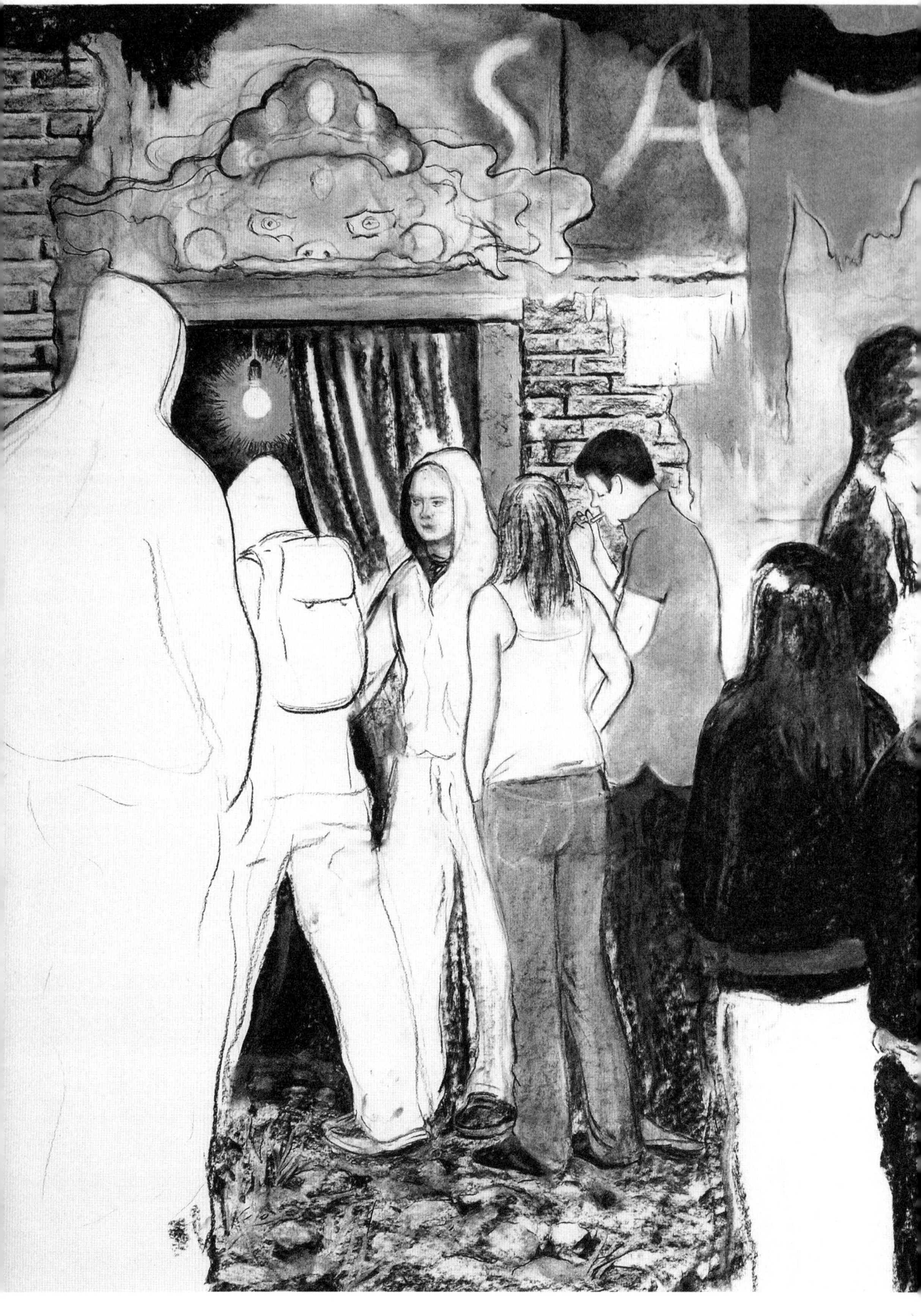

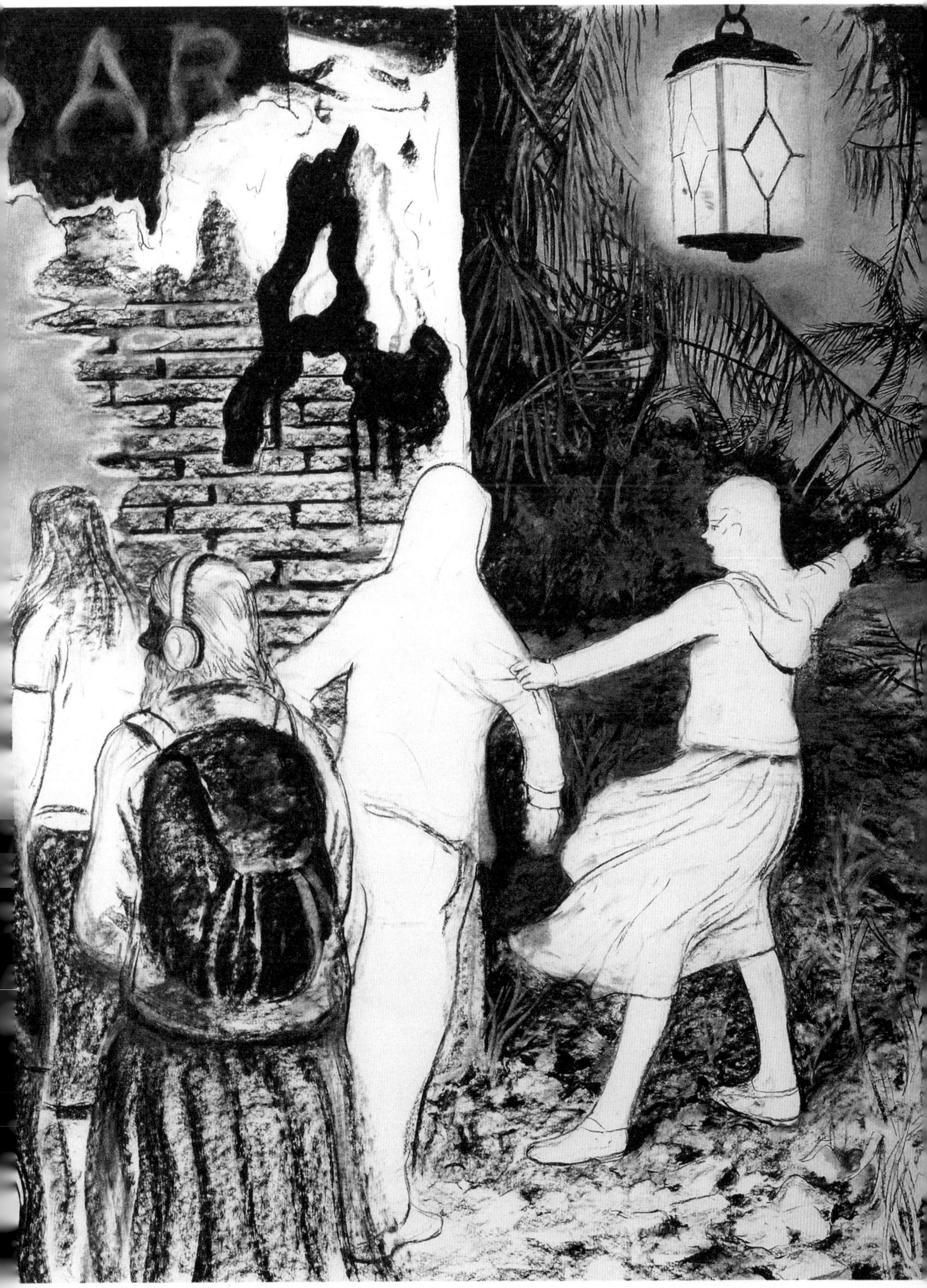

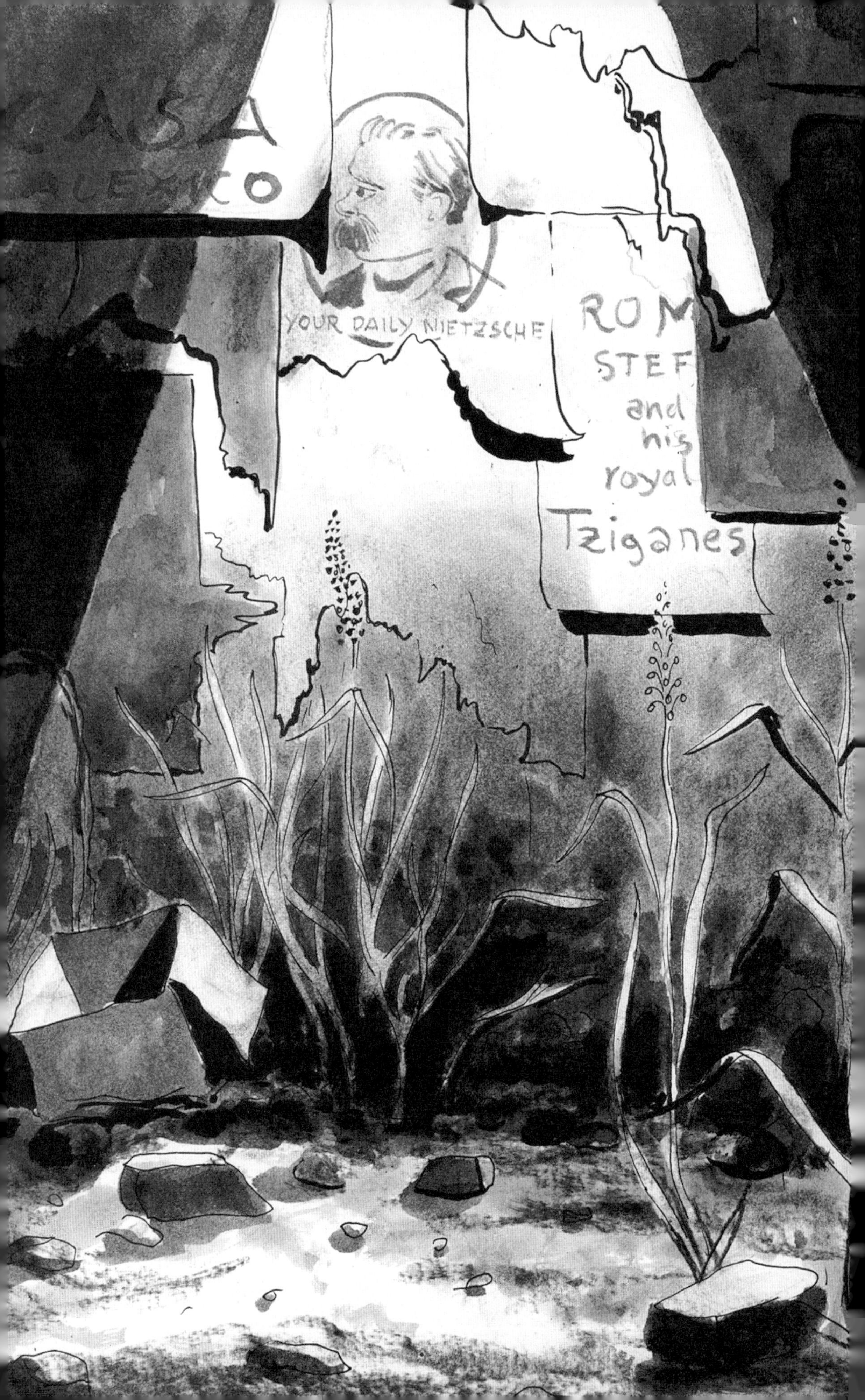
CASA
ALEXICO
YOUR DAILY NIETZSCHE
ROM
STEF
and
his
royal
Tziganes

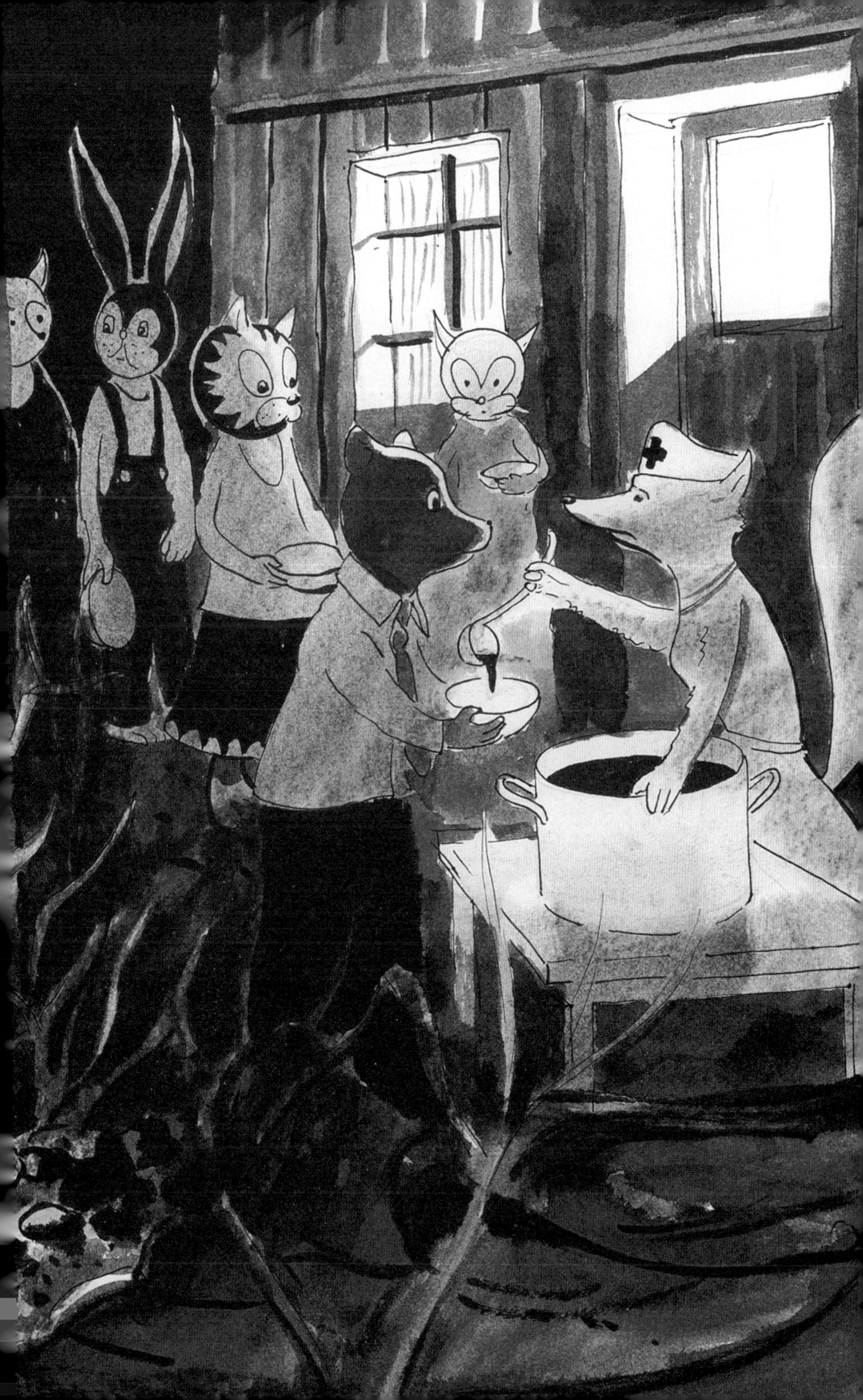

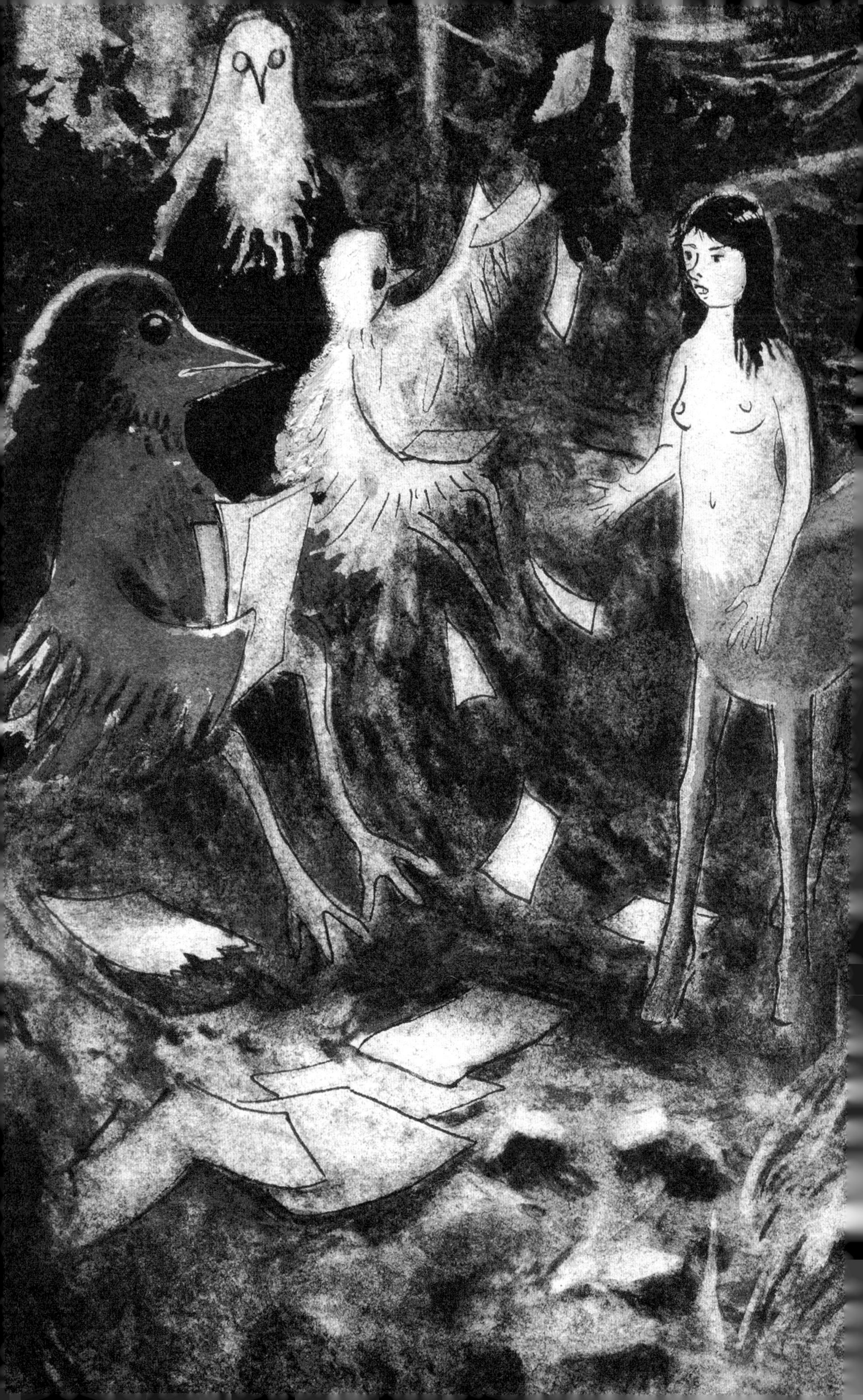

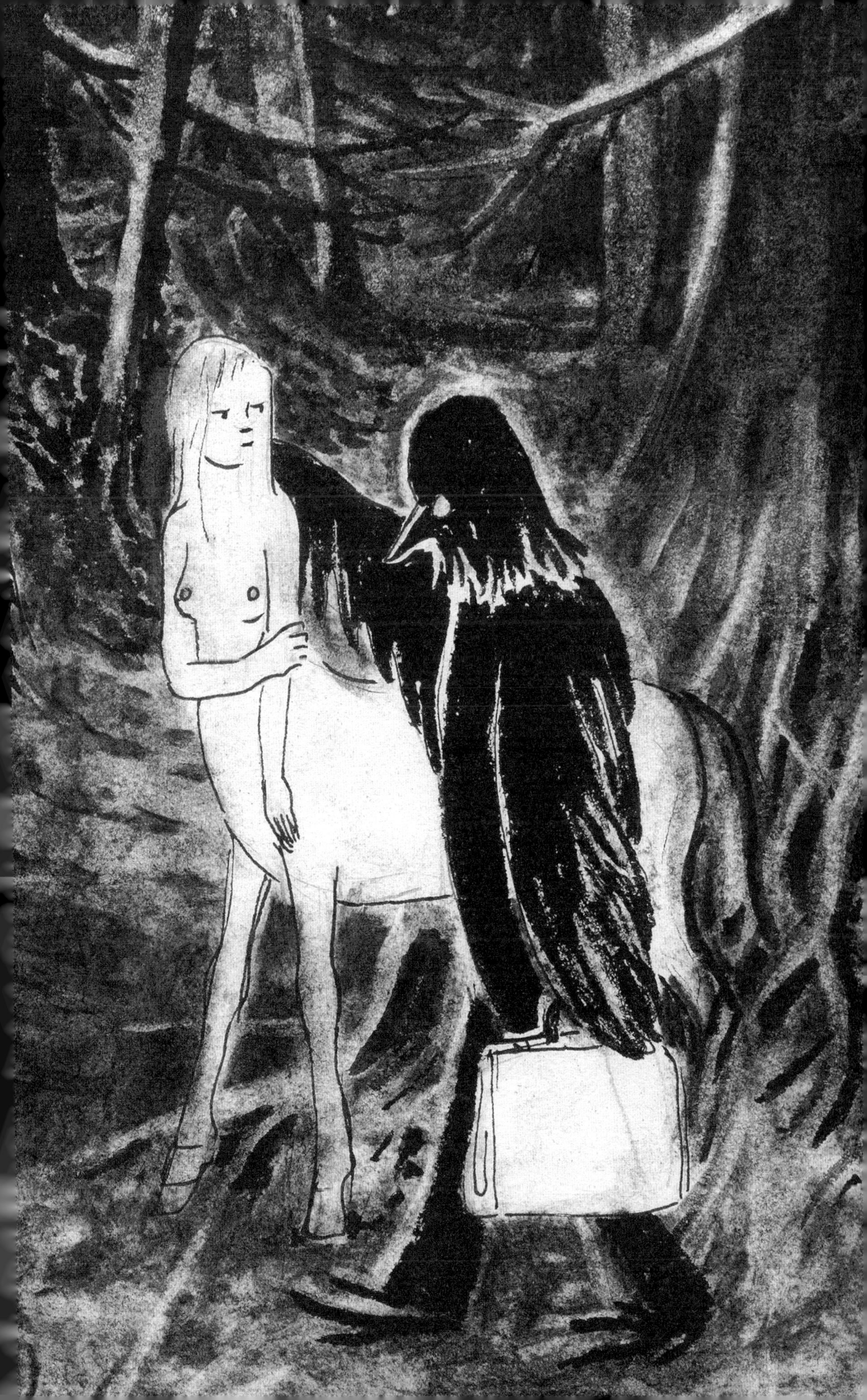

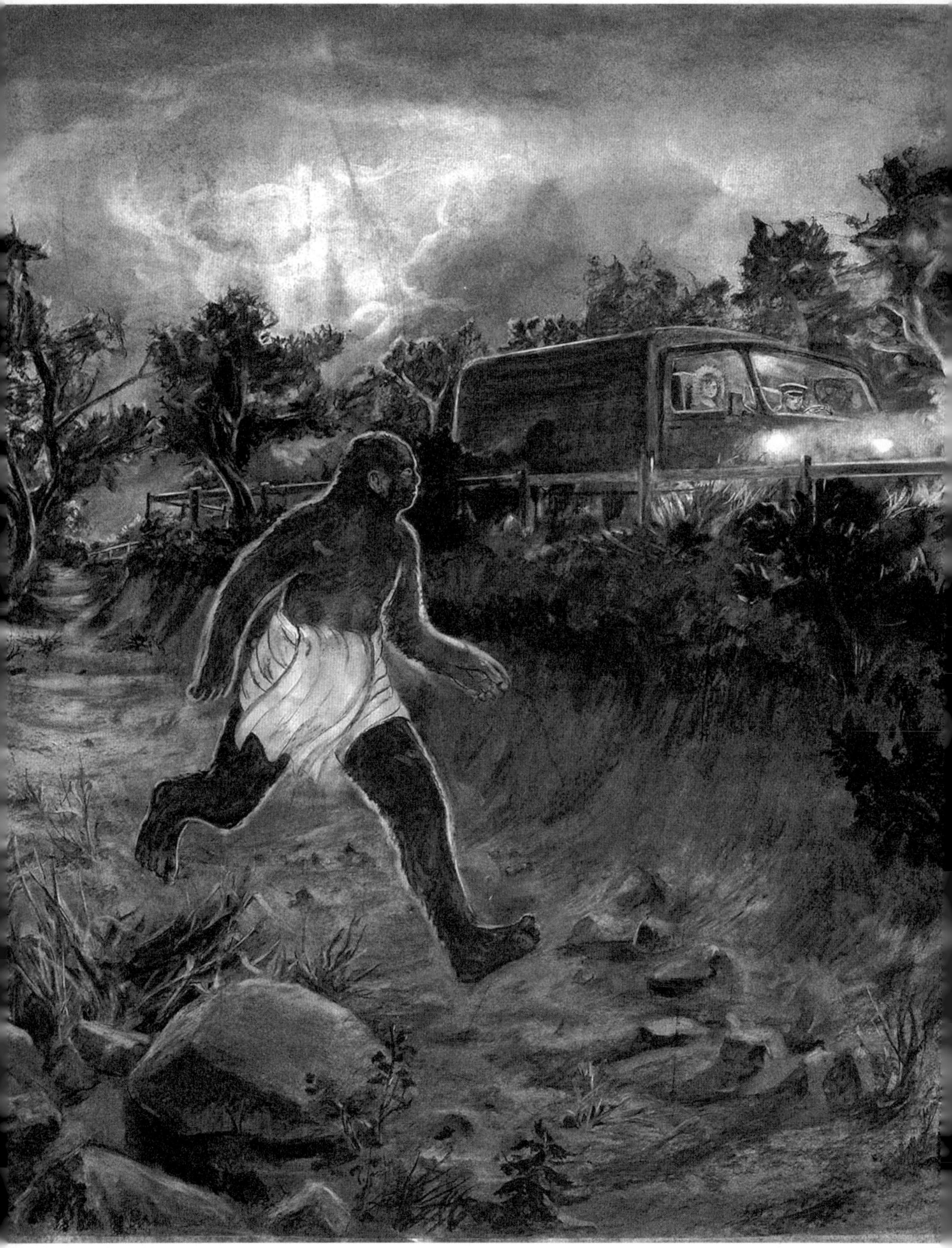

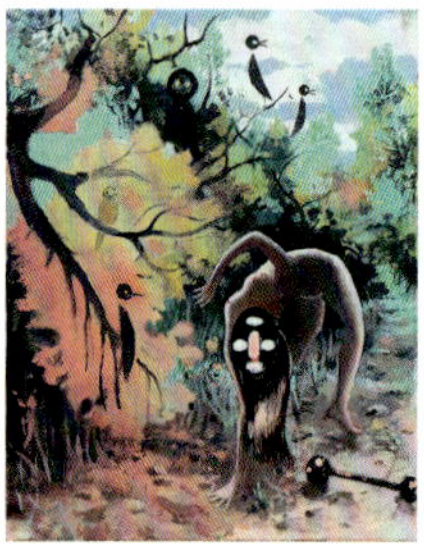

YOMA

2014, 50 × 40 cm
Öl auf Leinwand/oil on canvas

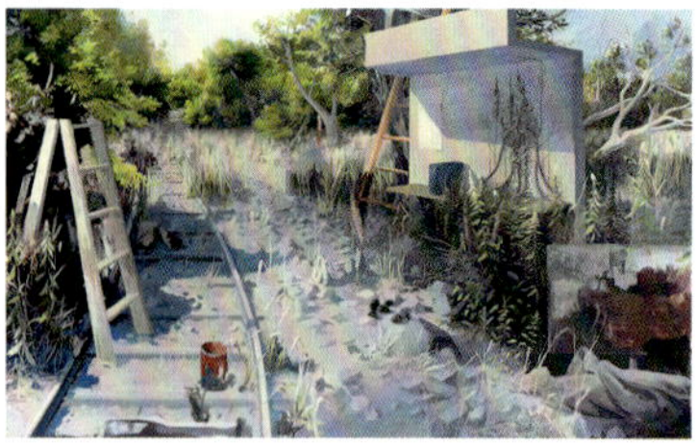

MOTIV

2009, 210 × 350 cm
Öl auf Leinwand/oil on canvas

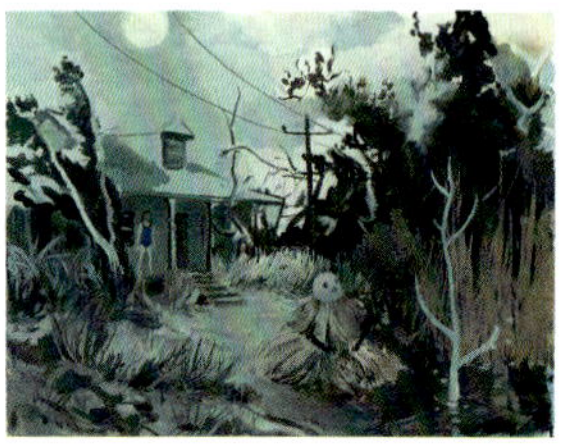

TRANSFORMER

2014, 60 × 80 cm
Öl auf Leinwand/oil on canvas

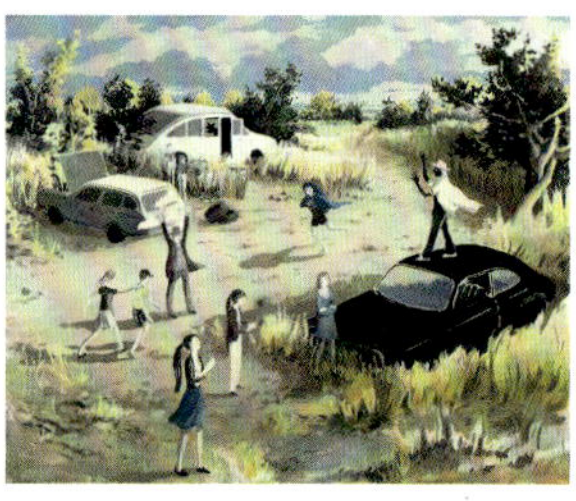

BRIDGE THE GAP

2015, 80 × 100 cm
Öl auf Leinwand/oil on canvas

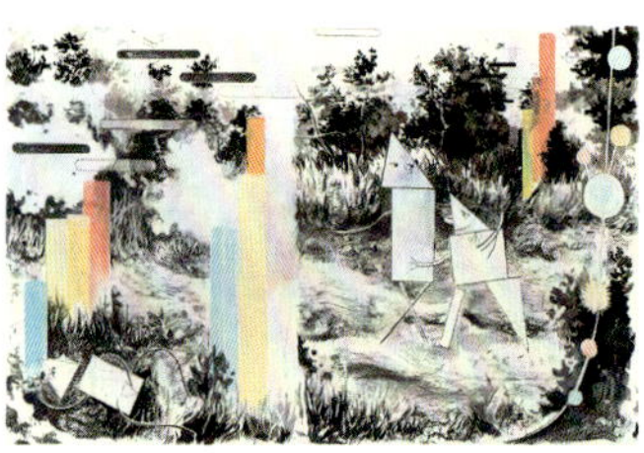

VABANQUE

2015, 140 × 205 cm
Kohle, Tusche und Pigment auf Papier/charcoal, ink and pigment on paper

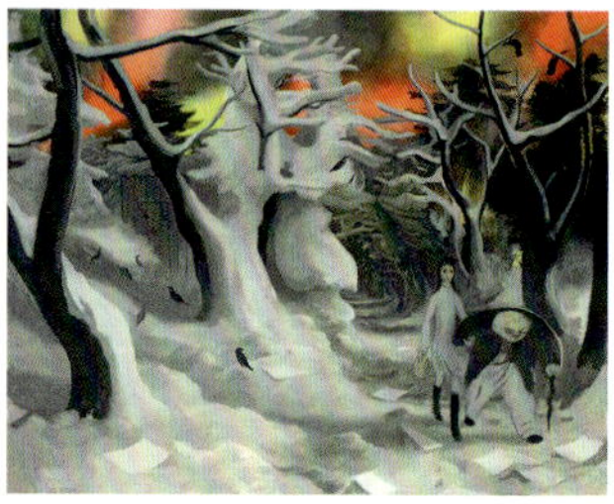

MUNK PARK

2011, 190 × 240 cm
Öl auf Leinwand/
oil on canvas

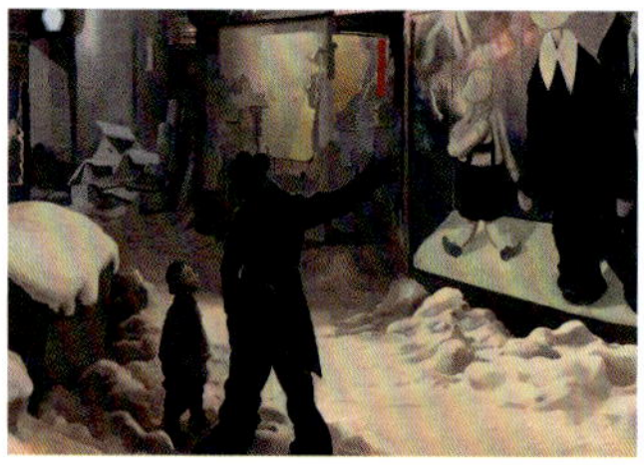

THE DEPENDENT INDEPENDENT

2009, 210 × 300 cm
Öl auf Leinwand/oil on canvas

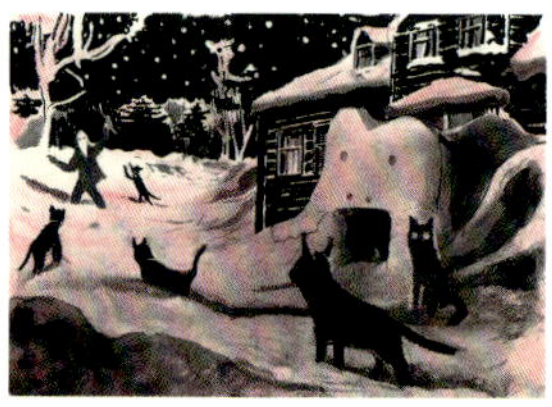

o.T. (SCHNEE)

2010, 30 × 42 cm
Kohle, Pastell auf Papier/
charcoal, pastel on paper

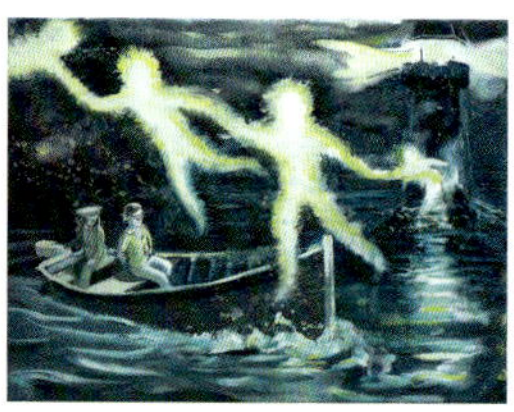

ELMSTURM

2012, 30 × 40 cm
Öl auf Leinwand/oil on canvas

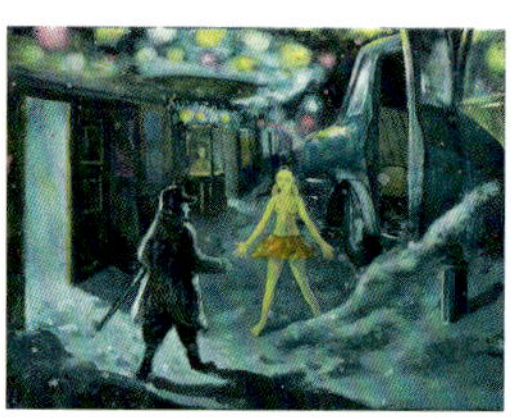

BANTU

2012, 30 × 40 cm
Öl auf Leinwand/oil on canvas

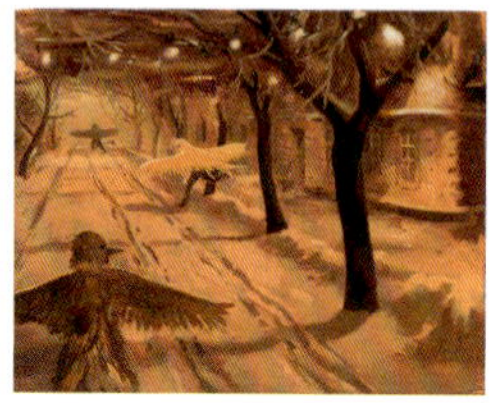

o.T.

2012, 40 × 50 cm
Öl auf Leinwand/oil on canvas

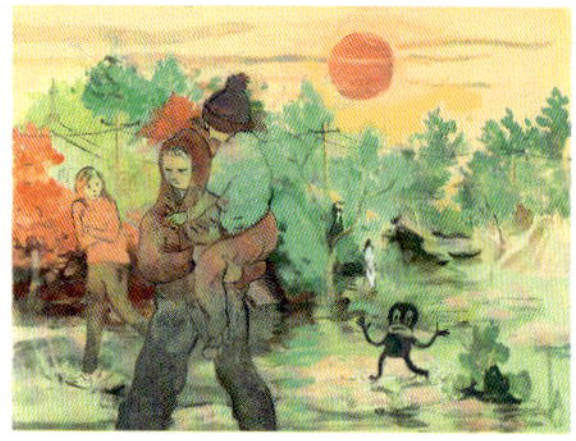

CARRIER

2014, 60 × 80 cm
Öl auf Leinwand/oil on canvas

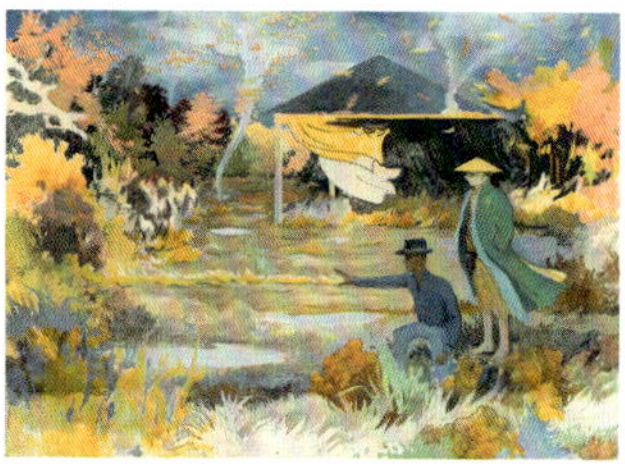

BLAST

2014, 150 × 205 cm
Öl auf Leinwand/oil on canvas

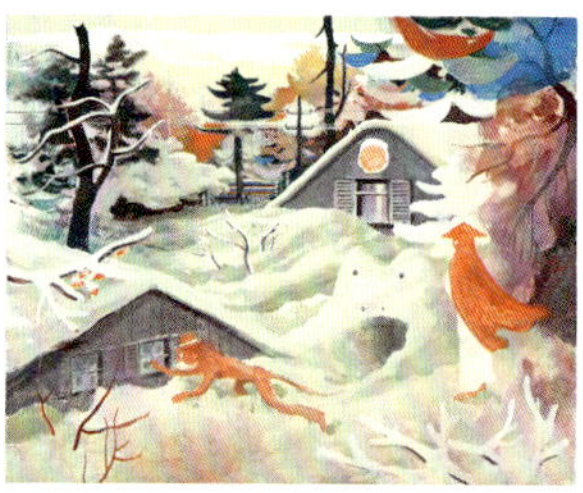

GARIN

2014, 200 × 250 cm
Öl auf Leinwand/oil on canvas

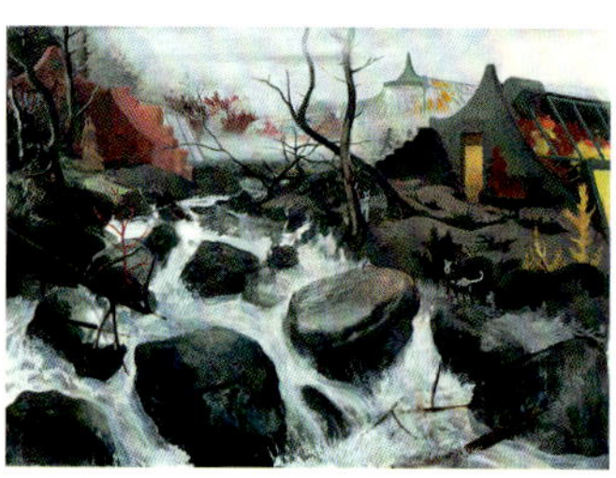

NEBELLEBEN

2014, 218 × 300 cm
Öl auf Papier/oil on paper

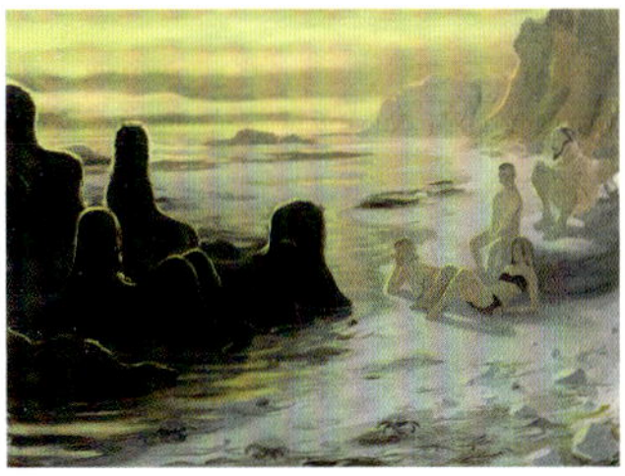

TONG

2011, 160 × 220 cm
Öl auf Leinwand/oil on canvas

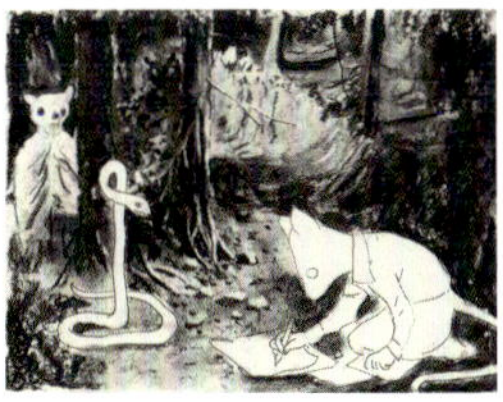

HALBWEISE

2012, 21 × 29 cm
Kohle, Tusche und Pastell auf Papier/charcoal, ink and pastel on paper

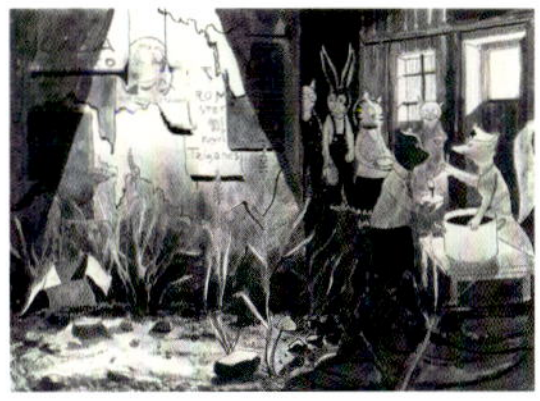

DAILY NIETZSCHE

2012, 21 × 29 cm
Kohle, Tusche und Pastell auf Papier/charcoal, ink and pastel on paper

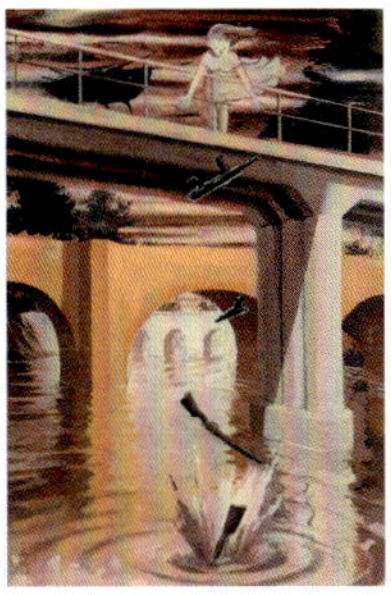

o.T. (HEDWIG)

2010, 65 × 40 cm
Öl auf MDF/oil on mdf

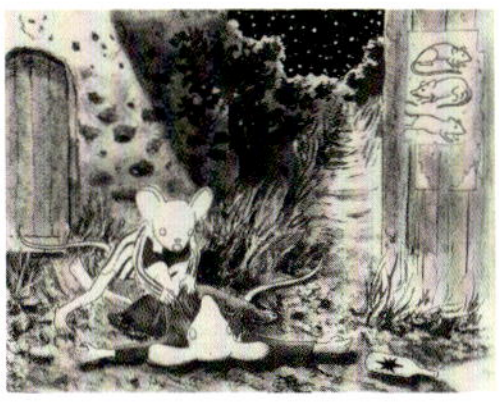

BAKBUK

2012, 25 × 32 cm
Kohle und Tusche auf Papier/charcoal and ink on paper

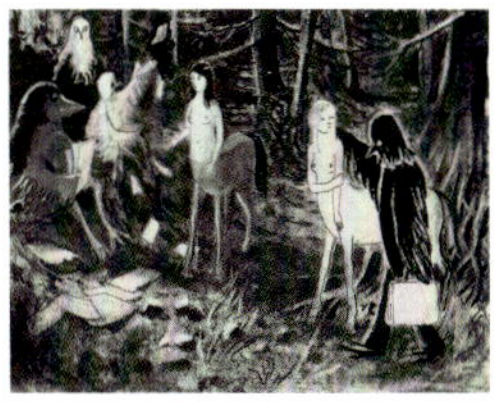

ZENSUR

2012, 21 × 29 cm
Kohle, Tusche und Pastell auf Papier/charcoal, ink and pastel on paper

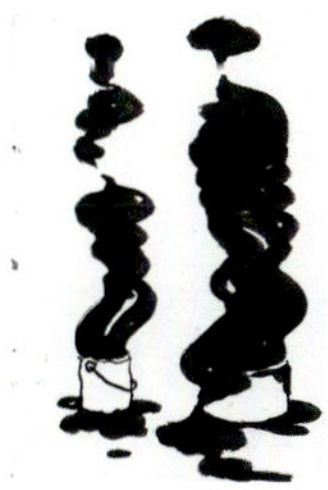

o.T.

2010, 25 × 18 cm
Tusche auf Papier/ink on paper

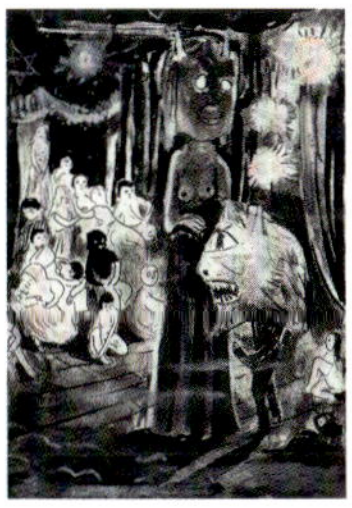

CAN CLUB

2014, 29 × 21 cm
Kohle, Tusche und Pastell auf Papier/charcoal, ink and pastel on paper

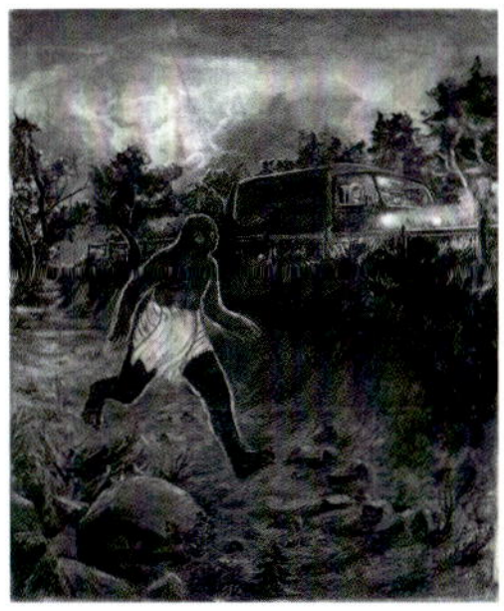

BEGLEITER

2009, 156 × 134 cm
Kohle auf Papier/charcoal on paper

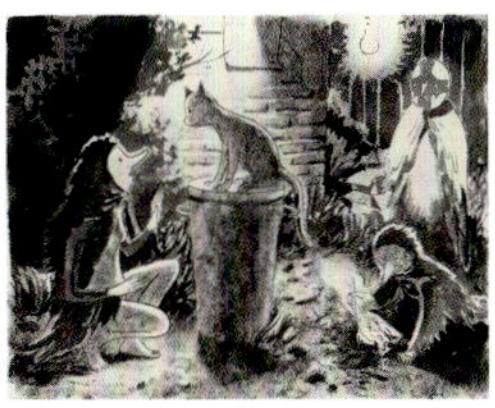

SAN SYLVESTRIS

2012, 21 × 29 cm
Kohle, Tusche und Pastell auf Papier/charcoal, ink and pastel on paper

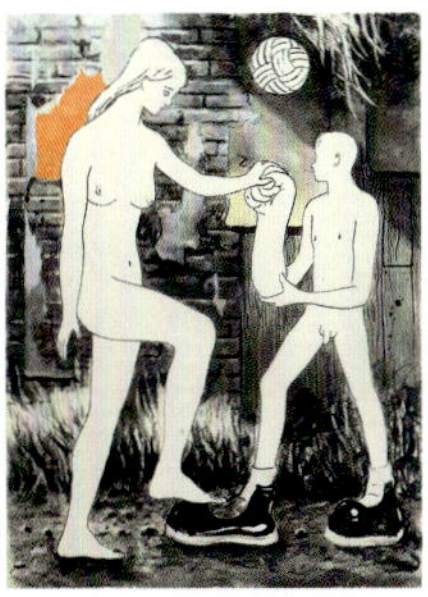

ANIMA

2015, 140 × 100 cm
Kohle, Tusche und Pigment auf Papier/charcoal, ink, oil and pigment on paper

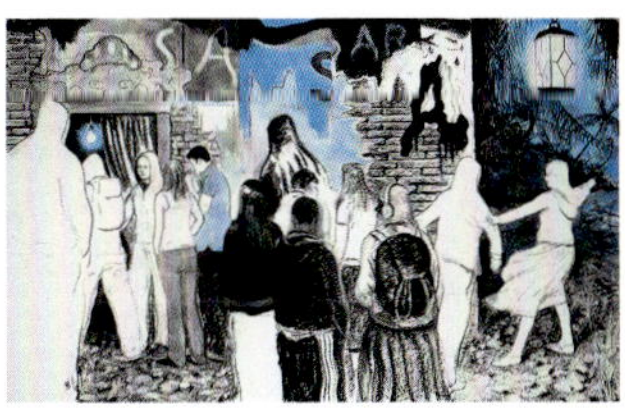

SAMSARA

2009, 125 × 200 cm
Kohle auf Papier/charcoal on paper

SENZA PAROLE

Herausgegeben von / Edited by:
Galerie Kleindienst und / and LUBOK Verlag, Leipzig

Gestaltung / Graphic Design: Andrej Loll (Büro Total)
Fotografie / Photography: Uwe Walter, Leipzig/Berlin
Bildbearbeitung / Image preparation: anna.k.o.
Übersetzung / Translation: Gunnar Wendel
Druck und Verarbeitung / Print and binding:
DZA Druckerei zu Altenburg GmbH

Auflage / Print run: 750
10 Exemplare erscheinen als Vorzugsausgabe im Schuber mit jeweils einer signierten Originalzeichnung /
10 copies come as collectors edition in a slipcase with a signed original drawing

Erschienen im / Published by:
LUBOK Verlag
Floßplatz 8
D-04107 Leipzig
www.lubok.de

ISBN 978-3-945111-18-5

Printed in Germany

Dieses Buch wurde gefördert durch die Kulturstiftung des Freistaates Sachsen / This publication has been supported by the Kulturstiftung des Freistaates Sachsen

Kulturstiftung des Freistaates Sachsen